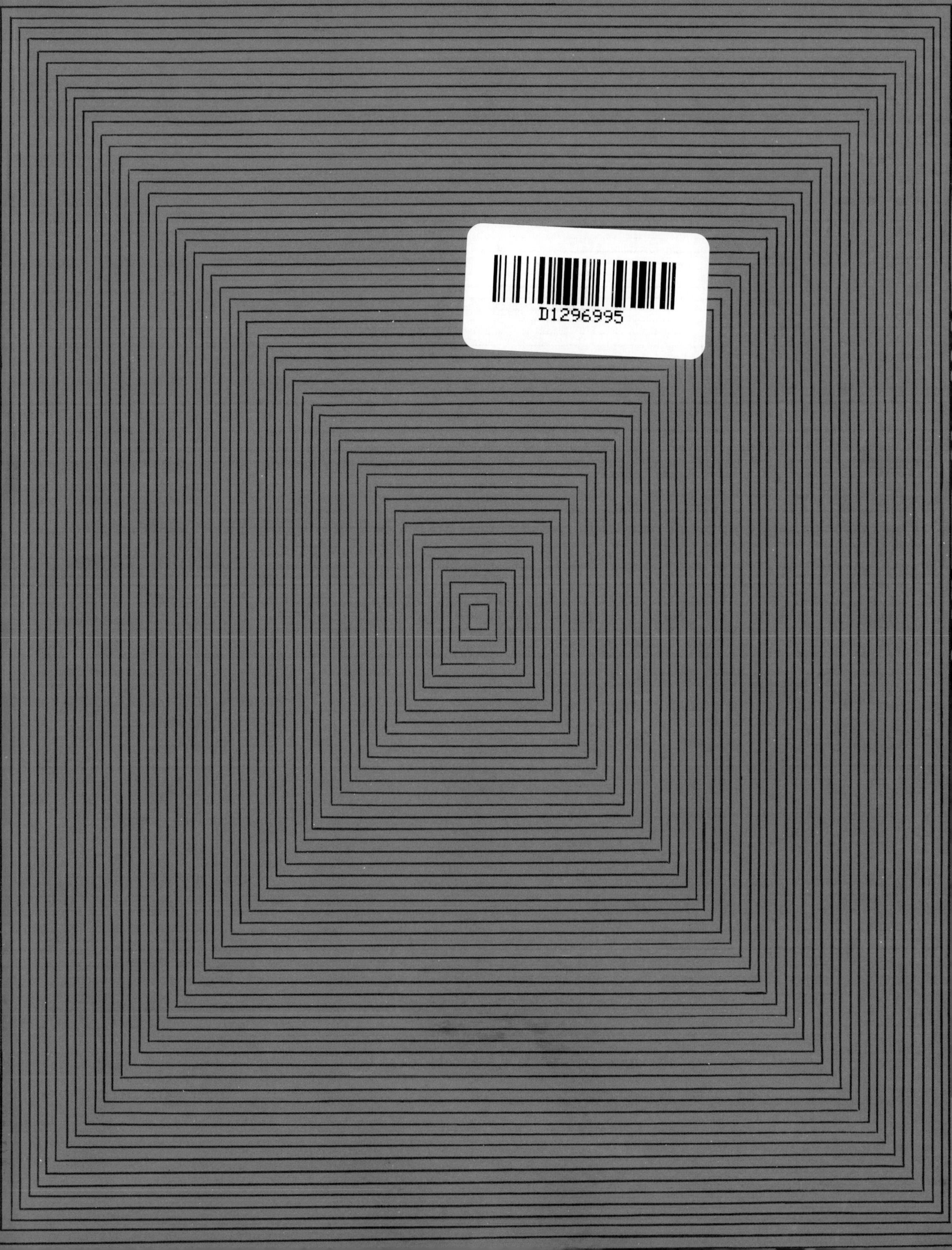

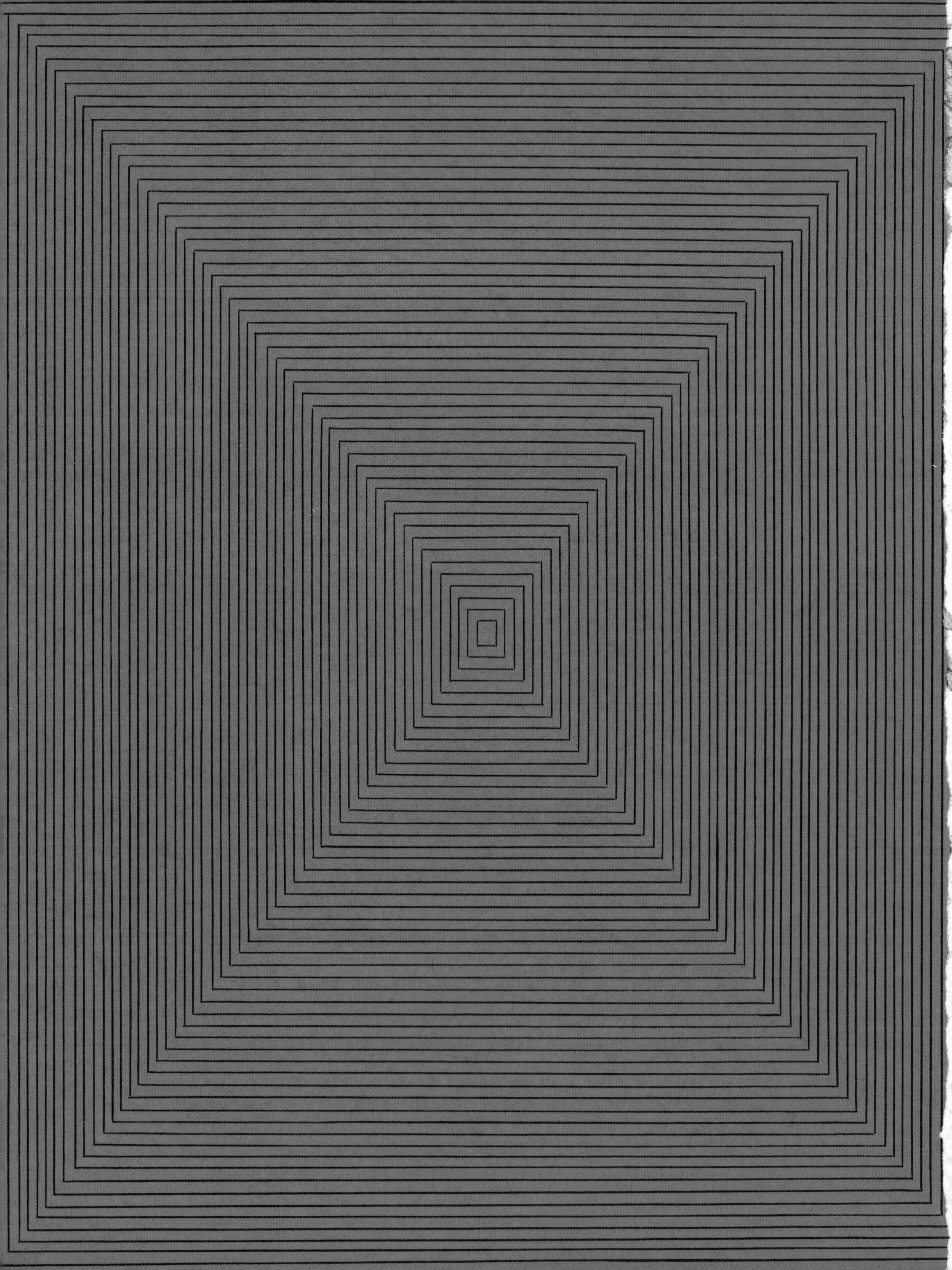

INFOMANIACS

MATTHEW THURBE

PICTUREBOX
BROOKLYN

INFOMANIACS
MATTHEW THURBER

dedicated to my parents

"MIRRORS ARE INSTRUMENTS OF A
UNIVERSAL MAGIC THAT CONVERTS THINGS
INTO SPECTACLE, SPECTACLE INTO THINGS,
MYSELF INTO ANOTHER, AND ANOTHER INTO MYSELF."

– MAURICE MERLEAU-PONTY, "EYE AND MIND"

THANKS TO THE PARTICIPANTS IN THE
"INFOMANIACS CHARACTER OFFER":
GRAHAM KOLBEINS, NEVA WHITE, PUAL N.,
PAUL DAVIS, JIM THOMAS...
THANKS TO DAVE WILFERT AT THE WORLD'S BEST EVER
FOR SERIALIZING THE WEBCOMIC.
THANKS OF COURSE TO DAN NADEL.
PRODUCTION/DESIGN ASSISTANCE BY ANGELA WYMAN.
SPECIAL THANKS TO REBECCA BIRD FOR THE
HORSE JOKE ON PAGE 186.

PICTURE BOX
P.O. BOX 24744
BROOKLYN, NY 11202
PICTUREBOXINC.COM

ISBN 978-1-939799-08-1
PRINTED IN CHINA.
DISTRIBUTION IN NORTH AMERICA:
ARTBOOK|DAP

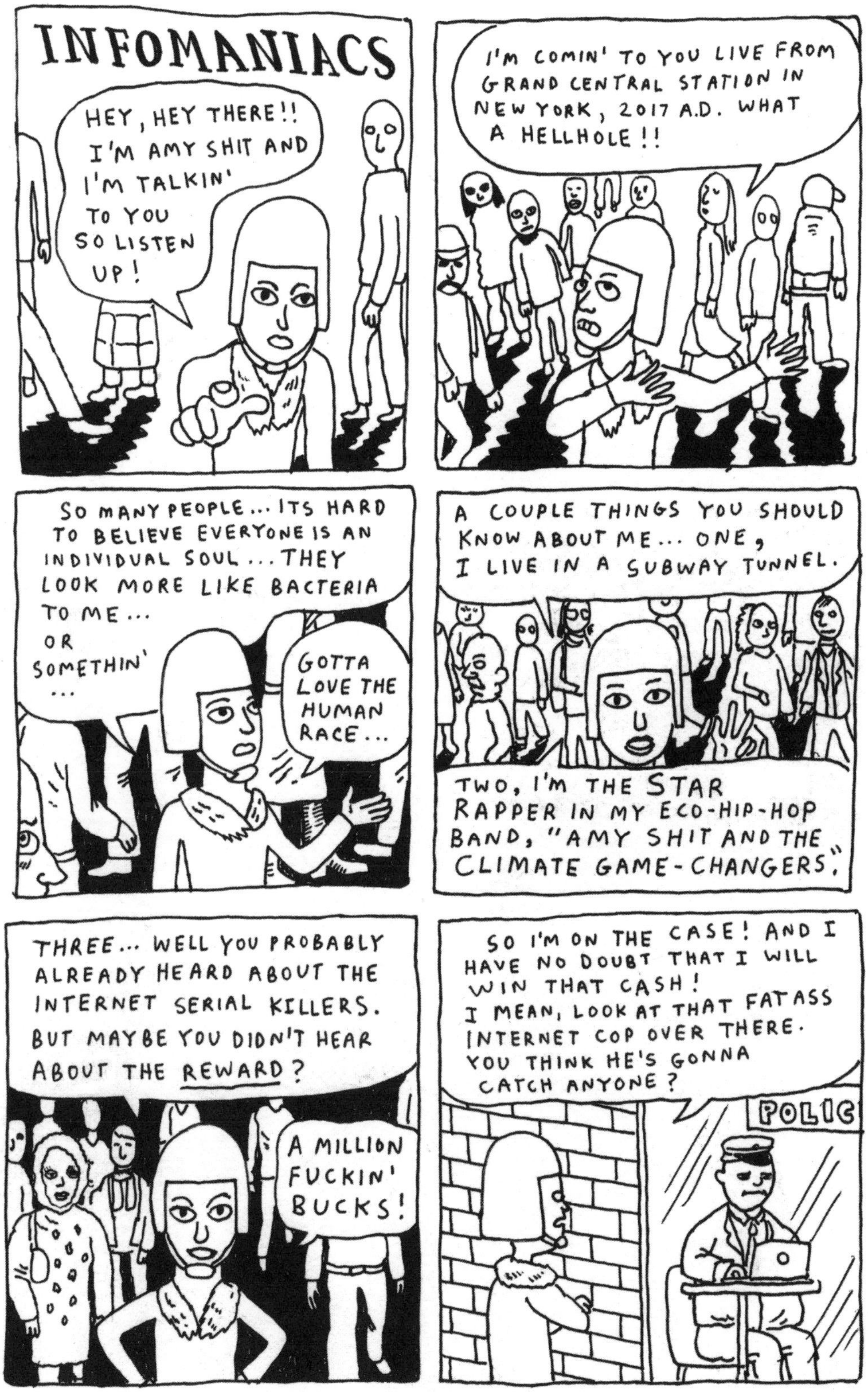

INFOMANIACS
HEY, HEY THERE!! I'M AMY SHIT AND I'M TALKIN' TO YOU SO LISTEN UP!
I'M COMIN' TO YOU LIVE FROM GRAND CENTRAL STATION IN NEW YORK, 2017 A.D. WHAT A HELLHOLE!!
SO MANY PEOPLE... ITS HARD TO BELIEVE EVERYONE IS AN INDIVIDUAL SOUL... THEY LOOK MORE LIKE BACTERIA TO ME... OR SOMETHIN' ...
GOTTA LOVE THE HUMAN RACE...
A COUPLE THINGS YOU SHOULD KNOW ABOUT ME... ONE, I LIVE IN A SUBWAY TUNNEL.
TWO, I'M THE STAR RAPPER IN MY ECO-HIP-HOP BAND, "AMY SHIT AND THE CLIMATE GAME-CHANGERS".
THREE... WELL YOU PROBABLY ALREADY HEARD ABOUT THE INTERNET SERIAL KILLERS. BUT MAYBE YOU DIDN'T HEAR ABOUT THE REWARD?
A MILLION FUCKIN' BUCKS!
SO I'M ON THE CASE! AND I HAVE NO DOUBT THAT I WILL WIN THAT CASH! I MEAN, LOOK AT THAT FAT ASS INTERNET COP OVER THERE. YOU THINK HE'S GONNA CATCH ANYONE?
POLIC

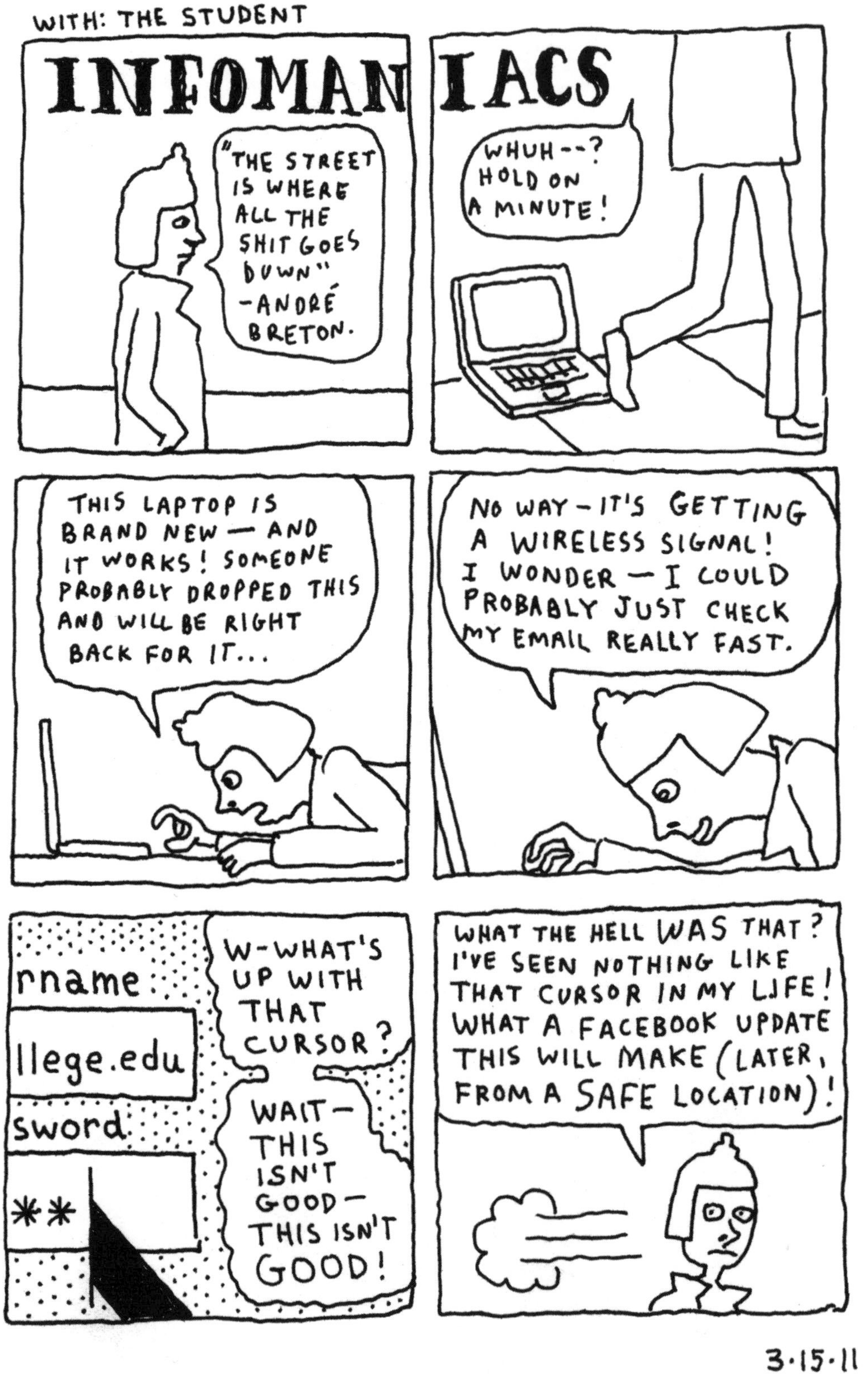
WITH: THE STUDENT
INFOMANIACS
"THE STREET IS WHERE ALL THE SHIT GOES DOWN" -ANDRÉ BRETON.
WHUH--? HOLD ON A MINUTE!
THIS LAPTOP IS BRAND NEW — AND IT WORKS! SOMEONE PROBABLY DROPPED THIS AND WILL BE RIGHT BACK FOR IT...
NO WAY - IT'S GETTING A WIRELESS SIGNAL! I WONDER — I COULD PROBABLY JUST CHECK MY EMAIL REALLY FAST.
rname
llege.edu
sword
**
W-WHAT'S UP WITH THAT CURSOR?
WAIT— THIS ISN'T GOOD— THIS ISN'T GOOD!
WHAT THE HELL WAS THAT? I'VE SEEN NOTHING LIKE THAT CURSOR IN MY LIFE! WHAT A FACEBOOK UPDATE THIS WILL MAKE (LATER, FROM A SAFE LOCATION)!
3·15·11

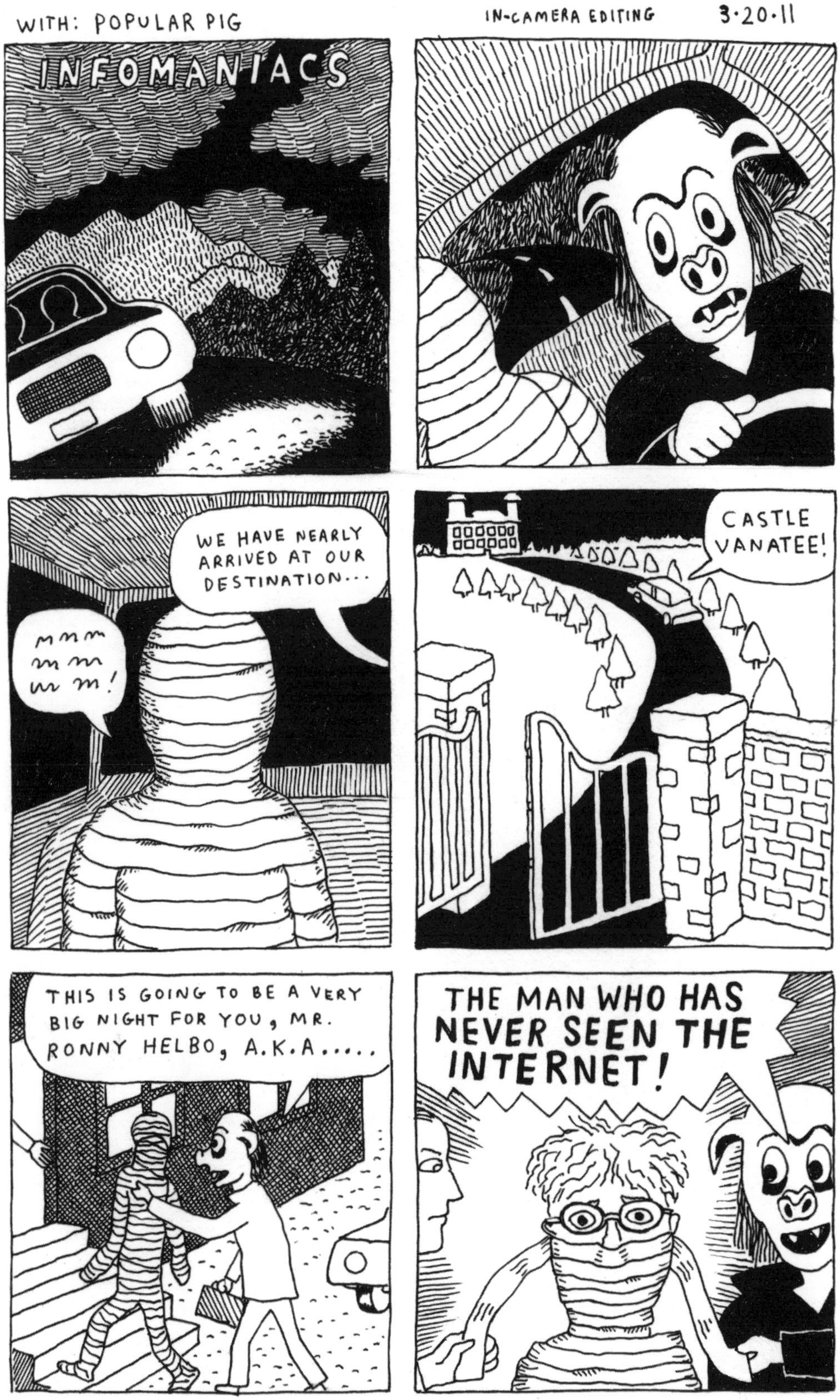
WITH: POPULAR PIG
IN-CAMERA EDITING
3·20·11
INFOMANIACS
WE HAVE NEARLY ARRIVED AT OUR DESTINATION...
CASTLE VANATEE!
THIS IS GOING TO BE A VERY BIG NIGHT FOR YOU, MR. RONNY HELBO, A.K.A.....
THE MAN WHO HAS NEVER SEEN THE INTERNET!

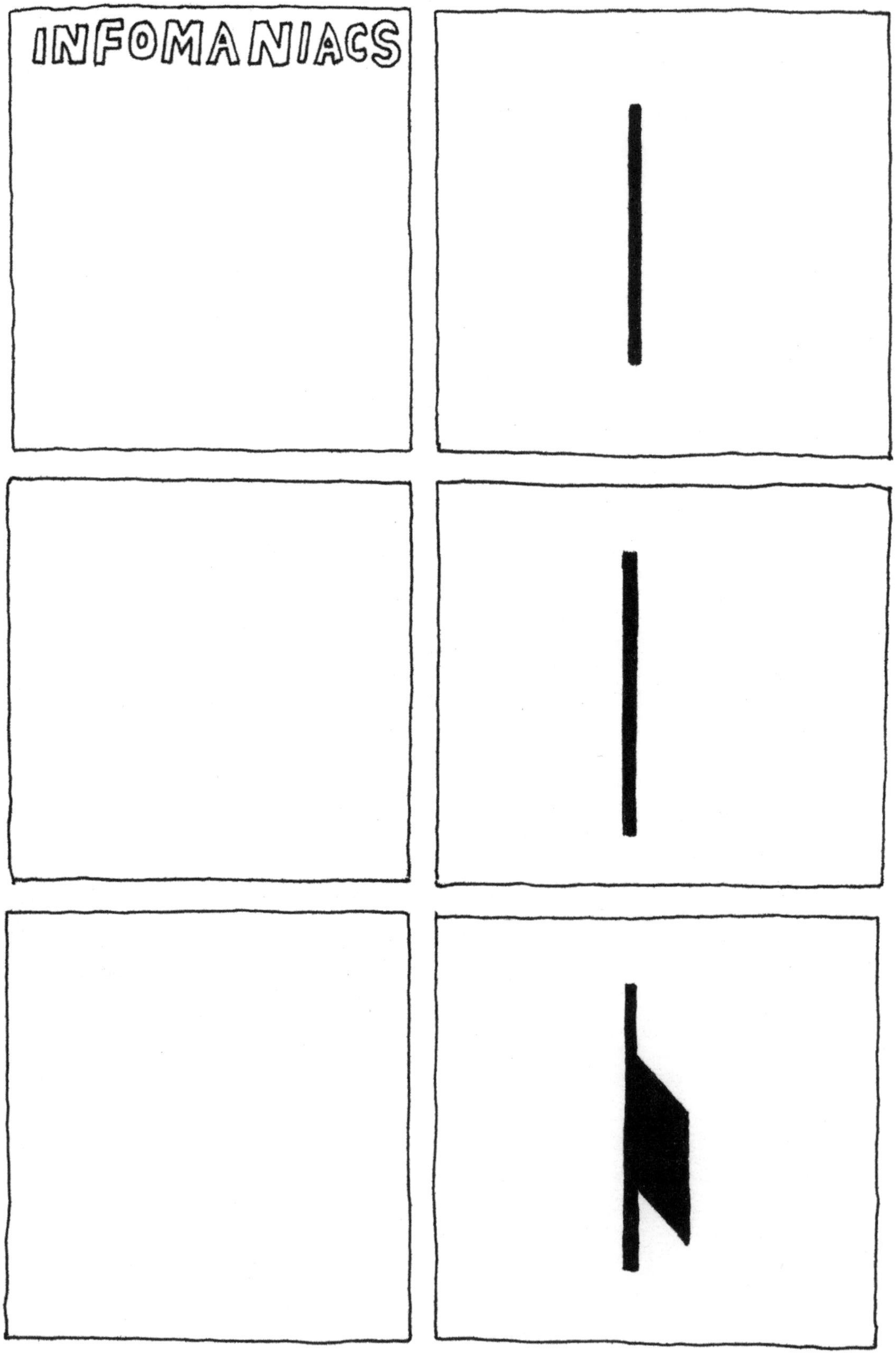
INFOMANIACS

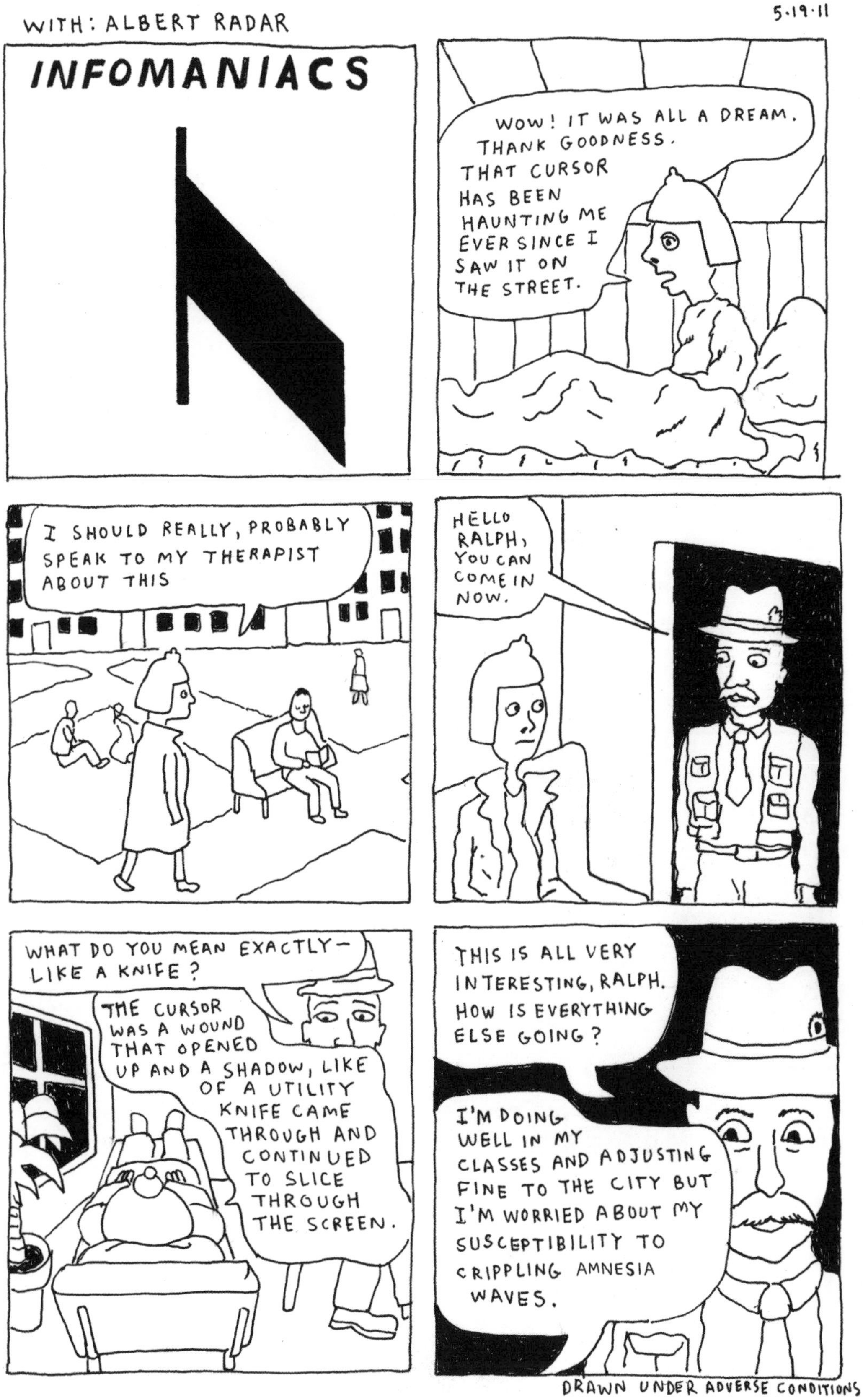
WITH: ALBERT RADAR
5·19·11
INFOMANIACS
WOW! IT WAS ALL A DREAM. THANK GOODNESS. THAT CURSOR HAS BEEN HAUNTING ME EVER SINCE I SAW IT ON THE STREET.
I SHOULD REALLY, PROBABLY SPEAK TO MY THERAPIST ABOUT THIS
HELLO RALPH, YOU CAN COME IN NOW.
WHAT DO YOU MEAN EXACTLY— LIKE A KNIFE?
THE CURSOR WAS A WOUND THAT OPENED UP AND A SHADOW, LIKE OF A UTILITY KNIFE CAME THROUGH AND CONTINUED TO SLICE THROUGH THE SCREEN.
THIS IS ALL VERY INTERESTING, RALPH. HOW IS EVERYTHING ELSE GOING?
I'M DOING WELL IN MY CLASSES AND ADJUSTING FINE TO THE CITY BUT I'M WORRIED ABOUT MY SUSCEPTIBILITY TO CRIPPLING AMNESIA WAVES.
DRAWN UNDER ADVERSE CONDITIONS

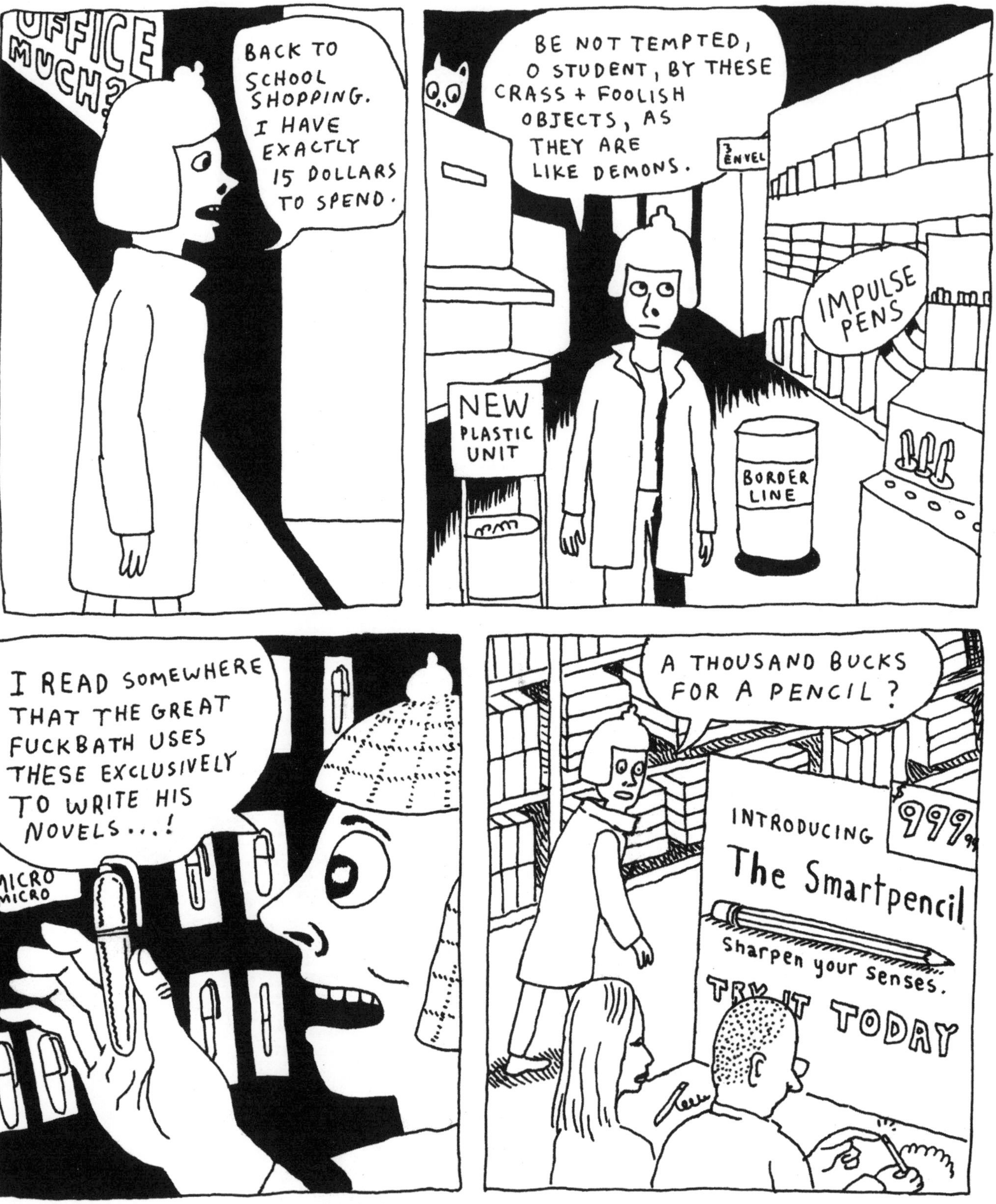
OFFICE MUCH?
BACK TO SCHOOL SHOPPING. I HAVE EXACTLY 15 DOLLARS TO SPEND.
BE NOT TEMPTED, O STUDENT, BY THESE CRASS + FOOLISH OBJECTS, AS THEY ARE LIKE DEMONS.
ENVEL
IMPULSE PENS
NEW PLASTIC UNIT
BORDER LINE
I READ SOMEWHERE THAT THE GREAT FUCKBATH USES THESE EXCLUSIVELY TO WRITE HIS NOVELS...!
MICRO MICRO
A THOUSAND BUCKS FOR A PENCIL?
INTRODUCING
999.99
The Smartpencil
Sharpen your senses.
TRY IT TODAY

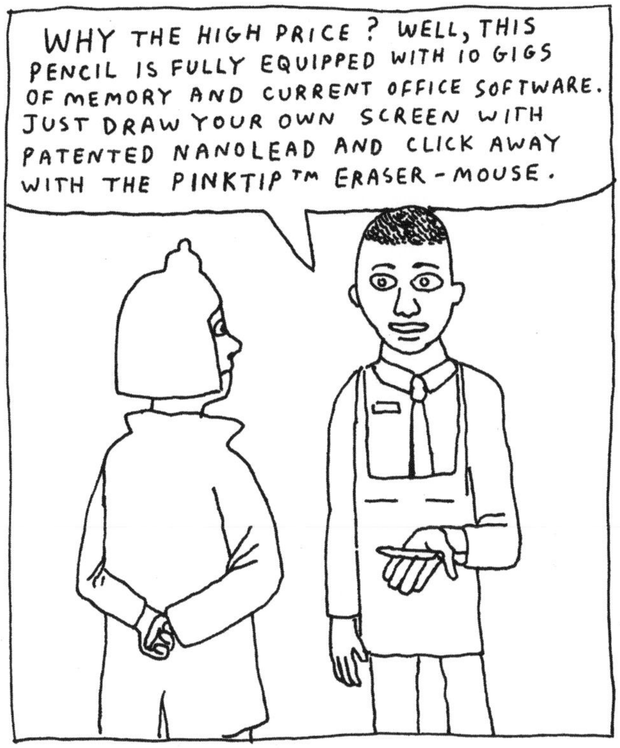
WHY THE HIGH PRICE? WELL, THIS PENCIL IS FULLY EQUIPPED WITH 10 GIGS OF MEMORY AND CURRENT OFFICE SOFTWARE. JUST DRAW YOUR OWN SCREEN WITH PATENTED NANOLEAD AND CLICK AWAY WITH THE PINKTIP™ ERASER-MOUSE.

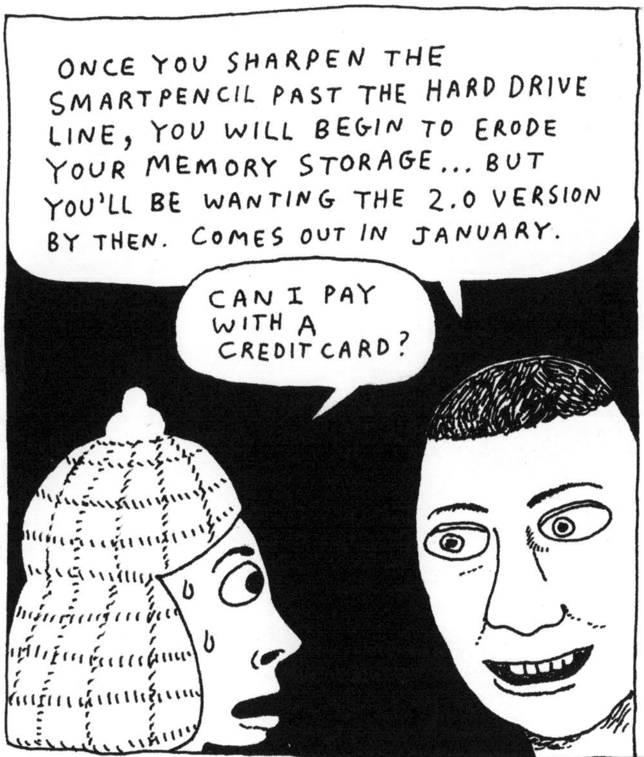
ONCE YOU SHARPEN THE SMARTPENCIL PAST THE HARD DRIVE LINE, YOU WILL BEGIN TO ERODE YOUR MEMORY STORAGE... BUT YOU'LL BE WANTING THE 2.0 VERSION BY THEN. COMES OUT IN JANUARY.
CAN I PAY WITH A CREDIT CARD?

IMA PELICAN LIVE & DIRECT 10-20-11

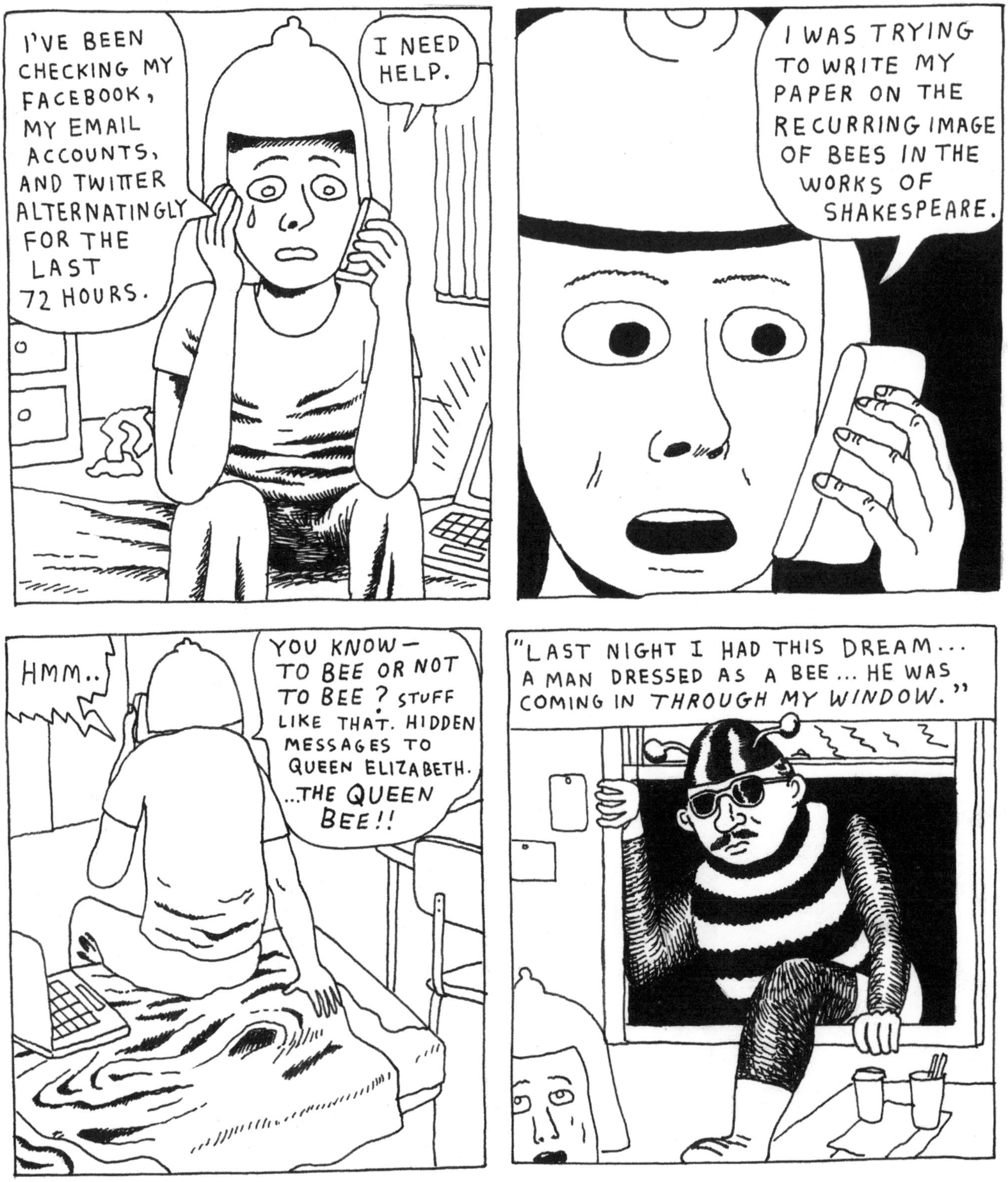
I'VE BEEN CHECKING MY FACEBOOK, MY EMAIL ACCOUNTS, AND TWITTER ALTERNATINGLY FOR THE LAST 72 HOURS.
I NEED HELP.
I WAS TRYING TO WRITE MY PAPER ON THE RECURRING IMAGE OF BEES IN THE WORKS OF SHAKESPEARE.
HMM..
YOU KNOW— TO BEE OR NOT TO BEE? STUFF LIKE THAT. HIDDEN MESSAGES TO QUEEN ELIZABETH. ...THE QUEEN BEE!!
"LAST NIGHT I HAD THIS DREAM... A MAN DRESSED AS A BEE... HE WAS COMING IN *THROUGH MY WINDOW*."

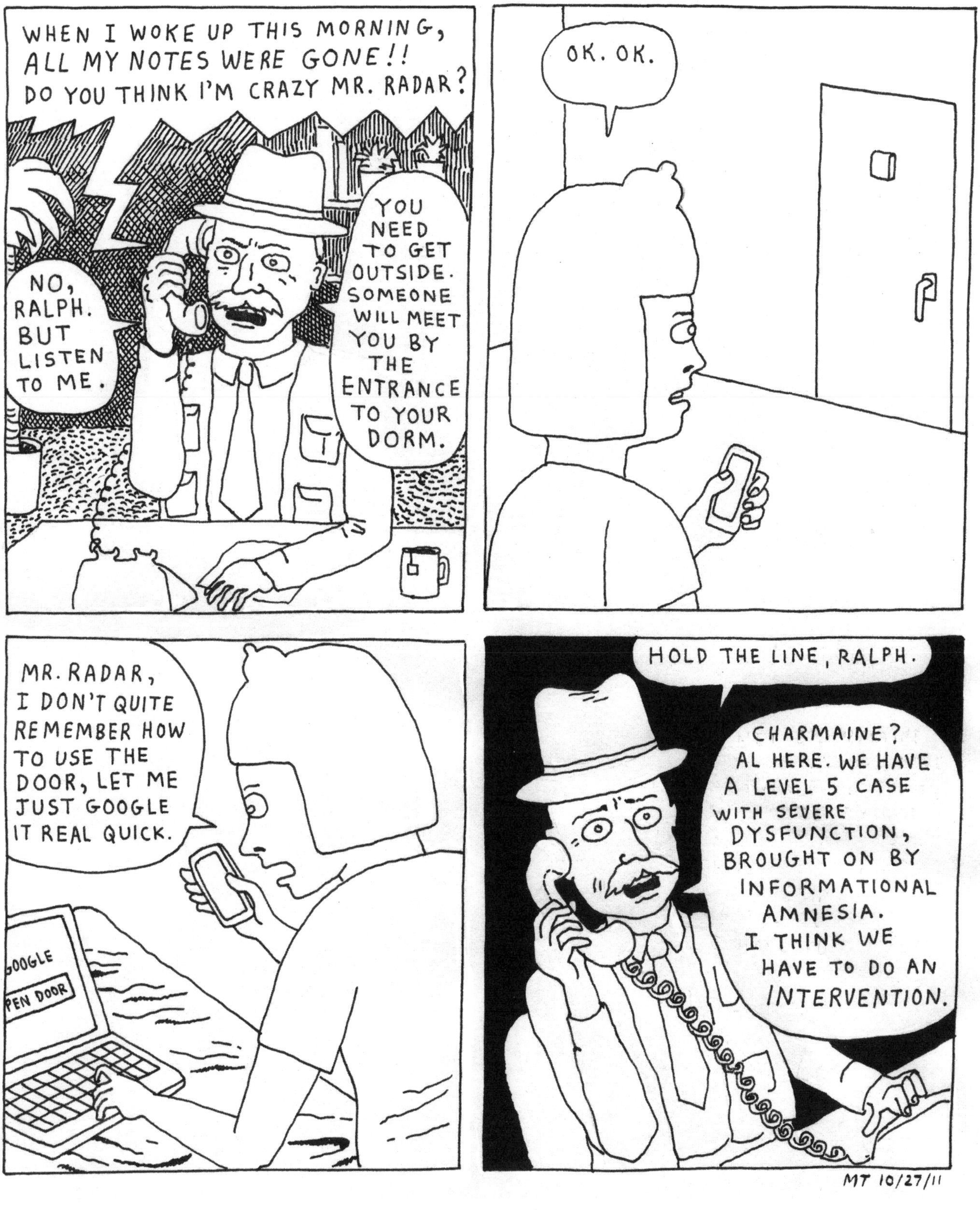
WHEN I WOKE UP THIS MORNING, ALL MY NOTES WERE GONE!! DO YOU THINK I'M CRAZY MR. RADAR?
NO, RALPH. BUT LISTEN TO ME.
YOU NEED TO GET OUTSIDE. SOMEONE WILL MEET YOU BY THE ENTRANCE TO YOUR DORM.
OK. OK.
MR. RADAR, I DON'T QUITE REMEMBER HOW TO USE THE DOOR, LET ME JUST GOOGLE IT REAL QUICK.
HOLD THE LINE, RALPH.
CHARMAINE? AL HERE. WE HAVE A LEVEL 5 CASE WITH SEVERE DYSFUNCTION, BROUGHT ON BY INFORMATIONAL AMNESIA. I THINK WE HAVE TO DO AN INTERVENTION.
MT 10/27/11

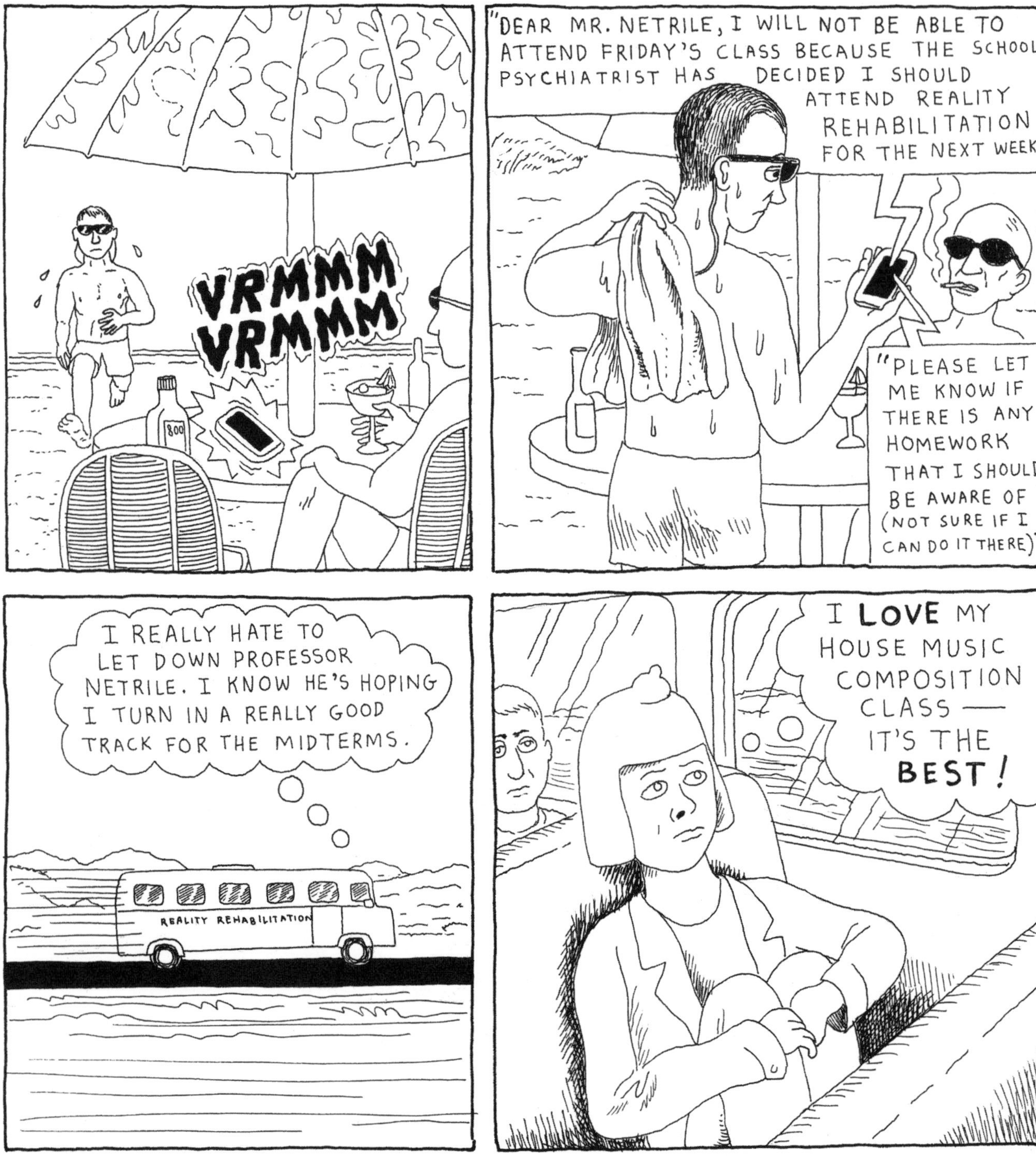
VRMMM VRMMM
"DEAR MR. NETRILE, I WILL NOT BE ABLE TO ATTEND FRIDAY'S CLASS BECAUSE THE SCHOOL PSYCHIATRIST HAS DECIDED I SHOULD ATTEND REALITY REHABILITATION FOR THE NEXT WEEK.
"PLEASE LET ME KNOW IF THERE IS ANY HOMEWORK THAT I SHOULD BE AWARE OF (NOT SURE IF I CAN DO IT THERE)"
I REALLY HATE TO LET DOWN PROFESSOR NETRILE. I KNOW HE'S HOPING I TURN IN A REALLY GOOD TRACK FOR THE MIDTERMS.
REALITY REHABILITATION
I **LOVE** MY HOUSE MUSIC COMPOSITION CLASS — IT'S THE **BEST**!

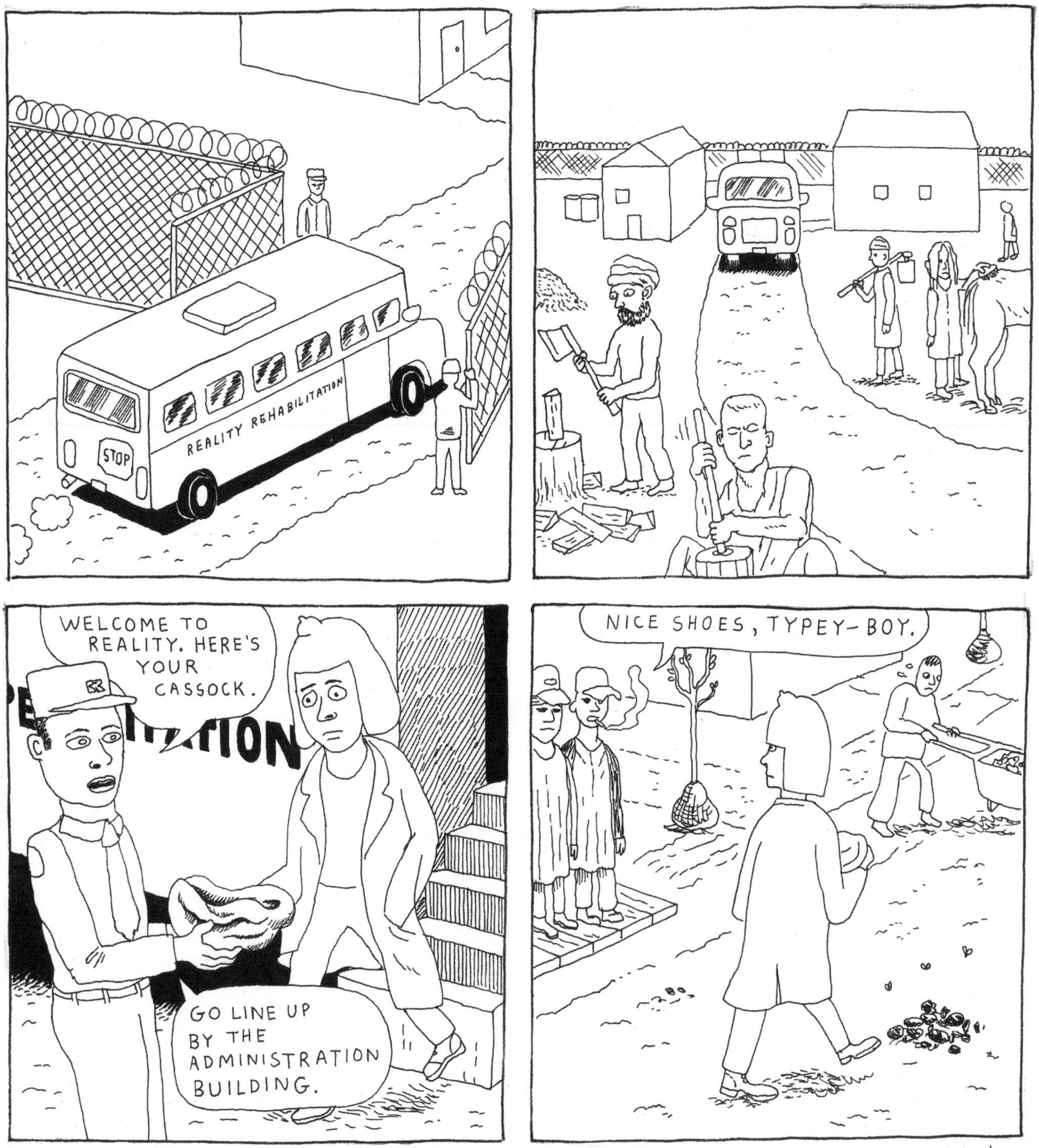
STOP
REALITY REHABILITATION
WELCOME TO REALITY. HERE'S YOUR CASSOCK.
GO LINE UP BY THE ADMINISTRATION BUILDING.
NICE SHOES, TYPEY-BOY.
MT 11/03/11

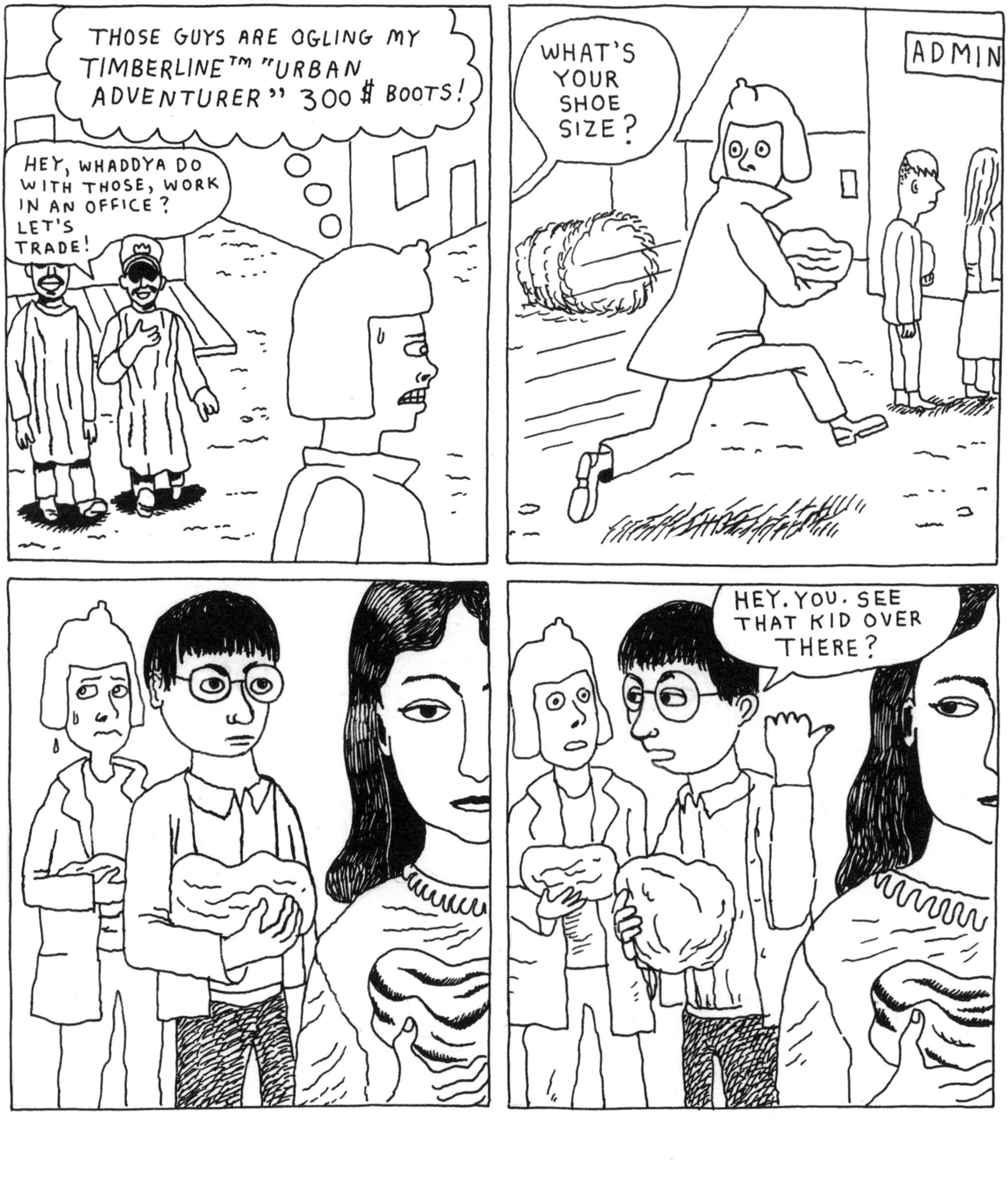
THOSE GUYS ARE OGLING MY TIMBERLINE™ "URBAN ADVENTURER" 300 $ BOOTS!
HEY, WHADDYA DO WITH THOSE, WORK IN AN OFFICE? LET'S TRADE!
WHAT'S YOUR SHOE SIZE?
ADMIN
HEY. YOU. SEE THAT KID OVER THERE?

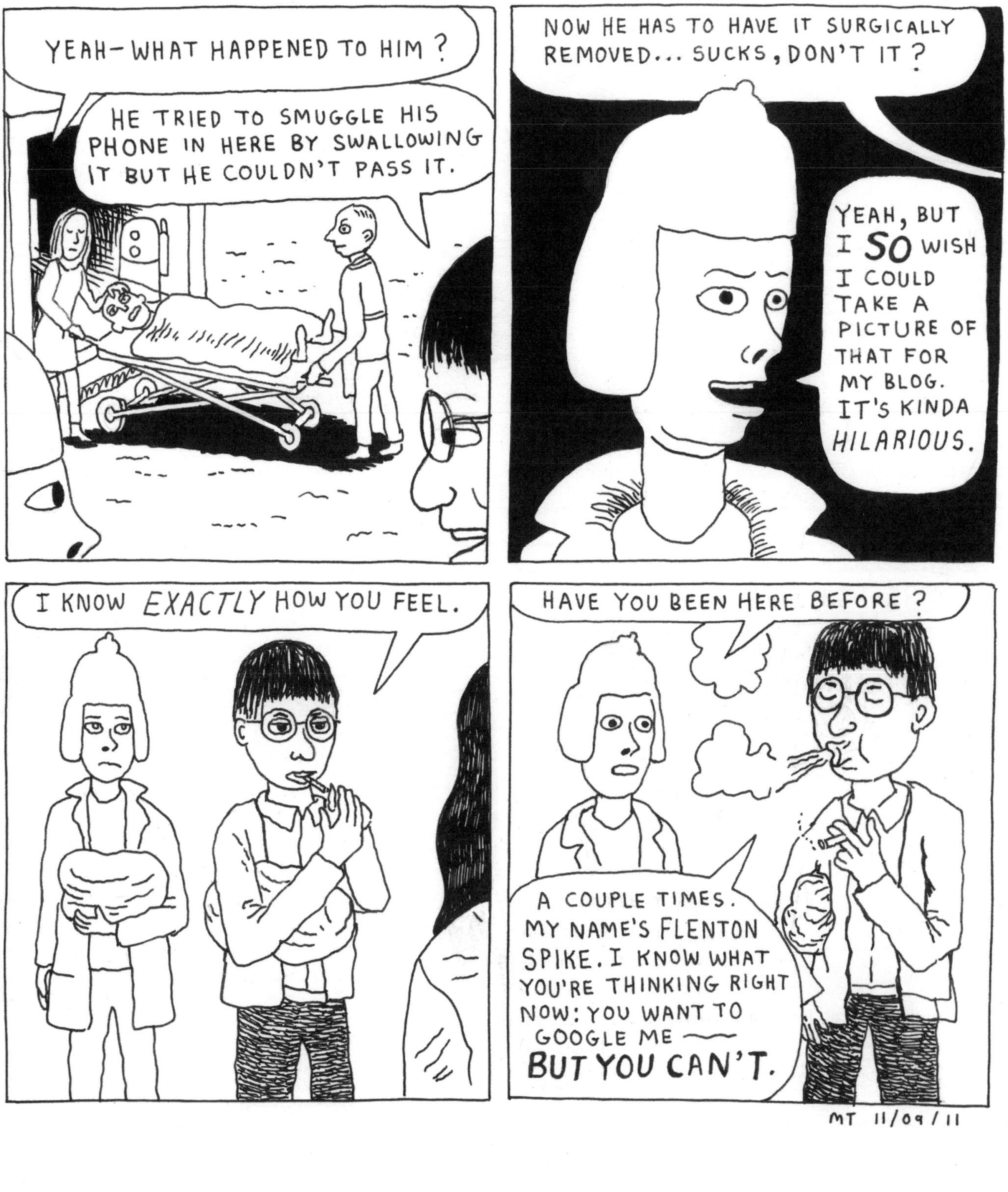
YEAH- WHAT HAPPENED TO HIM?
HE TRIED TO SMUGGLE HIS PHONE IN HERE BY SWALLOWING IT BUT HE COULDN'T PASS IT.
NOW HE HAS TO HAVE IT SURGICALLY REMOVED... SUCKS, DON'T IT?
YEAH, BUT I SO WISH I COULD TAKE A PICTURE OF THAT FOR MY BLOG. IT'S KINDA HILARIOUS.
I KNOW EXACTLY HOW YOU FEEL.
HAVE YOU BEEN HERE BEFORE?
A COUPLE TIMES. MY NAME'S FLENTON SPIKE. I KNOW WHAT YOU'RE THINKING RIGHT NOW: YOU WANT TO GOOGLE ME — BUT YOU CAN'T.
MT 11/09/11

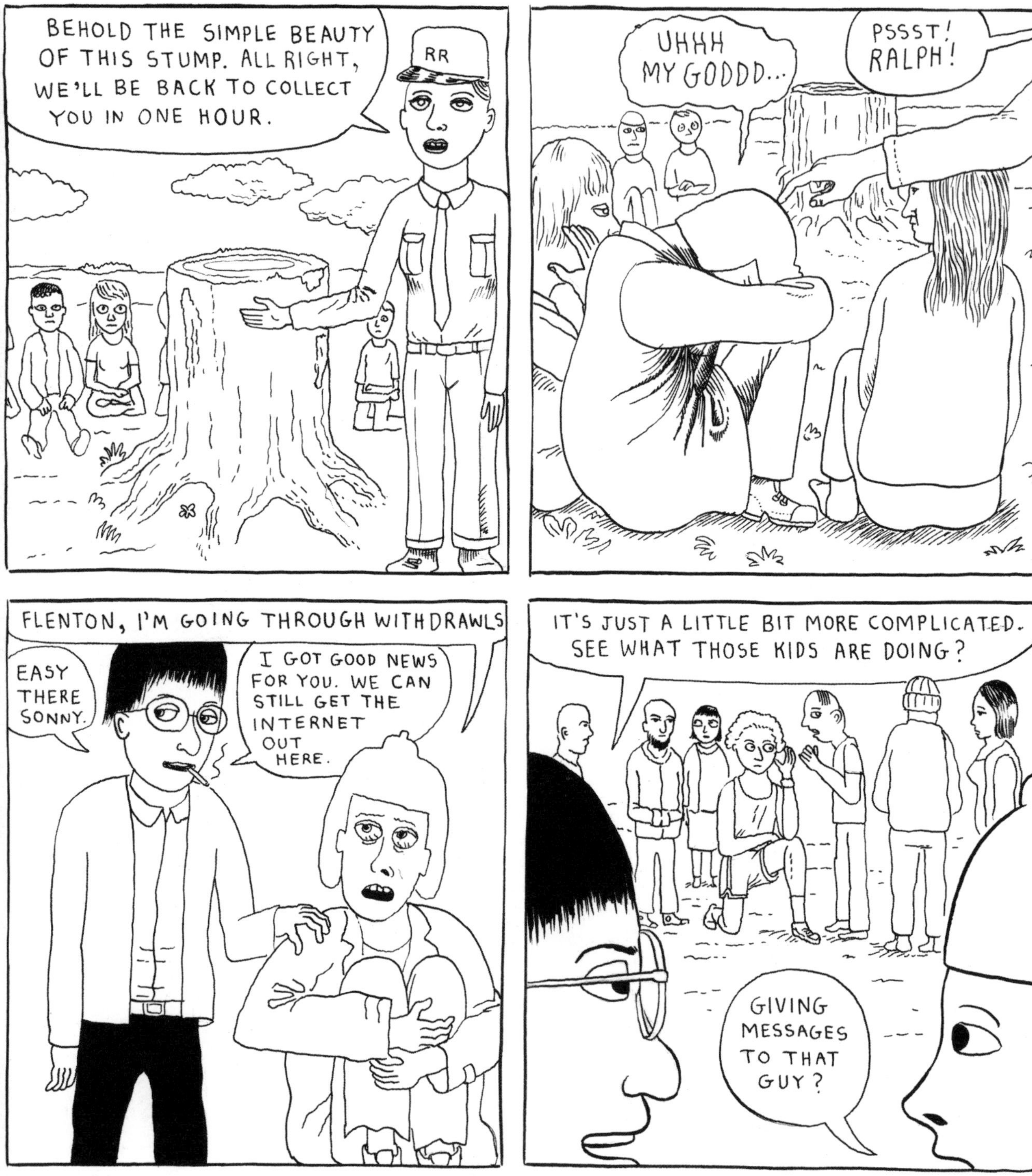

BEHOLD THE SIMPLE BEAUTY OF THIS STUMP. ALL RIGHT, WE'LL BE BACK TO COLLECT YOU IN ONE HOUR.
RR
UHHH MY GODDD...
PSSST! RALPH!
FLENTON, I'M GOING THROUGH WITHDRAWLS
EASY THERE SONNY.
I GOT GOOD NEWS FOR YOU. WE CAN STILL GET THE INTERNET OUT HERE.
IT'S JUST A LITTLE BIT MORE COMPLICATED. SEE WHAT THOSE KIDS ARE DOING?
GIVING MESSAGES TO THAT GUY?

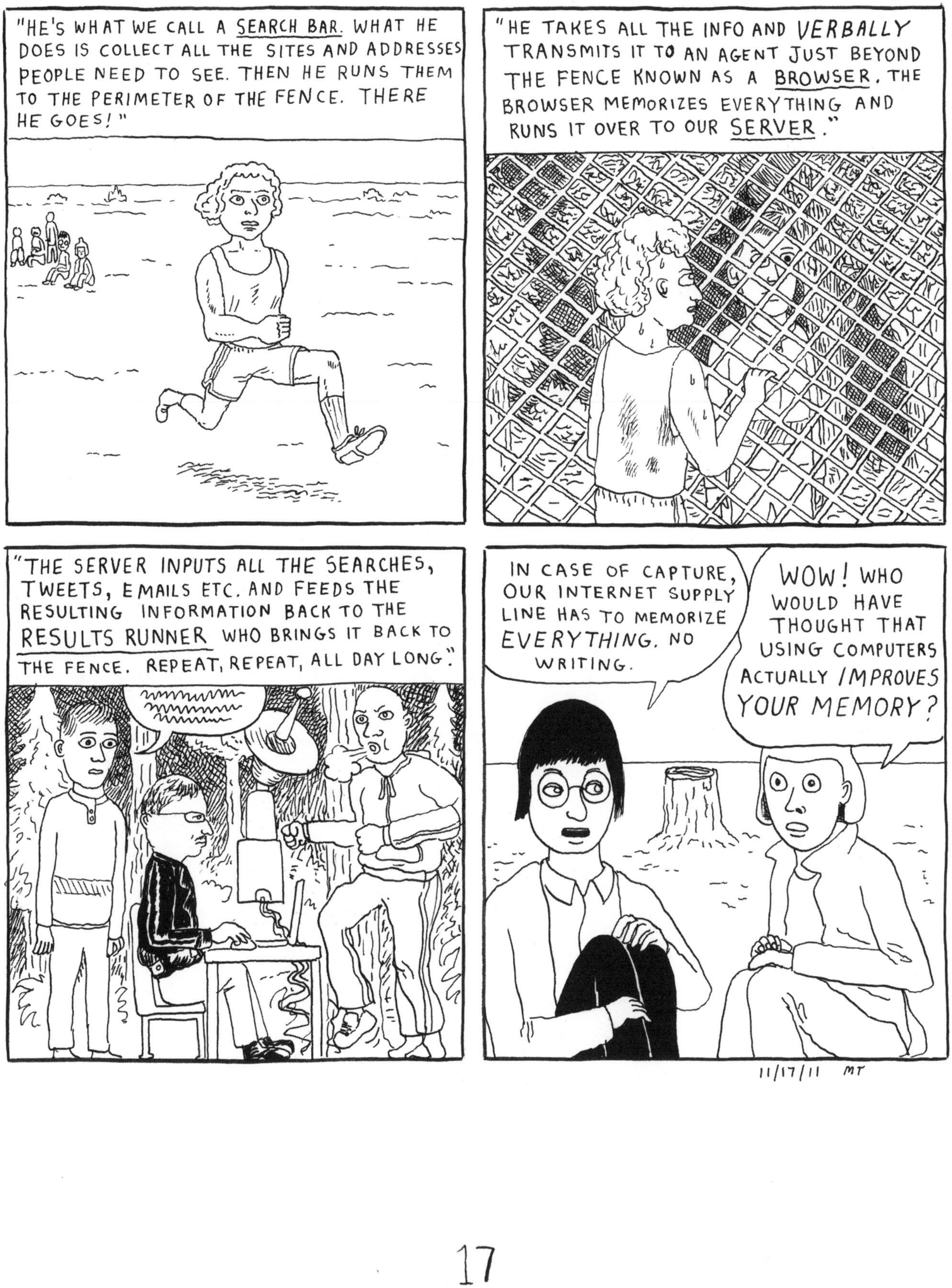
"HE'S WHAT WE CALL A SEARCH BAR. WHAT HE DOES IS COLLECT ALL THE SITES AND ADDRESSES PEOPLE NEED TO SEE. THEN HE RUNS THEM TO THE PERIMETER OF THE FENCE. THERE HE GOES!"
"HE TAKES ALL THE INFO AND VERBALLY TRANSMITS IT TO AN AGENT JUST BEYOND THE FENCE KNOWN AS A BROWSER. THE BROWSER MEMORIZES EVERYTHING AND RUNS IT OVER TO OUR SERVER."
"THE SERVER INPUTS ALL THE SEARCHES, TWEETS, EMAILS ETC. AND FEEDS THE RESULTING INFORMATION BACK TO THE RESULTS RUNNER WHO BRINGS IT BACK TO THE FENCE. REPEAT, REPEAT, ALL DAY LONG."
IN CASE OF CAPTURE, OUR INTERNET SUPPLY LINE HAS TO MEMORIZE EVERYTHING. NO WRITING.
WOW! WHO WOULD HAVE THOUGHT THAT USING COMPUTERS ACTUALLY IMPROVES YOUR MEMORY?
11/17/11 MT

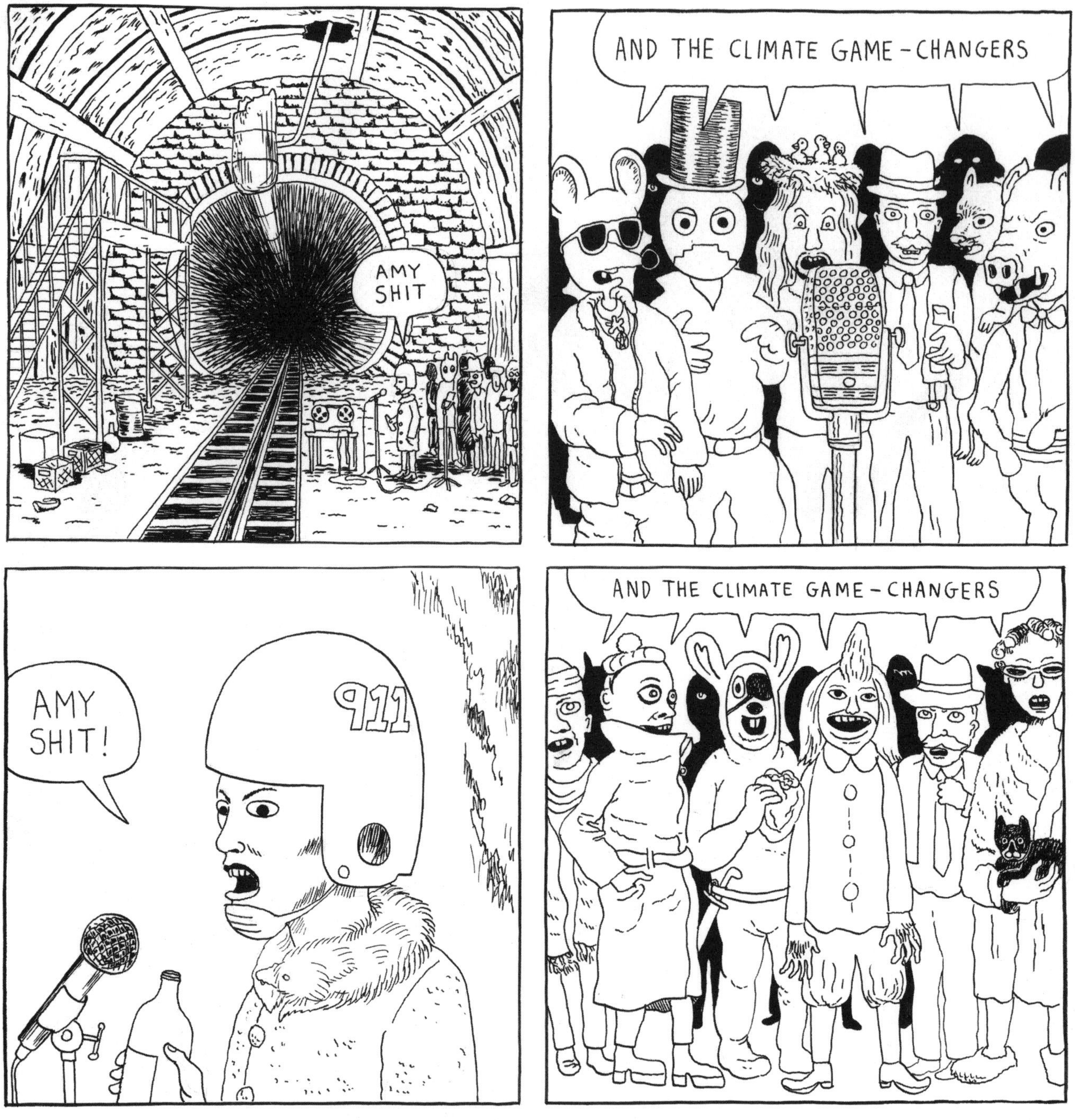
AMY SHIT
AND THE CLIMATE GAME-CHANGERS
AMY SHIT!
AND THE CLIMATE GAME-CHANGERS

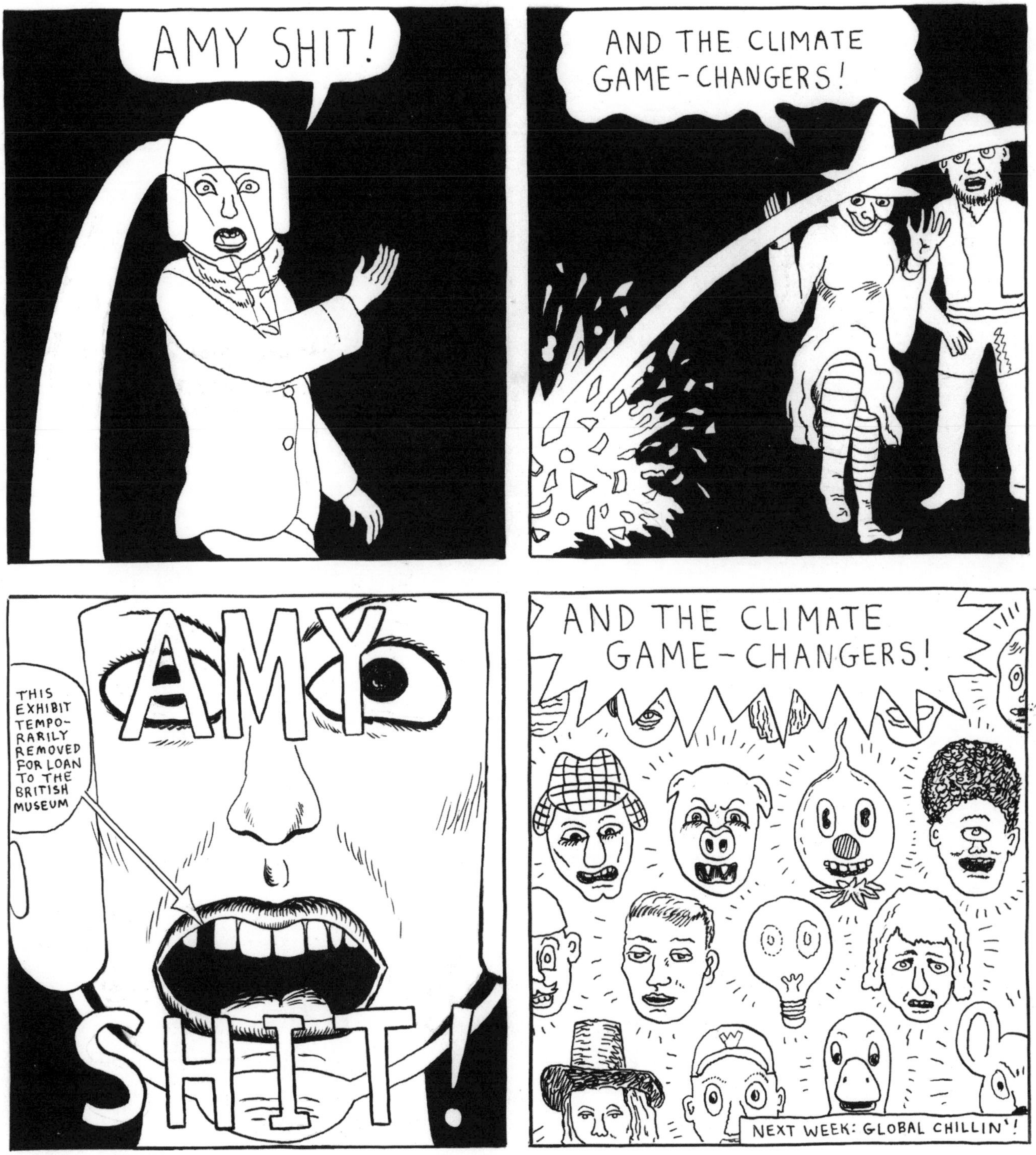
AMY SHIT!
AND THE CLIMATE GAME-CHANGERS!
AMY SHIT!
THIS EXHIBIT TEMPORARILY REMOVED FOR LOAN TO THE BRITISH MUSEUM
AND THE CLIMATE GAME-CHANGERS!
NEXT WEEK: GLOBAL CHILLIN'!

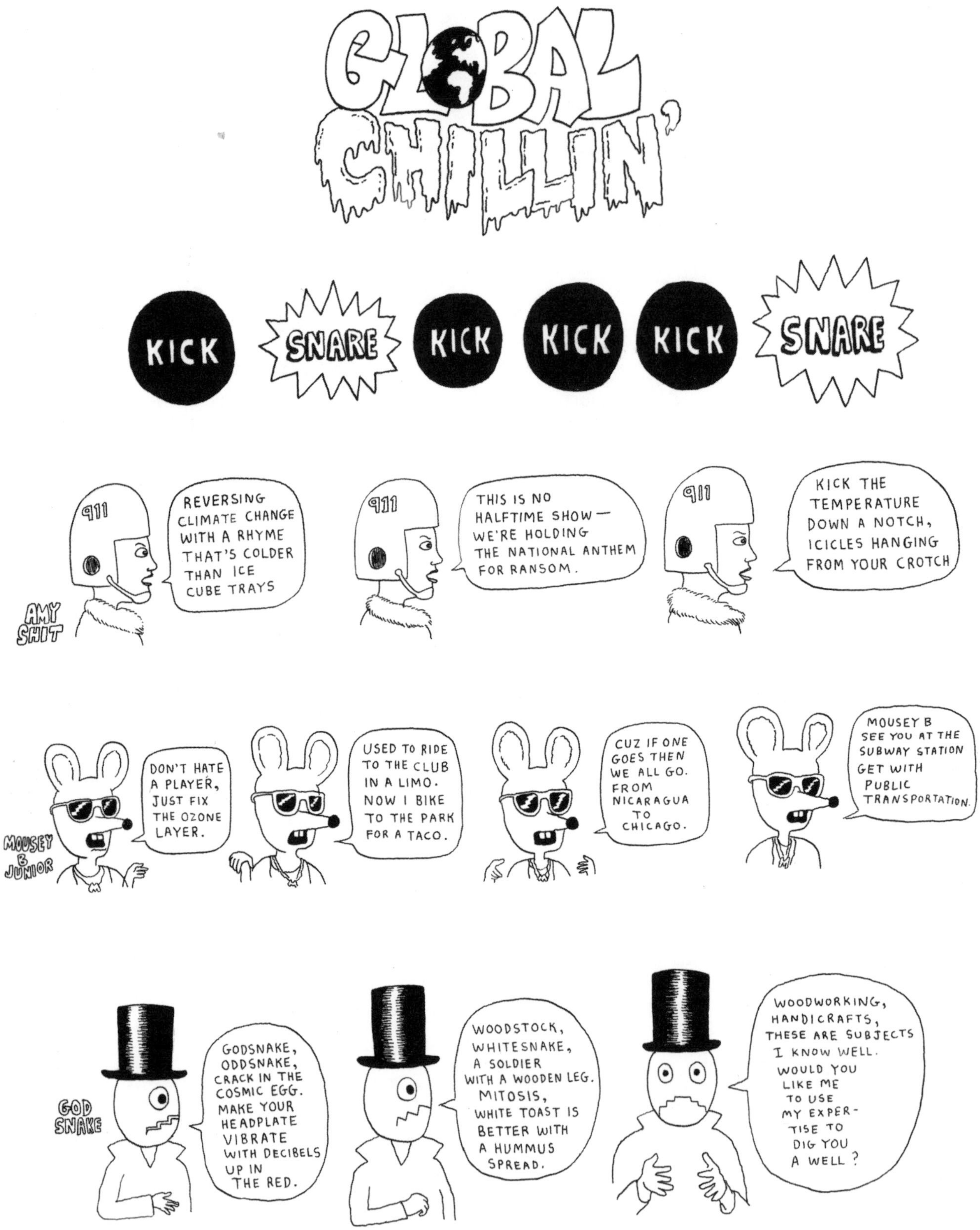
GLOBAL CHILLIN'
KICK
SNARE
KICK
KICK
KICK
SNARE
AMY SHIT
REVERSING CLIMATE CHANGE WITH A RHYME THAT'S COLDER THAN ICE CUBE TRAYS
THIS IS NO HALFTIME SHOW— WE'RE HOLDING THE NATIONAL ANTHEM FOR RANSOM.
KICK THE TEMPERATURE DOWN A NOTCH, ICICLES HANGING FROM YOUR CROTCH
MOUSEY B JUNIOR
DON'T HATE A PLAYER, JUST FIX THE OZONE LAYER.
USED TO RIDE TO THE CLUB IN A LIMO. NOW I BIKE TO THE PARK FOR A TACO.
CUZ IF ONE GOES THEN WE ALL GO. FROM NICARAGUA TO CHICAGO.
MOUSEY B SEE YOU AT THE SUBWAY STATION GET WITH PUBLIC TRANSPORTATION.
GOD SNAKE
GODSNAKE, ODDSNAKE, CRACK IN THE COSMIC EGG. MAKE YOUR HEADPLATE VIBRATE WITH DECIBELS UP IN THE RED.
WOODSTOCK, WHITESNAKE, A SOLDIER WITH A WOODEN LEG. MITOSIS, WHITE TOAST IS BETTER WITH A HUMMUS SPREAD.
WOODWORKING, HANDICRAFTS, THESE ARE SUBJECTS I KNOW WELL. WOULD YOU LIKE ME TO USE MY EXPER-TISE TO DIG YOU A WELL?

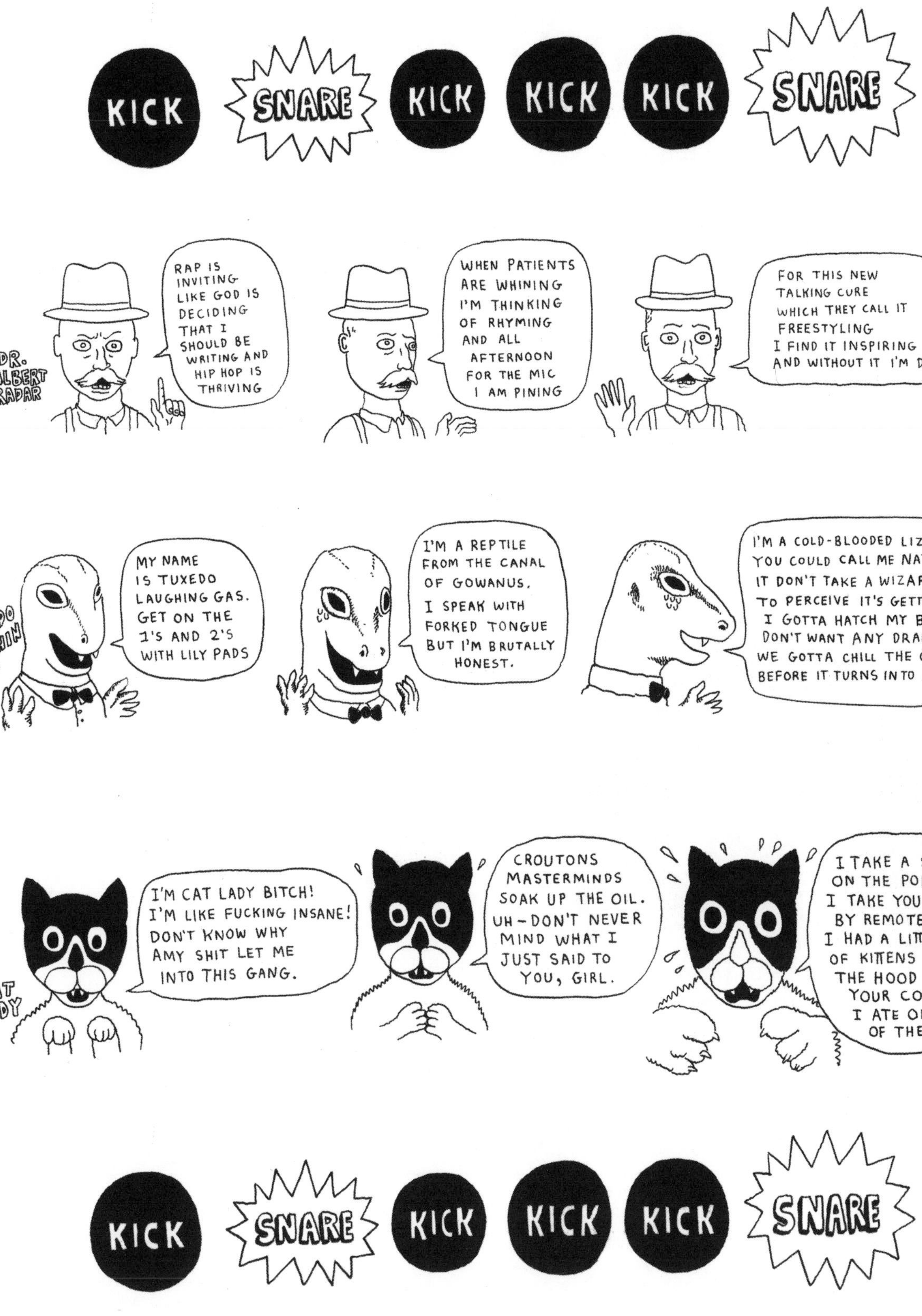

KICK
SNARE
KICK
KICK
KICK
SNARE
DR. ALBERT RADAR
RAP IS INVITING LIKE GOD IS DECIDING THAT I SHOULD BE WRITING AND HIP HOP IS THRIVING
WHEN PATIENTS ARE WHINING I'M THINKING OF RHYMING AND ALL AFTERNOON FOR THE MIC I AM PINING
FOR THIS NEW TALKING CURE WHICH THEY CALL IT FREESTYLING I FIND IT INSPIRING AND WITHOUT IT I'M DYING.
TUXEDO LAUGHIN GAS
MY NAME IS TUXEDO LAUGHING GAS. GET ON THE 1'S AND 2'S WITH LILY PADS
I'M A REPTILE FROM THE CANAL OF GOWANUS. I SPEAK WITH FORKED TONGUE BUT I'M BRUTALLY HONEST.
I'M A COLD-BLOODED LIZARD YOU COULD CALL ME NATIVE FAUNA IT DON'T TAKE A WIZARD TO PERCEIVE IT'S GETTING WARMER I GOTTA HATCH MY BABIES DON'T WANT ANY DRAMA WE GOTTA CHILL THE GLOBE BEFORE IT TURNS INTO A SAUNA.
CAT LADY
I'M CAT LADY BITCH! I'M LIKE FUCKING INSANE! DON'T KNOW WHY AMY SHIT LET ME INTO THIS GANG.
CROUTONS MASTERMINDS SOAK UP THE OIL. UH-DON'T NEVER MIND WHAT I JUST SAID TO YOU, GIRL.
I TAKE A SHIT ON THE POPE. I TAKE YOU OUT BY REMOTE. I HAD A LITTER OF KITTENS IN THE HOOD OF YOUR COAT. I ATE ONE OF THEM.
KICK
SNARE
KICK
KICK
KICK
SNARE

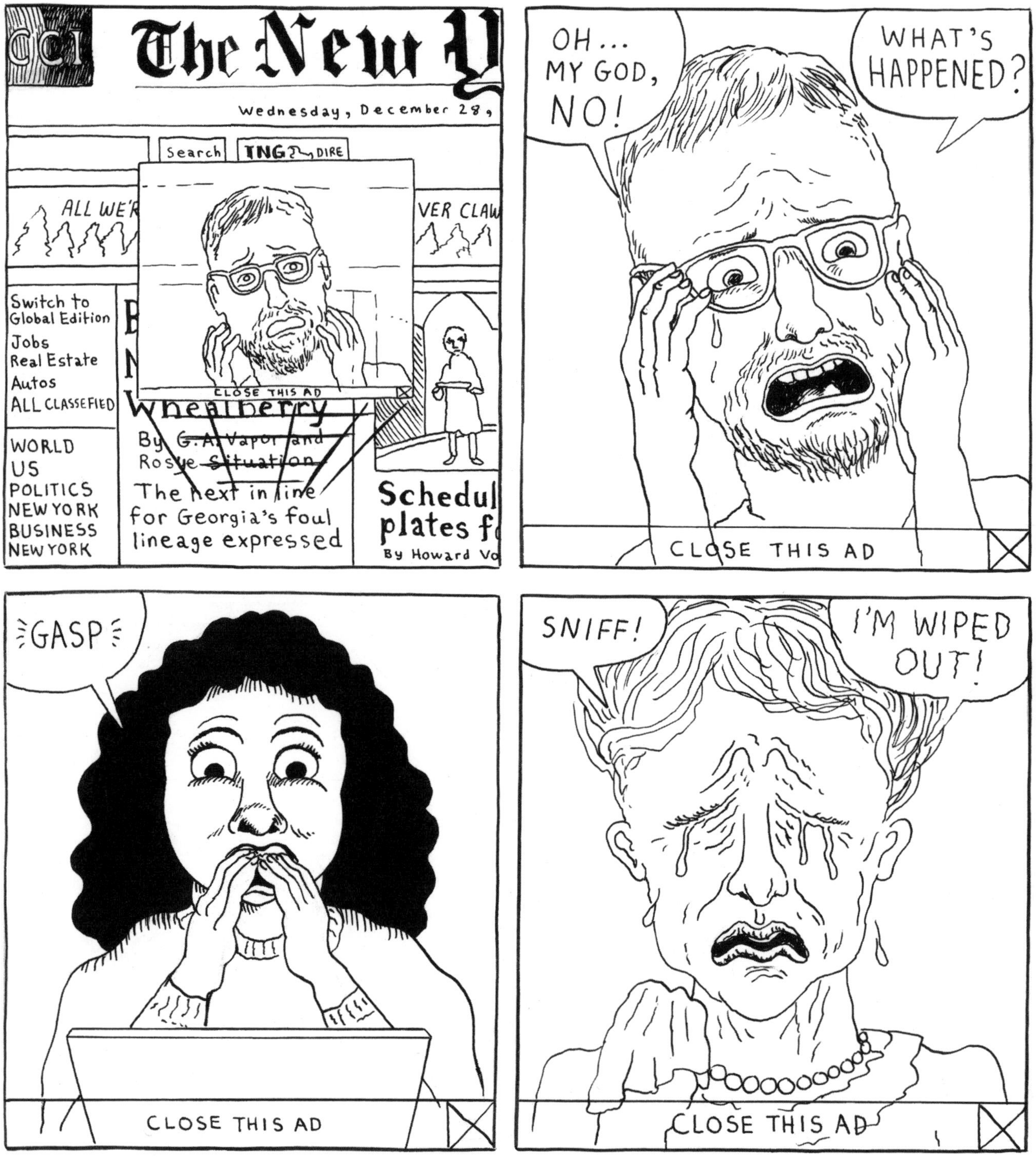

The New Y
Wednesday, December 28,
Search
TNG
DIRE
ALL WE'R
VER CLAW
Switch to Global Edition
Jobs
Real Estate
Autos
ALL CLASSEFIED
WORLD
US
POLITICS
NEW YORK
BUSINESS
NEW YORK
Whealberry
By G. A. Vapor and Rosye Situation
The next in line for Georgia's foul lineage expressed
Schedul plates f
By Howard Vo
CLOSE THIS AD
OH... MY GOD, NO!
WHAT'S HAPPENED?
CLOSE THIS AD
GASP
CLOSE THIS AD
SNIFF!
I'M WIPED OUT!
CLOSE THIS AD

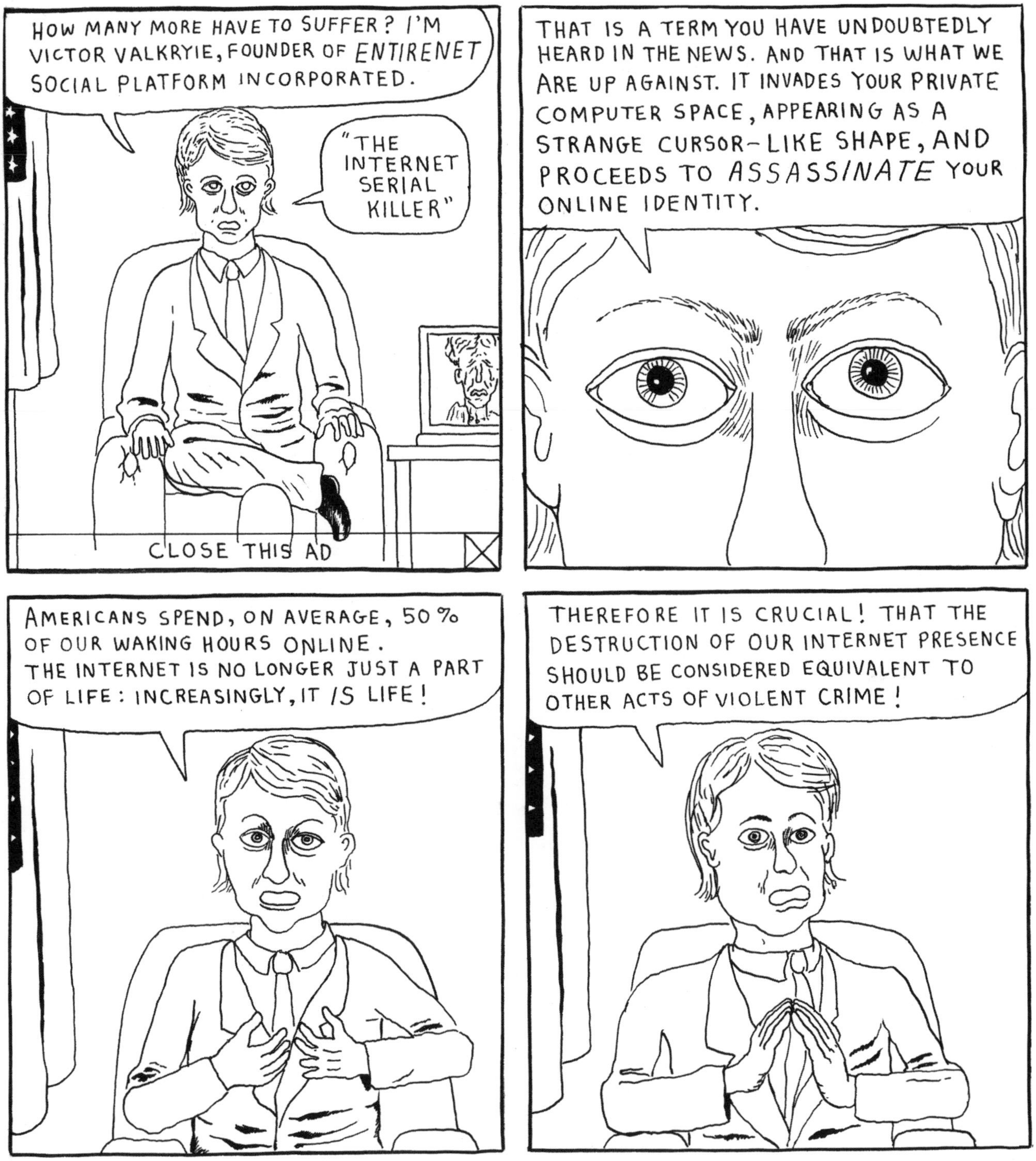
HOW MANY MORE HAVE TO SUFFER? I'M VICTOR VALKRYIE, FOUNDER OF ENTIRENET SOCIAL PLATFORM INCORPORATED.
"THE INTERNET SERIAL KILLER"
CLOSE THIS AD
THAT IS A TERM YOU HAVE UNDOUBTEDLY HEARD IN THE NEWS. AND THAT IS WHAT WE ARE UP AGAINST. IT INVADES YOUR PRIVATE COMPUTER SPACE, APPEARING AS A STRANGE CURSOR-LIKE SHAPE, AND PROCEEDS TO ASSASSINATE YOUR ONLINE IDENTITY.
AMERICANS SPEND, ON AVERAGE, 50% OF OUR WAKING HOURS ONLINE. THE INTERNET IS NO LONGER JUST A PART OF LIFE: INCREASINGLY, IT IS LIFE!
THEREFORE IT IS CRUCIAL! THAT THE DESTRUCTION OF OUR INTERNET PRESENCE SHOULD BE CONSIDERED EQUIVALENT TO OTHER ACTS OF VIOLENT CRIME!

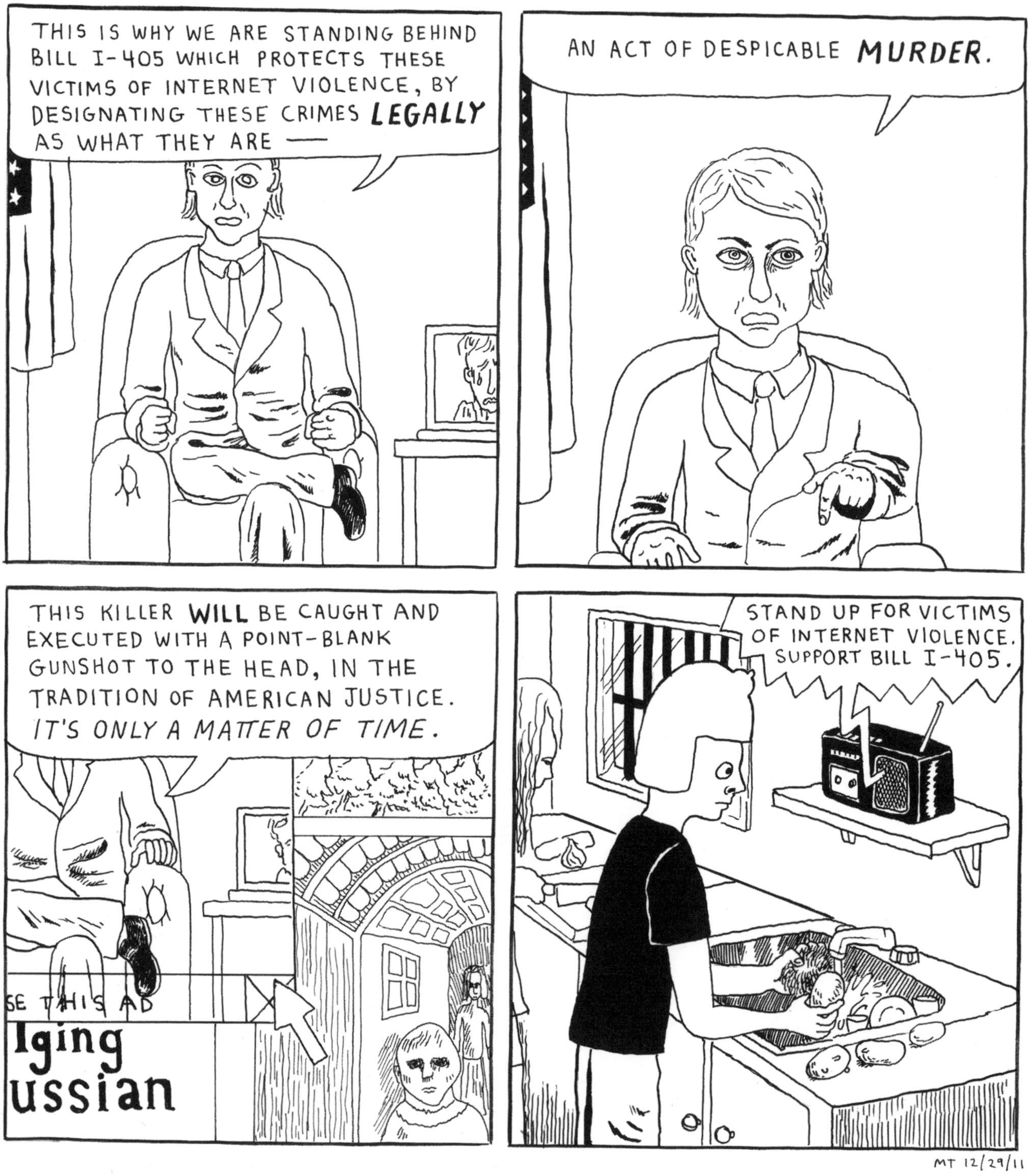
THIS IS WHY WE ARE STANDING BEHIND BILL I-405 WHICH PROTECTS THESE VICTIMS OF INTERNET VIOLENCE, BY DESIGNATING THESE CRIMES LEGALLY AS WHAT THEY ARE —
AN ACT OF DESPICABLE MURDER.
THIS KILLER WILL BE CAUGHT AND EXECUTED WITH A POINT-BLANK GUNSHOT TO THE HEAD, IN THE TRADITION OF AMERICAN JUSTICE. IT'S ONLY A MATTER OF TIME.
SE THIS AD
lging
ussian
STAND UP FOR VICTIMS OF INTERNET VIOLENCE. SUPPORT BILL I-405.
MT 12/29/11

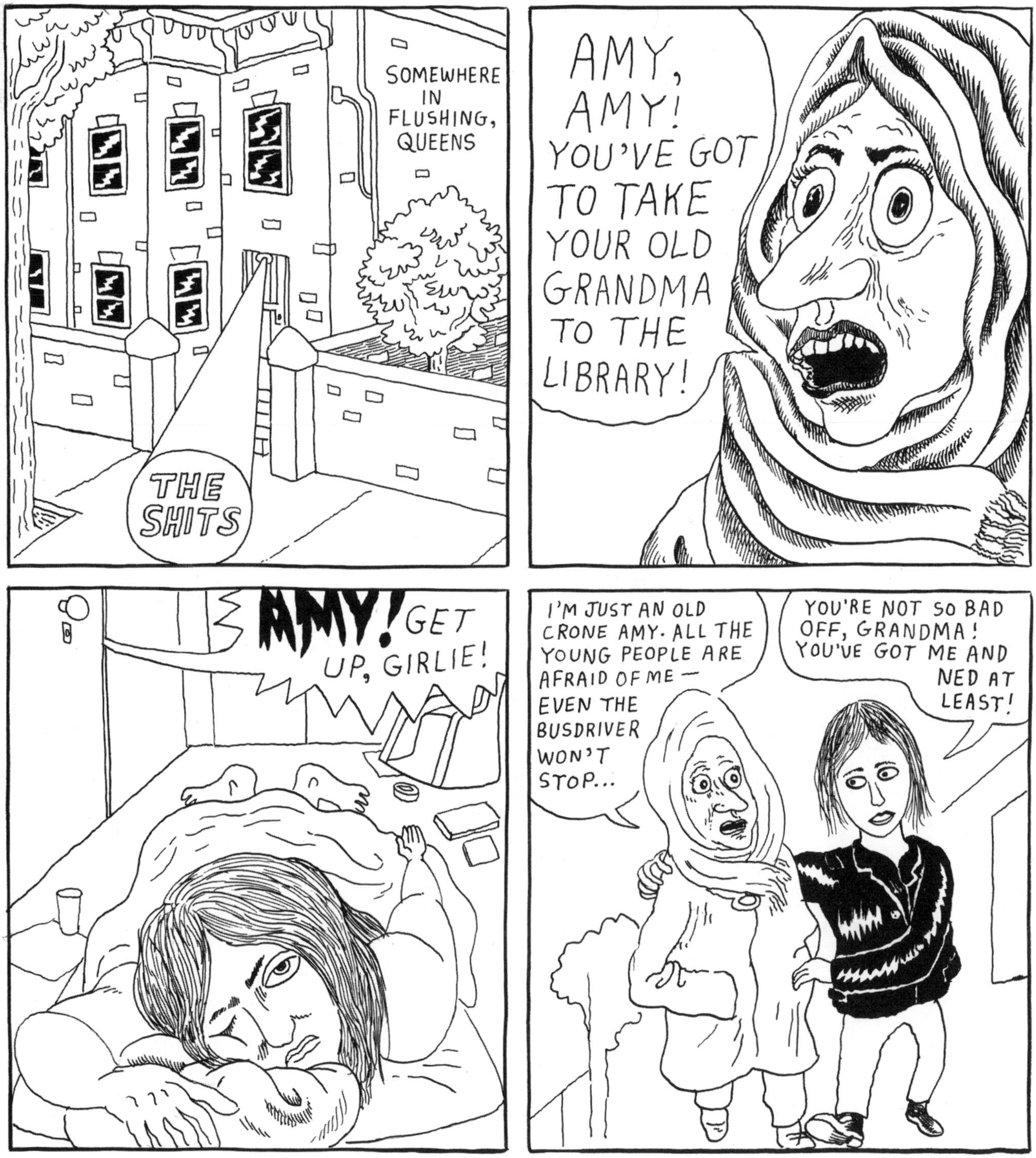
SOMEWHERE IN FLUSHING, QUEENS
THE SHITS
AMY, AMY! YOU'VE GOT TO TAKE YOUR OLD GRANDMA TO THE LIBRARY!
AMY! GET UP, GIRLIE!
I'M JUST AN OLD CRONE AMY. ALL THE YOUNG PEOPLE ARE AFRAID OF ME — EVEN THE BUSDRIVER WON'T STOP...
YOU'RE NOT SO BAD OFF, GRANDMA! YOU'VE GOT ME AND NED AT LEAST!

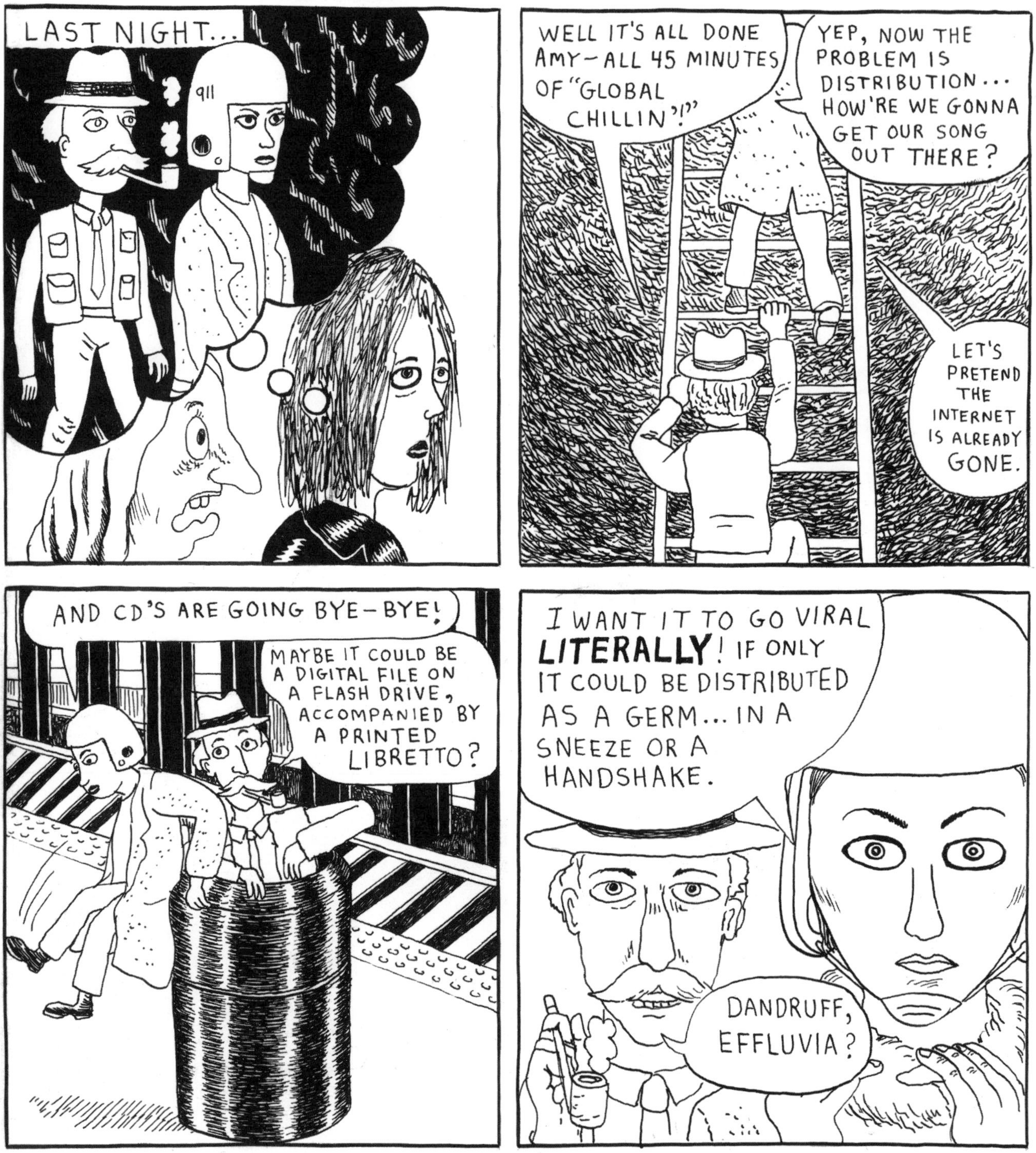

LAST NIGHT...
911
WELL IT'S ALL DONE AMY—ALL 45 MINUTES OF "GLOBAL CHILLIN'!"
YEP, NOW THE PROBLEM IS DISTRIBUTION... HOW'RE WE GONNA GET OUR SONG OUT THERE?
LET'S PRETEND THE INTERNET IS ALREADY GONE.
AND CD'S ARE GOING BYE-BYE!
MAYBE IT COULD BE A DIGITAL FILE ON A FLASH DRIVE, ACCOMPANIED BY A PRINTED LIBRETTO?
I WANT IT TO GO VIRAL **LITERALLY**! IF ONLY IT COULD BE DISTRIBUTED AS A GERM... IN A SNEEZE OR A HANDSHAKE.
DANDRUFF, EFFLUVIA?

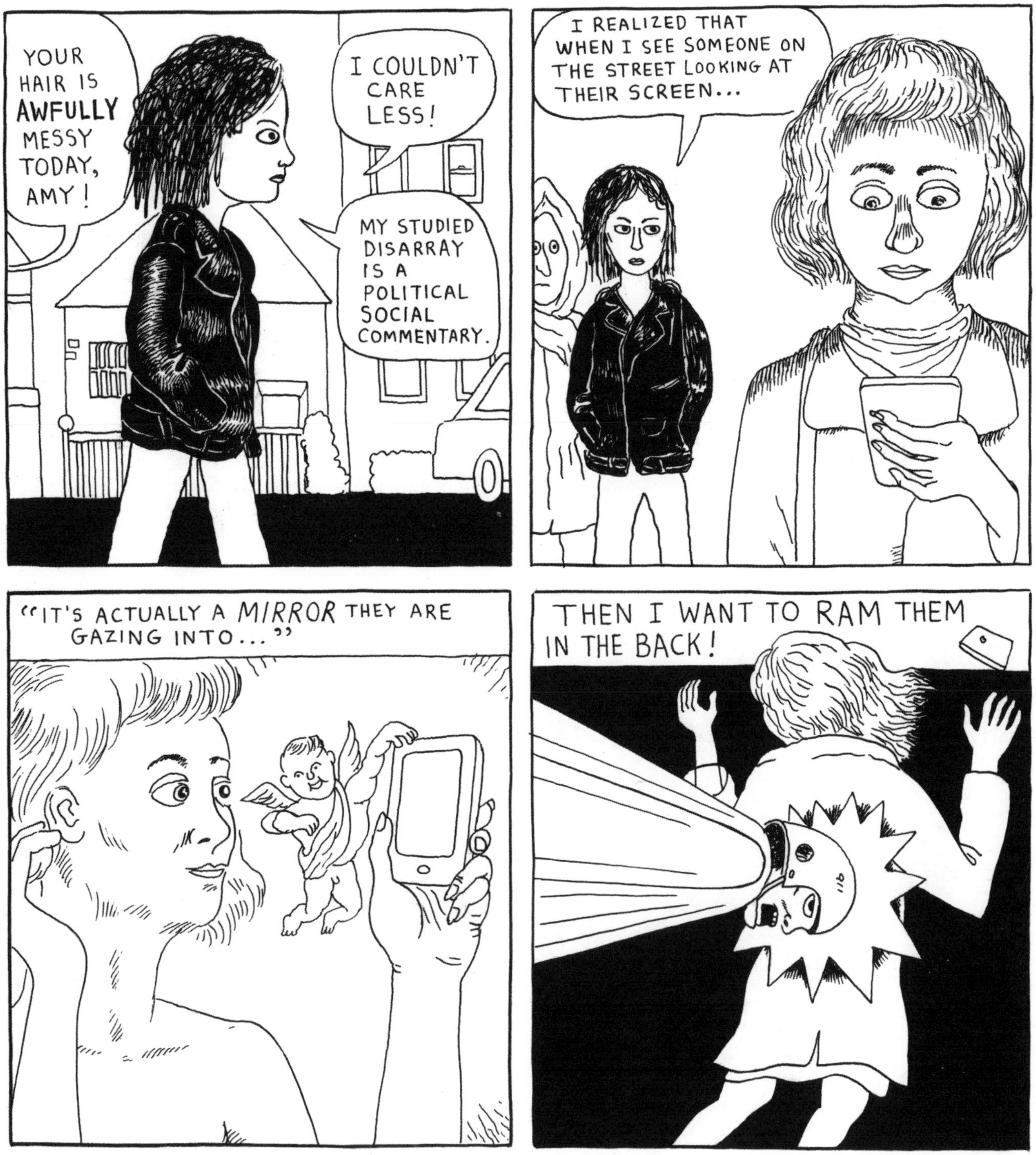
YOUR HAIR IS **AWFULLY** MESSY TODAY, AMY!
I COULDN'T CARE LESS!
MY STUDIED DISARRAY IS A POLITICAL SOCIAL COMMENTARY.
I REALIZED THAT WHEN I SEE SOMEONE ON THE STREET LOOKING AT THEIR SCREEN...
"IT'S ACTUALLY A *MIRROR* THEY ARE GAZING INTO..."
THEN I WANT TO RAM THEM IN THE BACK!

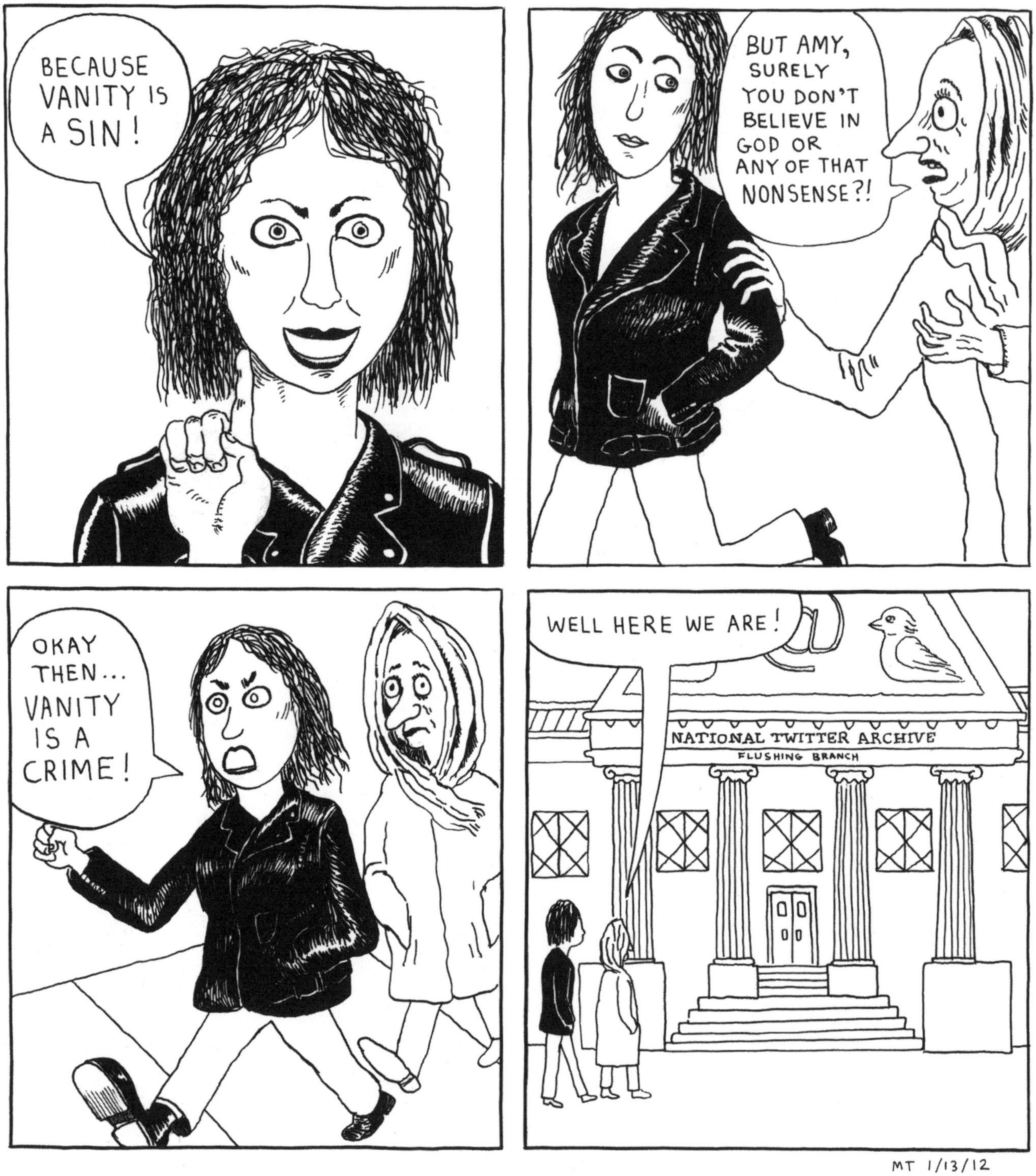
BECAUSE VANITY IS A SIN!
BUT AMY, SURELY YOU DON'T BELIEVE IN GOD OR ANY OF THAT NONSENSE?!
OKAY THEN... VANITY IS A CRIME!
WELL HERE WE ARE!
NATIONAL TWITTER ARCHIVE
FLUSHING BRANCH
MT 1/13/12

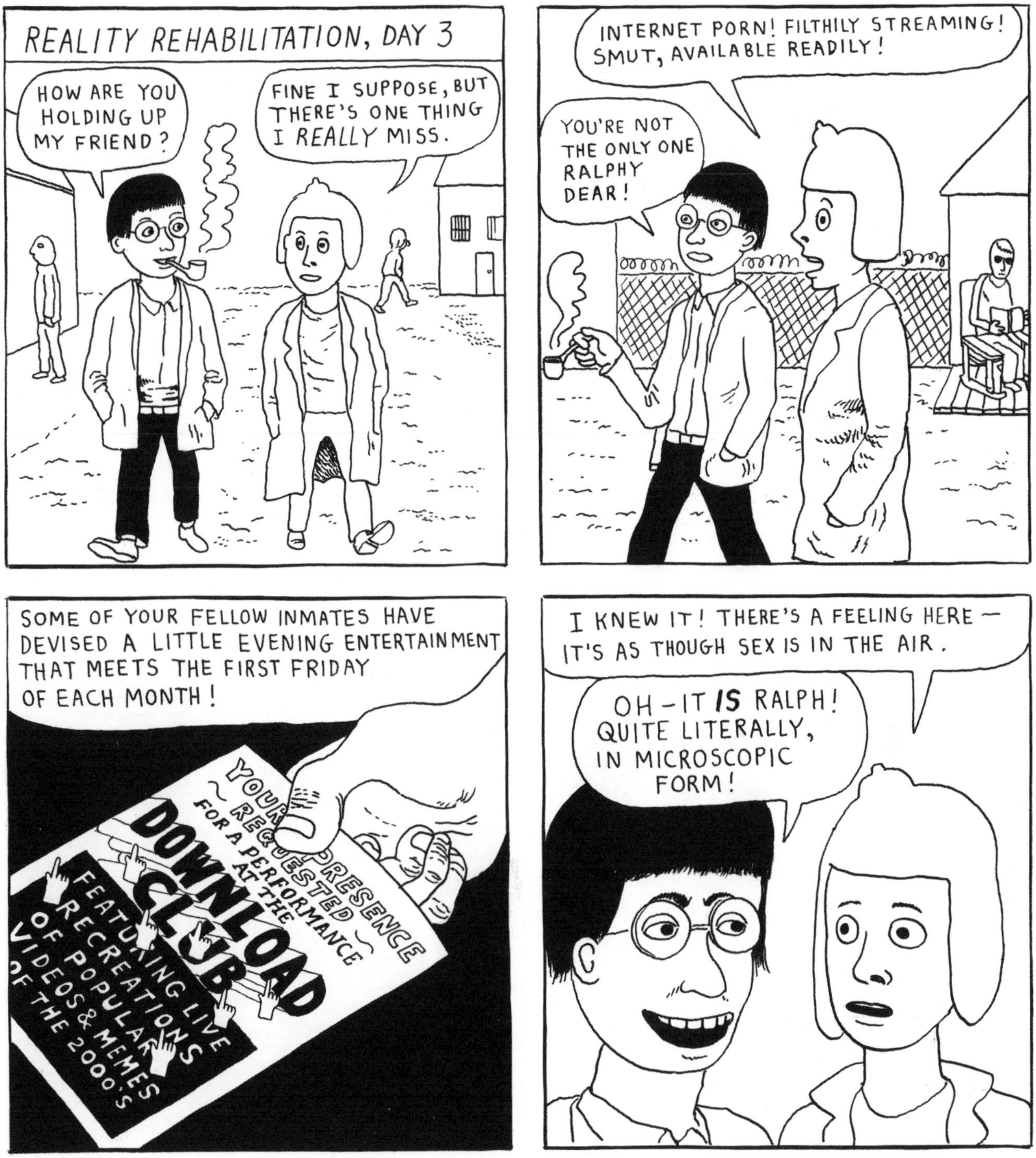
REALITY REHABILITATION, DAY 3
HOW ARE YOU HOLDING UP MY FRIEND?
FINE I SUPPOSE, BUT THERE'S ONE THING I *REALLY* MISS.
INTERNET PORN! FILTHILY STREAMING! SMUT, AVAILABLE READILY!
YOU'RE NOT THE ONLY ONE RALPHY DEAR!
SOME OF YOUR FELLOW INMATES HAVE DEVISED A LITTLE EVENING ENTERTAINMENT THAT MEETS THE FIRST FRIDAY OF EACH MONTH!
YOUR PRESENCE ~ REQUESTED ~ FOR A PERFORMANCE AT THE
DOWNLOAD CLUB
FEATURING LIVE RECREATIONS OF POPULAR VIDEOS & MEMES OF THE 2000'S
I KNEW IT! THERE'S A FEELING HERE — IT'S AS THOUGH SEX IS IN THE AIR.
OH — IT **IS** RALPH! QUITE LITERALLY, IN MICROSCOPIC FORM!

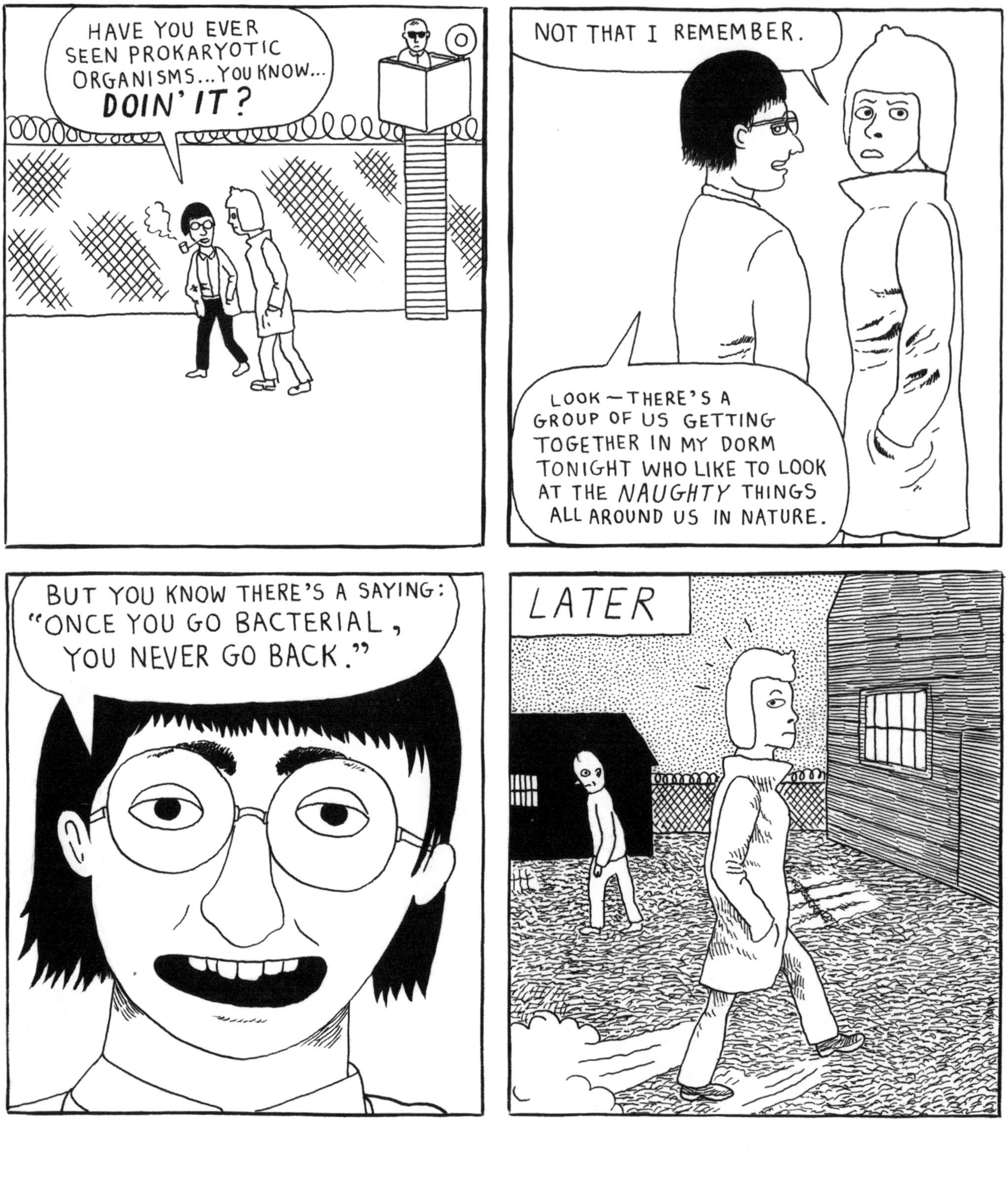

HAVE YOU EVER SEEN PROKARYOTIC ORGANISMS... YOU KNOW... DOIN' IT?
NOT THAT I REMEMBER.
LOOK — THERE'S A GROUP OF US GETTING TOGETHER IN MY DORM TONIGHT WHO LIKE TO LOOK AT THE NAUGHTY THINGS ALL AROUND US IN NATURE.
BUT YOU KNOW THERE'S A SAYING: "ONCE YOU GO BACTERIAL, YOU NEVER GO BACK."
LATER

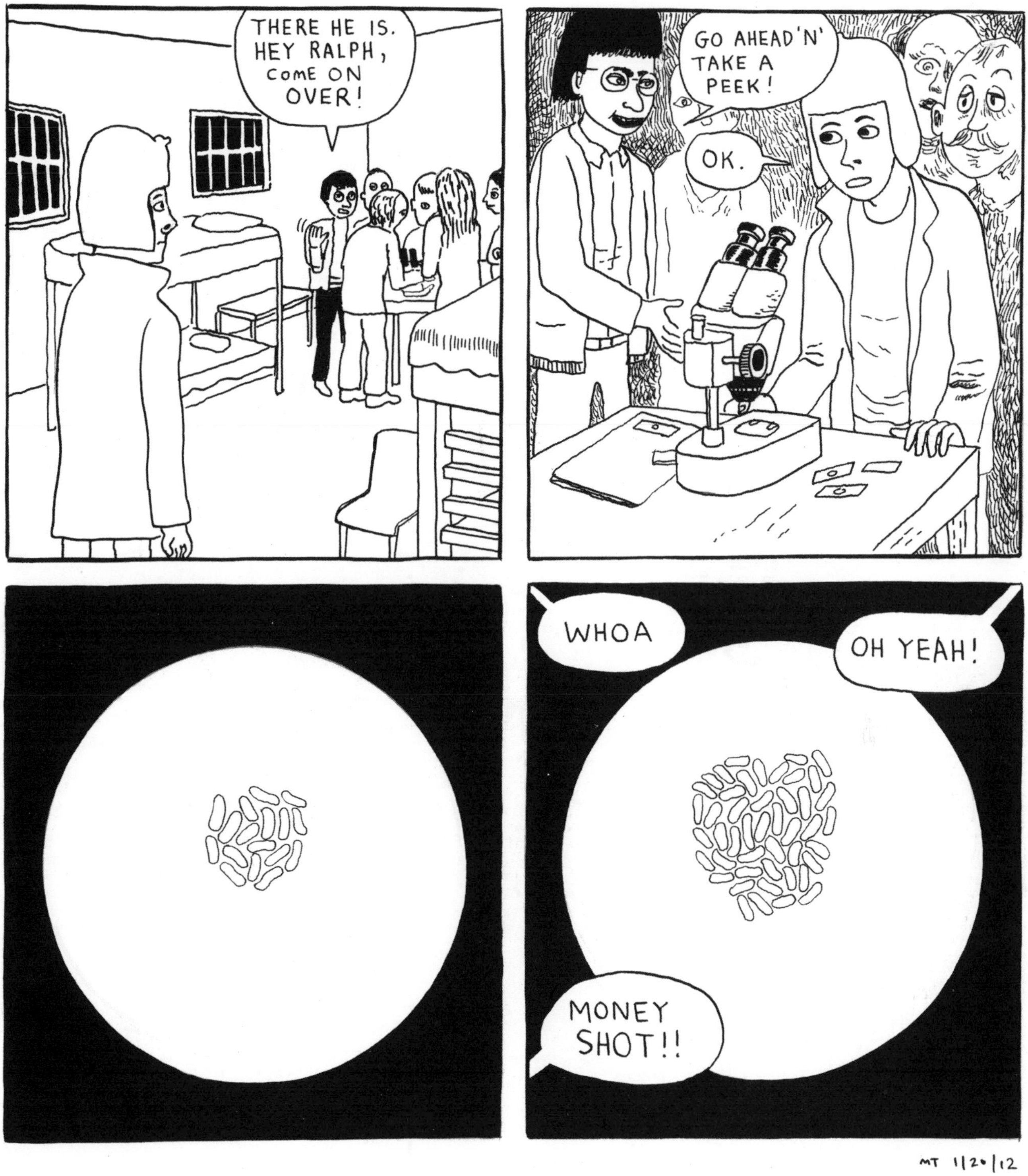
THERE HE IS. HEY RALPH, COME ON OVER!
GO AHEAD'N' TAKE A PEEK!
OK.
WHOA
OH YEAH!
MONEY SHOT!!
MT 1/20/12

I'LL BE OUTSIDE, GRANDMA.
THERE THEY ARE... THE SCRIVENERS OF TWEET STREET!
FOR A PRICE THEY'LL COMPOSE A POST FOR A TONGUE-TIED TYPIST... GHOST-WRITE YOUR BLOG...
NEED A JOKE, MISS?
LOL'S MY SPECIAL-TY
ELQQUENT RESPONSE TO CELEB DEATH?
DESTITUTE WRITERS, THEIR PUBLISHING OPPORTUNITIES VAPORIZED BY THE INTERNET. CHAMELEONS OF PROSE!
YOUTUBE LINKAGE?
HOW ABOUT A LUNCH TWEET, MA'AM? TELL YOUR FRIENDS WHAT YOU'RE EATIN'?
NON SEQUITUR?

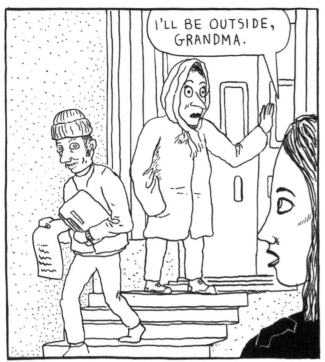

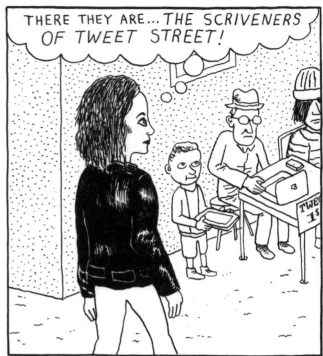

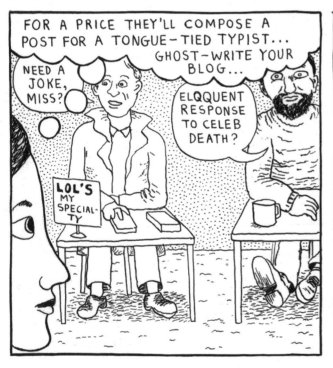

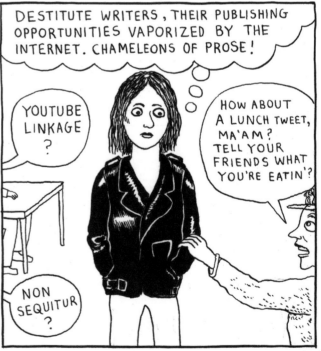

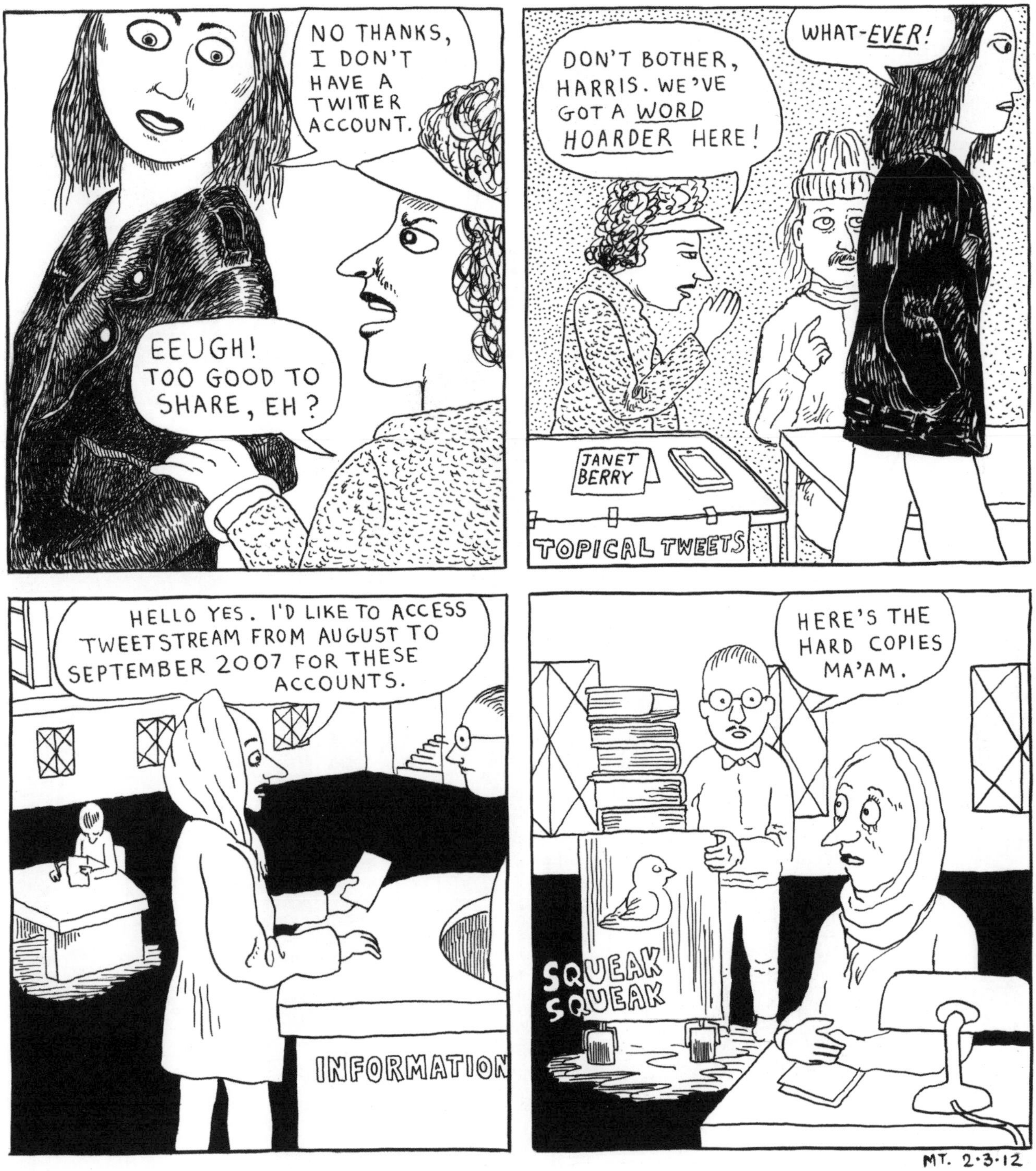
NO THANKS, I DON'T HAVE A TWITTER ACCOUNT.
EEUGH! TOO GOOD TO SHARE, EH?
DON'T BOTHER, HARRIS. WE'VE GOT A WORD HOARDER HERE!
WHAT-EVER!
JANET BERRY
TOPICAL TWEETS
HELLO YES. I'D LIKE TO ACCESS TWEETSTREAM FROM AUGUST TO SEPTEMBER 2007 FOR THESE ACCOUNTS.
INFORMATION
HERE'S THE HARD COPIES MA'AM.
SQUEAK SQUEAK
MT. 2·3·12

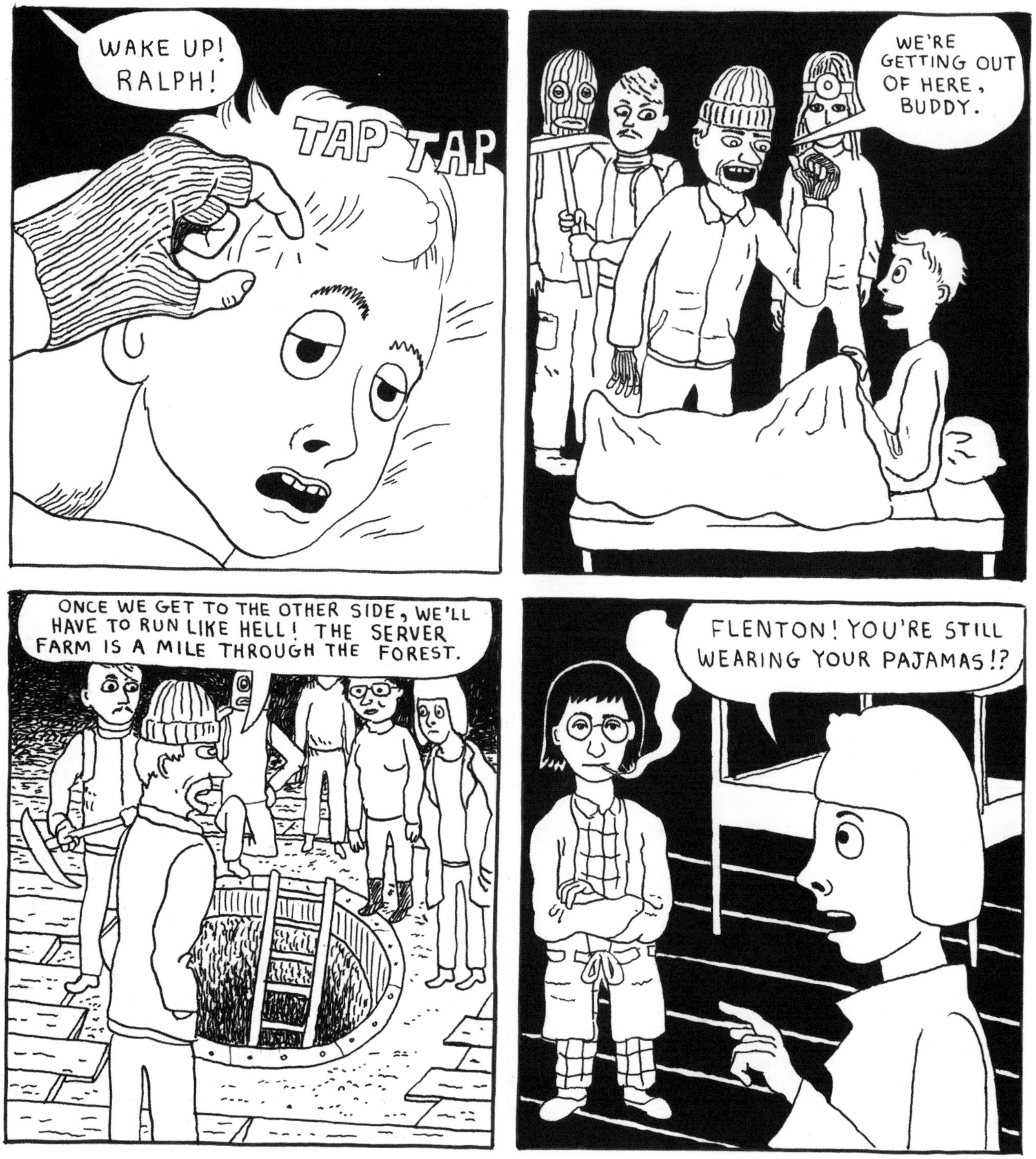
WAKE UP! RALPH!
TAP TAP
WE'RE GETTING OUT OF HERE, BUDDY.
ONCE WE GET TO THE OTHER SIDE, WE'LL HAVE TO RUN LIKE HELL! THE SERVER FARM IS A MILE THROUGH THE FOREST.
FLENTON! YOU'RE STILL WEARING YOUR PAJAMAS!?

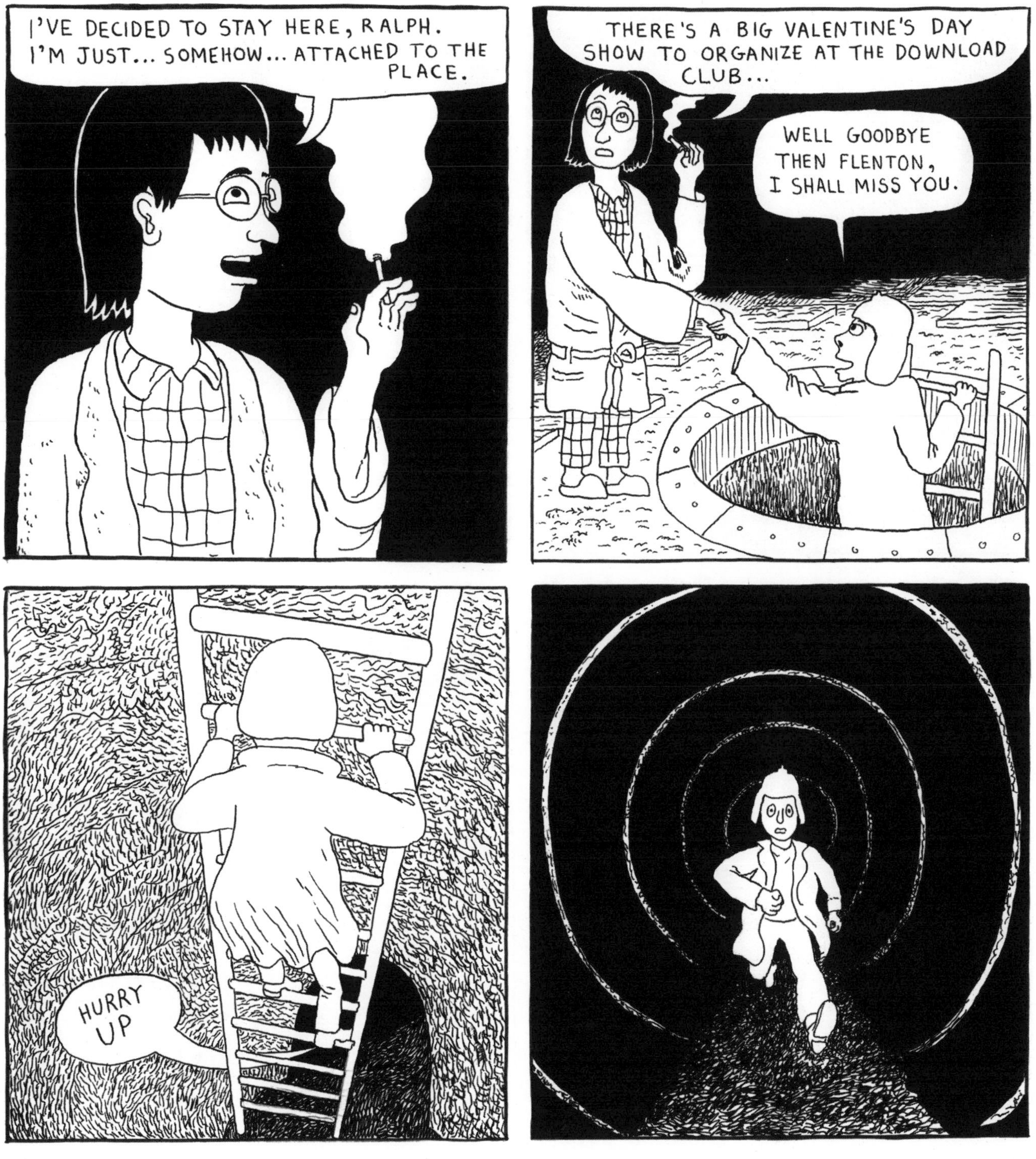
I'VE DECIDED TO STAY HERE, RALPH. I'M JUST... SOMEHOW... ATTACHED TO THE PLACE.
THERE'S A BIG VALENTINE'S DAY SHOW TO ORGANIZE AT THE DOWNLOAD CLUB...
WELL GOODBYE THEN FLENTON, I SHALL MISS YOU.
HURRY UP

MT 2/12/12

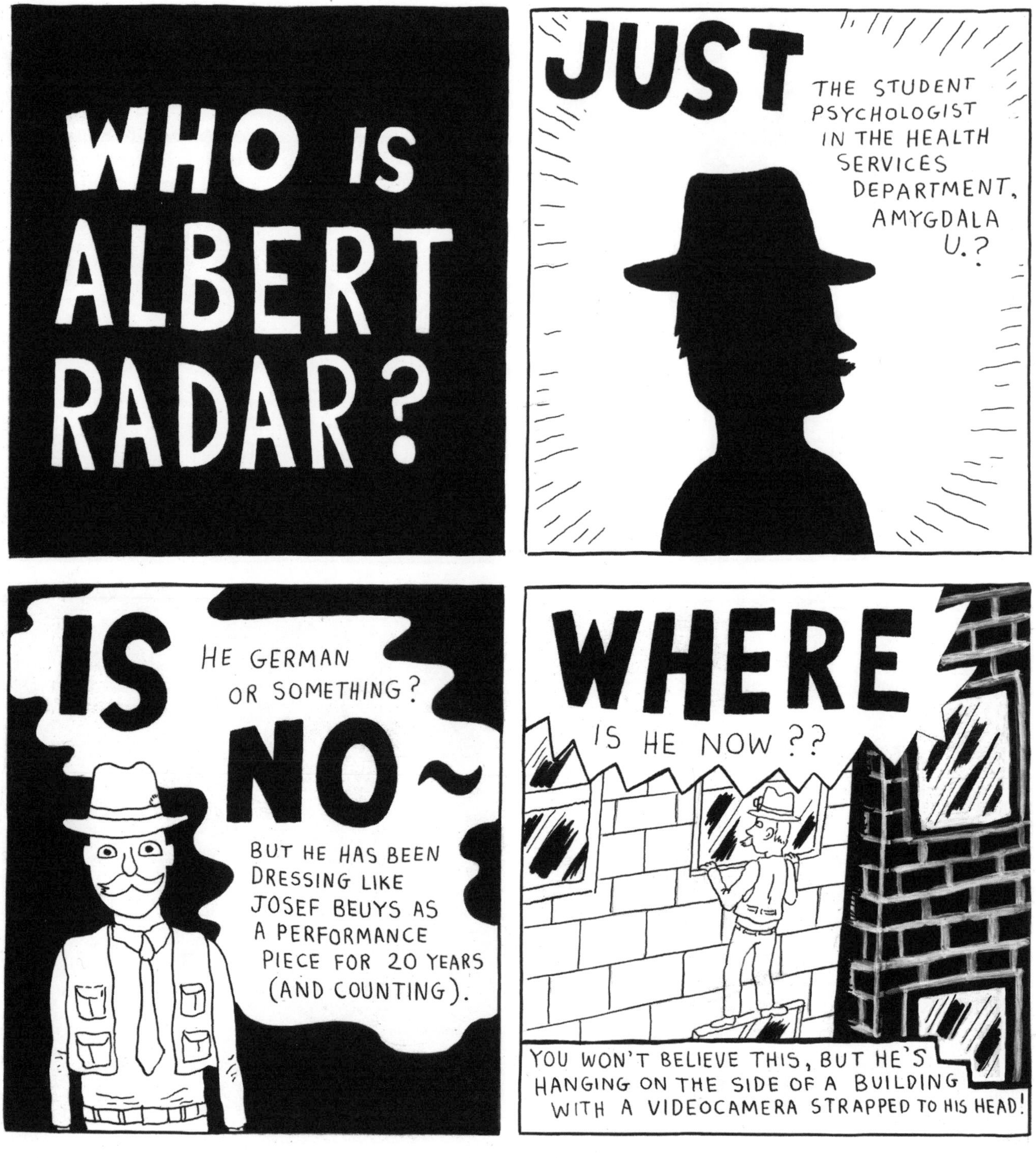
WHO IS ALBERT RADAR?
JUST
THE STUDENT PSYCHOLOGIST IN THE HEALTH SERVICES DEPARTMENT, AMYGDALA U.?
IS
HE GERMAN OR SOMETHING?
NO~
BUT HE HAS BEEN DRESSING LIKE JOSEF BEUYS AS A PERFORMANCE PIECE FOR 20 YEARS (AND COUNTING).
WHERE
IS HE NOW??
YOU WON'T BELIEVE THIS, BUT HE'S HANGING ON THE SIDE OF A BUILDING WITH A VIDEOCAMERA STRAPPED TO HIS HEAD!

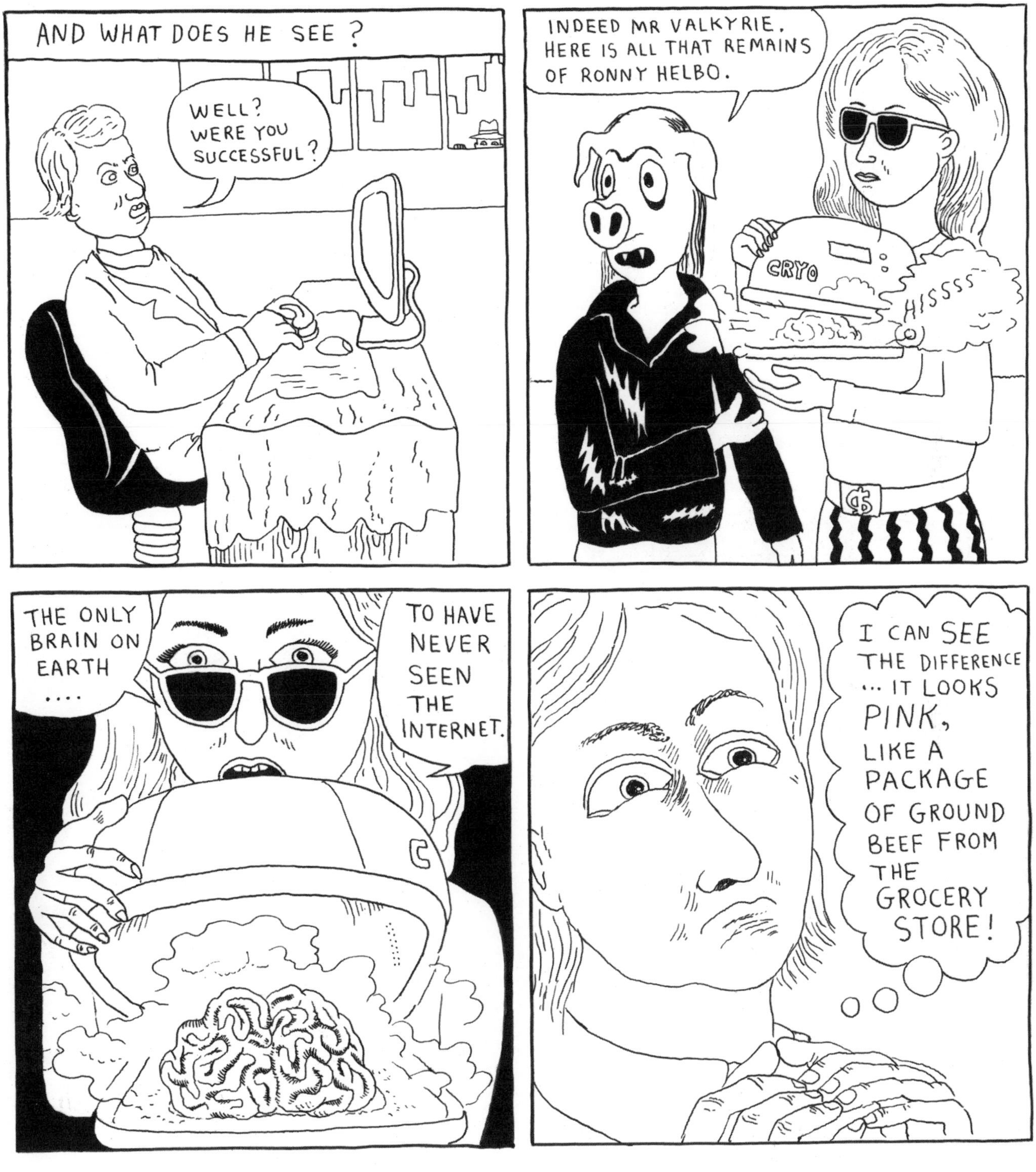
AND WHAT DOES HE SEE?
WELL? WERE YOU SUCCESSFUL?
INDEED MR VALKYRIE. HERE IS ALL THAT REMAINS OF RONNY HELBO.
CRYO
HISSSS
THE ONLY BRAIN ON EARTH ....
TO HAVE NEVER SEEN THE INTERNET.
I CAN SEE THE DIFFERENCE ... IT LOOKS PINK, LIKE A PACKAGE OF GROUND BEEF FROM THE GROCERY STORE!

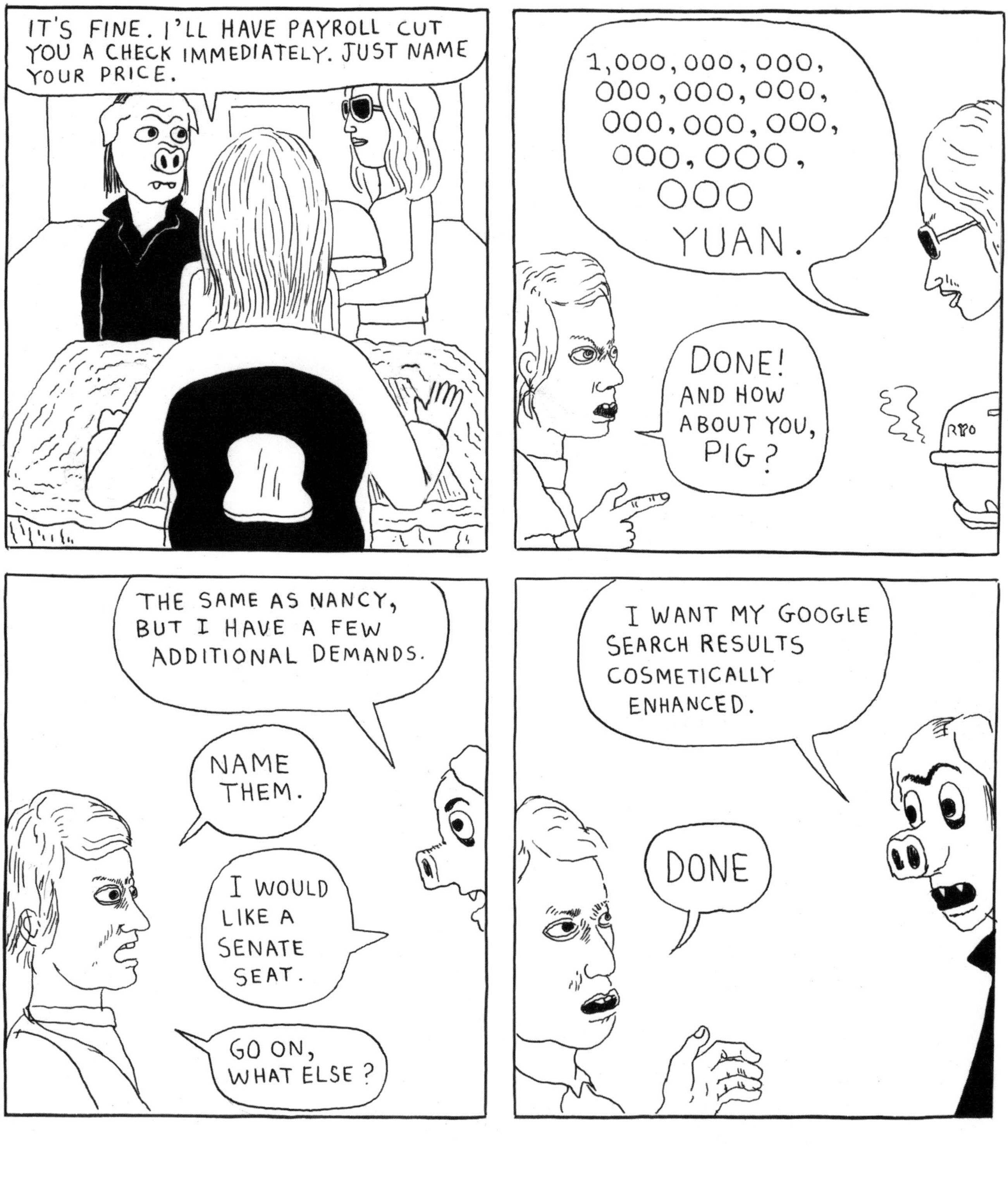
IT'S FINE. I'LL HAVE PAYROLL CUT YOU A CHECK IMMEDIATELY. JUST NAME YOUR PRICE.
1,000,000,000, 000,000,000, 000,000,000, 000,000, 000 YUAN.
DONE! AND HOW ABOUT YOU, PIG?
THE SAME AS NANCY, BUT I HAVE A FEW ADDITIONAL DEMANDS.
NAME THEM.
I WOULD LIKE A SENATE SEAT.
GO ON, WHAT ELSE?
I WANT MY GOOGLE SEARCH RESULTS COSMETICALLY ENHANCED.
DONE

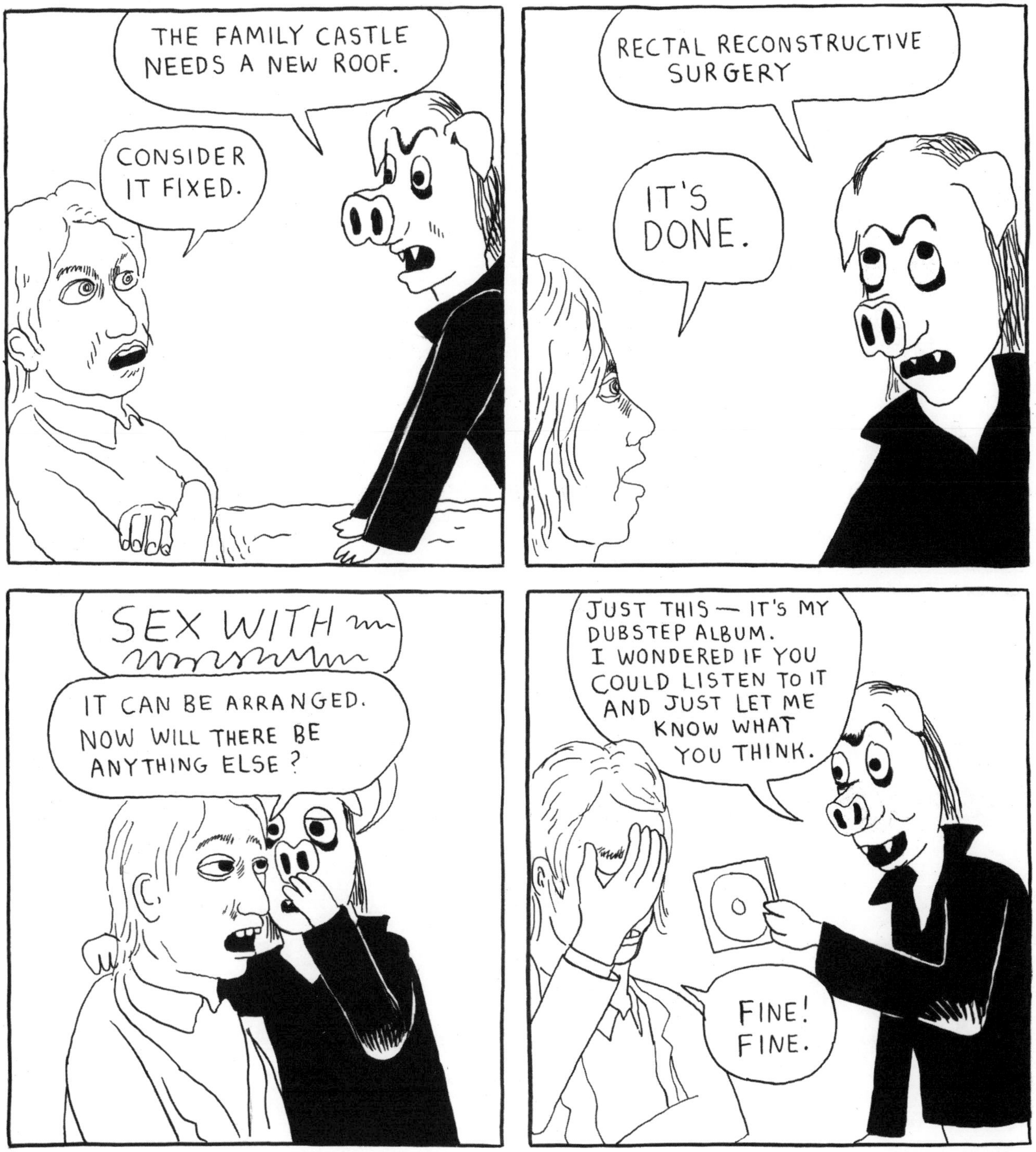
THE FAMILY CASTLE NEEDS A NEW ROOF.
CONSIDER IT FIXED.
RECTAL RECONSTRUCTIVE SURGERY
IT'S DONE.
SEX WITH
IT CAN BE ARRANGED. NOW WILL THERE BE ANYTHING ELSE?
JUST THIS — IT'S MY DUBSTEP ALBUM. I WONDERED IF YOU COULD LISTEN TO IT AND JUST LET ME KNOW WHAT YOU THINK.
FINE! FINE.
MT 2·23·12

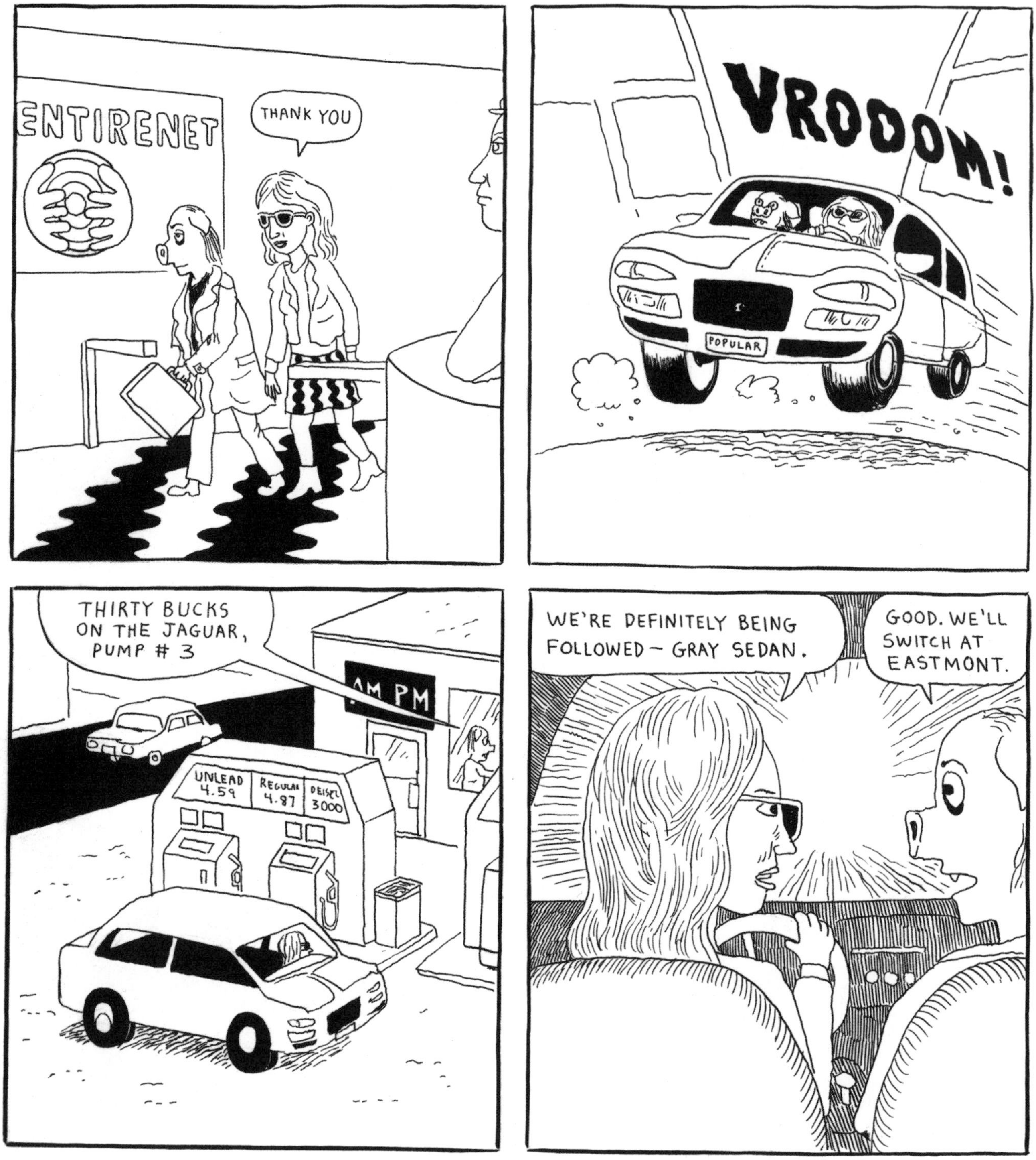
ENTIRENET
THANK YOU
VROOOM!
POPULAR
THIRTY BUCKS ON THE JAGUAR, PUMP # 3
AM PM
UNLEAD 4.59
REGULAR 4.87
DEISEL 3000
WE'RE DEFINITELY BEING FOLLOWED — GRAY SEDAN.
GOOD. WE'LL SWITCH AT EASTMONT.

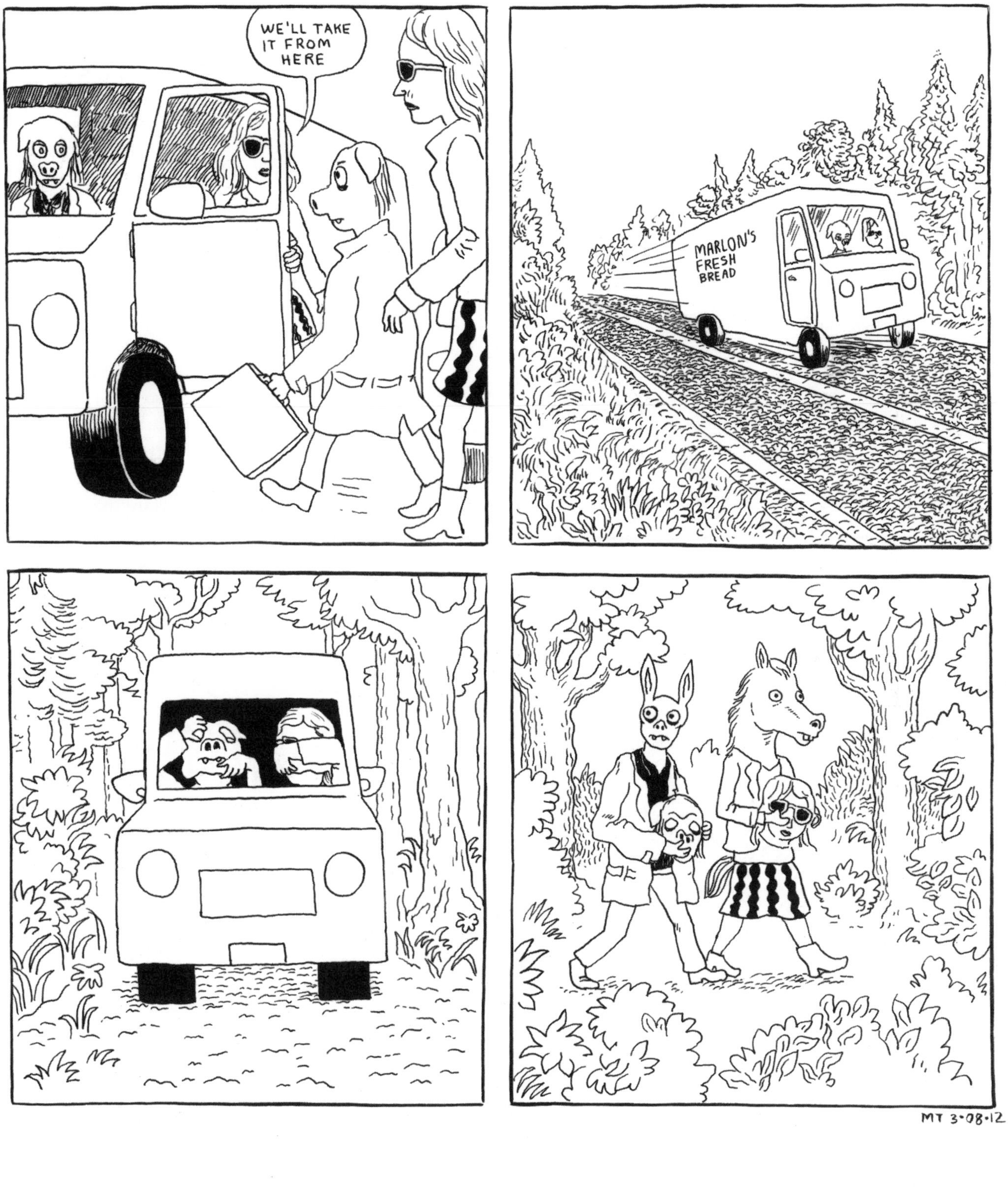
WE'LL TAKE IT FROM HERE
MARLON'S FRESH BREAD
MT 3-08-12

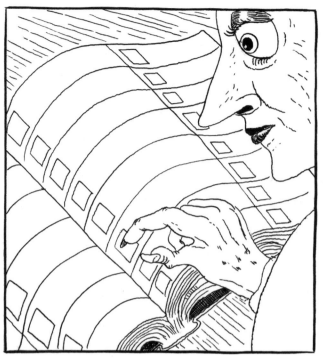

HERE! THE *FINAL TWEETS* BETWEEN RANDALL AND VIOLA!

GOODNESS, THEY SOUND SO AFFECTIONATE, SO IN LOVE!

WHAT CAN HAVE HAPPENED TO THEM? MY DAUGHTER, HER HUSBAND?

RandallShit @Hair... What do you want fro... store? #groceries

Hairballcapture or catfood

RandallShit ...people who work b... ...se your own bag?

allcapture just stuff your pockets!

THEY DISAPPEARED OFF THE FACE OF THE EARTH ONE DAY LIKE THEY NEVER EXISTED...

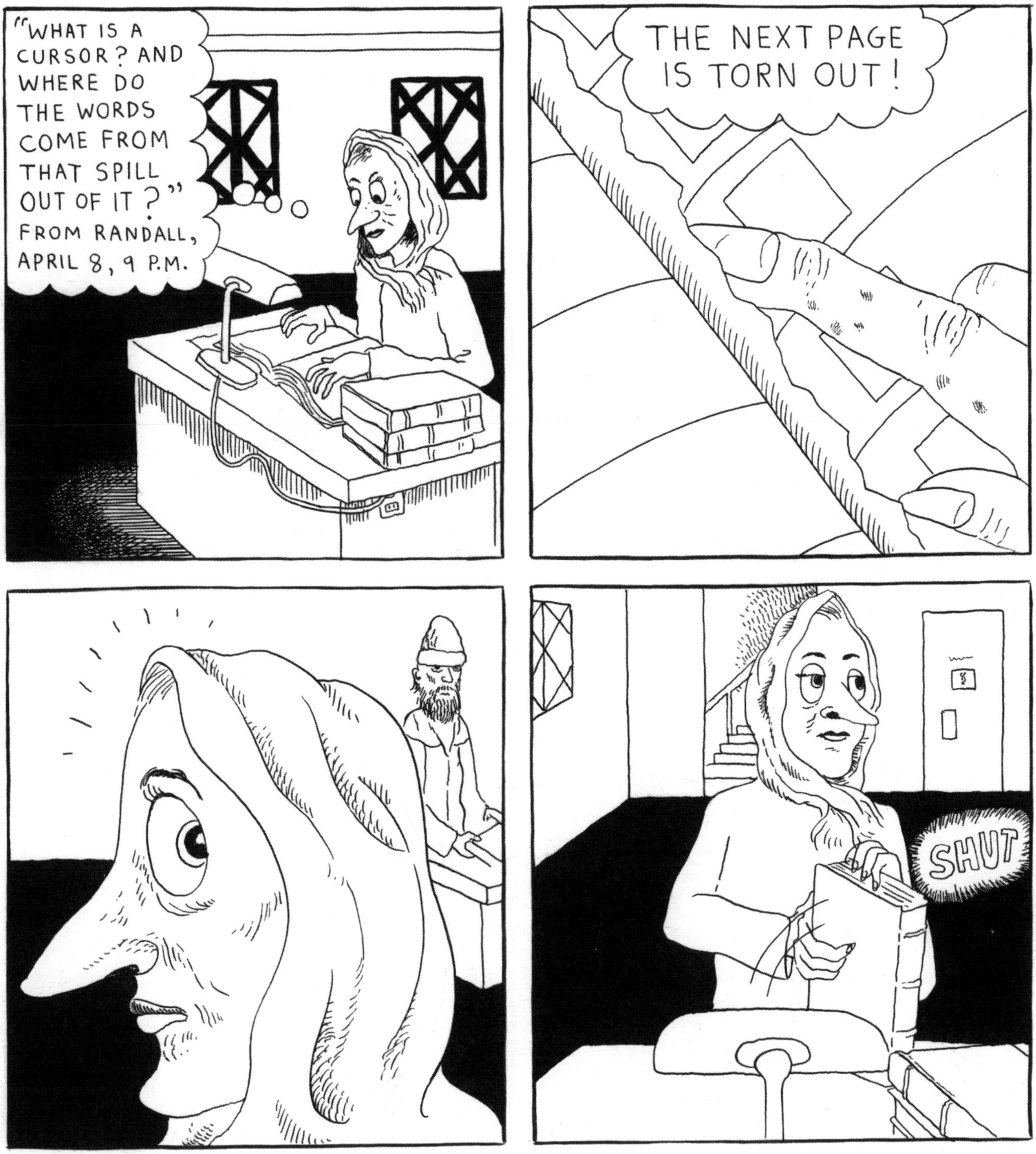
"WHAT IS A CURSOR? AND WHERE DO THE WORDS COME FROM THAT SPILL OUT OF IT?" FROM RANDALL, APRIL 8, 9 P.M.
THE NEXT PAGE IS TORN OUT!
SHUT

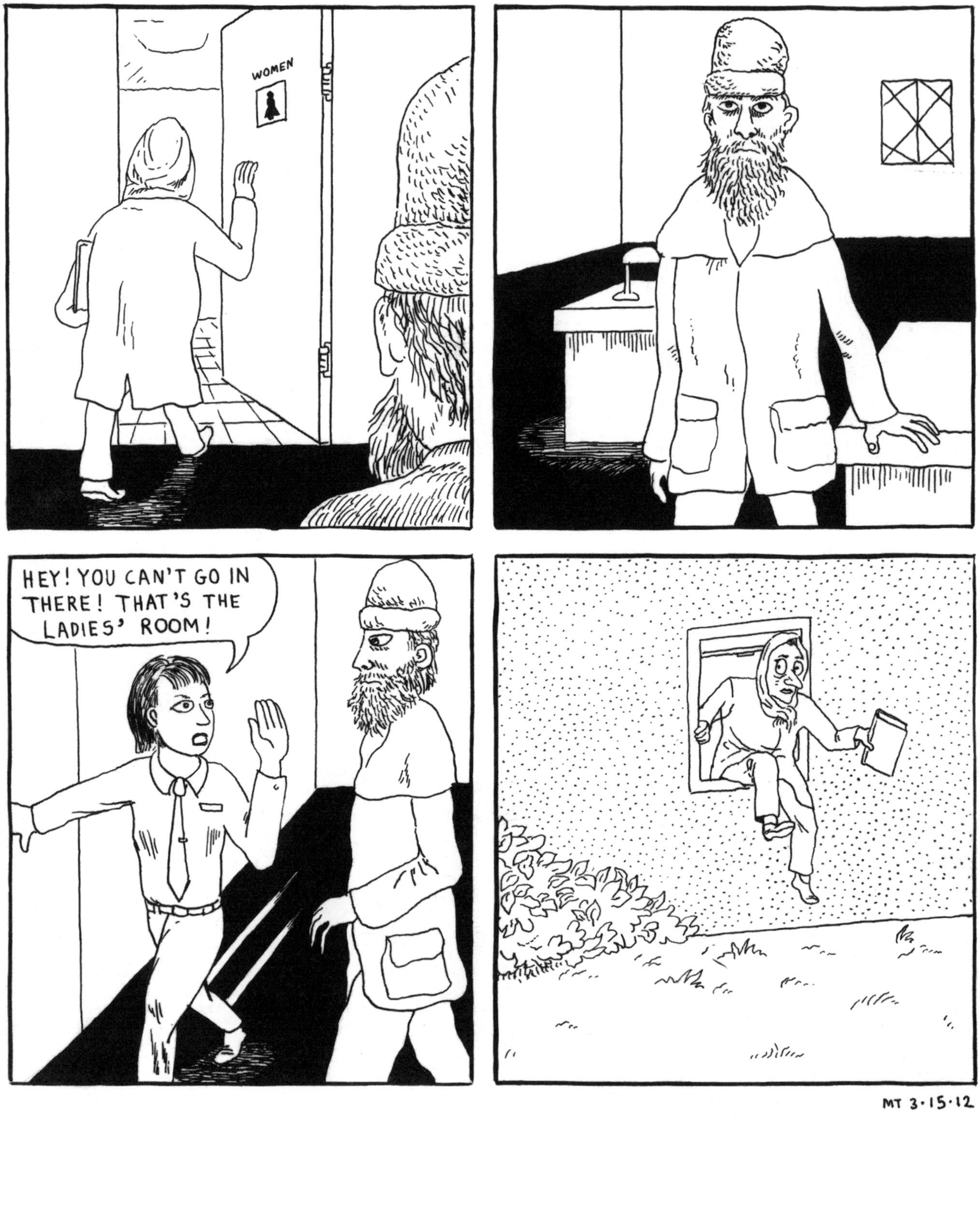
WOMEN
HEY! YOU CAN'T GO IN THERE! THAT'S THE LADIES' ROOM!
MT 3·15·12

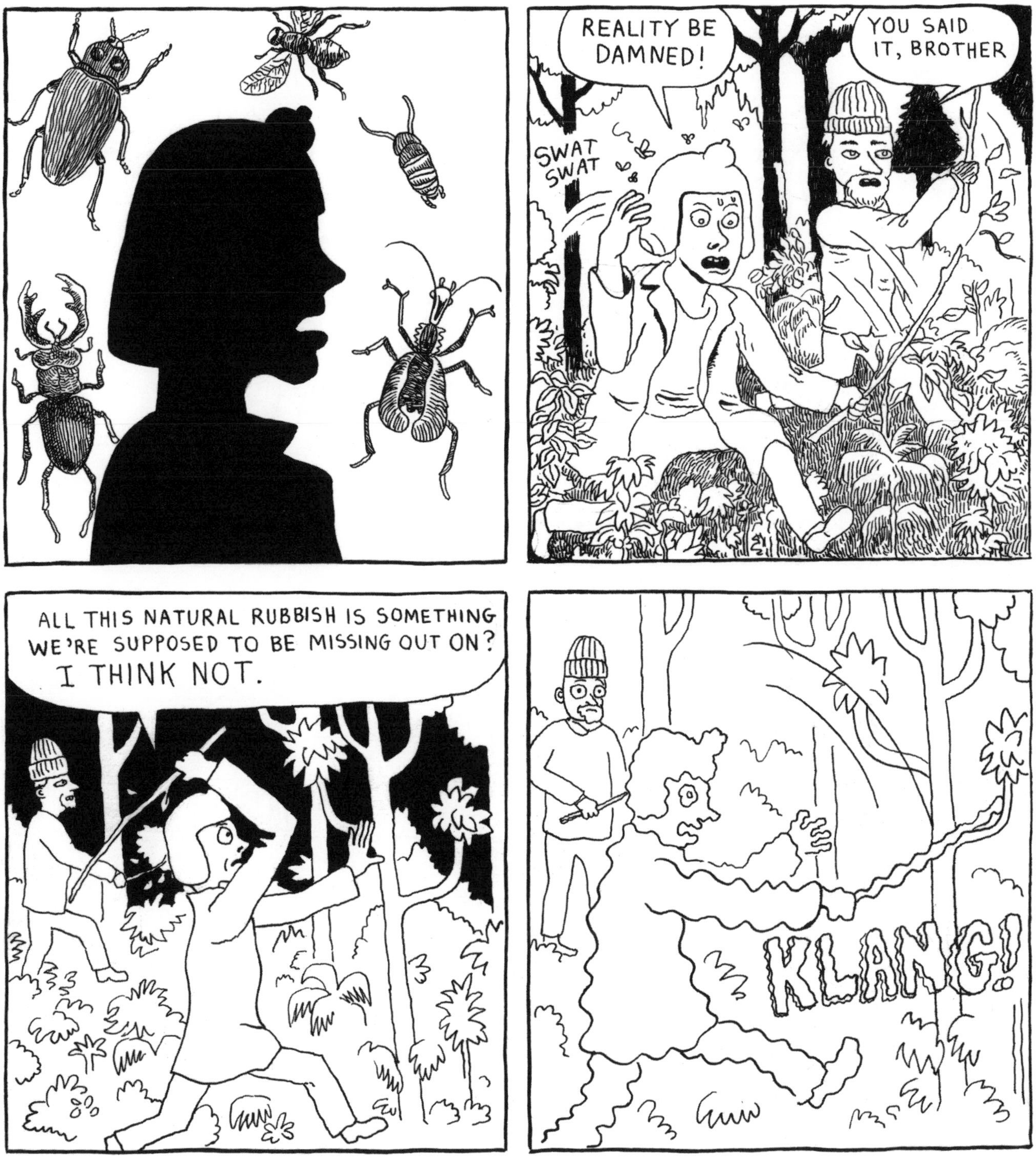

REALITY BE DAMNED!
YOU SAID IT, BROTHER
SWAT SWAT
ALL THIS NATURAL RUBBISH IS SOMETHING WE'RE SUPPOSED TO BE MISSING OUT ON? I THINK NOT.
KLANG!

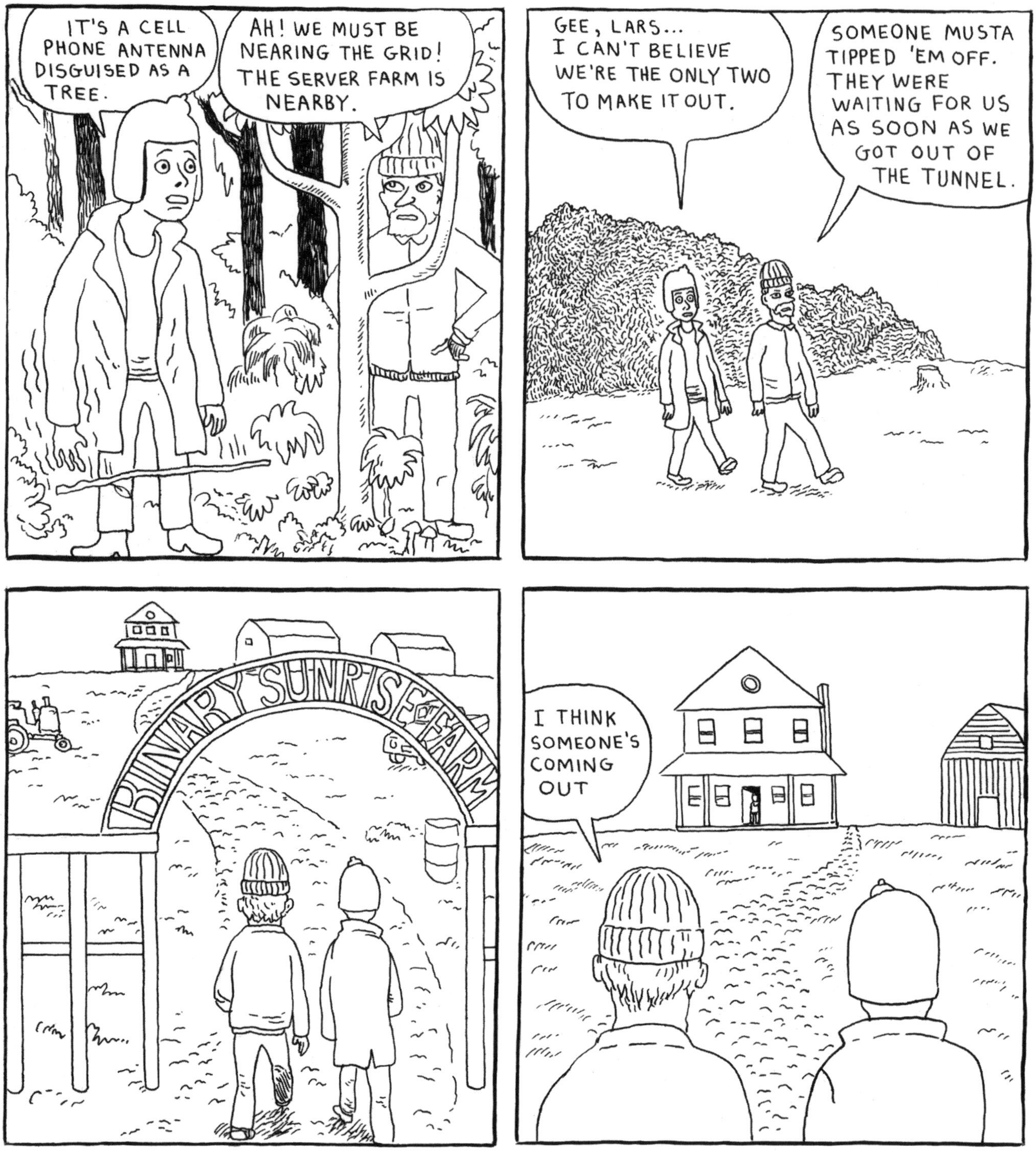
IT'S A CELL PHONE ANTENNA DISGUISED AS A TREE.
AH! WE MUST BE NEARING THE GRID! THE SERVER FARM IS NEARBY.
GEE, LARS... I CAN'T BELIEVE WE'RE THE ONLY TWO TO MAKE IT OUT.
SOMEONE MUSTA TIPPED 'EM OFF. THEY WERE WAITING FOR US AS SOON AS WE GOT OUT OF THE TUNNEL.
BINARY SUNRISE FARM
I THINK SOMEONE'S COMING OUT

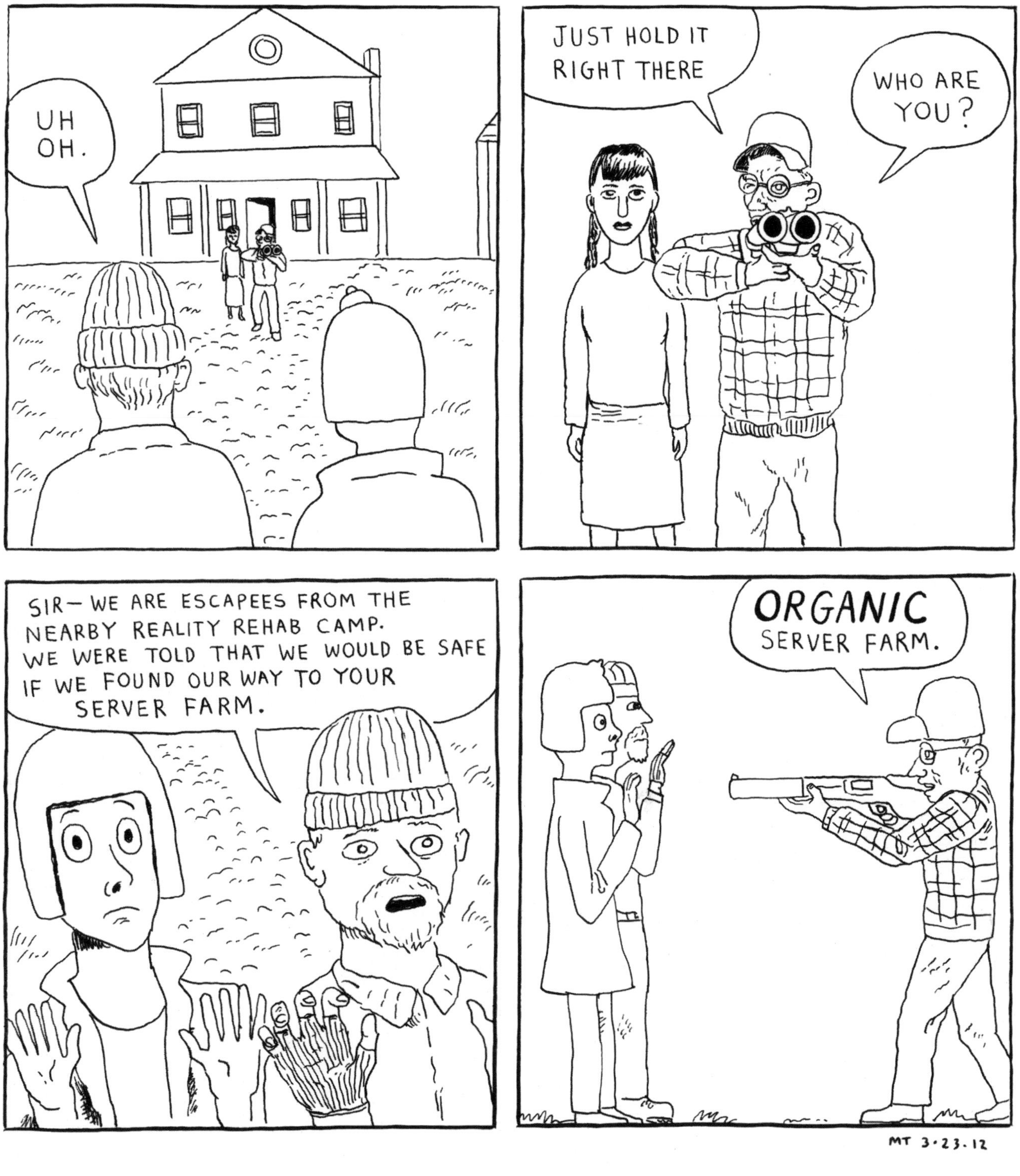

UH OH.
JUST HOLD IT RIGHT THERE
WHO ARE YOU?
SIR— WE ARE ESCAPEES FROM THE NEARBY REALITY REHAB CAMP. WE WERE TOLD THAT WE WOULD BE SAFE IF WE FOUND OUR WAY TO YOUR SERVER FARM.
ORGANIC SERVER FARM.
MT 3·23·12

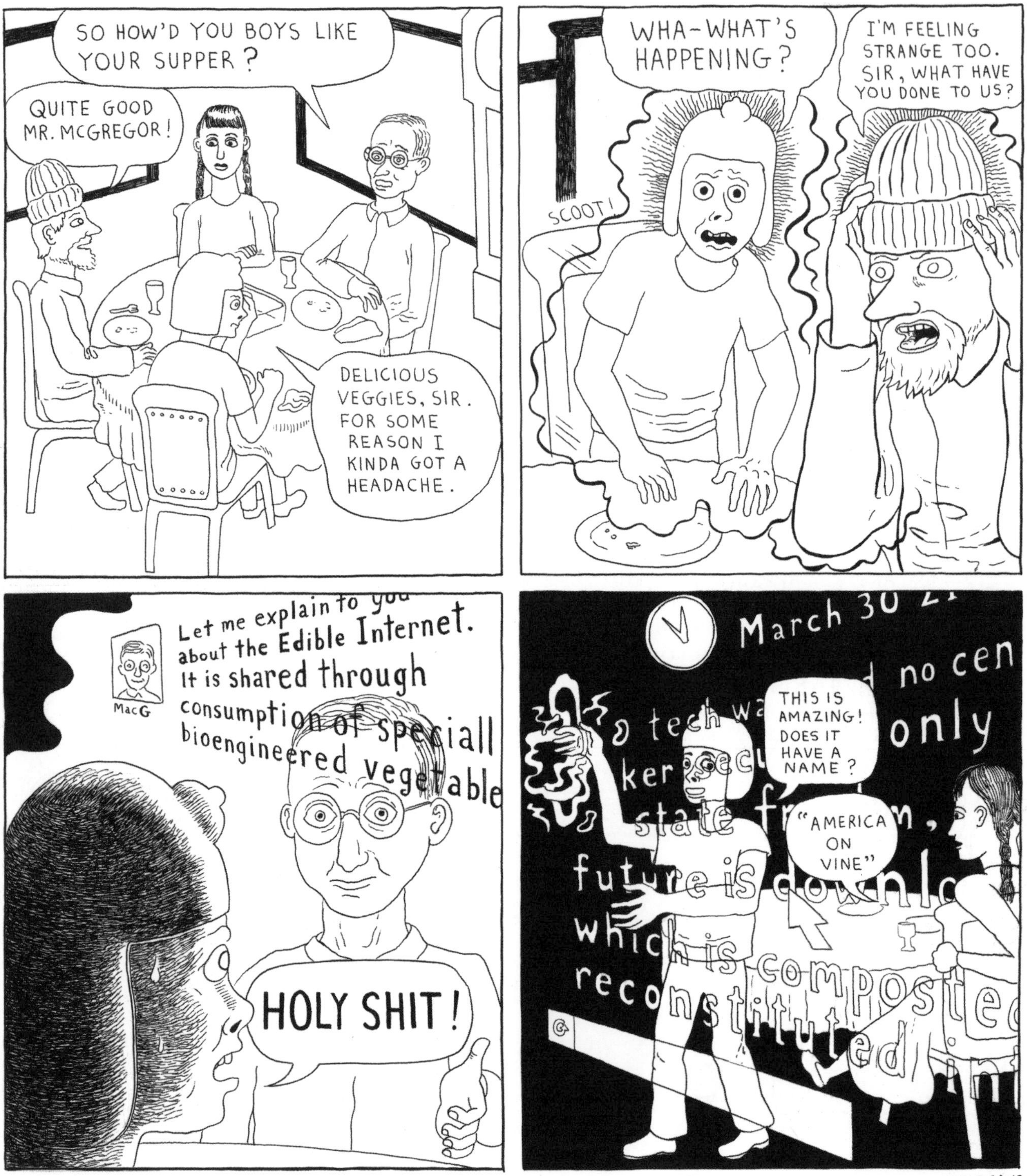

SO HOW'D YOU BOYS LIKE YOUR SUPPER?
QUITE GOOD MR. MCGREGOR!
DELICIOUS VEGGIES, SIR. FOR SOME REASON I KINDA GOT A HEADACHE.
WHA-WHAT'S HAPPENING?
SCOOT!
I'M FEELING STRANGE TOO. SIR, WHAT HAVE YOU DONE TO US?
MacG
Let me explain to you about the Edible Internet. It is shared through consumption of speciall bioengineered vegetable
HOLY SHIT!
March 30
no cen
tech wa
only
ker secu
state fr m,
future is downl
which is composted
reconstituted
THIS IS AMAZING! DOES IT HAVE A NAME?
"AMERICA ON VINE"

MT 3.30.12

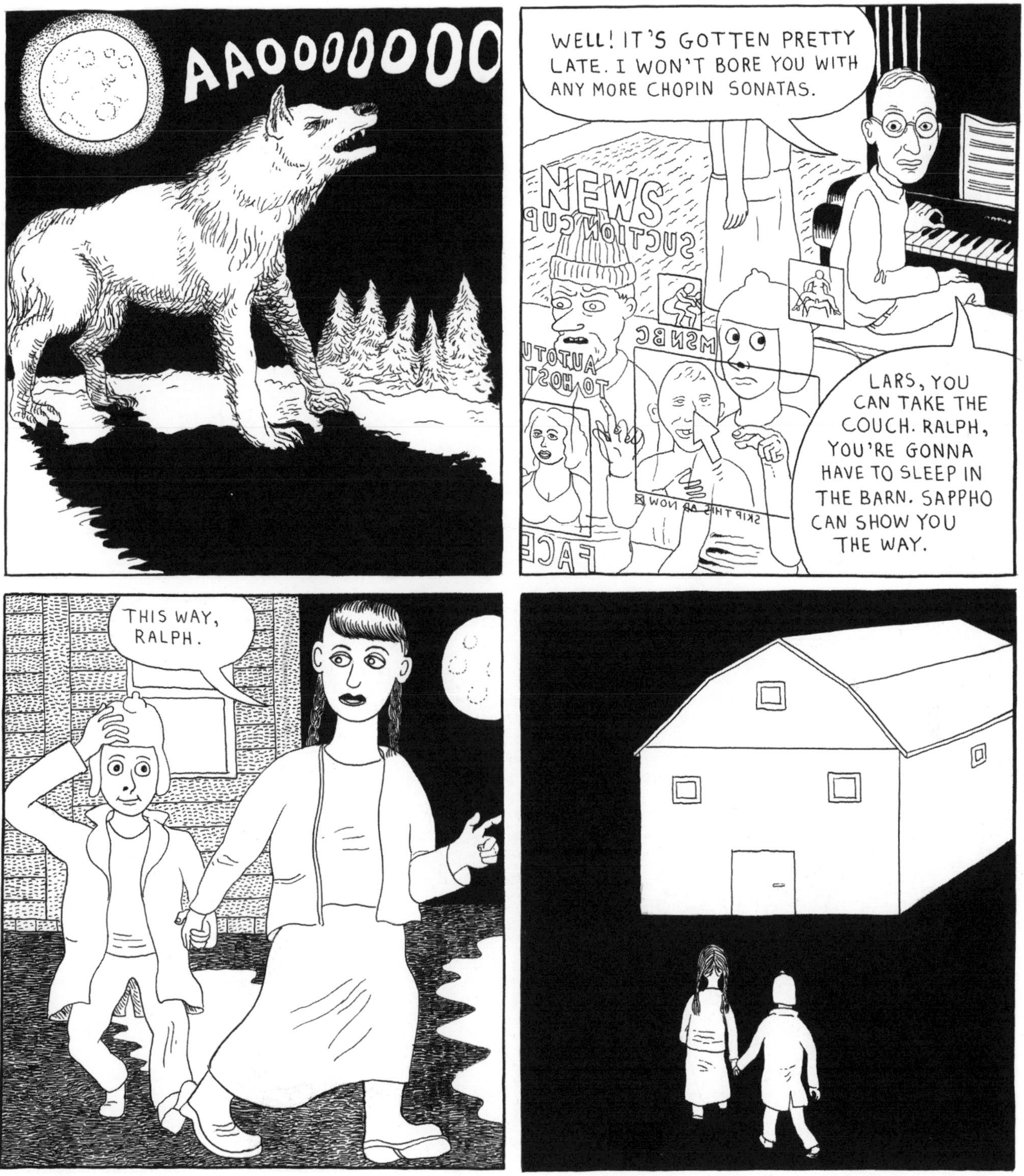
AAOOOOOOO
WELL! IT'S GOTTEN PRETTY LATE. I WON'T BORE YOU WITH ANY MORE CHOPIN SONATAS.
NEWS
LARS, YOU CAN TAKE THE COUCH. RALPH, YOU'RE GONNA HAVE TO SLEEP IN THE BARN. SAPPHO CAN SHOW YOU THE WAY.
THIS WAY, RALPH.

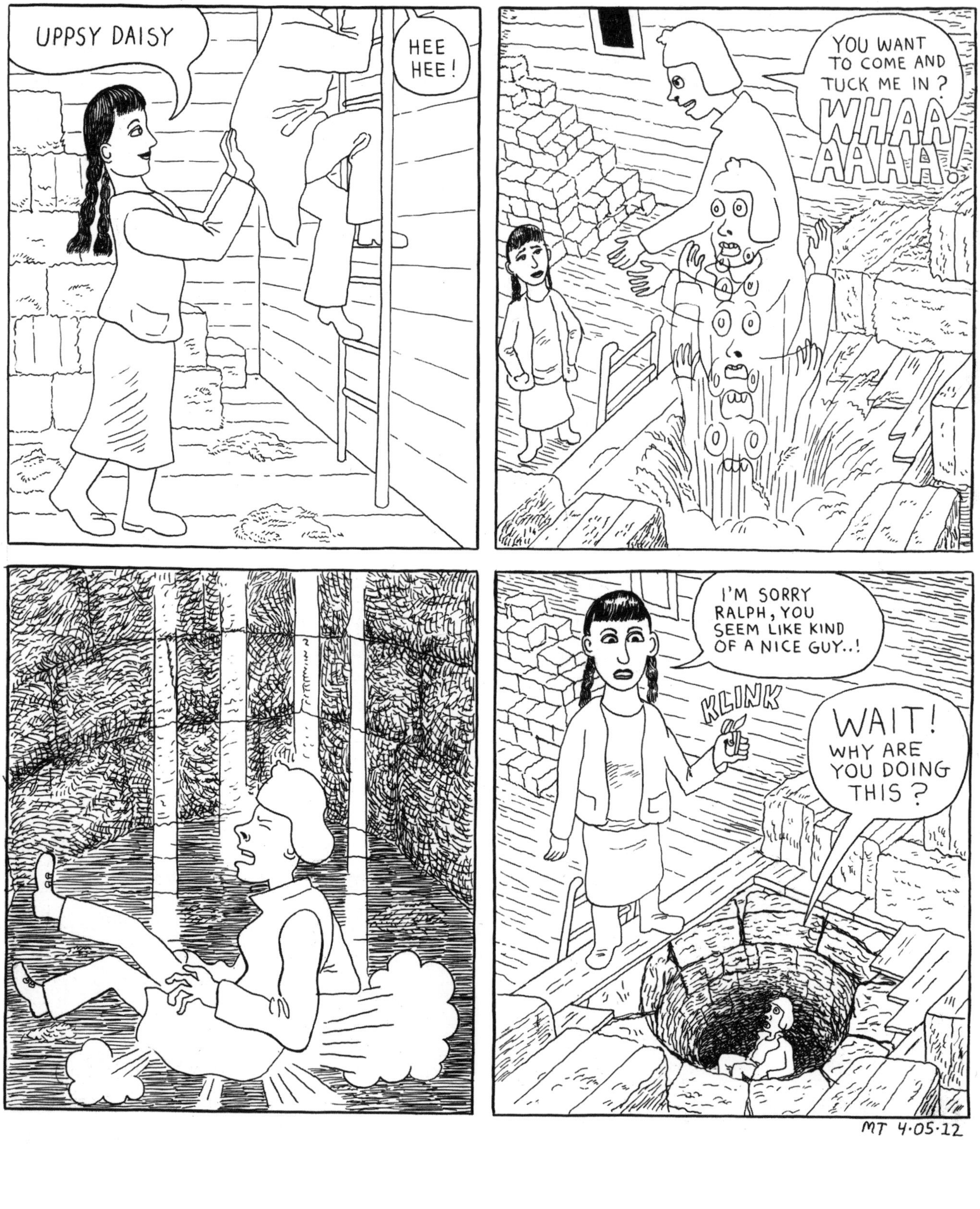
UPPSY DAISY
HEE HEE!
YOU WANT TO COME AND TUCK ME IN?
WHAA AAAA!
I'M SORRY RALPH, YOU SEEM LIKE KIND OF A NICE GUY..!
KLINK
WAIT! WHY ARE YOU DOING THIS?
MT 4·05·12

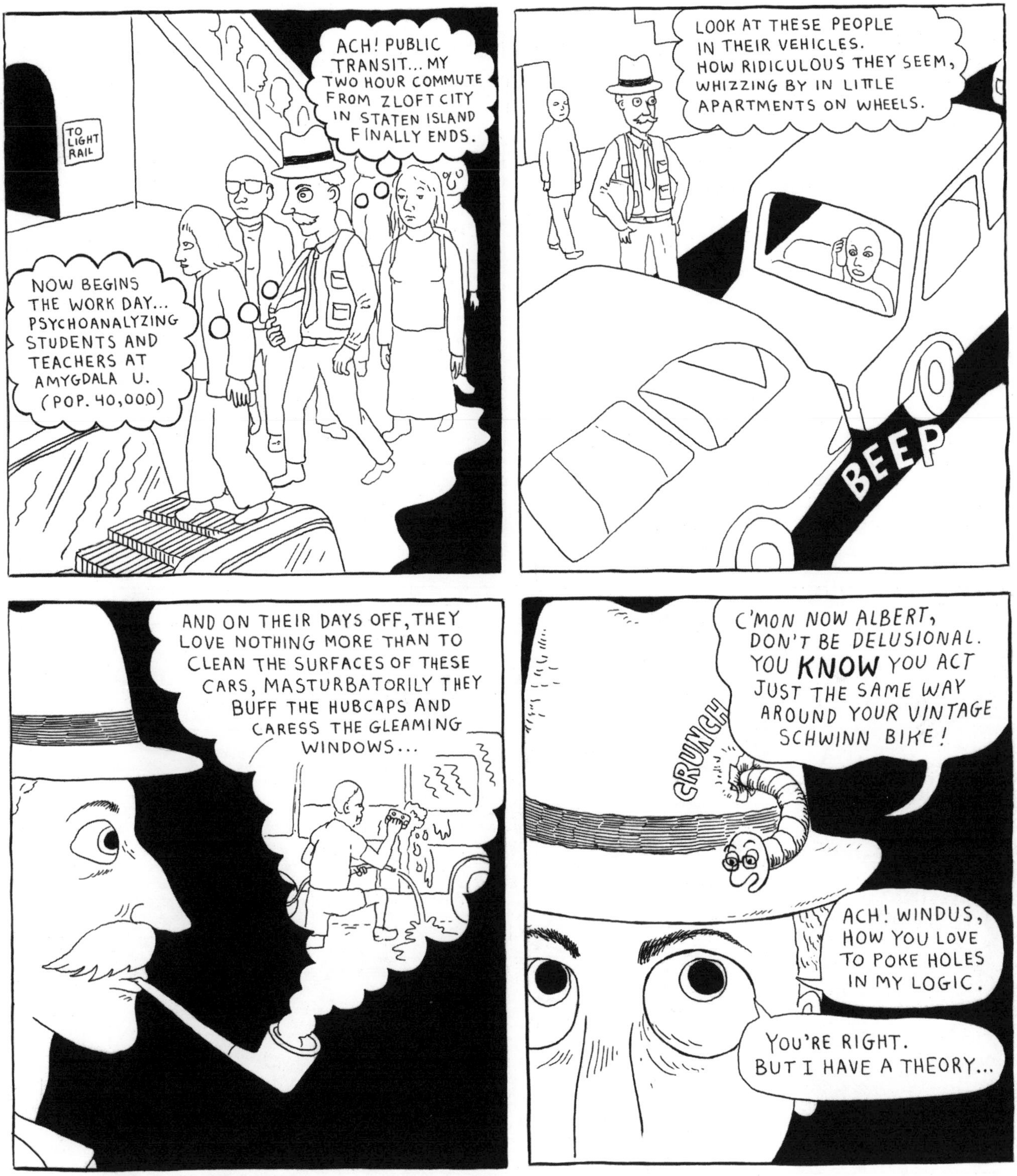
ACH! PUBLIC TRANSIT... MY TWO HOUR COMMUTE FROM ZLOFT CITY IN STATEN ISLAND FINALLY ENDS.
TO LIGHT RAIL
NOW BEGINS THE WORK DAY... PSYCHOANALYZING STUDENTS AND TEACHERS AT AMYGDALA U. (POP. 40,000)
LOOK AT THESE PEOPLE IN THEIR VEHICLES. HOW RIDICULOUS THEY SEEM, WHIZZING BY IN LITTLE APARTMENTS ON WHEELS.
BEEP
AND ON THEIR DAYS OFF, THEY LOVE NOTHING MORE THAN TO CLEAN THE SURFACES OF THESE CARS, MASTURBATORILY THEY BUFF THE HUBCAPS AND CARESS THE GLEAMING WINDOWS...
C'MON NOW ALBERT, DON'T BE DELUSIONAL. YOU KNOW YOU ACT JUST THE SAME WAY AROUND YOUR VINTAGE SCHWINN BIKE!
CRUNCH
ACH! WINDUS, HOW YOU LOVE TO POKE HOLES IN MY LOGIC.
YOU'RE RIGHT. BUT I HAVE A THEORY...

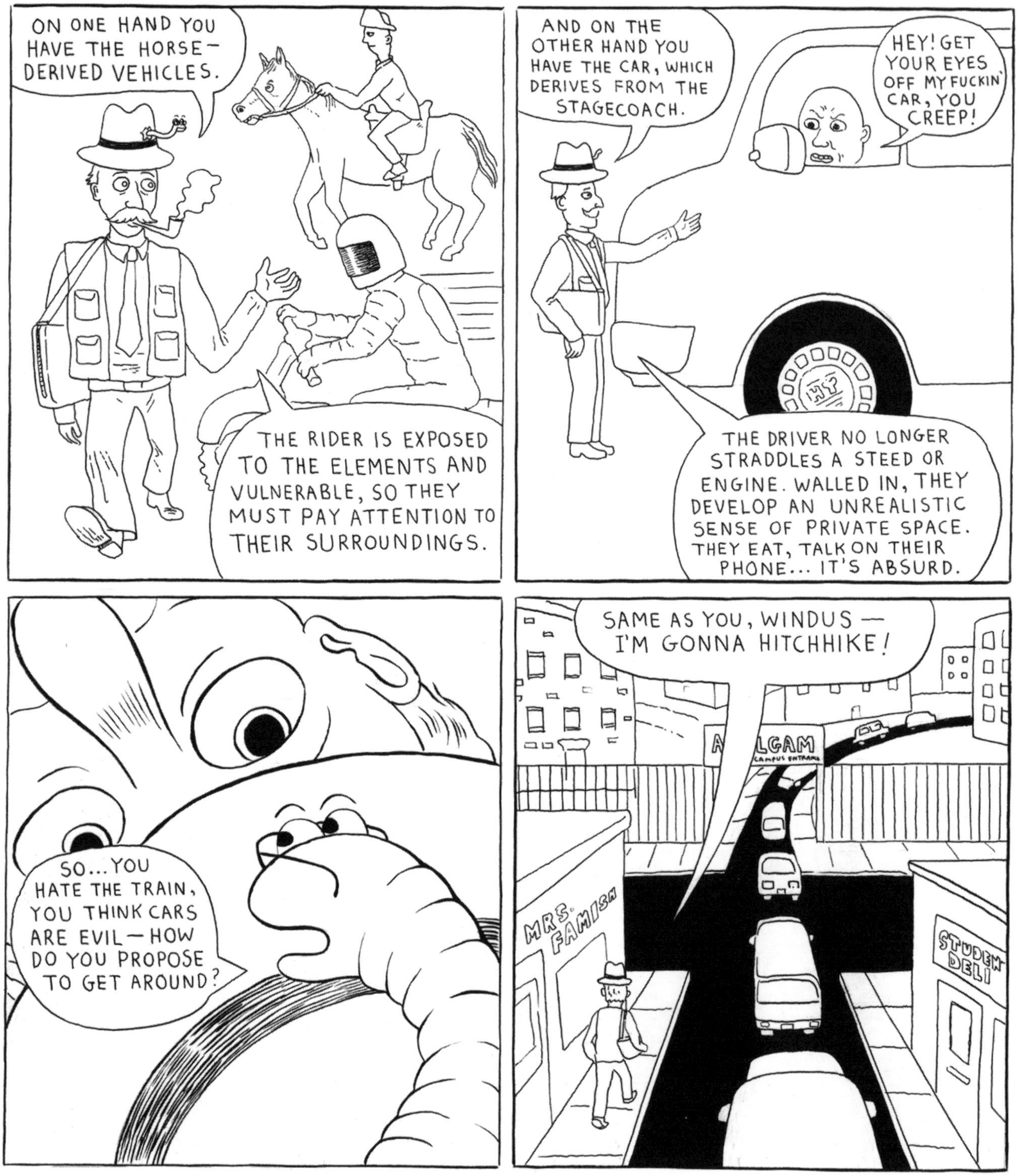
ON ONE HAND YOU HAVE THE HORSE-DERIVED VEHICLES.
THE RIDER IS EXPOSED TO THE ELEMENTS AND VULNERABLE, SO THEY MUST PAY ATTENTION TO THEIR SURROUNDINGS.
AND ON THE OTHER HAND YOU HAVE THE CAR, WHICH DERIVES FROM THE STAGECOACH.
HEY! GET YOUR EYES OFF MY FUCKIN' CAR, YOU CREEP!
THE DRIVER NO LONGER STRADDLES A STEED OR ENGINE. WALLED IN, THEY DEVELOP AN UNREALISTIC SENSE OF PRIVATE SPACE. THEY EAT, TALK ON THEIR PHONE... IT'S ABSURD.
SO... YOU HATE THE TRAIN, YOU THINK CARS ARE EVIL—HOW DO YOU PROPOSE TO GET AROUND?
SAME AS YOU, WINDUS — I'M GONNA HITCHHIKE!
MRS. FAMISH

MT 4/25/12

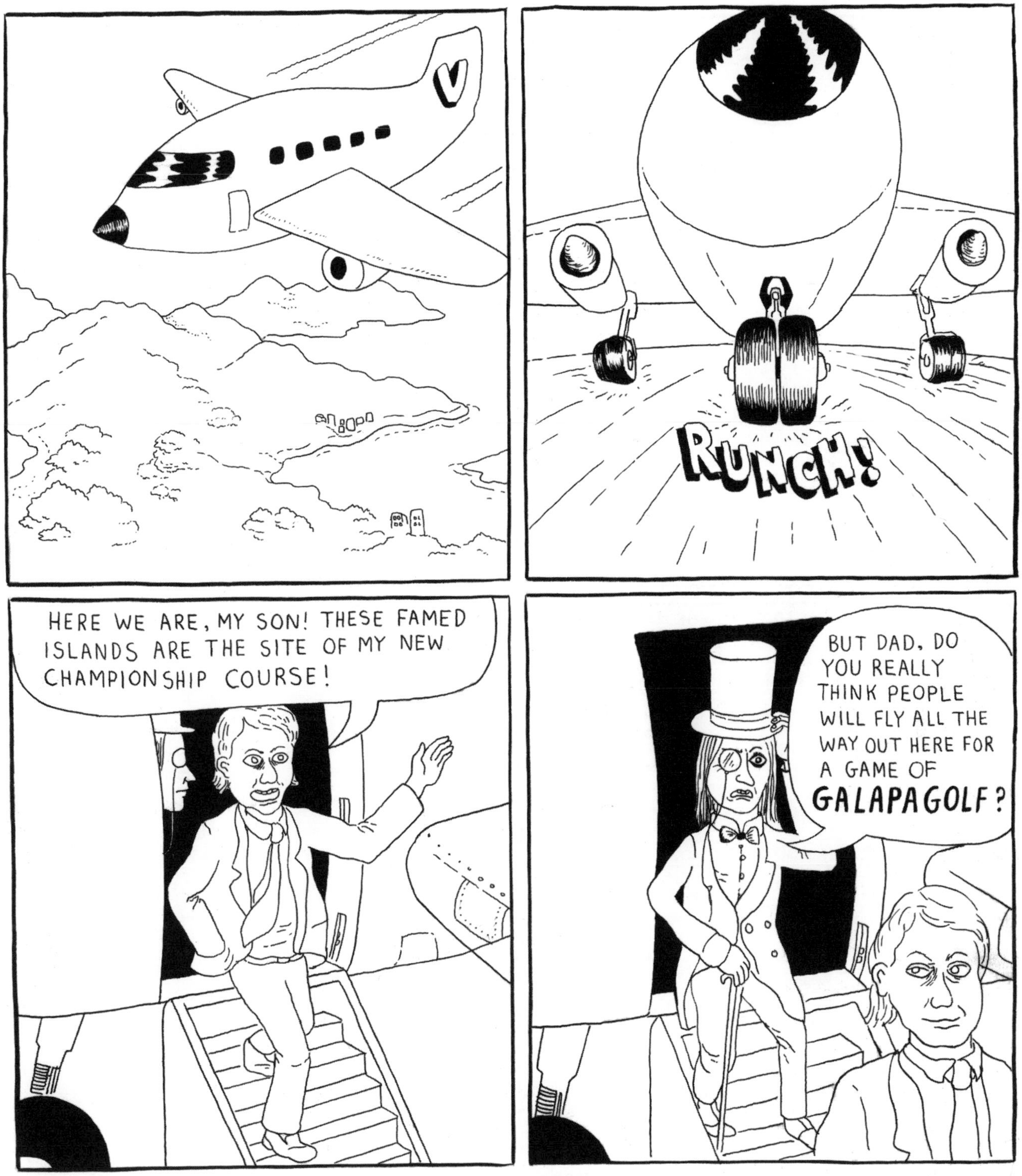
RUNCH!
HERE WE ARE, MY SON! THESE FAMED ISLANDS ARE THE SITE OF MY NEW CHAMPIONSHIP COURSE!
BUT DAD, DO YOU REALLY THINK PEOPLE WILL FLY ALL THE WAY OUT HERE FOR A GAME OF GALAPAGOLF?

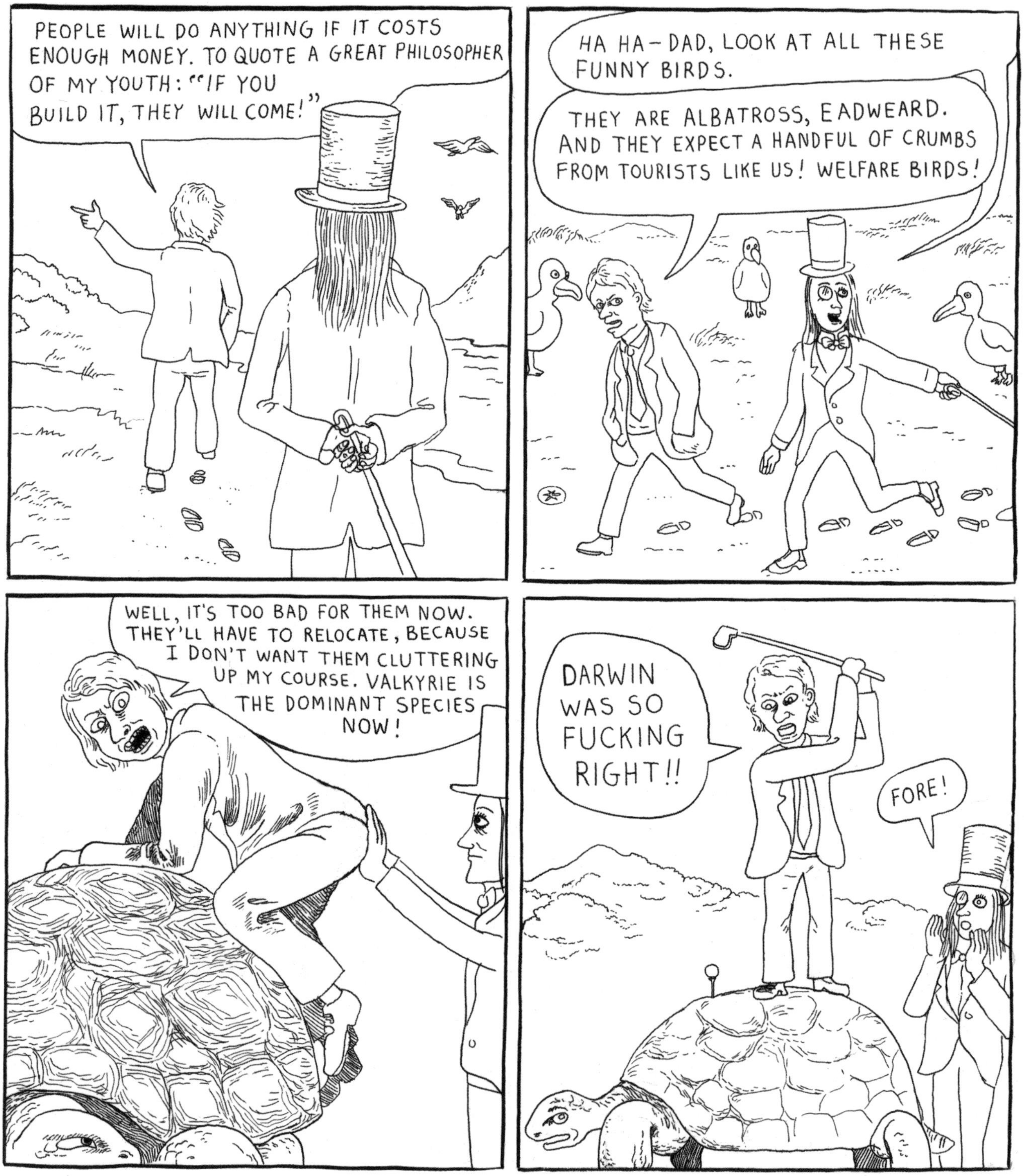
PEOPLE WILL DO ANYTHING IF IT COSTS ENOUGH MONEY. TO QUOTE A GREAT PHILOSOPHER OF MY YOUTH: "IF YOU BUILD IT, THEY WILL COME!"
HA HA - DAD, LOOK AT ALL THESE FUNNY BIRDS.
THEY ARE ALBATROSS, EADWEARD. AND THEY EXPECT A HANDFUL OF CRUMBS FROM TOURISTS LIKE US! WELFARE BIRDS!
WELL, IT'S TOO BAD FOR THEM NOW. THEY'LL HAVE TO RELOCATE, BECAUSE I DON'T WANT THEM CLUTTERING UP MY COURSE. VALKYRIE IS THE DOMINANT SPECIES NOW!
DARWIN WAS SO FUCKING RIGHT!!
FORE!

WHACK!
THERE'S REALLY ONLY ONE ANIMAL I HAVE ANY REASON TO WORRY ABOUT...
WHAT COULD IT POSSIBLY BE, DAD?
A MOLE. I FEAR THERE MAY BE A TRAITOR IN VALKYRIE CORPORATION. SECRETS ARE LEAKING OUT ABOUT OUR REAL ESTATE HOLDINGS, OUR ART INVESTMENTS...
LOOSE LIPS SINK SHIPS, SON. I HOPE YOU HAVEN'T BEEN BLABBING TO ANY OF YOUR STEAMPUNK FRIENDS...
AW JEEZ POP!
MT 5/08/12

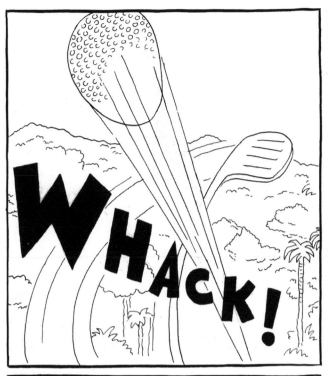

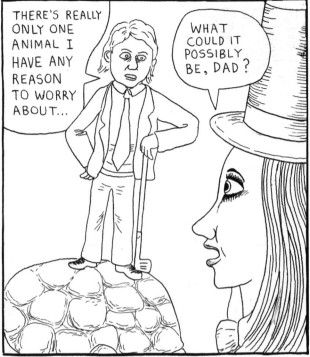

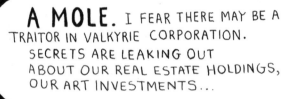

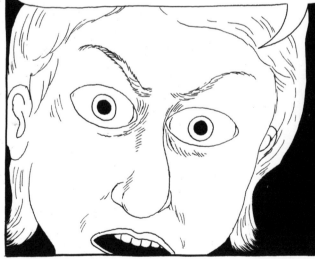

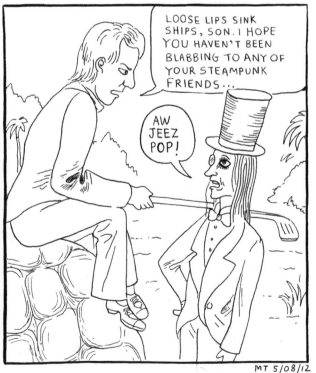

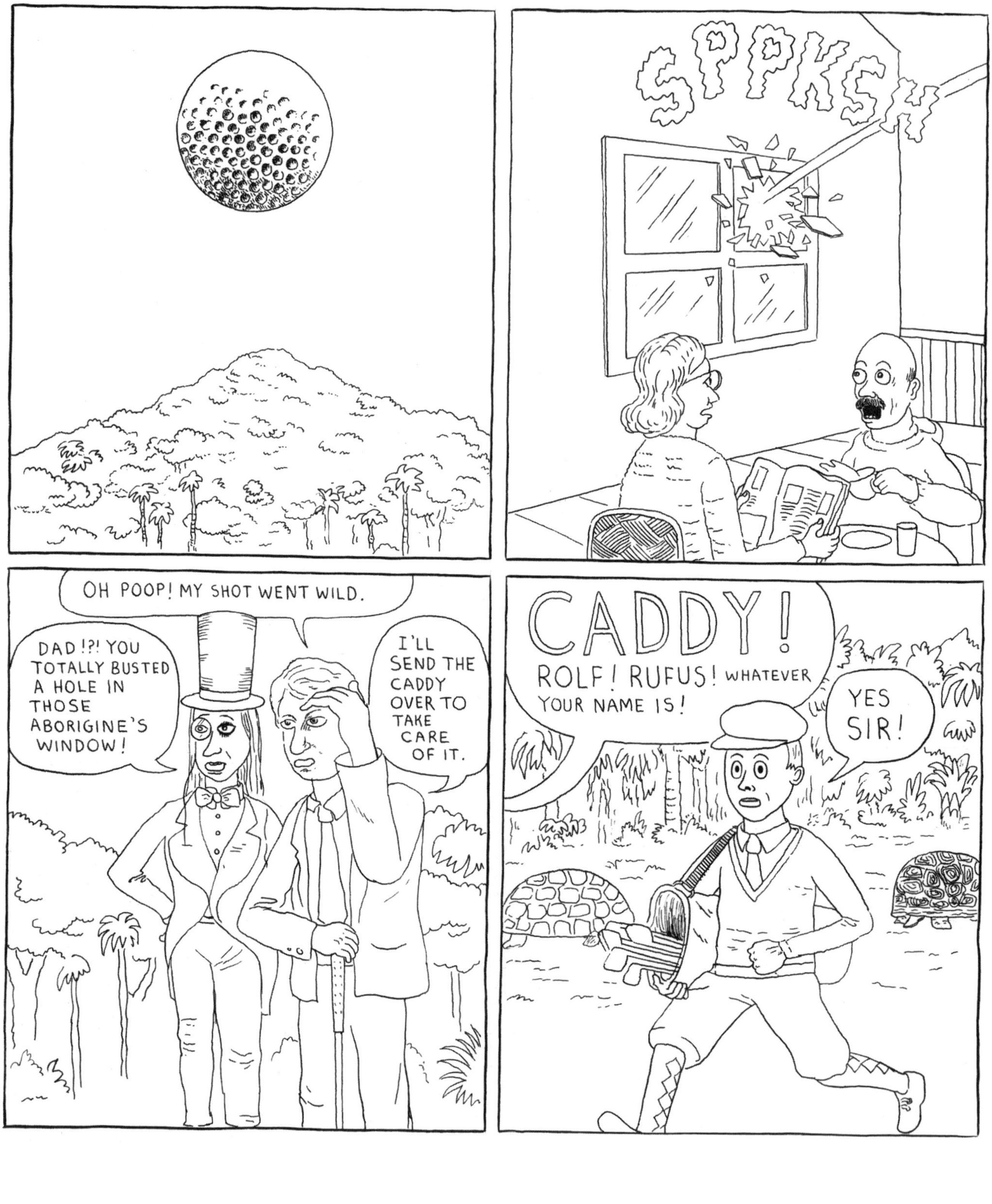

SPPKSH
OH POOP! MY SHOT WENT WILD.
DAD!?! YOU TOTALLY BUSTED A HOLE IN THOSE ABORIGINE'S WINDOW!
I'LL SEND THE CADDY OVER TO TAKE CARE OF IT.
CADDY! ROLF! RUFUS! WHATEVER YOUR NAME IS!
YES SIR!

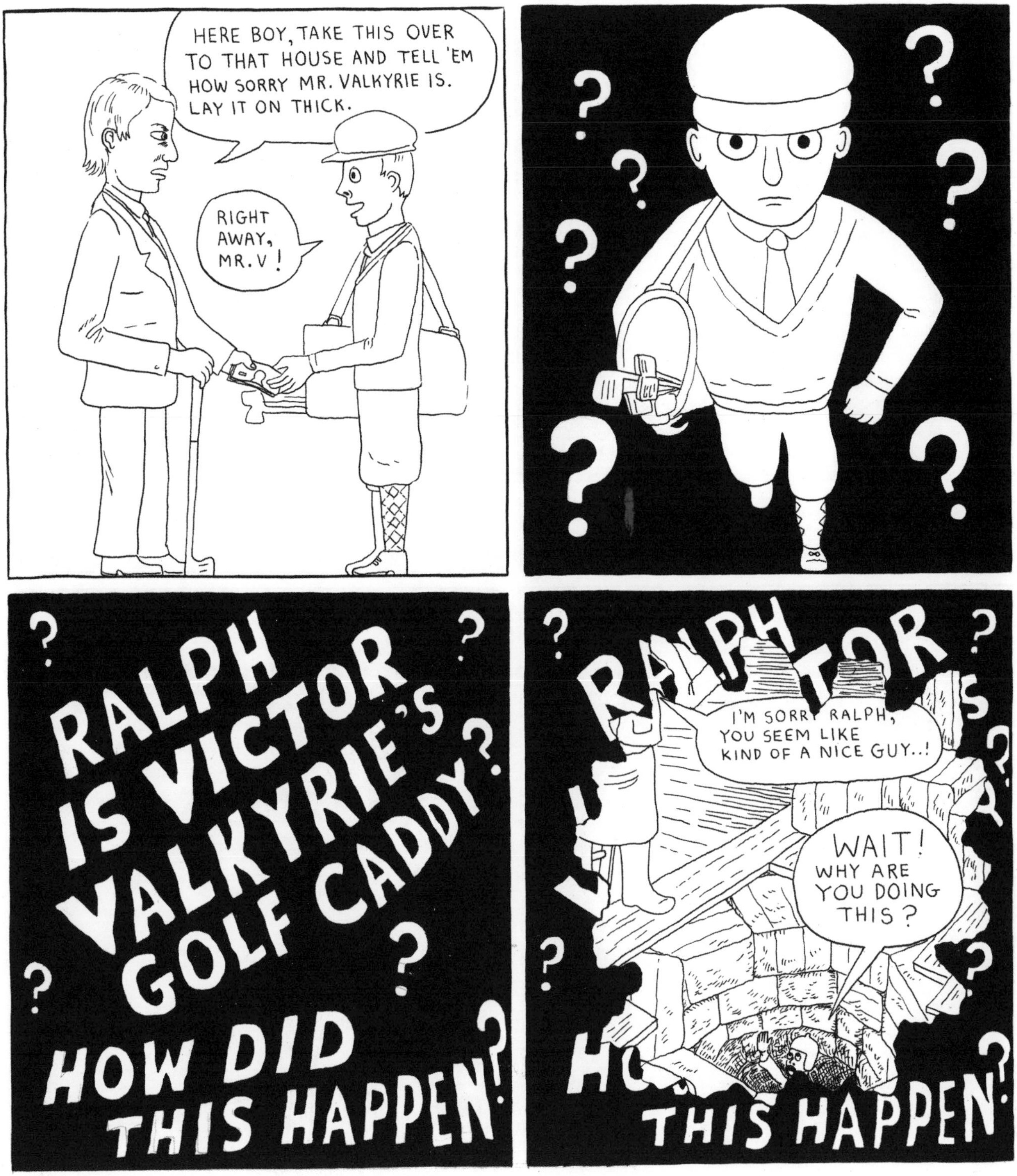

HERE BOY, TAKE THIS OVER TO THAT HOUSE AND TELL 'EM HOW SORRY MR. VALKYRIE IS. LAY IT ON THICK.
RIGHT AWAY, MR. V!
RALPH IS VICTOR VALKYRIE'S GOLF CADDY?
HOW DID THIS HAPPEN?
I'M SORRY RALPH, YOU SEEM LIKE KIND OF A NICE GUY..!
WAIT! WHY ARE YOU DOING THIS?
THIS HAPPEN?

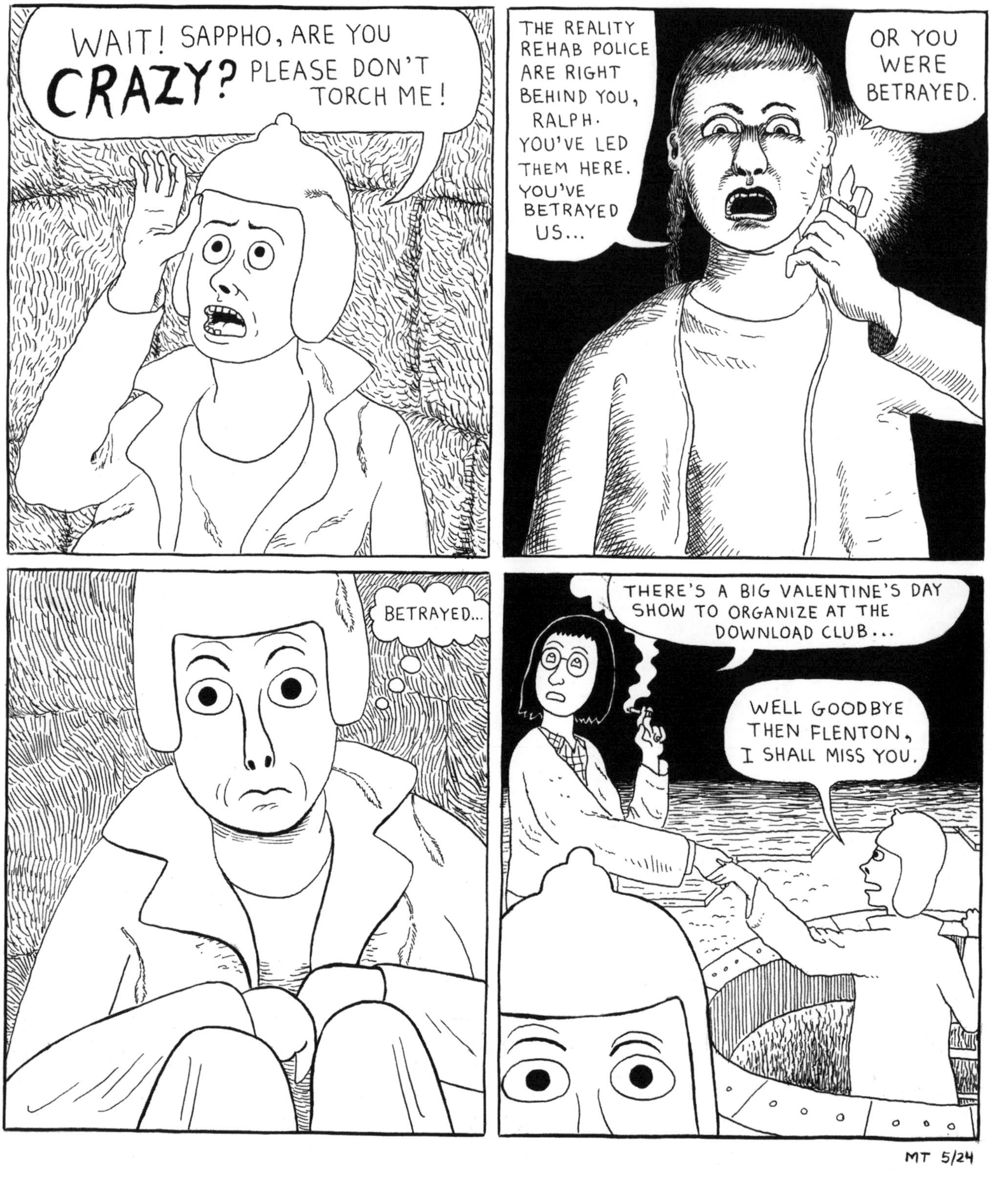
WAIT! SAPPHO, ARE YOU CRAZY? PLEASE DON'T TORCH ME!
THE REALITY REHAB POLICE ARE RIGHT BEHIND YOU, RALPH. YOU'VE LED THEM HERE. YOU'VE BETRAYED US...
OR YOU WERE BETRAYED.
BETRAYED...
THERE'S A BIG VALENTINE'S DAY SHOW TO ORGANIZE AT THE DOWNLOAD CLUB...
WELL GOODBYE THEN FLENTON, I SHALL MISS YOU.
MT 5/24

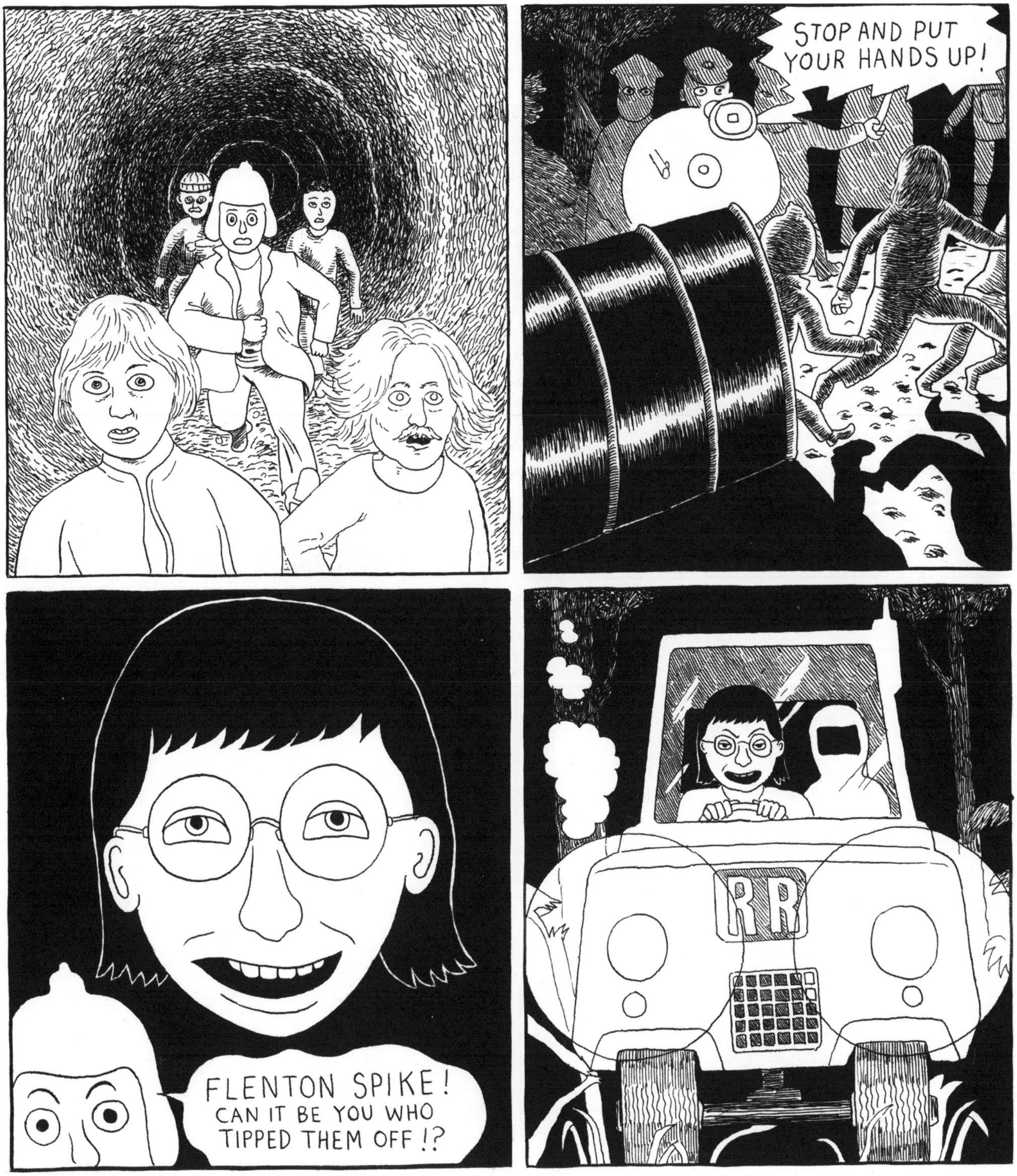
STOP AND PUT YOUR HANDS UP!
FLENTON SPIKE! CAN IT BE YOU WHO TIPPED THEM OFF!?
RR

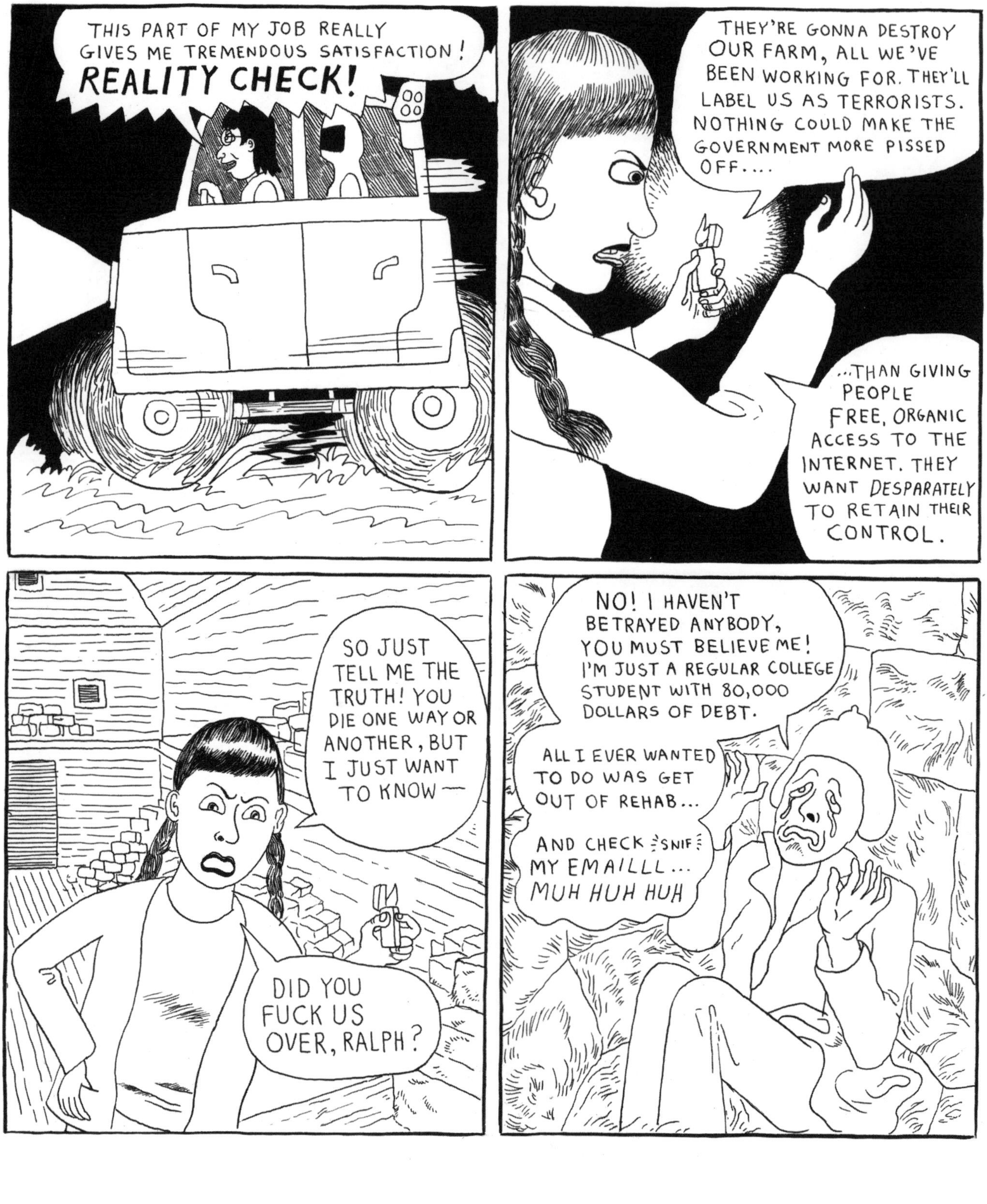
THIS PART OF MY JOB REALLY GIVES ME TREMENDOUS SATISFACTION! REALITY CHECK!
THEY'RE GONNA DESTROY OUR FARM, ALL WE'VE BEEN WORKING FOR. THEY'LL LABEL US AS TERRORISTS. NOTHING COULD MAKE THE GOVERNMENT MORE PISSED OFF....
...THAN GIVING PEOPLE FREE, ORGANIC ACCESS TO THE INTERNET. THEY WANT DESPARATELY TO RETAIN THEIR CONTROL.
SO JUST TELL ME THE TRUTH! YOU DIE ONE WAY OR ANOTHER, BUT I JUST WANT TO KNOW—
DID YOU FUCK US OVER, RALPH?
NO! I HAVEN'T BETRAYED ANYBODY, YOU MUST BELIEVE ME! I'M JUST A REGULAR COLLEGE STUDENT WITH 80,000 DOLLARS OF DEBT.
ALL I EVER WANTED TO DO WAS GET OUT OF REHAB...
AND CHECK SNIF MY EMAILLL... MUH HUH HUH

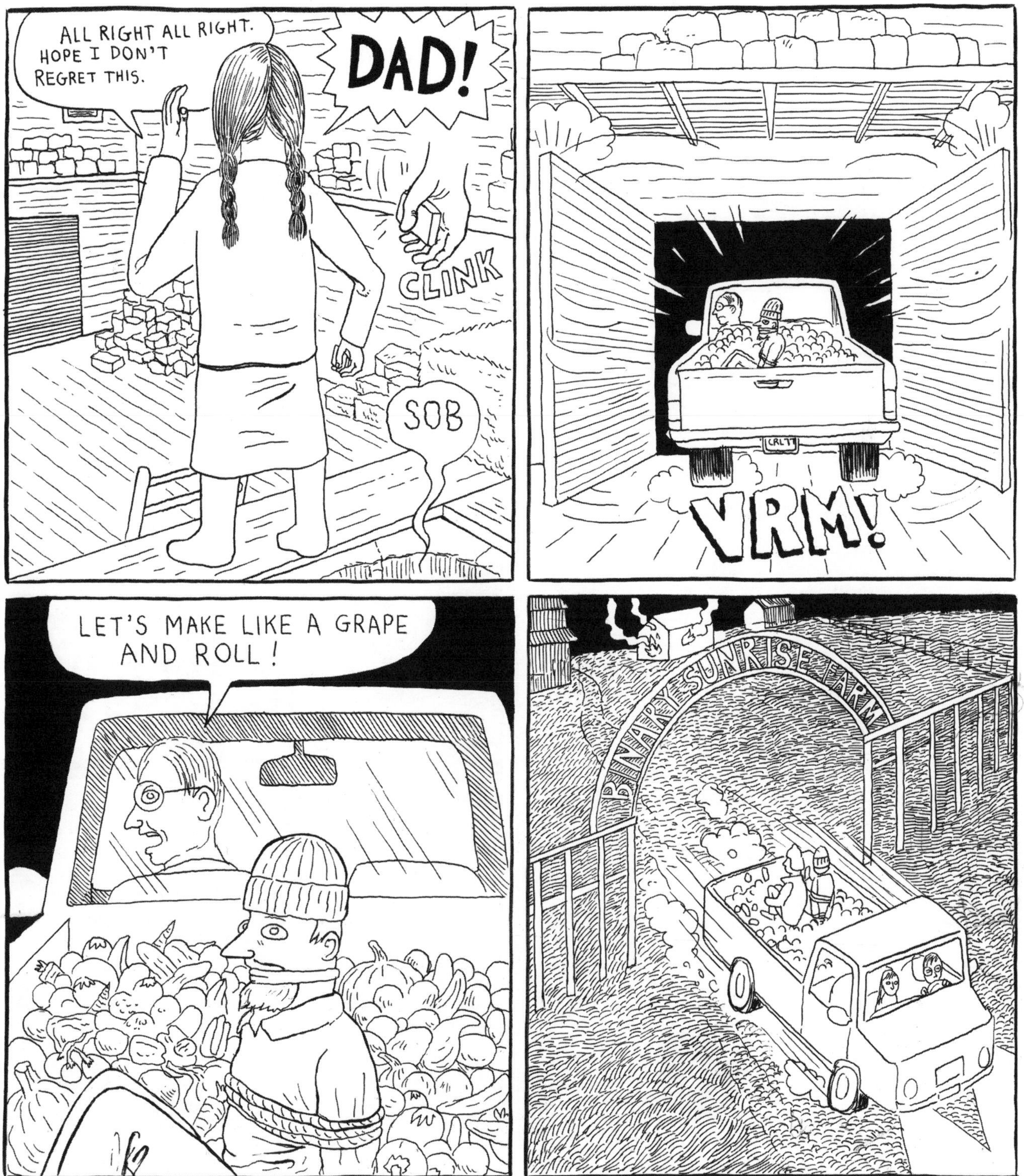

ALL RIGHT ALL RIGHT. HOPE I DON'T REGRET THIS.
DAD!
CLINK
SOB
VRM!
CRLT
LET'S MAKE LIKE A GRAPE AND ROLL!
BINARY SUNRISE FARM

INCH BY INCH

M.T. 6/2/12

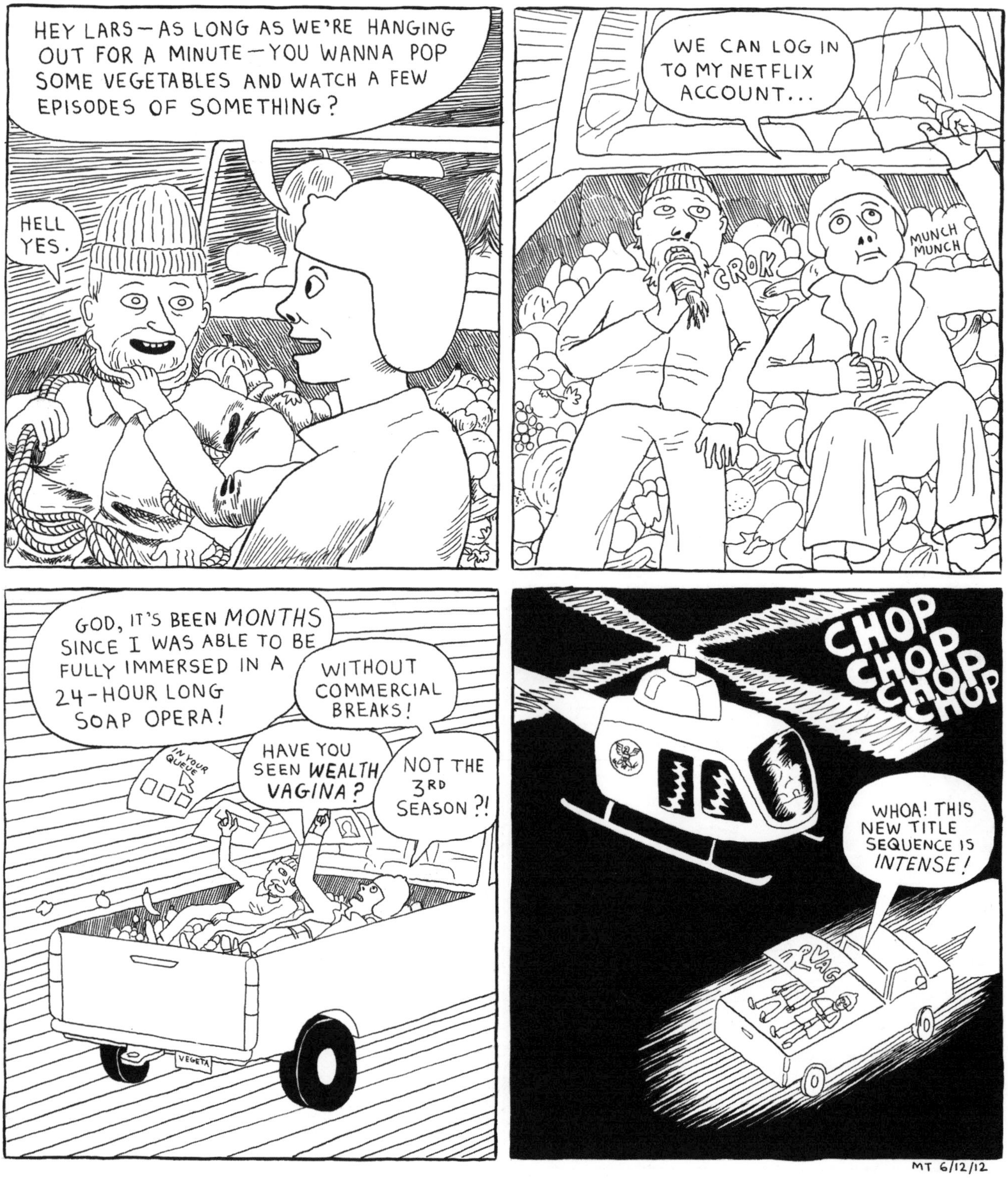
HEY LARS—AS LONG AS WE'RE HANGING OUT FOR A MINUTE—YOU WANNA POP SOME VEGETABLES AND WATCH A FEW EPISODES OF SOMETHING?
HELL YES.
WE CAN LOG IN TO MY NETFLIX ACCOUNT...
CROK
MUNCH MUNCH
GOD, IT'S BEEN MONTHS SINCE I WAS ABLE TO BE FULLY IMMERSED IN A 24-HOUR LONG SOAP OPERA!
WITHOUT COMMERCIAL BREAKS!
HAVE YOU SEEN WEALTH VAGINA?
NOT THE 3RD SEASON?!
IN YOUR QUEUE
VEGETA
CHOP CHOP CHOP CHOP
WHOA! THIS NEW TITLE SEQUENCE IS INTENSE!
VAG
MT 6/12/12

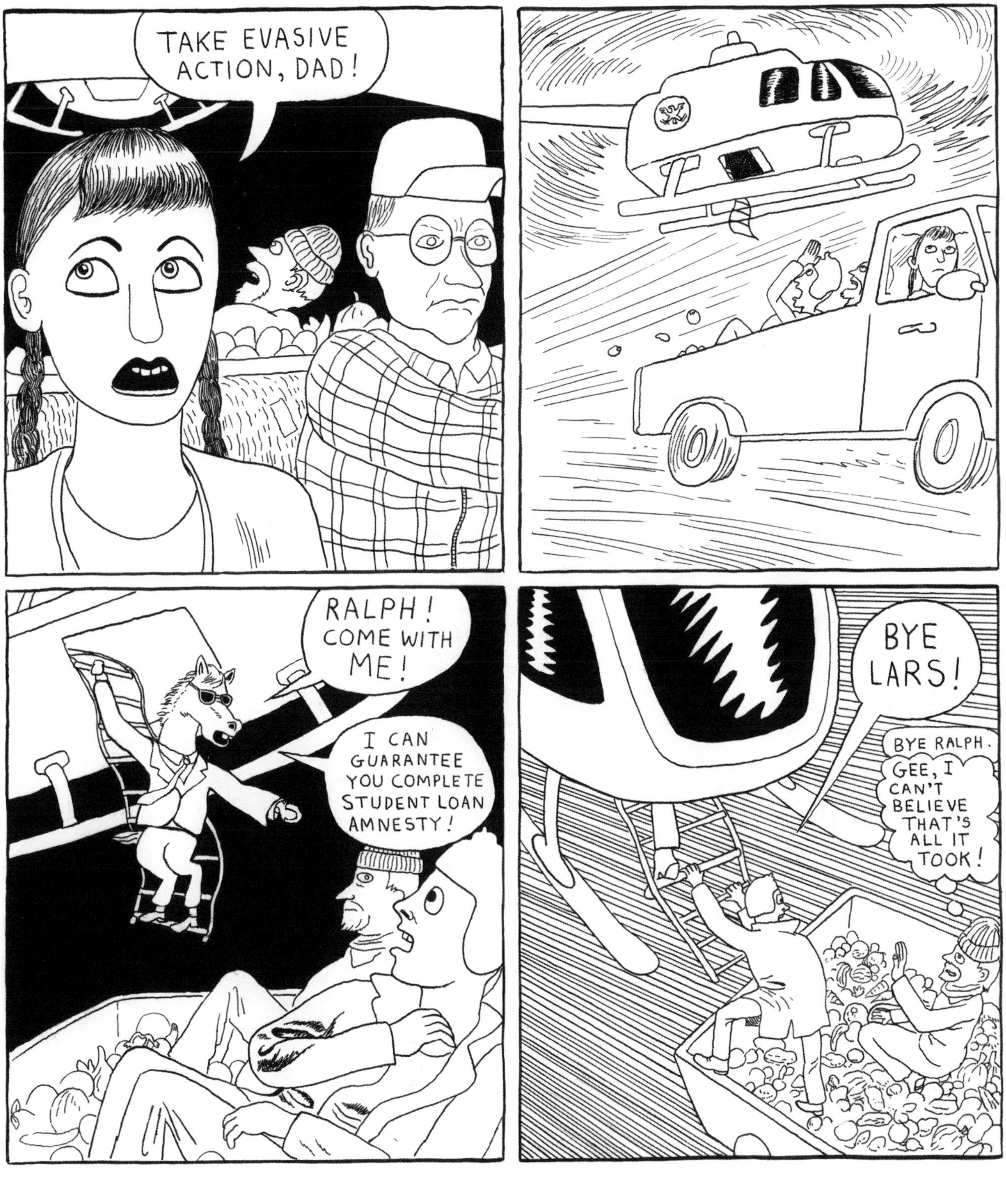
TAKE EVASIVE ACTION, DAD!
RALPH! COME WITH ME!
I CAN GUARANTEE YOU COMPLETE STUDENT LOAN AMNESTY!
BYE LARS!
BYE RALPH.
GEE, I CAN'T BELIEVE THAT'S ALL IT TOOK!

SIT DOWN AND STRAP IN, RALPH. I'M SPECIAL AGENT COLOSTOMY. THIS IS OFFICER FOX.
YOU DON'T KNOW US, BUT WE KNOW YOU. WE LIKE THE WAY YOU THINK... THE WAY YOU WRITE. YOU'RE NOT IN TROUBLE HERE. YOU'RE A GOOD AMERICAN — THE KIND WE'RE INTERESTED IN.
ARE YOU THE CIA?
FIRST AID
SORT OF. WE'RE A MICRO-AGENCY IN THE INTELLIGENCE COMMUNITY. THE ATF. IT STANDS FOR ANTHROPOMORPHIC TASK FORCE.
WE WANT TO OFFER YOU A PART-TIME JOB— WHILE YOU FINISH YOUR STUDIES.
THAT IS — IF YOU CAN PASS OUR STRINGENT HIRING PROCESS.
OKAY... BUT WHERE ARE WE HEADED?
LANGLEY, VIRGINIA, FOR YOUR TRAINING IN THE CRAFT OF CLANDESTINE OPERATIONS.
M.T. 6/15/12

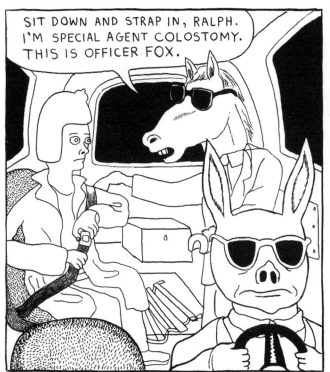

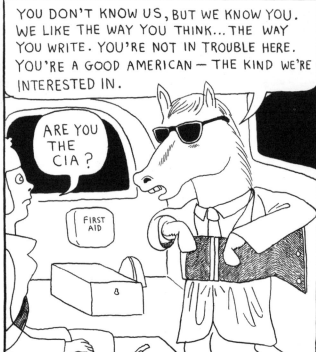

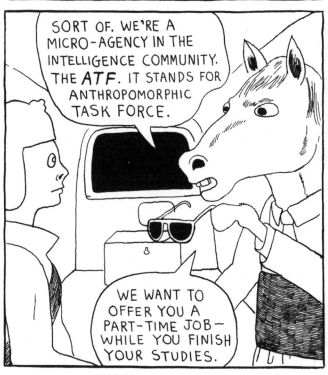

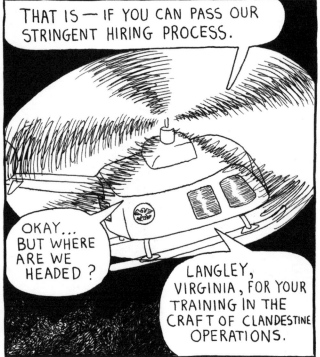

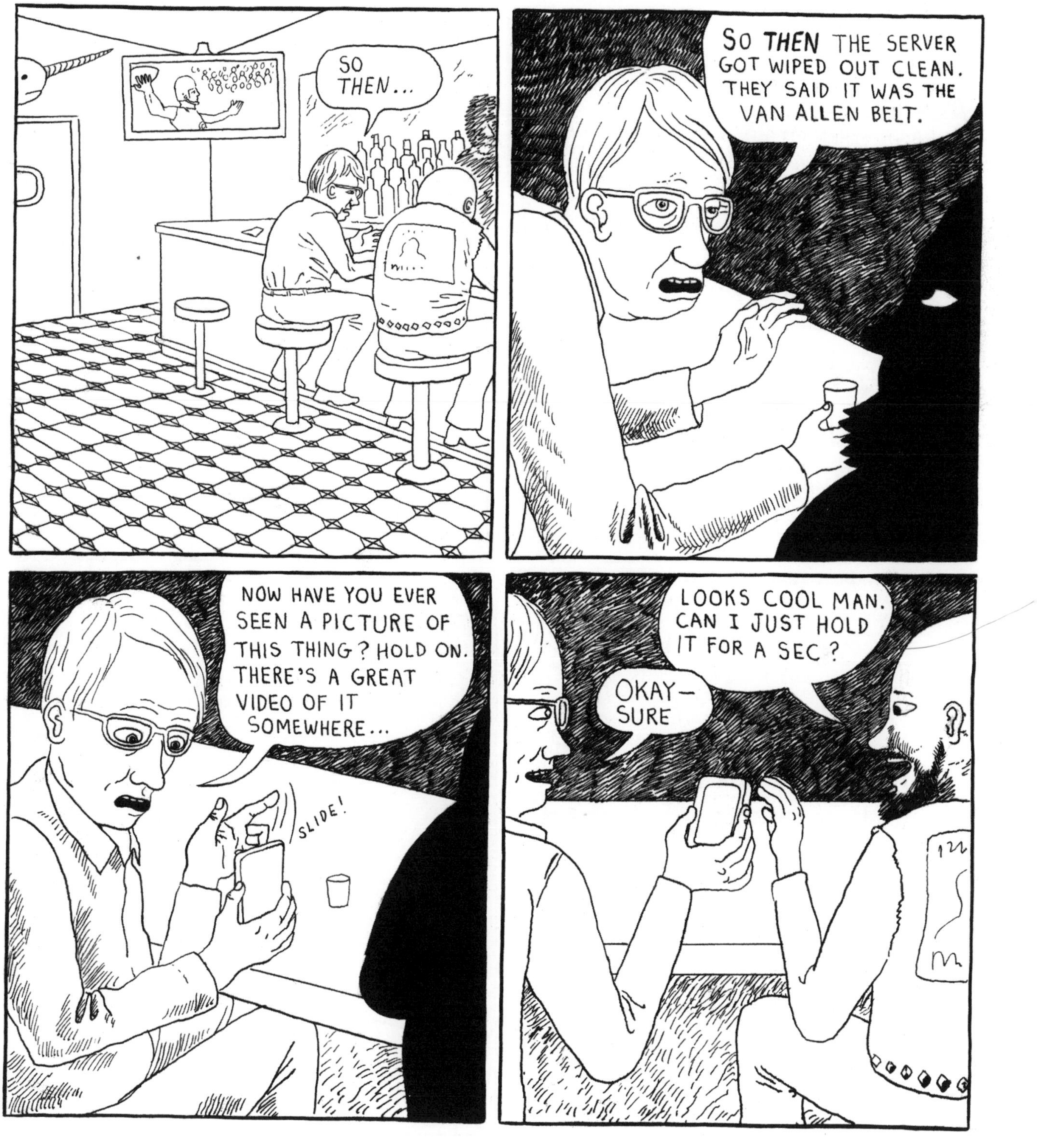
SO THEN...
SO THEN THE SERVER GOT WIPED OUT CLEAN. THEY SAID IT WAS THE VAN ALLEN BELT.
NOW HAVE YOU EVER SEEN A PICTURE OF THIS THING? HOLD ON. THERE'S A GREAT VIDEO OF IT SOMEWHERE...
SLIDE!
LOOKS COOL MAN. CAN I JUST HOLD IT FOR A SEC?
OKAY- SURE

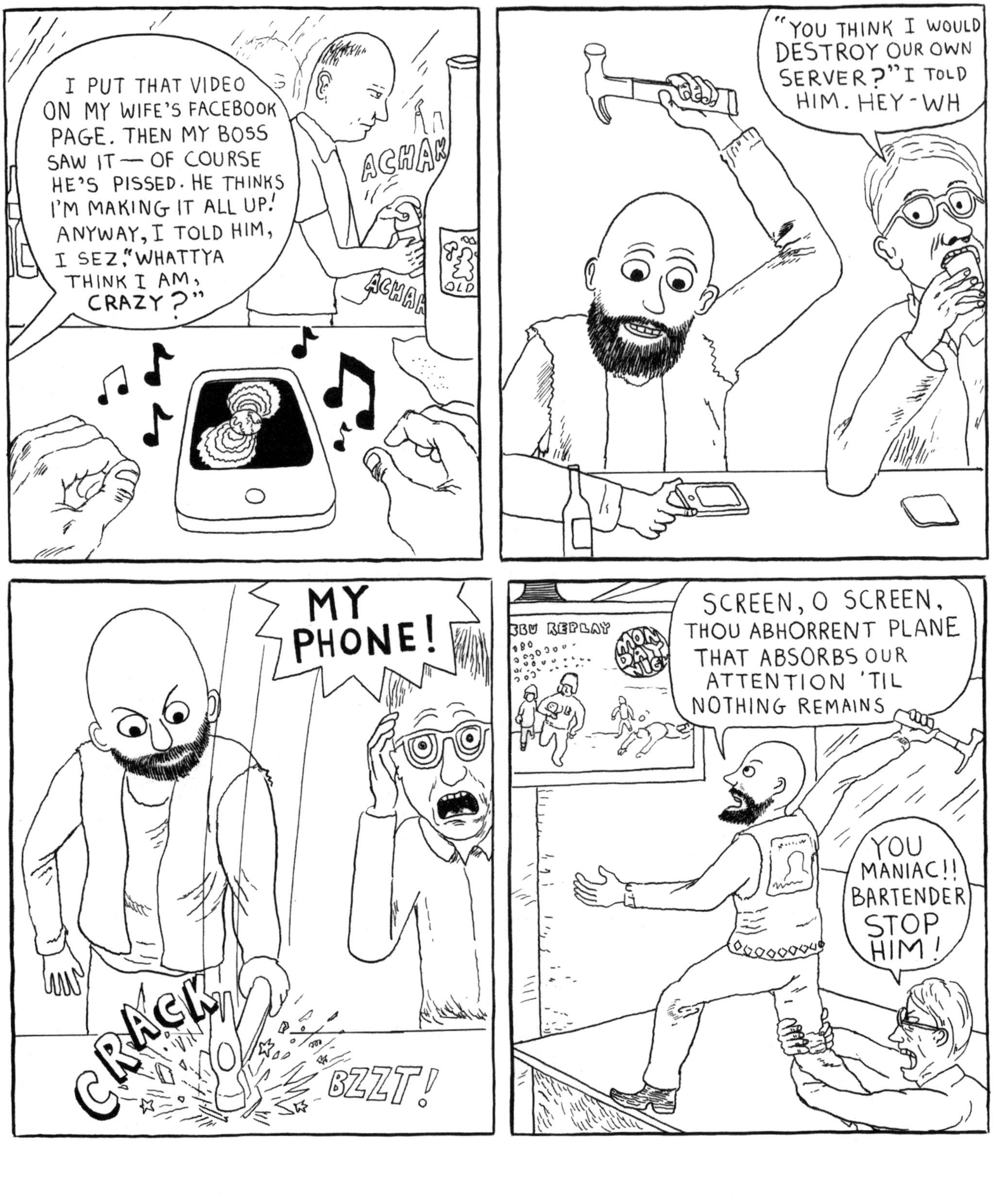
I PUT THAT VIDEO ON MY WIFE'S FACEBOOK PAGE. THEN MY BOSS SAW IT — OF COURSE HE'S PISSED. HE THINKS I'M MAKING IT ALL UP! ANYWAY, I TOLD HIM, I SEZ, "WHATTYA THINK I AM, CRAZY?"
ACHAK
ACHAK
"YOU THINK I WOULD DESTROY OUR OWN SERVER?" I TOLD HIM. HEY-WH
MY PHONE!
CRACK
BZZT!
SCREEN, O SCREEN, THOU ABHORRENT PLANE THAT ABSORBS OUR ATTENTION 'TIL NOTHING REMAINS
YOU MANIAC!! BARTENDER STOP HIM!

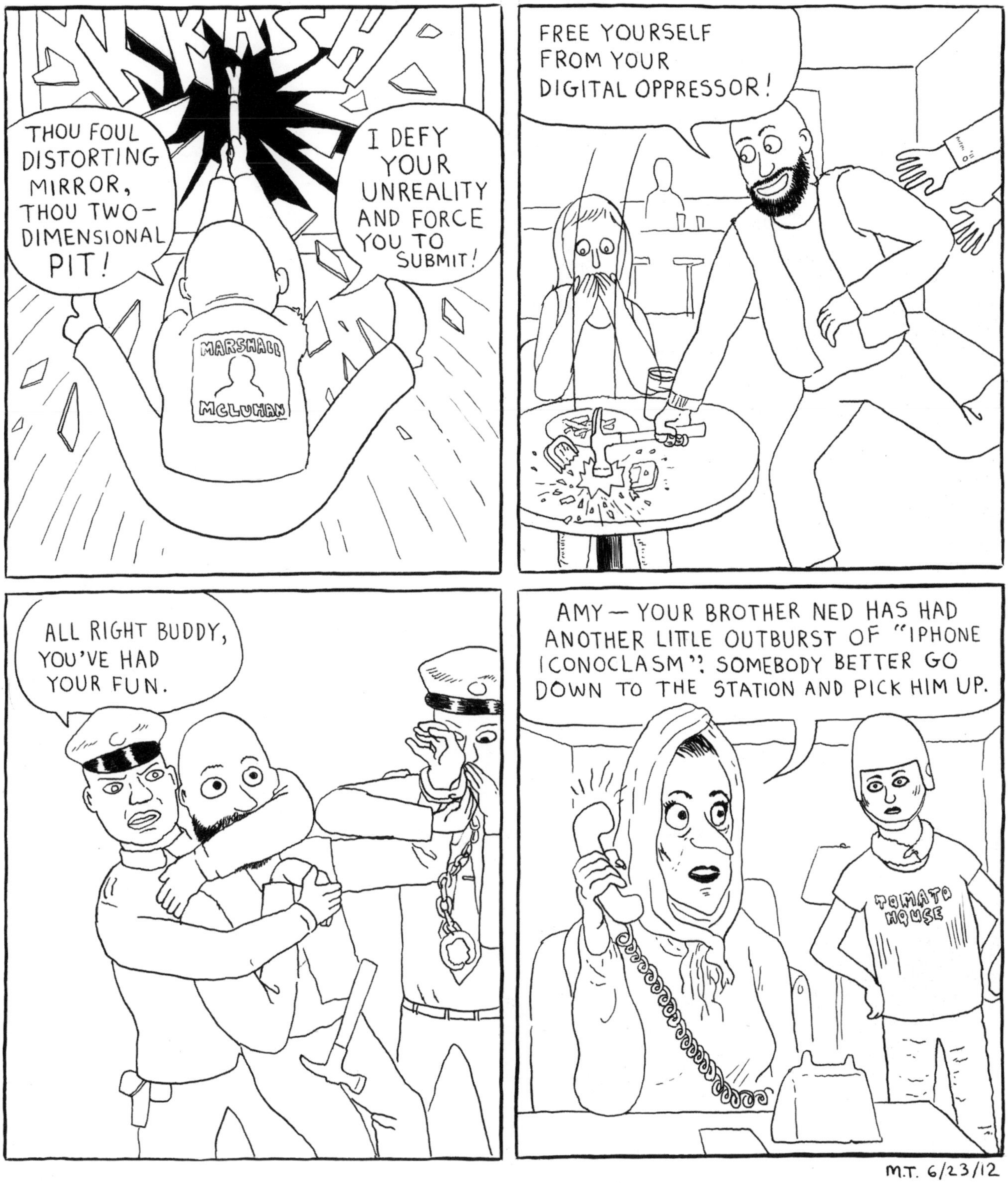
KRASH
THOU FOUL DISTORTING MIRROR, THOU TWO-DIMENSIONAL PIT!
I DEFY YOUR UNREALITY AND FORCE YOU TO SUBMIT!
MARSHALL MCLUHAN
FREE YOURSELF FROM YOUR DIGITAL OPPRESSOR!
ALL RIGHT BUDDY, YOU'VE HAD YOUR FUN.
AMY — YOUR BROTHER NED HAS HAD ANOTHER LITTLE OUTBURST OF "IPHONE ICONOCLASM". SOMEBODY BETTER GO DOWN TO THE STATION AND PICK HIM UP.
TOMATO HOUSE
M.T. 6/23/12

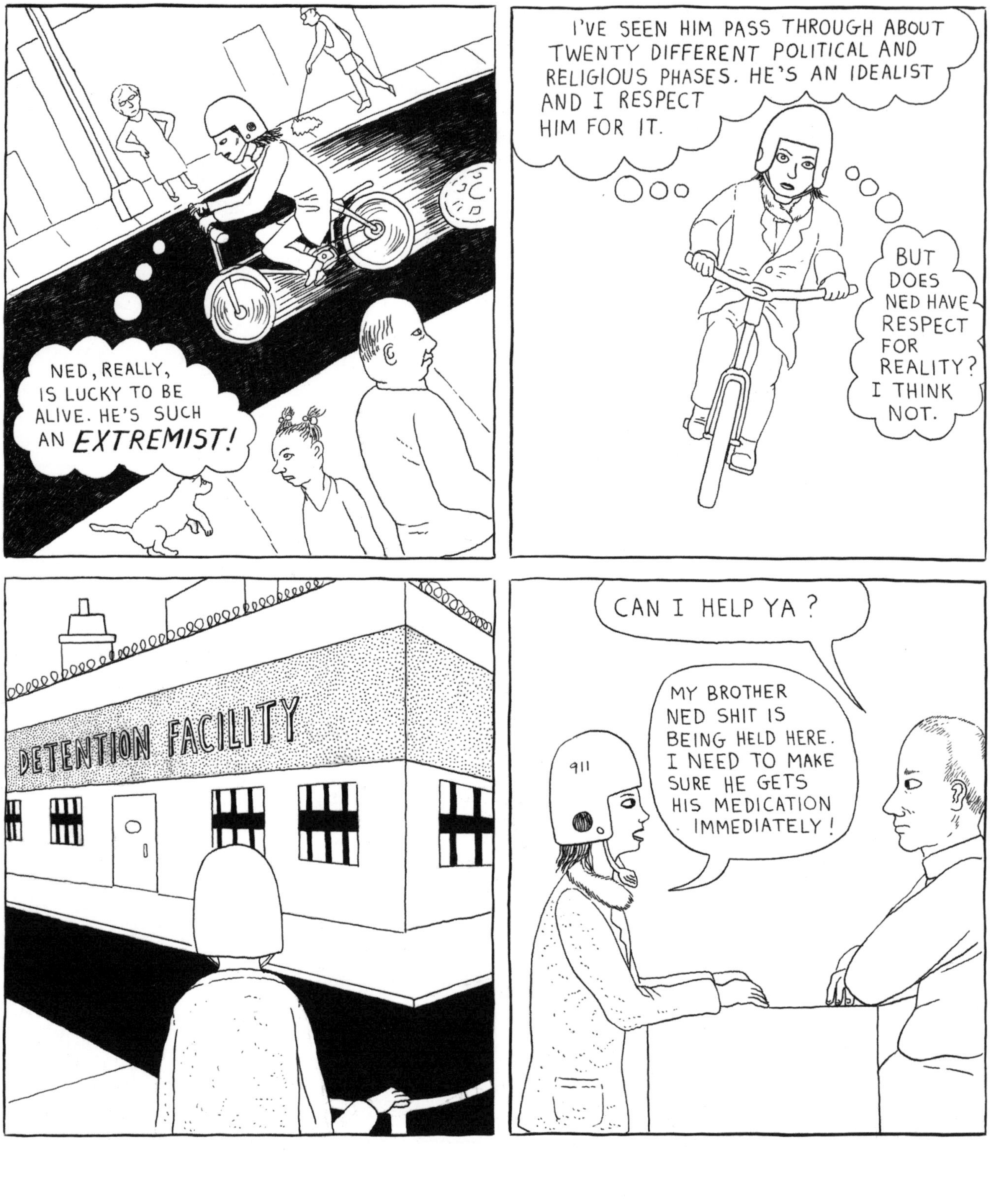
NED, REALLY, IS LUCKY TO BE ALIVE. HE'S SUCH AN *EXTREMIST!*
I'VE SEEN HIM PASS THROUGH ABOUT TWENTY DIFFERENT POLITICAL AND RELIGIOUS PHASES. HE'S AN IDEALIST AND I RESPECT HIM FOR IT.
BUT DOES NED HAVE RESPECT FOR REALITY? I THINK NOT.
DETENTION FACILITY
CAN I HELP YA?
911
MY BROTHER NED SHIT IS BEING HELD HERE. I NEED TO MAKE SURE HE GETS HIS MEDICATION IMMEDIATELY!

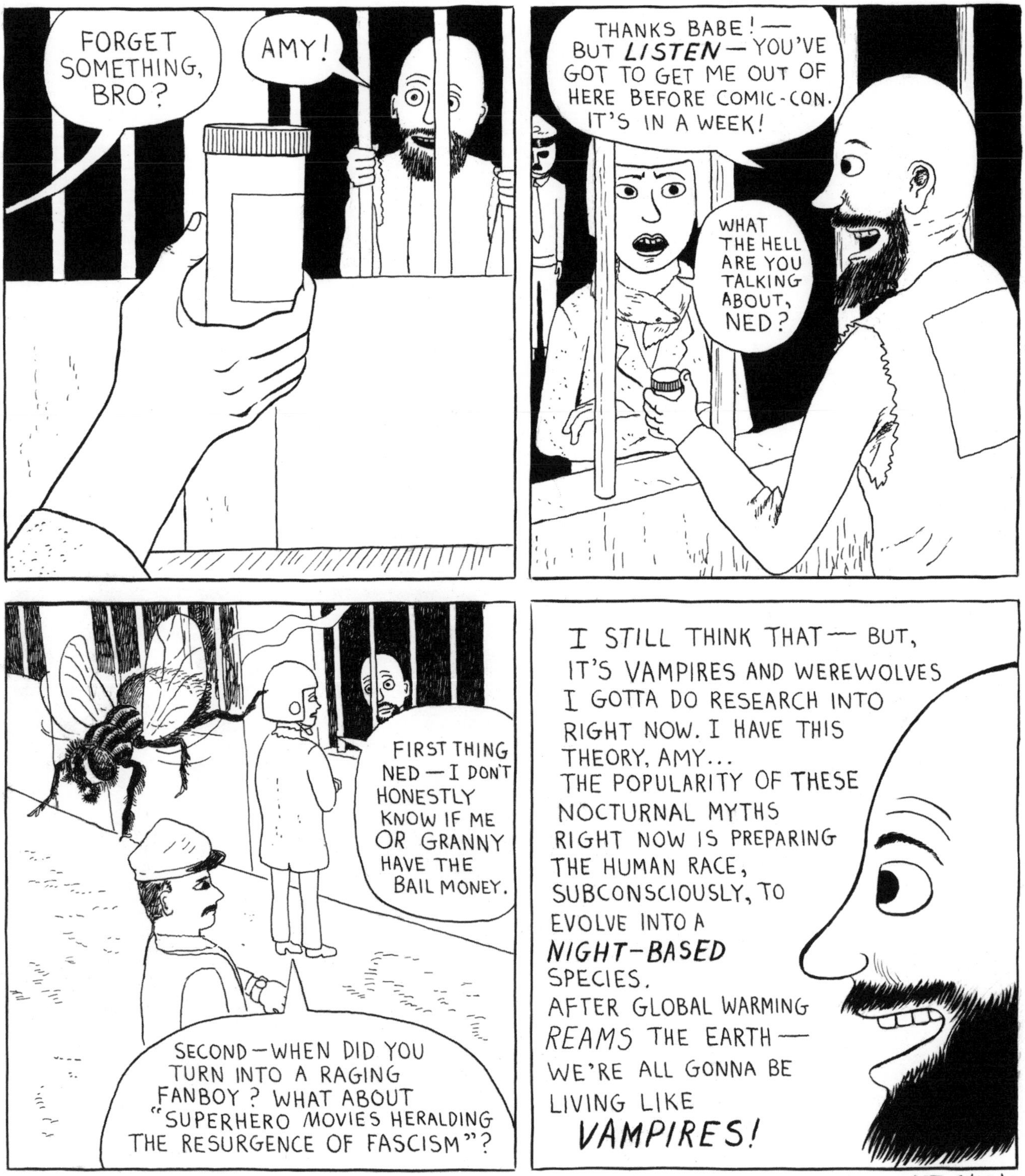
FORGET SOMETHING, BRO?
AMY!
THANKS BABE!— BUT LISTEN— YOU'VE GOT TO GET ME OUT OF HERE BEFORE COMIC-CON. IT'S IN A WEEK!
WHAT THE HELL ARE YOU TALKING ABOUT, NED?
FIRST THING NED— I DON'T HONESTLY KNOW IF ME OR GRANNY HAVE THE BAIL MONEY.
SECOND— WHEN DID YOU TURN INTO A RAGING FANBOY? WHAT ABOUT "SUPERHERO MOVIES HERALDING THE RESURGENCE OF FASCISM"?
I STILL THINK THAT— BUT, IT'S VAMPIRES AND WEREWOLVES I GOTTA DO RESEARCH INTO RIGHT NOW. I HAVE THIS THEORY, AMY... THE POPULARITY OF THESE NOCTURNAL MYTHS RIGHT NOW IS PREPARING THE HUMAN RACE, SUBCONSCIOUSLY, TO EVOLVE INTO A NIGHT-BASED SPECIES. AFTER GLOBAL WARMING REAMS THE EARTH— WE'RE ALL GONNA BE LIVING LIKE VAMPIRES!

MT 6/30/12

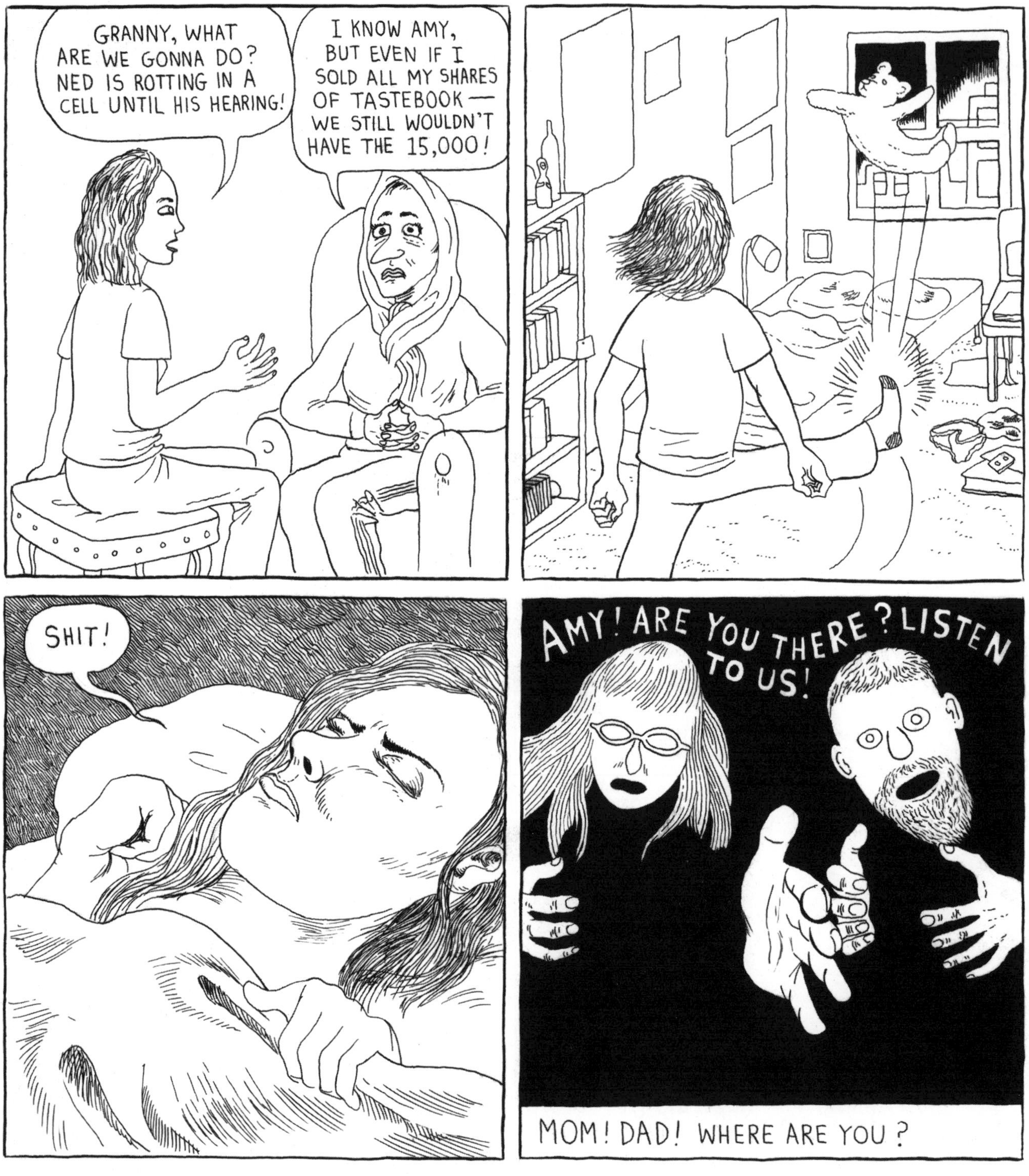
GRANNY, WHAT ARE WE GONNA DO? NED IS ROTTING IN A CELL UNTIL HIS HEARING!
I KNOW AMY, BUT EVEN IF I SOLD ALL MY SHARES OF TASTEBOOK — WE STILL WOULDN'T HAVE THE 15,000!
SHIT!
AMY! ARE YOU THERE? LISTEN TO US!
MOM! DAD! WHERE ARE YOU?

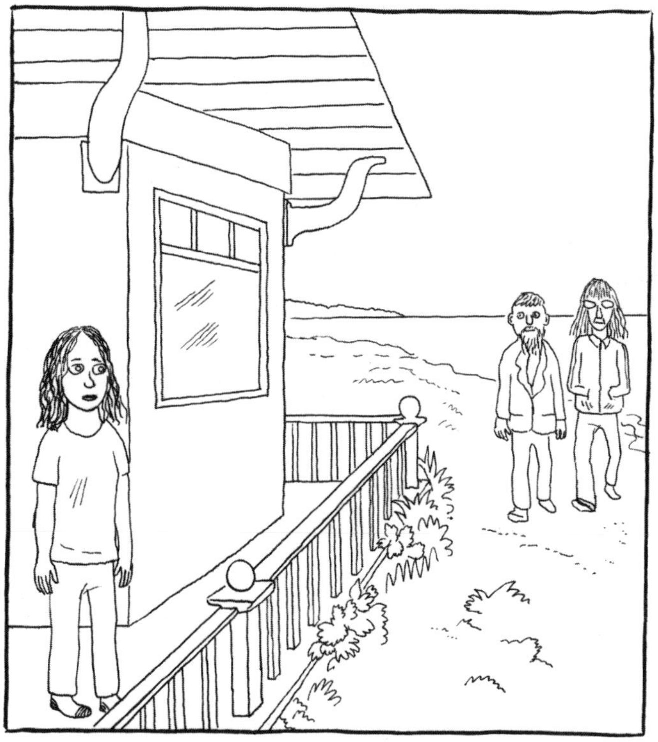

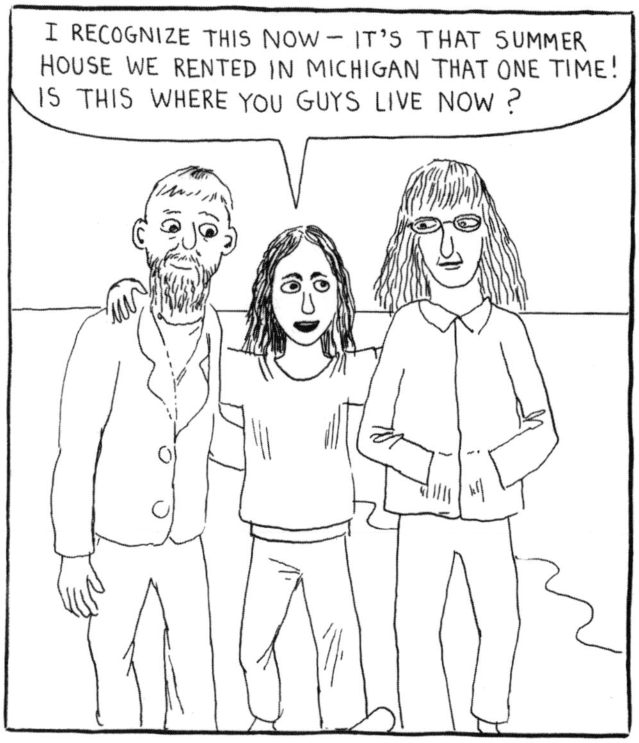
I RECOGNIZE THIS NOW – IT'S THAT SUMMER HOUSE WE RENTED IN MICHIGAN THAT ONE TIME! IS THIS WHERE YOU GUYS LIVE NOW?

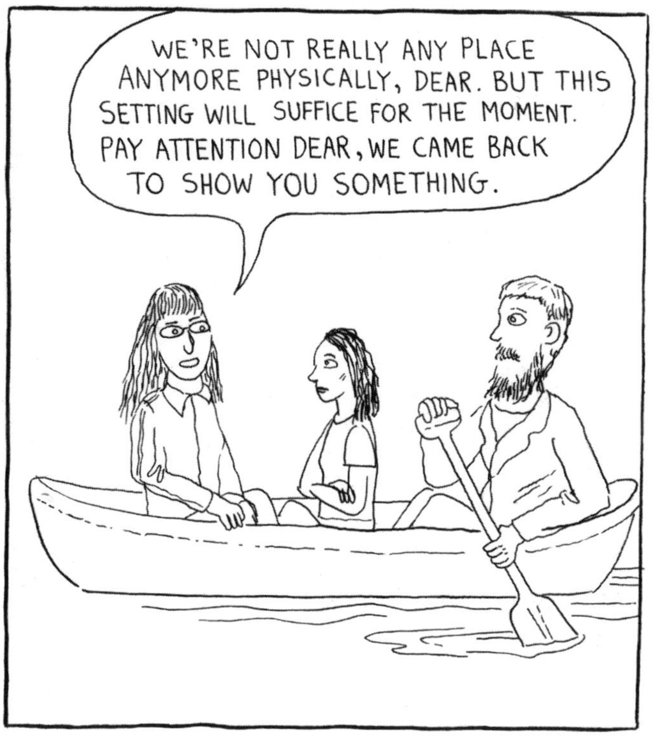
WE'RE NOT REALLY ANY PLACE ANYMORE PHYSICALLY, DEAR. BUT THIS SETTING WILL SUFFICE FOR THE MOMENT. PAY ATTENTION DEAR, WE CAME BACK TO SHOW YOU SOMETHING.

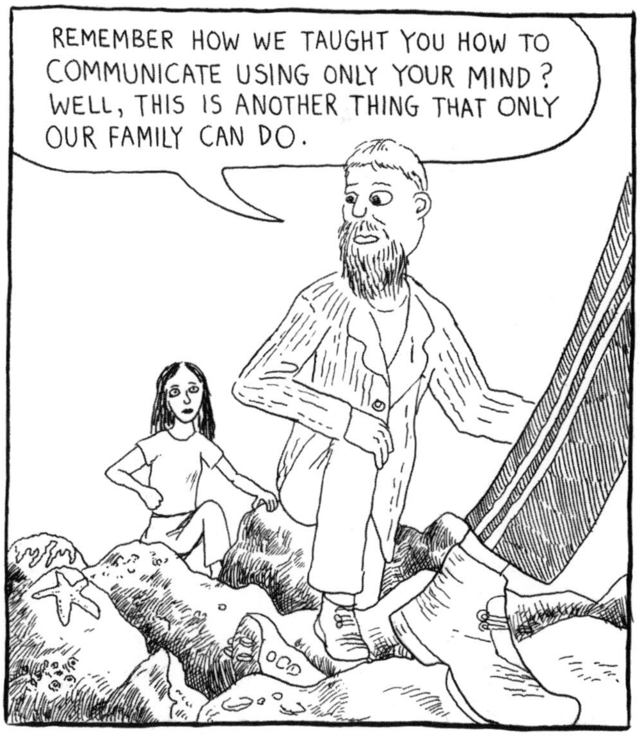
REMEMBER HOW WE TAUGHT YOU HOW TO COMMUNICATE USING ONLY YOUR MIND? WELL, THIS IS ANOTHER THING THAT ONLY OUR FAMILY CAN DO.

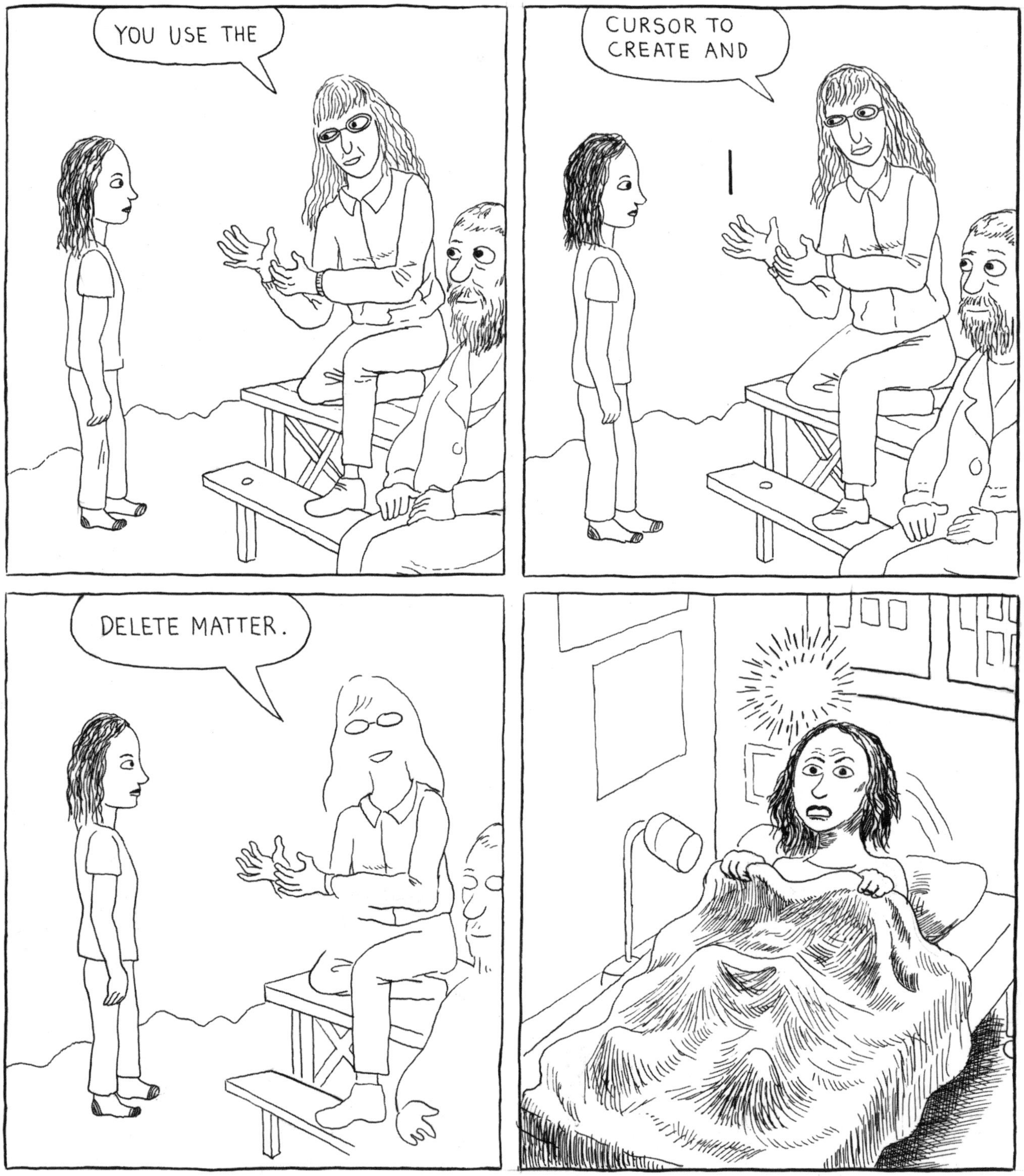
YOU USE THE
CURSOR TO CREATE AND
DELETE MATTER.
MT 7/4/12

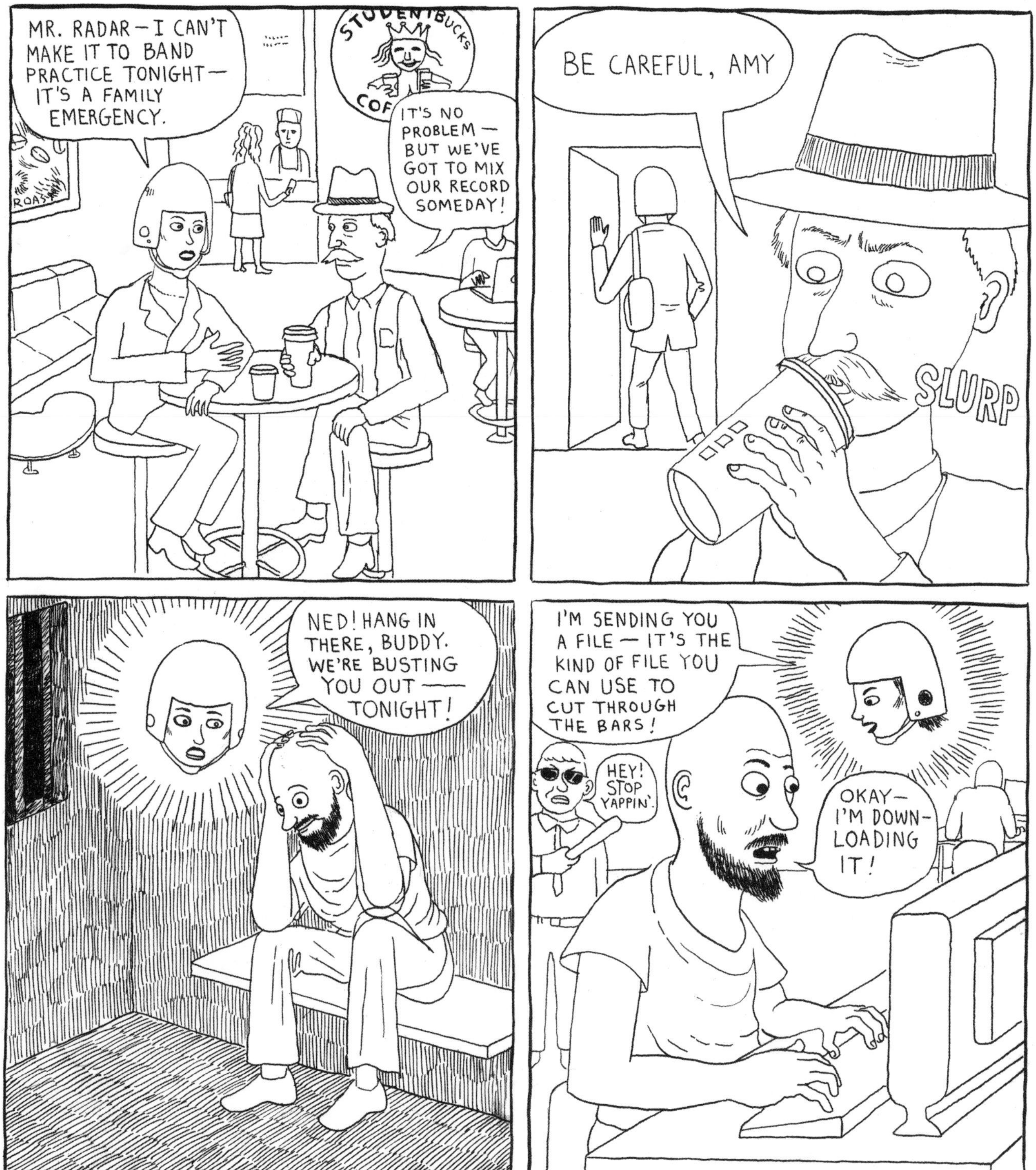
MR. RADAR — I CAN'T MAKE IT TO BAND PRACTICE TONIGHT — IT'S A FAMILY EMERGENCY.
STUDENTBUCKS COF
IT'S NO PROBLEM — BUT WE'VE GOT TO MIX OUR RECORD SOMEDAY!
BE CAREFUL, AMY
SLURP
NED! HANG IN THERE, BUDDY. WE'RE BUSTING YOU OUT — TONIGHT!
I'M SENDING YOU A FILE — IT'S THE KIND OF FILE YOU CAN USE TO CUT THROUGH THE BARS!
HEY! STOP YAPPIN'.
OKAY— I'M DOWN-LOADING IT!

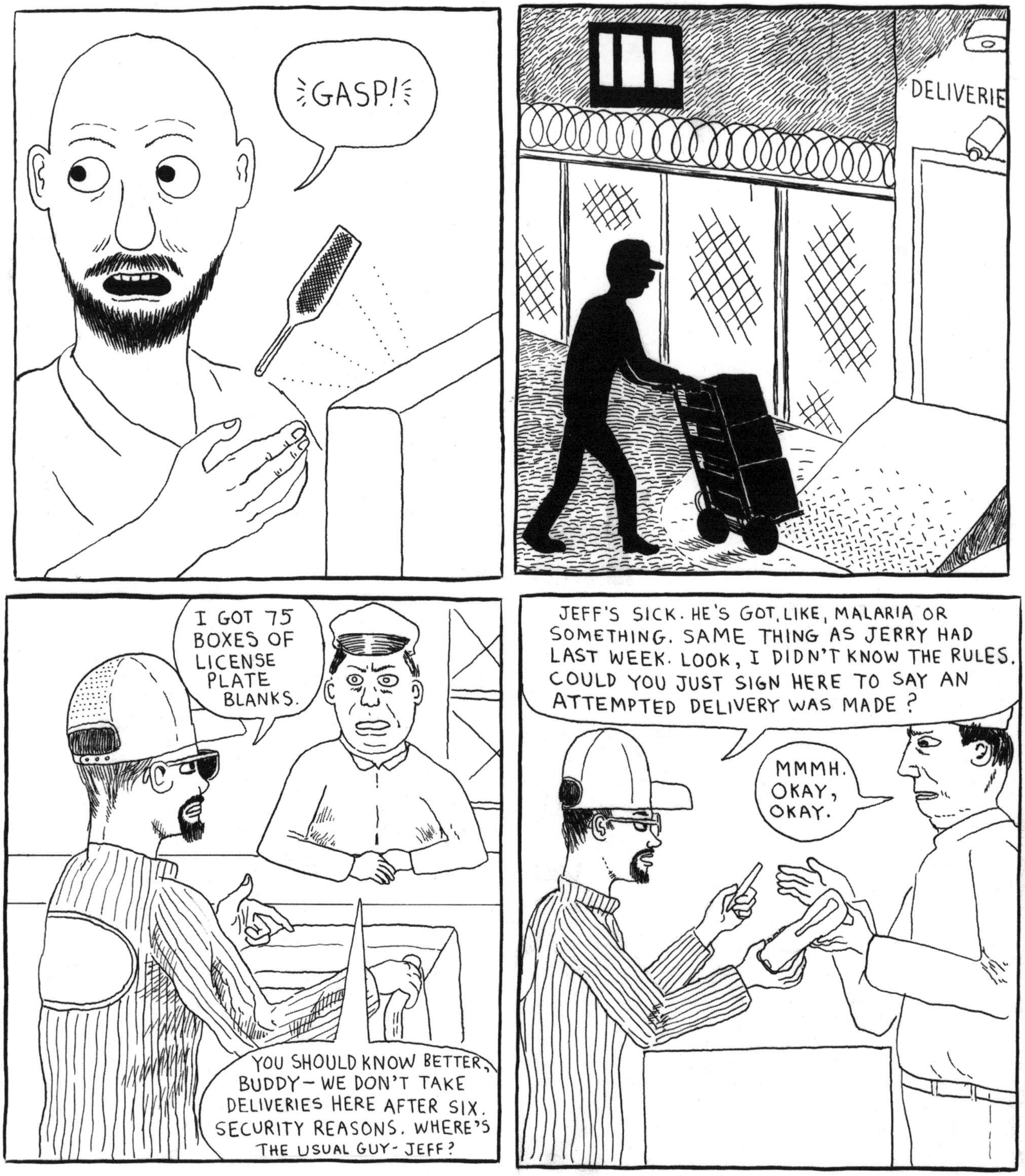

GASP!
DELIVERIE
I GOT 75 BOXES OF LICENSE PLATE BLANKS.
YOU SHOULD KNOW BETTER, BUDDY— WE DON'T TAKE DELIVERIES HERE AFTER SIX. SECURITY REASONS. WHERE'S THE USUAL GUY- JEFF?
JEFF'S SICK. HE'S GOT, LIKE, MALARIA OR SOMETHING. SAME THING AS JERRY HAD LAST WEEK. LOOK, I DIDN'T KNOW THE RULES. COULD YOU JUST SIGN HERE TO SAY AN ATTEMPTED DELIVERY WAS MADE?
MMMH. OKAY, OKAY.

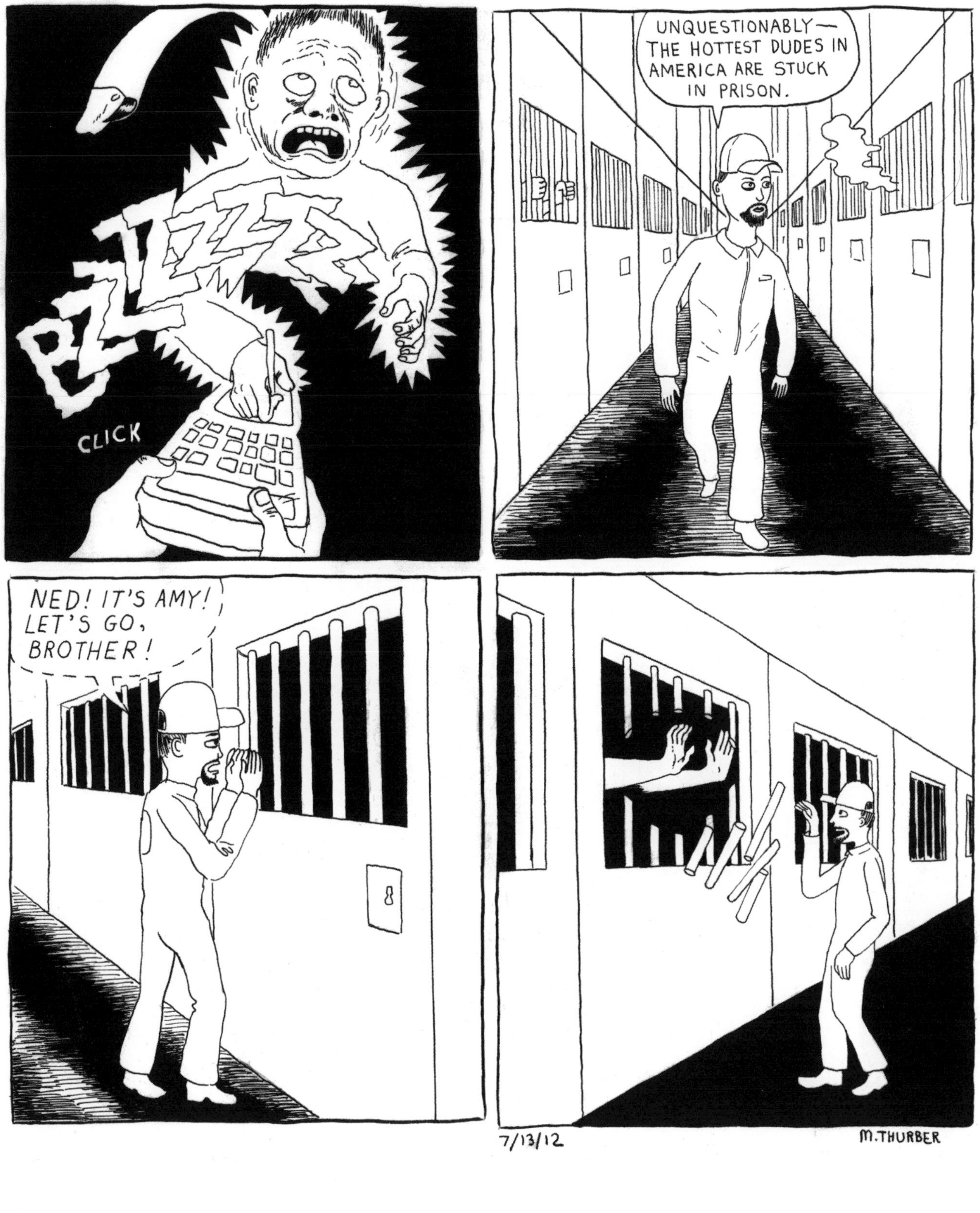
BZZZZZZZT
CLICK
UNQUESTIONABLY— THE HOTTEST DUDES IN AMERICA ARE STUCK IN PRISON.
NED! IT'S AMY! LET'S GO, BROTHER!
7/13/12
M.THURBER

AMY!
DON'T COME BACK TO THE HOUSE!
STICK TO PUBLIC SPACES FOR NOW!
I'M BEING FOLLOWED AND IT'S LIKELY THAT YOU ARE TOO. TAKE CARE, DEARIE!
OKAY GRANNY. I'LL ZIG-ZAG MY WAY TO BAND PRACTICE!
SLOW DOWN! NO NEED TO RUN - NOT YET. NO ONE ON MY TAIL - AND GRANNY SWEARS OUR "CHATTING" IS SECURE!
WHO'S MY ENEMY? THE PEOPLE WHO PUT MY PARENTS AWAY? RANDALL AND VIOLET— WHAT BECAME OF YOU, WHERE DID YOU GO?

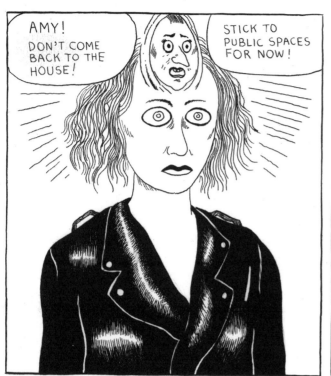

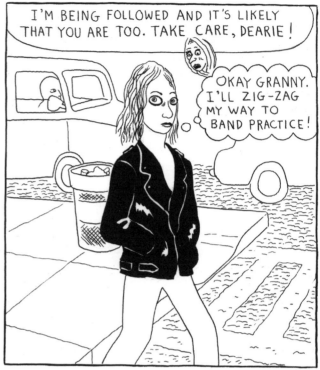

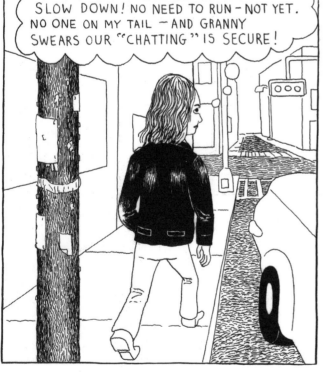

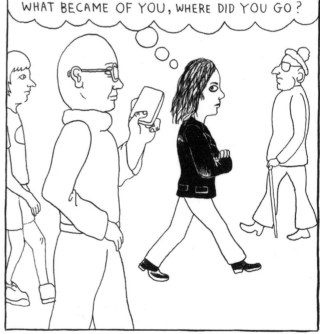

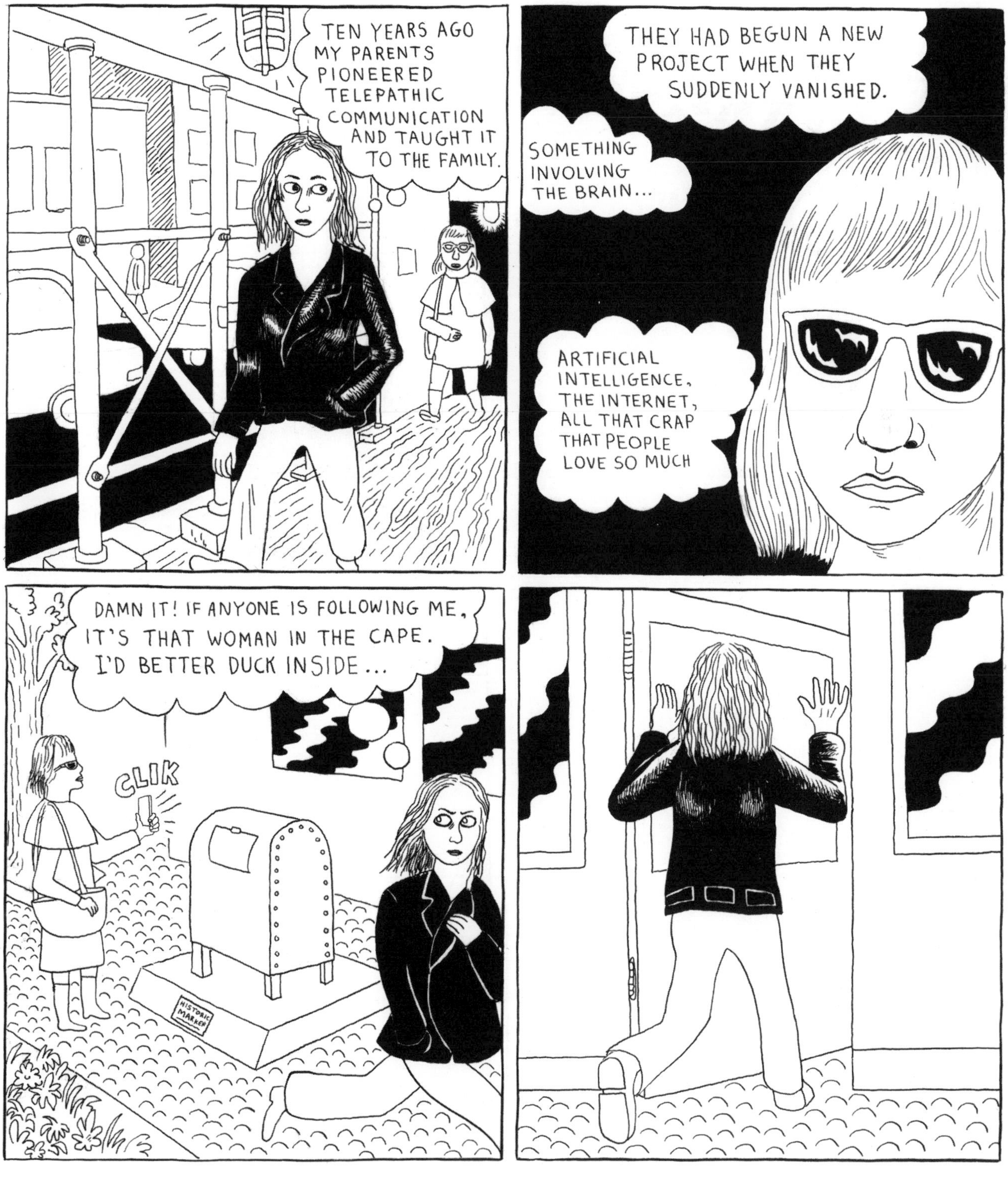
TEN YEARS AGO MY PARENTS PIONEERED TELEPATHIC COMMUNICATION AND TAUGHT IT TO THE FAMILY.
THEY HAD BEGUN A NEW PROJECT WHEN THEY SUDDENLY VANISHED.
SOMETHING INVOLVING THE BRAIN...
ARTIFICIAL INTELLIGENCE, THE INTERNET, ALL THAT CRAP THAT PEOPLE LOVE SO MUCH
DAMN IT! IF ANYONE IS FOLLOWING ME, IT'S THAT WOMAN IN THE CAPE. I'D BETTER DUCK INSIDE...
CLIK
HISTORIC MARKER

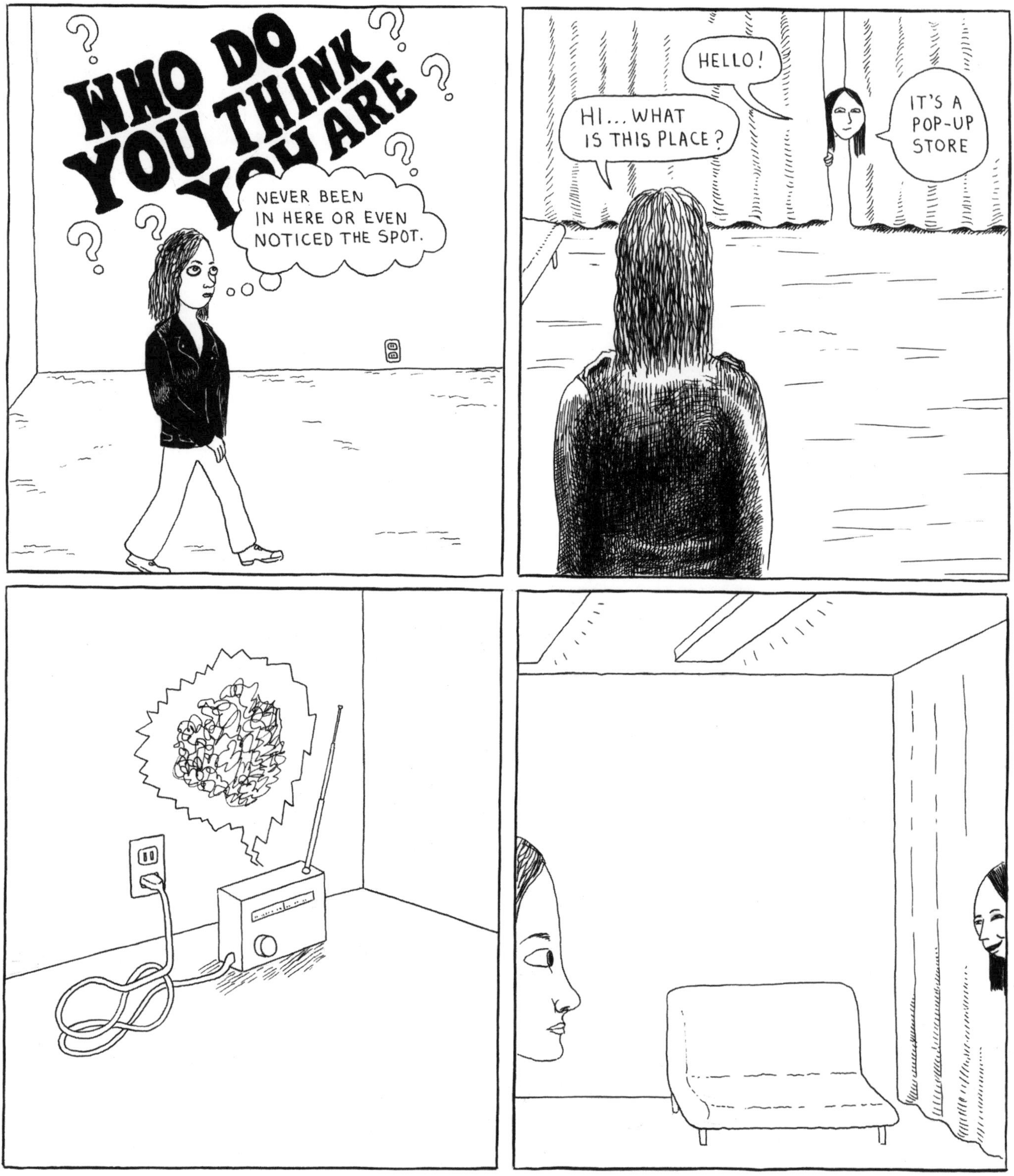
WHO DO YOU THINK YOU ARE
NEVER BEEN IN HERE OR EVEN NOTICED THE SPOT.
HELLO!
HI... WHAT IS THIS PLACE?
IT'S A POP-UP STORE

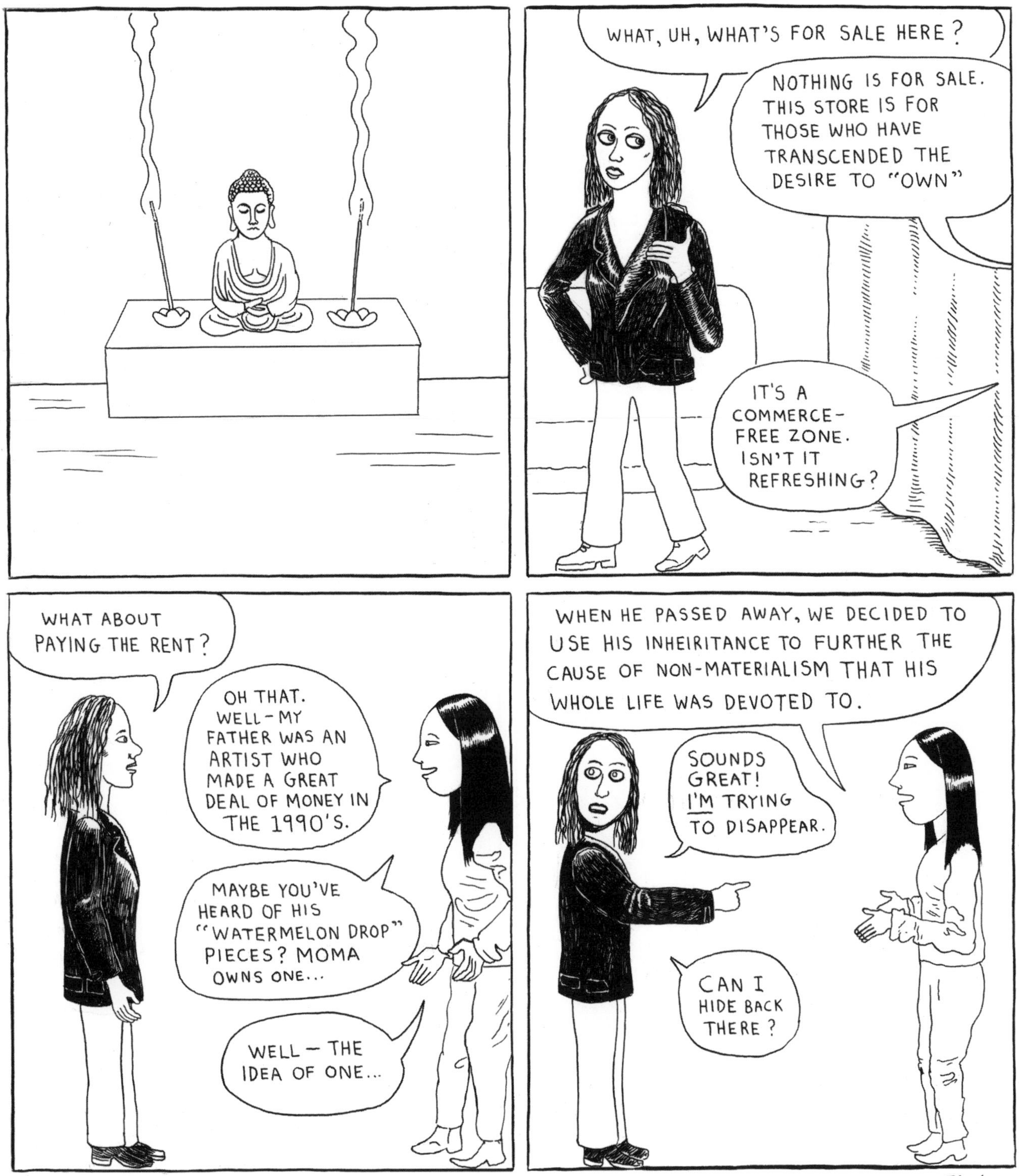
WHAT, UH, WHAT'S FOR SALE HERE?
NOTHING IS FOR SALE. THIS STORE IS FOR THOSE WHO HAVE TRANSCENDED THE DESIRE TO "OWN"
IT'S A COMMERCE-FREE ZONE. ISN'T IT REFRESHING?
WHAT ABOUT PAYING THE RENT?
OH THAT. WELL- MY FATHER WAS AN ARTIST WHO MADE A GREAT DEAL OF MONEY IN THE 1990'S.
MAYBE YOU'VE HEARD OF HIS "WATERMELON DROP" PIECES? MOMA OWNS ONE...
WELL - THE IDEA OF ONE...
WHEN HE PASSED AWAY, WE DECIDED TO USE HIS INHEIRITANCE TO FURTHER THE CAUSE OF NON-MATERIALISM THAT HIS WHOLE LIFE WAS DEVOTED TO.
SOUNDS GREAT! I'M TRYING TO DISAPPEAR.
CAN I HIDE BACK THERE?

MT 5/19/2012

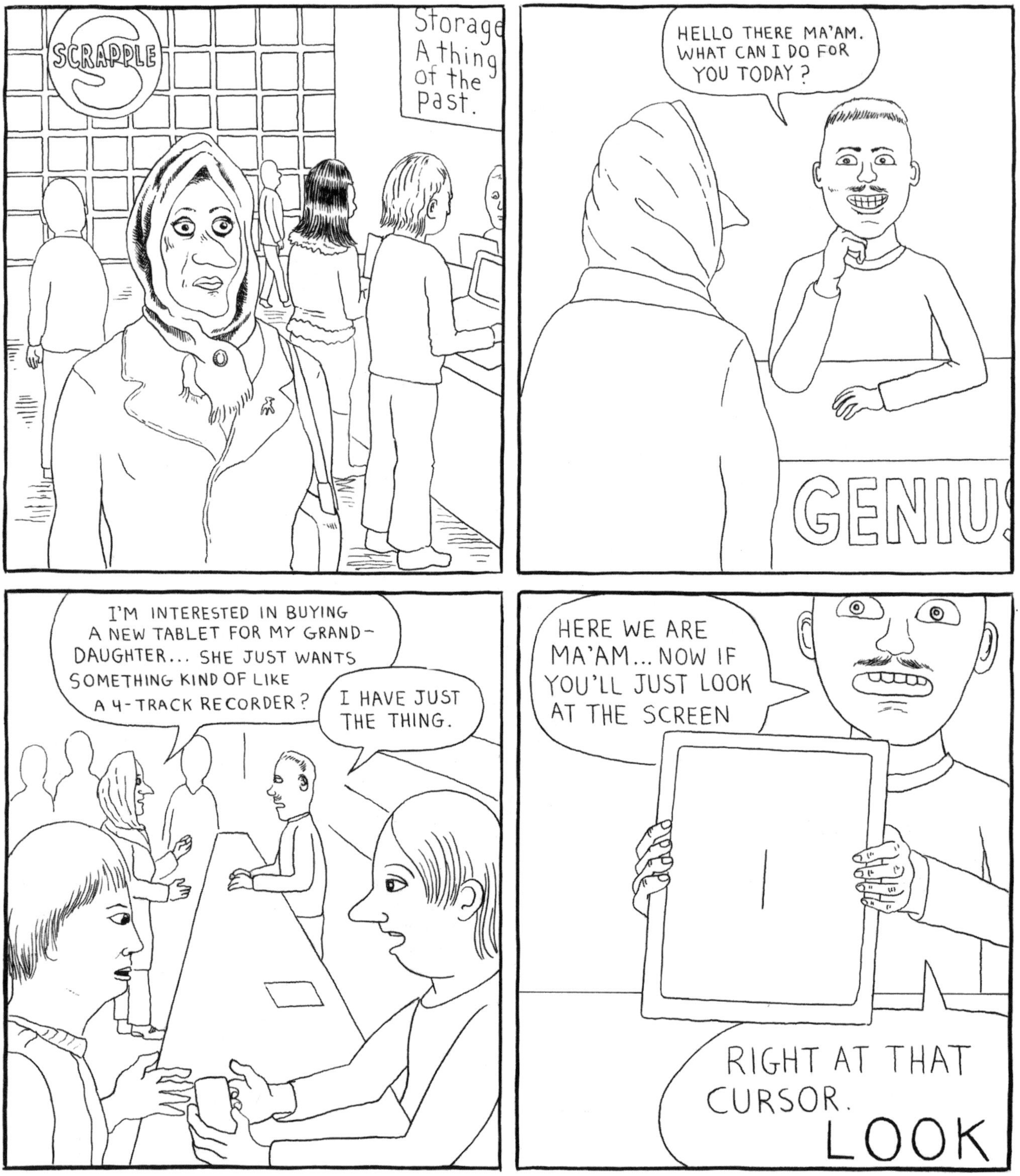
SCRAPPLE
Storage A thing of the past.
HELLO THERE MA'AM. WHAT CAN I DO FOR YOU TODAY?
GENIUS
I'M INTERESTED IN BUYING A NEW TABLET FOR MY GRAND-DAUGHTER... SHE JUST WANTS SOMETHING KIND OF LIKE A 4-TRACK RECORDER?
I HAVE JUST THE THING.
HERE WE ARE MA'AM... NOW IF YOU'LL JUST LOOK AT THE SCREEN
RIGHT AT THAT CURSOR. LOOK

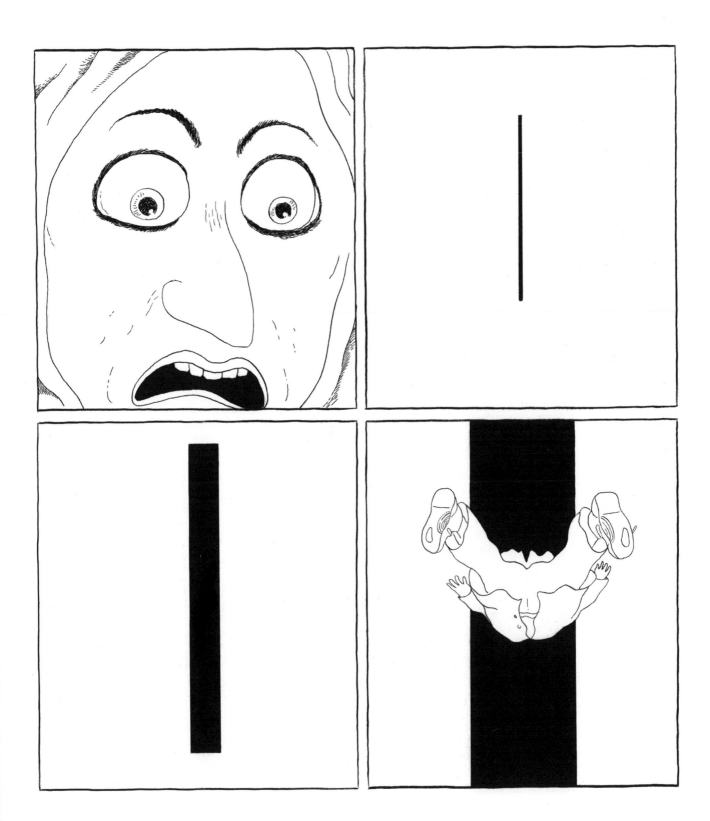

PERVERSE TEEN 93 WANTS TO CHAT!
PROMOTE
BOB DYLAN
TERMS OF SERVICE
YES I AGREE
ENTIRENET

MT 12/21/12

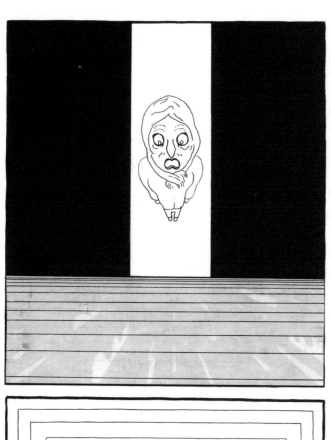

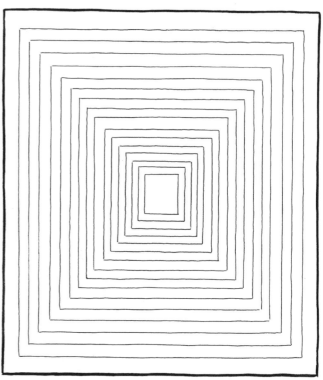

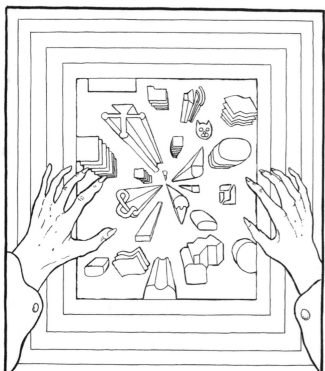

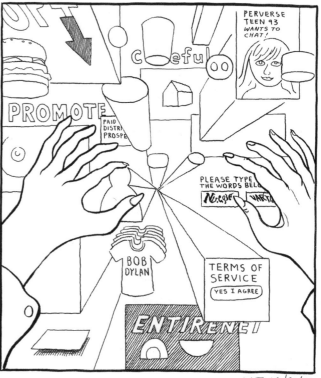

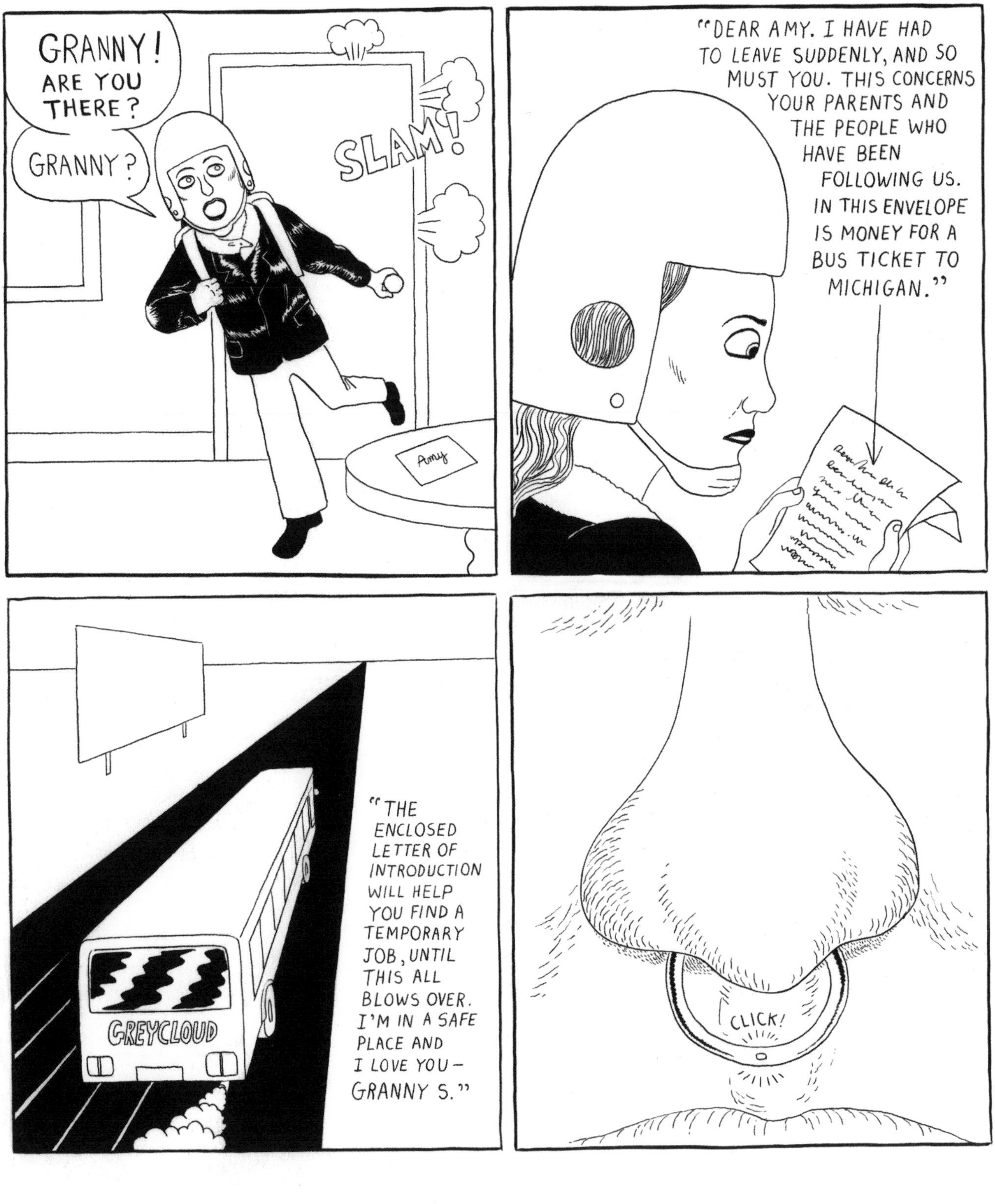
GRANNY! ARE YOU THERE?
GRANNY?
SLAM!
Amy
"DEAR AMY. I HAVE HAD TO LEAVE SUDDENLY, AND SO MUST YOU. THIS CONCERNS YOUR PARENTS AND THE PEOPLE WHO HAVE BEEN FOLLOWING US. IN THIS ENVELOPE IS MONEY FOR A BUS TICKET TO MICHIGAN."
GREYCLOUD
"THE ENCLOSED LETTER OF INTRODUCTION WILL HELP YOU FIND A TEMPORARY JOB, UNTIL THIS ALL BLOWS OVER. I'M IN A SAFE PLACE AND I LOVE YOU - GRANNY S."
CLICK!

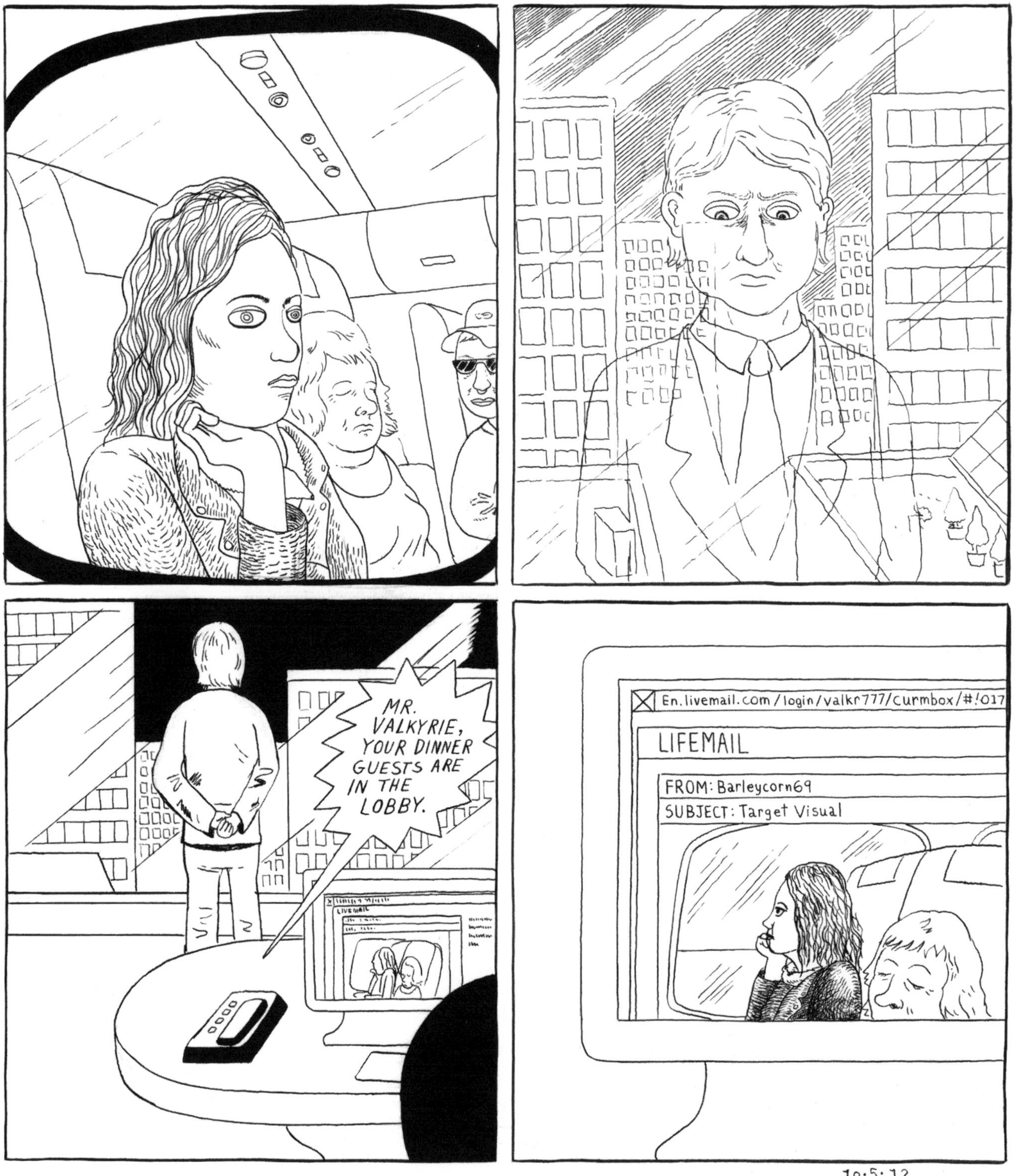
MR. VALKYRIE, YOUR DINNER GUESTS ARE IN THE LOBBY.
En.livemail.com/login/valkr777/curmbox/#!017
LIFEMAIL
FROM: Barleycorn69
SUBJECT: Target Visual

10·5·12

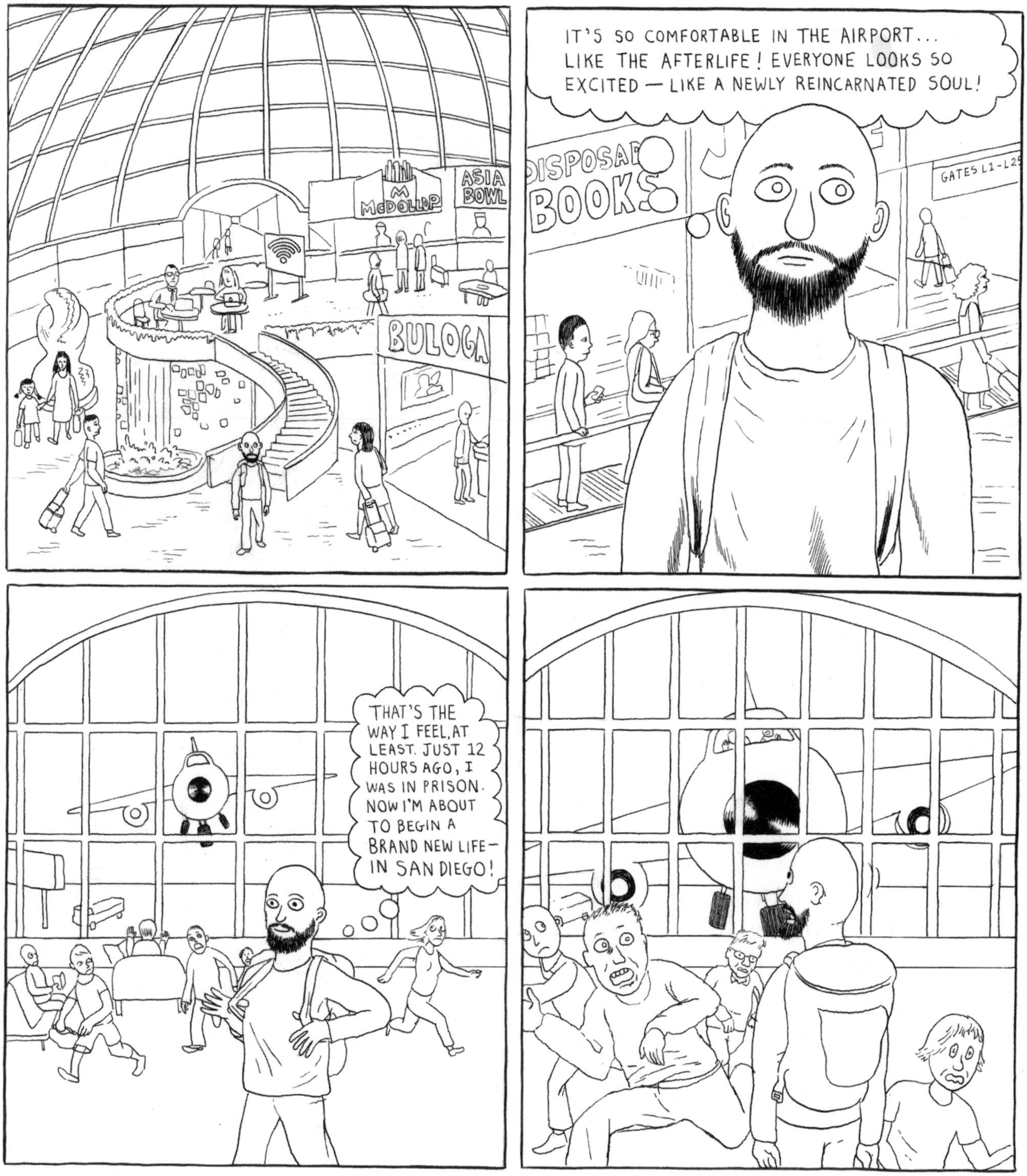
McDOLLOP
ASIA BOWL
BULOGA
IT'S SO COMFORTABLE IN THE AIRPORT... LIKE THE AFTERLIFE! EVERYONE LOOKS SO EXCITED — LIKE A NEWLY REINCARNATED SOUL!
DISPOSAB
BOOKS
GATES L1-L25
THAT'S THE WAY I FEEL, AT LEAST. JUST 12 HOURS AGO, I WAS IN PRISON. NOW I'M ABOUT TO BEGIN A BRAND NEW LIFE— IN SAN DIEGO!

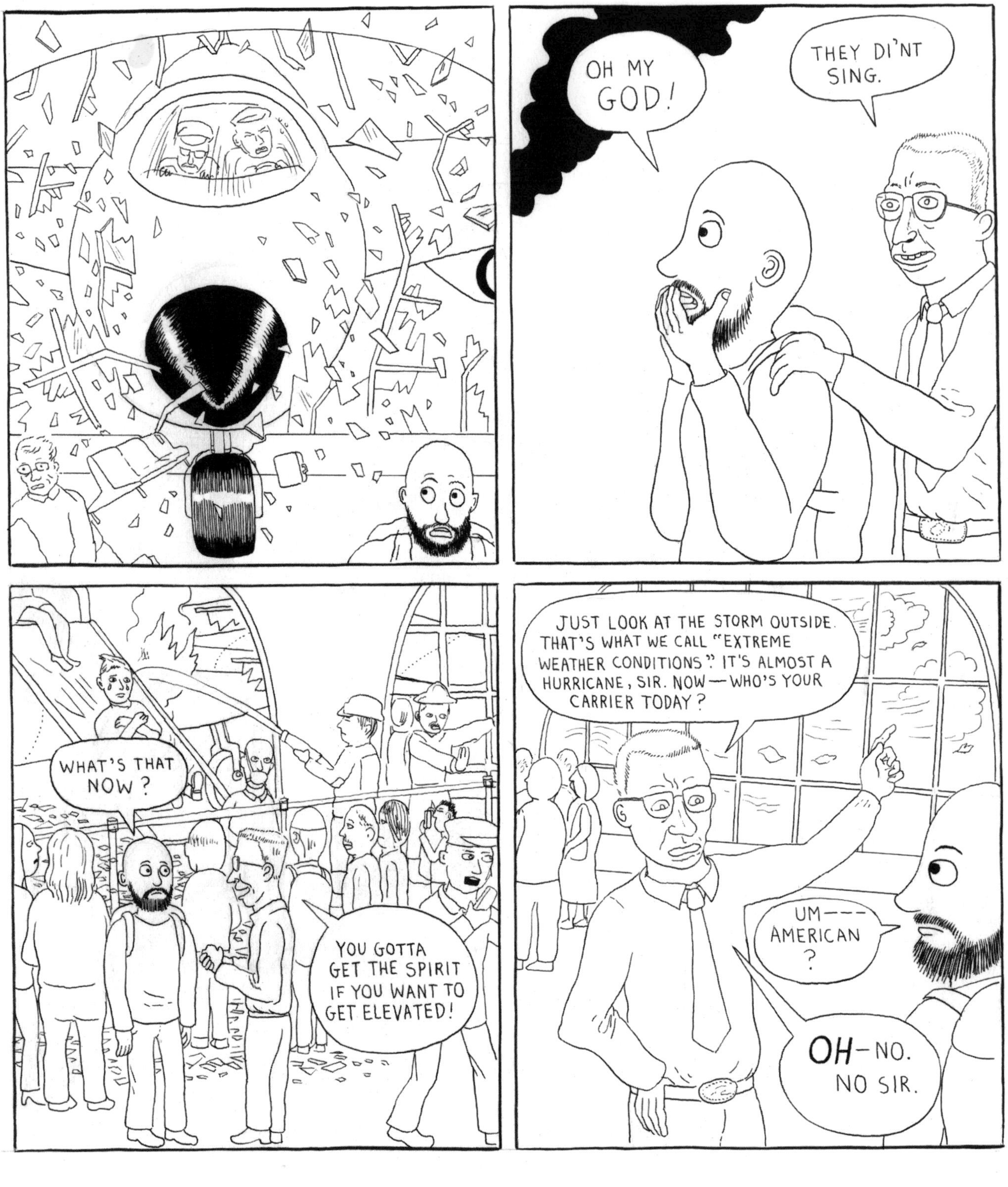
OH MY GOD!
THEY DI'NT SING.
WHAT'S THAT NOW?
YOU GOTTA GET THE SPIRIT IF YOU WANT TO GET ELEVATED!
JUST LOOK AT THE STORM OUTSIDE. THAT'S WHAT WE CALL "EXTREME WEATHER CONDITIONS." IT'S ALMOST A HURRICANE, SIR. NOW—WHO'S YOUR CARRIER TODAY?
UM——— AMERICAN ?
OH-NO. NO SIR.

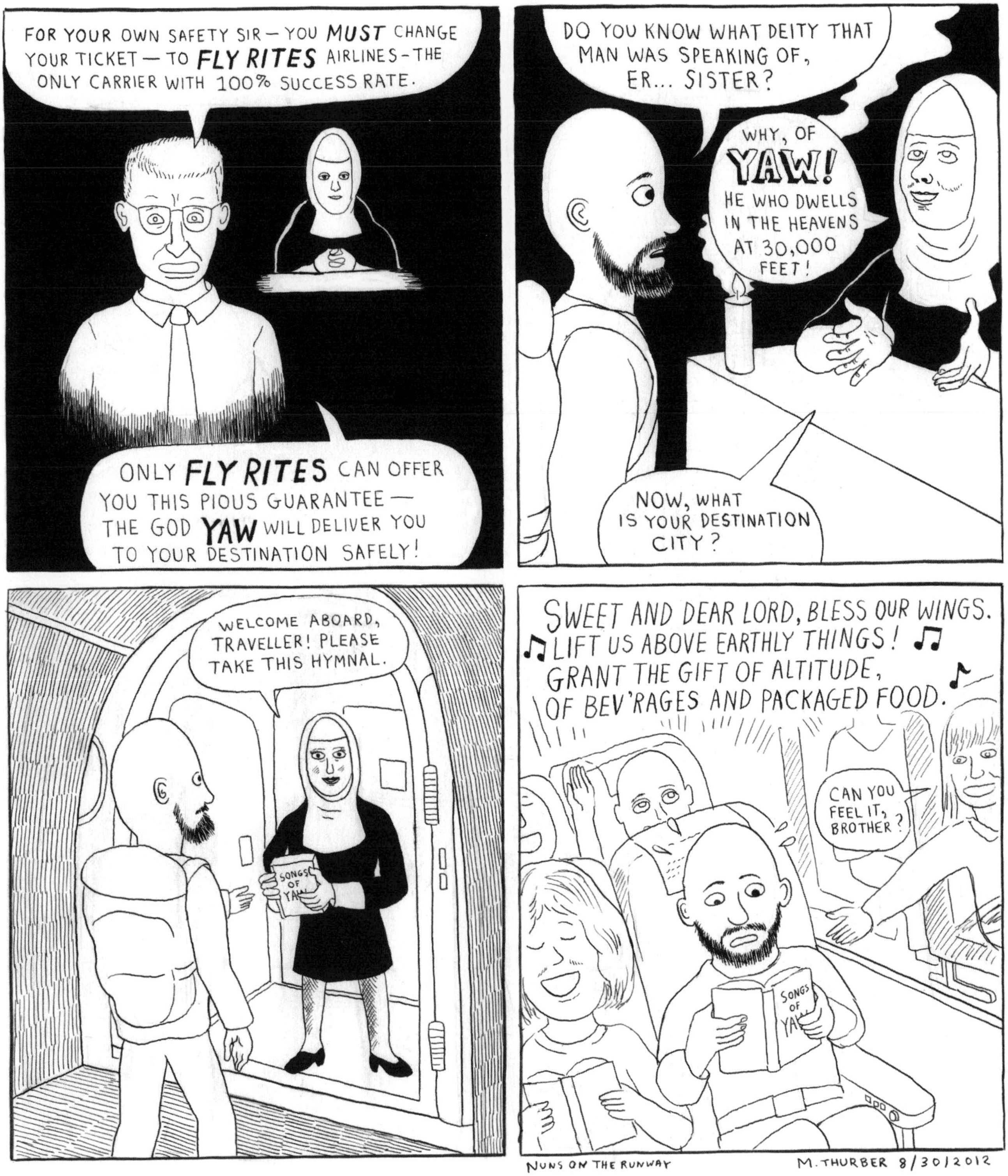
FOR YOUR OWN SAFETY SIR — YOU MUST CHANGE YOUR TICKET — TO FLY RITES AIRLINES - THE ONLY CARRIER WITH 100% SUCCESS RATE.
ONLY FLY RITES CAN OFFER YOU THIS PIOUS GUARANTEE — THE GOD YAW WILL DELIVER YOU TO YOUR DESTINATION SAFELY!
DO YOU KNOW WHAT DEITY THAT MAN WAS SPEAKING OF, ER... SISTER?
WHY, OF YAW! HE WHO DWELLS IN THE HEAVENS AT 30,000 FEET!
NOW, WHAT IS YOUR DESTINATION CITY?
WELCOME ABOARD, TRAVELLER! PLEASE TAKE THIS HYMNAL.
SONGS OF YAW
SWEET AND DEAR LORD, BLESS OUR WINGS. LIFT US ABOVE EARTHLY THINGS! GRANT THE GIFT OF ALTITUDE, OF BEV'RAGES AND PACKAGED FOOD.
CAN YOU FEEL IT, BROTHER?
SONGS OF YA

NUNS ON THE RUNWAY M. THURBER 8/30/2012

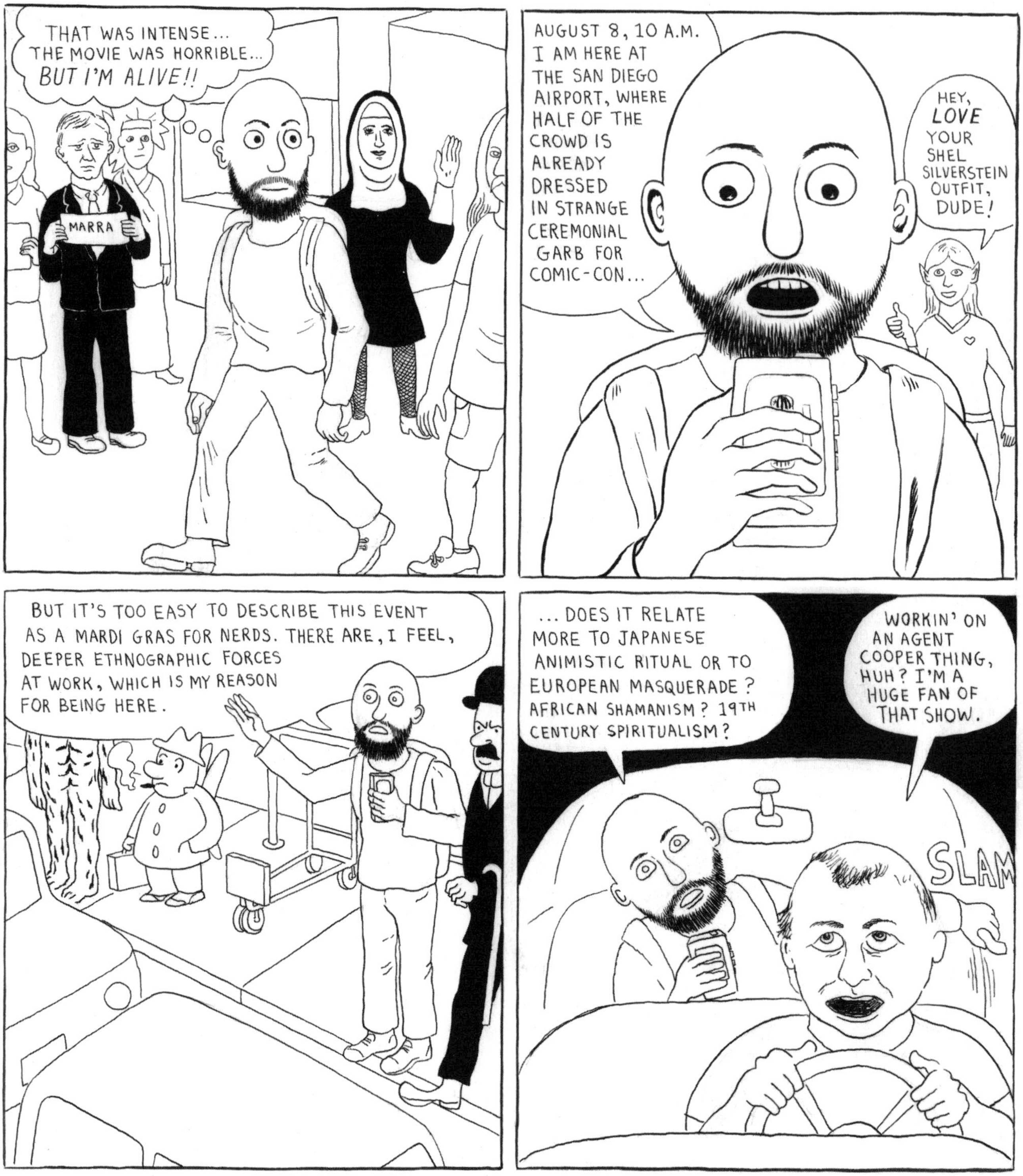
THAT WAS INTENSE... THE MOVIE WAS HORRIBLE... BUT I'M ALIVE!!
MARRA
AUGUST 8, 10 A.M. I AM HERE AT THE SAN DIEGO AIRPORT, WHERE HALF OF THE CROWD IS ALREADY DRESSED IN STRANGE CEREMONIAL GARB FOR COMIC-CON...
HEY, LOVE YOUR SHEL SILVERSTEIN OUTFIT, DUDE!
BUT IT'S TOO EASY TO DESCRIBE THIS EVENT AS A MARDI GRAS FOR NERDS. THERE ARE, I FEEL, DEEPER ETHNOGRAPHIC FORCES AT WORK, WHICH IS MY REASON FOR BEING HERE.
... DOES IT RELATE MORE TO JAPANESE ANIMISTIC RITUAL OR TO EUROPEAN MASQUERADE? AFRICAN SHAMANISM? 19TH CENTURY SPIRITUALISM?
WORKIN' ON AN AGENT COOPER THING, HUH? I'M A HUGE FAN OF THAT SHOW.
SLAM

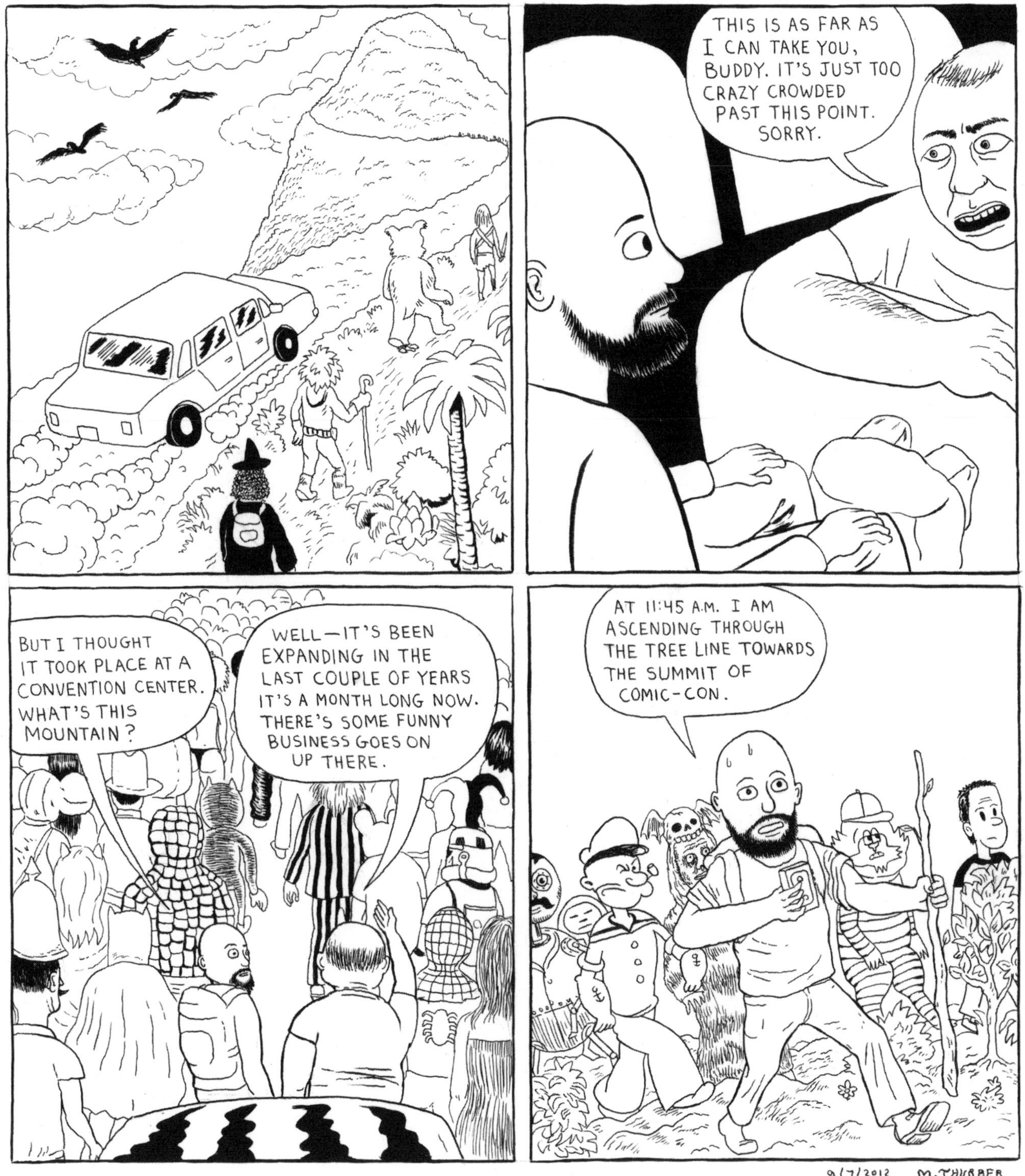

THIS IS AS FAR AS I CAN TAKE YOU, BUDDY. IT'S JUST TOO CRAZY CROWDED PAST THIS POINT. SORRY.
BUT I THOUGHT IT TOOK PLACE AT A CONVENTION CENTER. WHAT'S THIS MOUNTAIN?
WELL—IT'S BEEN EXPANDING IN THE LAST COUPLE OF YEARS IT'S A MONTH LONG NOW. THERE'S SOME FUNNY BUSINESS GOES ON UP THERE.
AT 11:45 A.M. I AM ASCENDING THROUGH THE TREE LINE TOWARDS THE SUMMIT OF COMIC-CON.
9/7/2012 M. THURBER

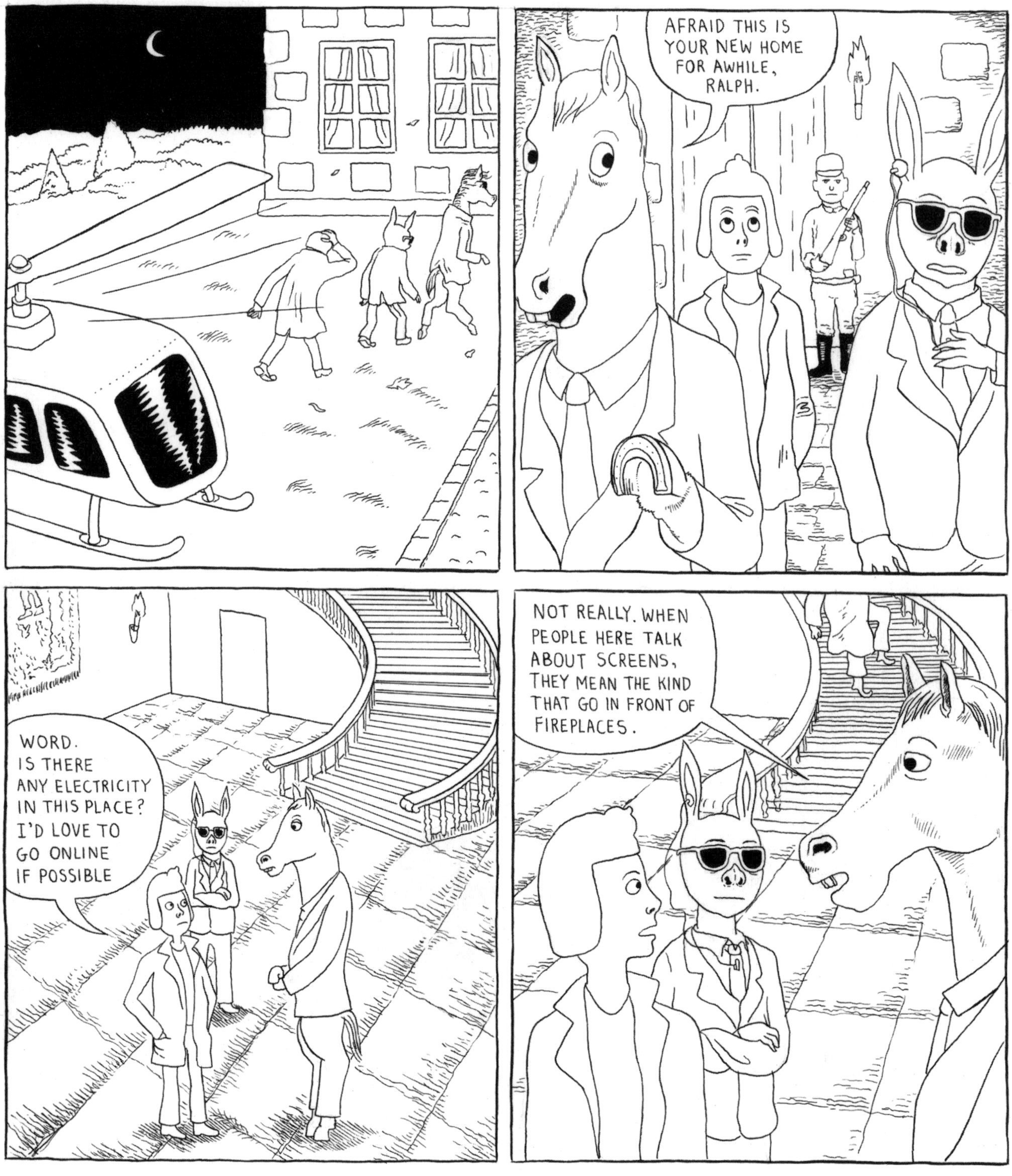
AFRAID THIS IS YOUR NEW HOME FOR AWHILE, RALPH.
WORD. IS THERE ANY ELECTRICITY IN THIS PLACE? I'D LOVE TO GO ONLINE IF POSSIBLE
NOT REALLY. WHEN PEOPLE HERE TALK ABOUT SCREENS, THEY MEAN THE KIND THAT GO IN FRONT OF FIREPLACES.

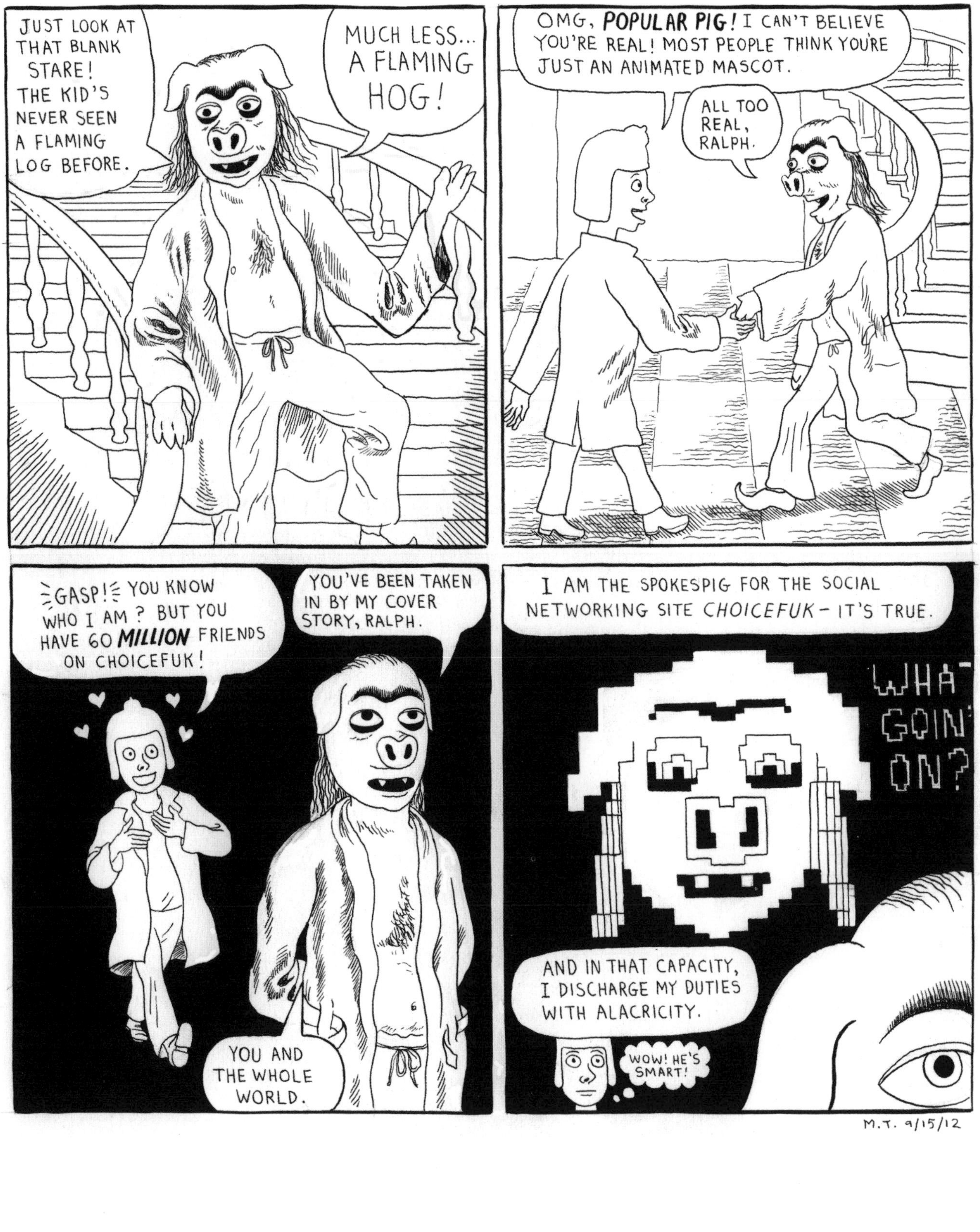
JUST LOOK AT THAT BLANK STARE! THE KID'S NEVER SEEN A FLAMING LOG BEFORE.
MUCH LESS... A FLAMING HOG!
OMG, POPULAR PIG! I CAN'T BELIEVE YOU'RE REAL! MOST PEOPLE THINK YOU'RE JUST AN ANIMATED MASCOT.
ALL TOO REAL, RALPH.
GASP! YOU KNOW WHO I AM? BUT YOU HAVE 60 MILLION FRIENDS ON CHOICEFUK!
YOU'VE BEEN TAKEN IN BY MY COVER STORY, RALPH.
YOU AND THE WHOLE WORLD.
I AM THE SPOKESPIG FOR THE SOCIAL NETWORKING SITE CHOICEFUK - IT'S TRUE.
WHA- GOIN' ON?
AND IN THAT CAPACITY, I DISCHARGE MY DUTIES WITH ALACRICITY.
WOW! HE'S SMART!
M.T. 9/15/12

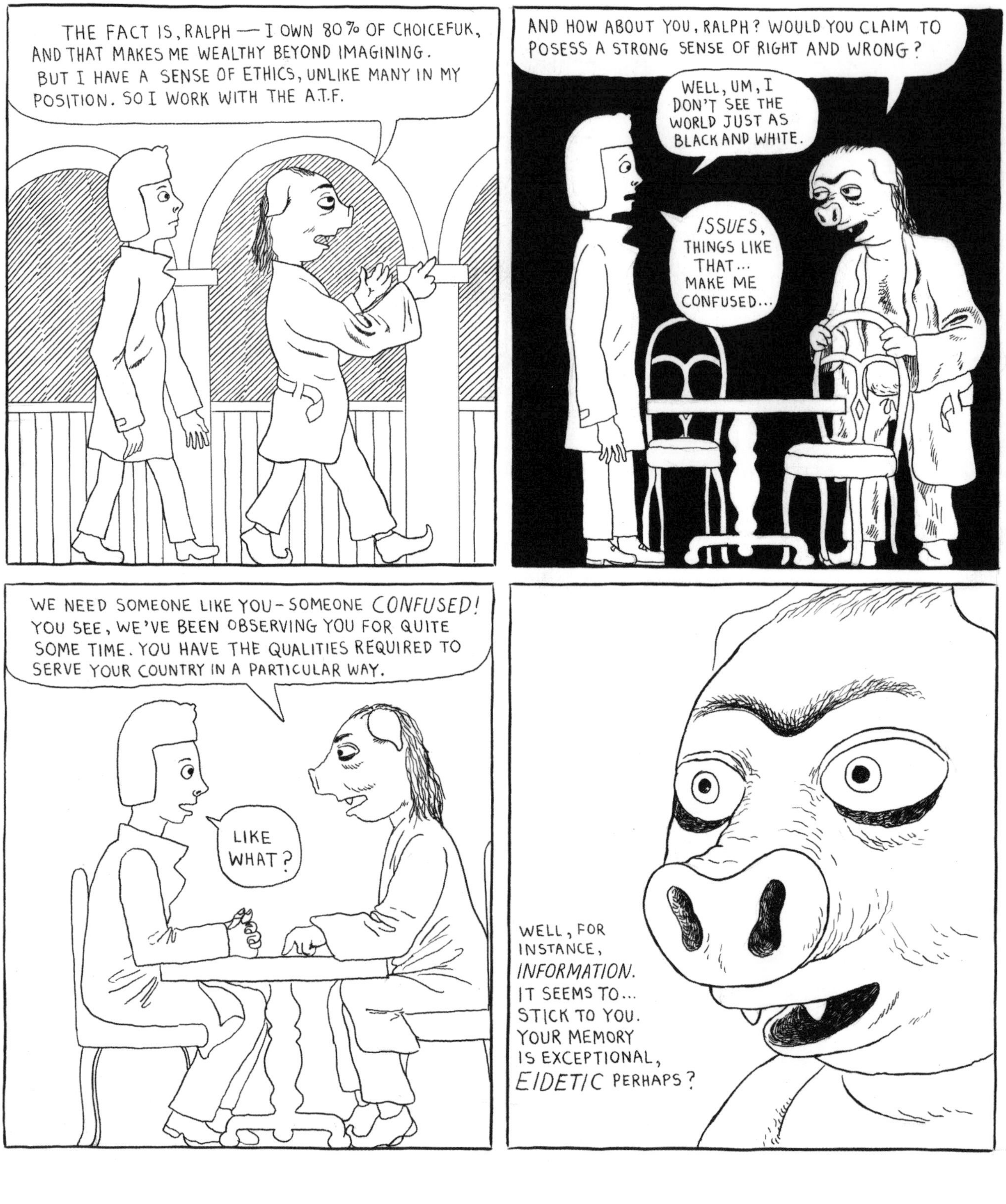
THE FACT IS, RALPH — I OWN 80% OF CHOICEFUK, AND THAT MAKES ME WEALTHY BEYOND IMAGINING. BUT I HAVE A SENSE OF ETHICS, UNLIKE MANY IN MY POSITION. SO I WORK WITH THE A.T.F.
AND HOW ABOUT YOU, RALPH? WOULD YOU CLAIM TO POSESS A STRONG SENSE OF RIGHT AND WRONG?
WELL, UM, I DON'T SEE THE WORLD JUST AS BLACK AND WHITE.
ISSUES, THINGS LIKE THAT... MAKE ME CONFUSED...
WE NEED SOMEONE LIKE YOU - SOMEONE CONFUSED! YOU SEE, WE'VE BEEN OBSERVING YOU FOR QUITE SOME TIME. YOU HAVE THE QUALITIES REQUIRED TO SERVE YOUR COUNTRY IN A PARTICULAR WAY.
LIKE WHAT?
WELL, FOR INSTANCE, INFORMATION. IT SEEMS TO... STICK TO YOU. YOUR MEMORY IS EXCEPTIONAL, EIDETIC PERHAPS?

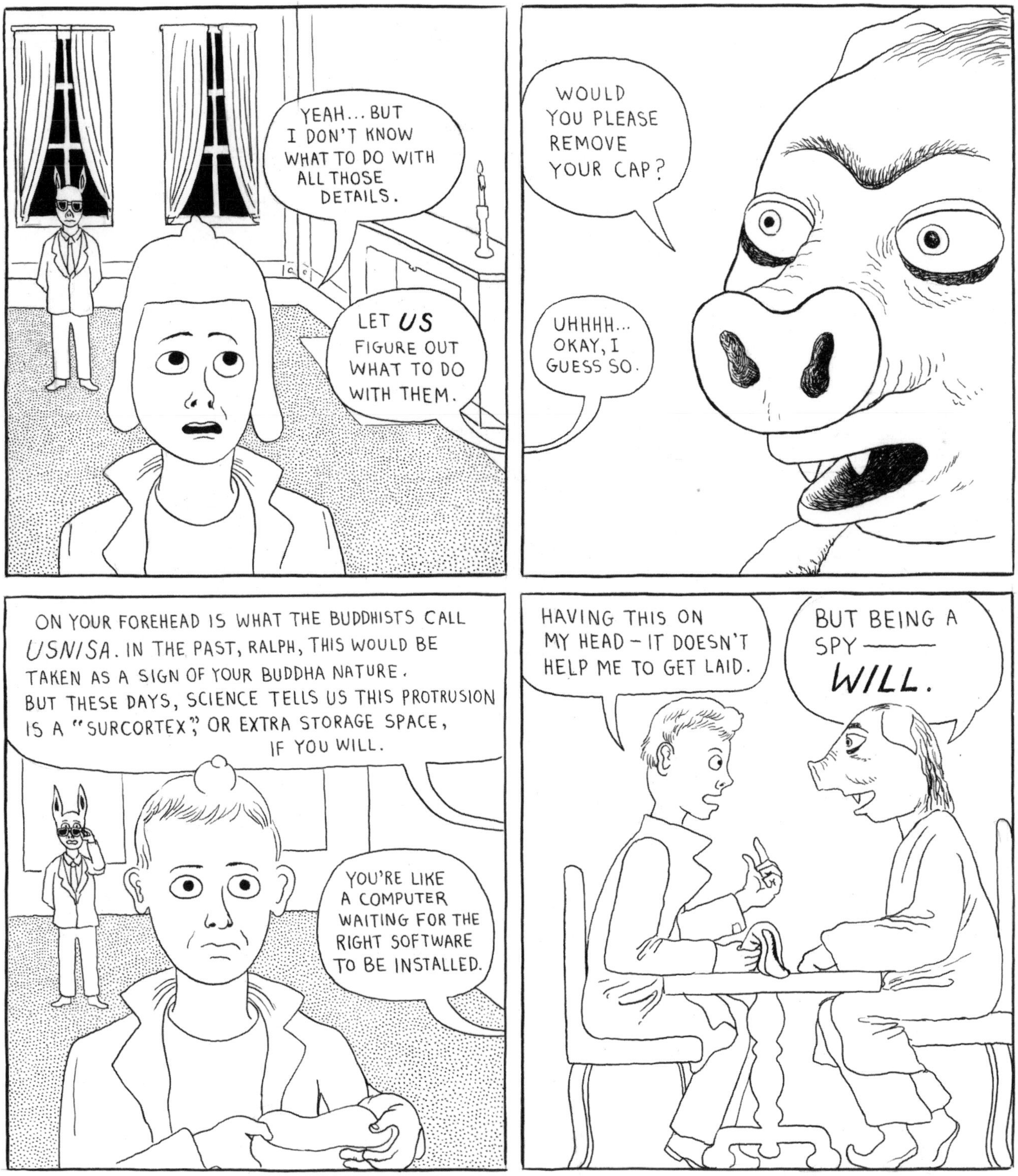
YEAH... BUT I DON'T KNOW WHAT TO DO WITH ALL THOSE DETAILS.
LET *US* FIGURE OUT WHAT TO DO WITH THEM.
WOULD YOU PLEASE REMOVE YOUR CAP?
UHHHH... OKAY, I GUESS SO.
ON YOUR FOREHEAD IS WHAT THE BUDDHISTS CALL *USNISA*. IN THE PAST, RALPH, THIS WOULD BE TAKEN AS A SIGN OF YOUR BUDDHA NATURE. BUT THESE DAYS, SCIENCE TELLS US THIS PROTRUSION IS A "SURCORTEX," OR EXTRA STORAGE SPACE, IF YOU WILL.
YOU'RE LIKE A COMPUTER WAITING FOR THE RIGHT SOFTWARE TO BE INSTALLED.
HAVING THIS ON MY HEAD – IT DOESN'T HELP ME TO GET LAID.
BUT BEING A SPY —— *WILL*.

9/19 M THURBER 2012

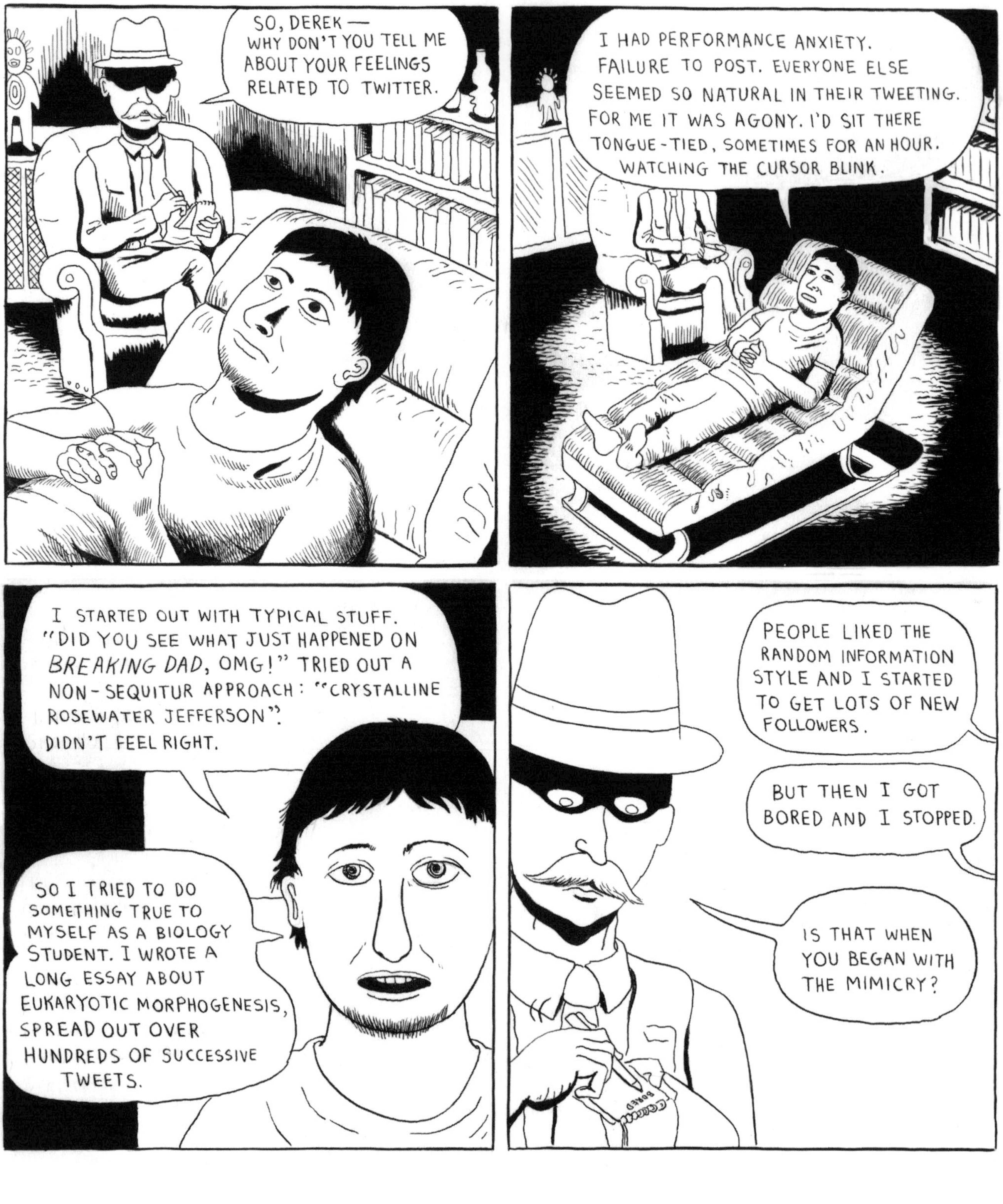
SO, DEREK — WHY DON'T YOU TELL ME ABOUT YOUR FEELINGS RELATED TO TWITTER.
I HAD PERFORMANCE ANXIETY. FAILURE TO POST. EVERYONE ELSE SEEMED SO NATURAL IN THEIR TWEETING. FOR ME IT WAS AGONY. I'D SIT THERE TONGUE-TIED, SOMETIMES FOR AN HOUR. WATCHING THE CURSOR BLINK.
I STARTED OUT WITH TYPICAL STUFF. "DID YOU SEE WHAT JUST HAPPENED ON *BREAKING DAD*, OMG!" TRIED OUT A NON-SEQUITUR APPROACH: "CRYSTALLINE ROSEWATER JEFFERSON". DIDN'T FEEL RIGHT.
SO I TRIED TO DO SOMETHING TRUE TO MYSELF AS A BIOLOGY STUDENT. I WROTE A LONG ESSAY ABOUT EUKARYOTIC MORPHOGENESIS, SPREAD OUT OVER HUNDREDS OF SUCCESSIVE TWEETS.
PEOPLE LIKED THE RANDOM INFORMATION STYLE AND I STARTED TO GET LOTS OF NEW FOLLOWERS.
BUT THEN I GOT BORED AND I STOPPED.
IS THAT WHEN YOU BEGAN WITH THE MIMICRY?
BORED

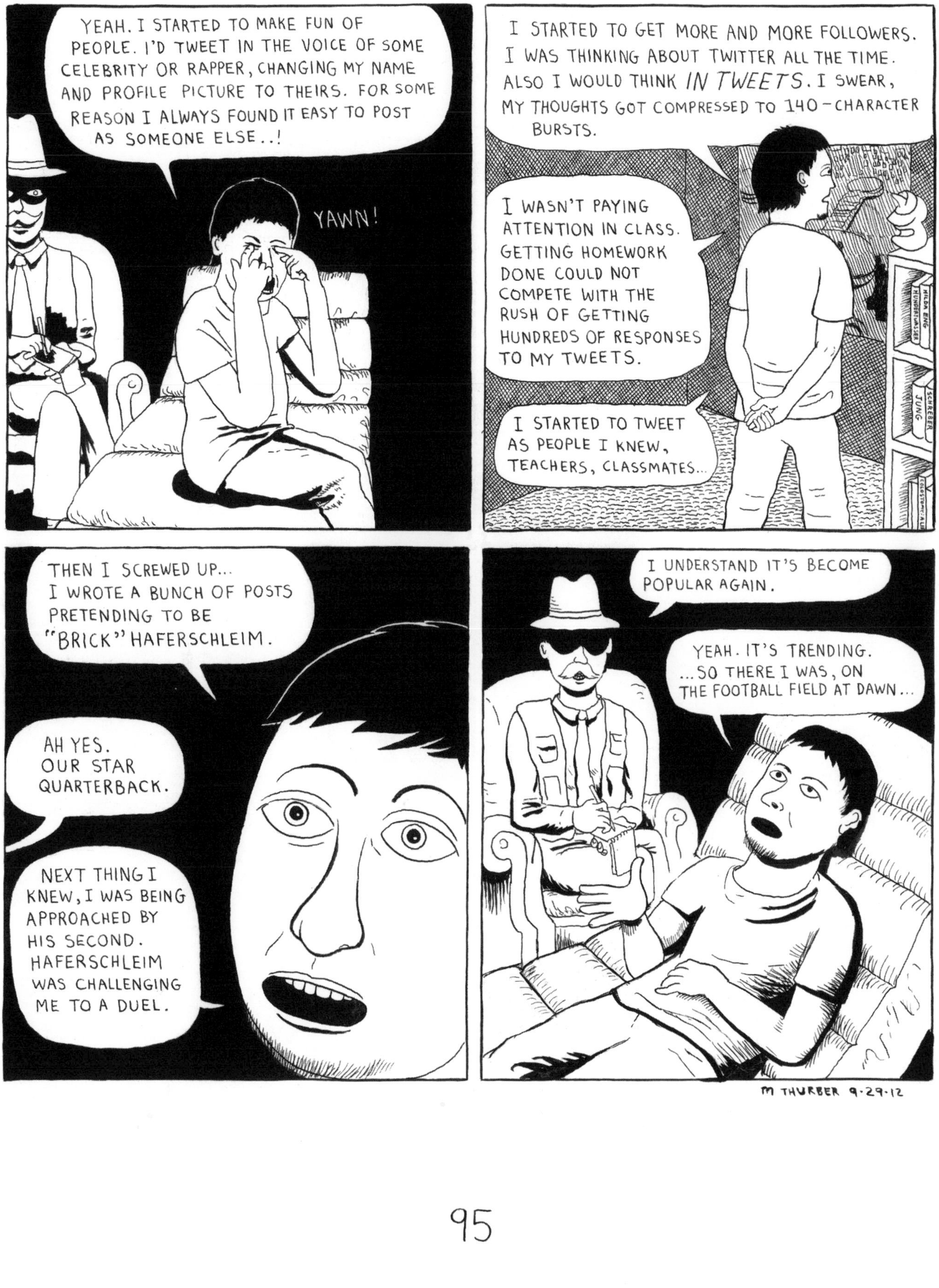
YEAH. I STARTED TO MAKE FUN OF PEOPLE. I'D TWEET IN THE VOICE OF SOME CELEBRITY OR RAPPER, CHANGING MY NAME AND PROFILE PICTURE TO THEIRS. FOR SOME REASON I ALWAYS FOUND IT EASY TO POST AS SOMEONE ELSE..!
YAWN!
I STARTED TO GET MORE AND MORE FOLLOWERS. I WAS THINKING ABOUT TWITTER ALL THE TIME. ALSO I WOULD THINK *IN TWEETS*. I SWEAR, MY THOUGHTS GOT COMPRESSED TO 140-CHARACTER BURSTS.
I WASN'T PAYING ATTENTION IN CLASS. GETTING HOMEWORK DONE COULD NOT COMPETE WITH THE RUSH OF GETTING HUNDREDS OF RESPONSES TO MY TWEETS.
I STARTED TO TWEET AS PEOPLE I KNEW, TEACHERS, CLASSMATES...
SCHREBER
JUNG
THEN I SCREWED UP... I WROTE A BUNCH OF POSTS PRETENDING TO BE "BRICK" HAFERSCHLEIM.
AH YES. OUR STAR QUARTERBACK.
NEXT THING I KNEW, I WAS BEING APPROACHED BY HIS SECOND. HAFERSCHLEIM WAS CHALLENGING ME TO A DUEL.
I UNDERSTAND IT'S BECOME POPULAR AGAIN.
YEAH. IT'S TRENDING. ...SO THERE I WAS, ON THE FOOTBALL FIELD AT DAWN...
M THURBER 9·29·12

ZUMBA STUDIO
OPEN
SO YOU SEE, RALPH, WE LIVE IN A WORLD OF SIGNS.
UH-HUH.
FIRST STREET
NO STAND
A LOT OF THEM ARE SECRET. I.E: LOOK AT THIS GRAFFITTI.
THAT IS AN ENCODED AGENCY MESSAGE. IT READS AS FOLLOWS: "MARCH 28, IVORY AND MCALPINE DISCUSSED TROOP MOVEMENTS ALONG THE ARIZONA BORDER IN BACK ROOM OF STARBUCKS ON 11 CASTLE BLVD."
I CAN'T UNDERSTAND A THING.
REALLY, IT SAYS ALL THAT? TO ME IT KIND OF LOOKS LIKE "ZWOOP".
SNAP
WE WILL TEACH YOU HOW TO ENCODE YOUR DAILY REPORTS INTO GRAFFITTI. YOU CAN PUT UP YOUR TAG ON *ANY* WALL — WE'LL BE WATCHING.
HEY! WHY DON'T I JUST SEND YOU A **TEXT MESSAGE?** IT'LL BE SO MUCH MORE EFFICIENT!

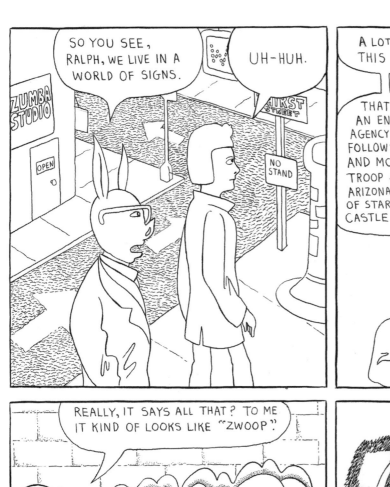

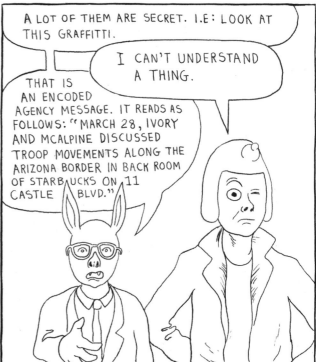

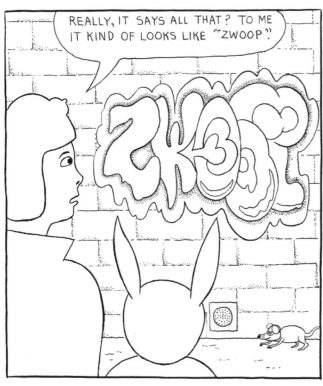

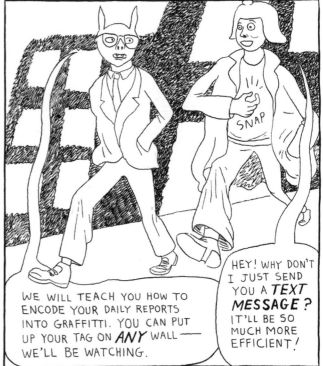

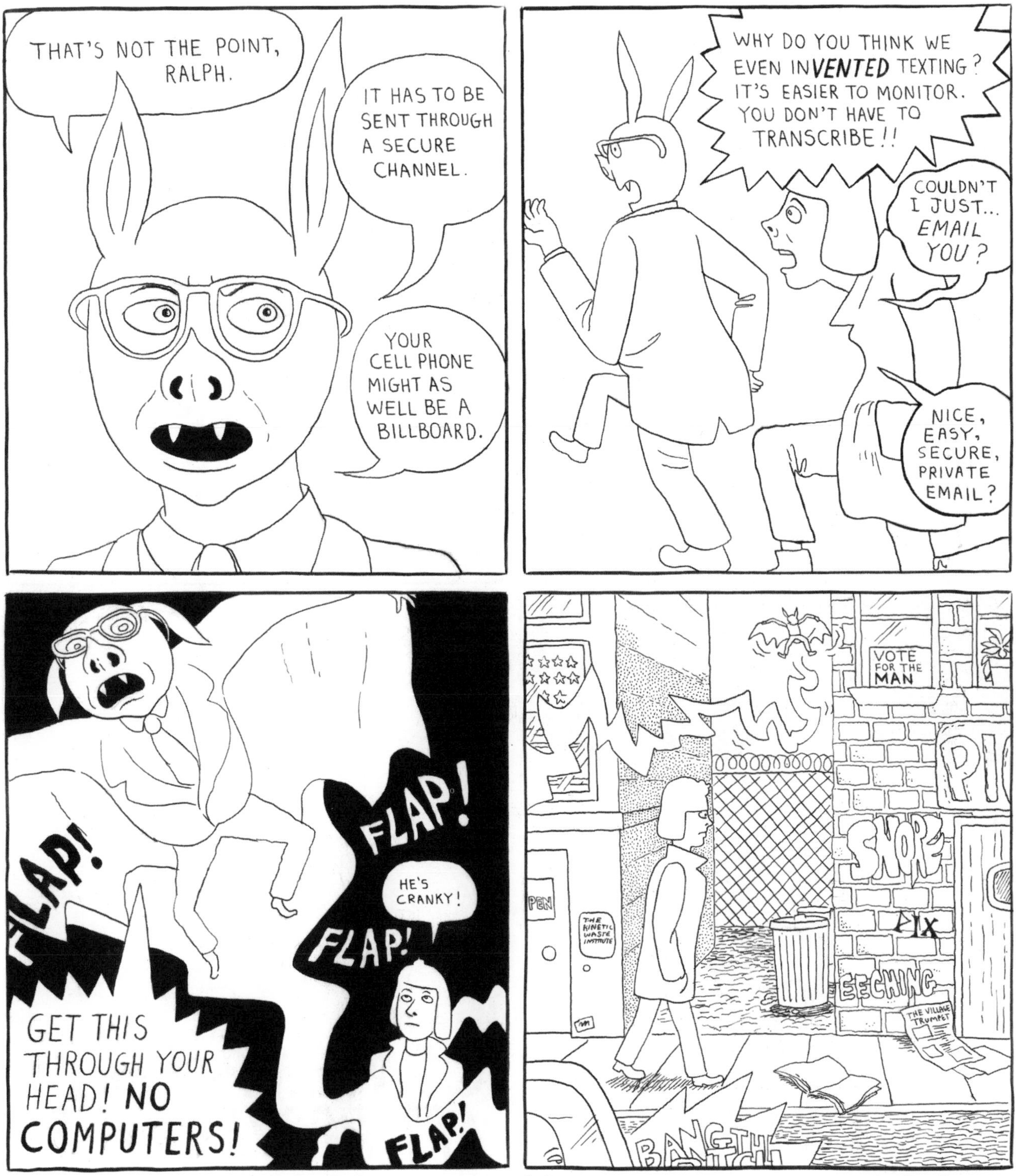
THAT'S NOT THE POINT, RALPH.
IT HAS TO BE SENT THROUGH A SECURE CHANNEL.
YOUR CELL PHONE MIGHT AS WELL BE A BILLBOARD.
WHY DO YOU THINK WE EVEN IN**VENTED** TEXTING? IT'S EASIER TO MONITOR. YOU DON'T HAVE TO TRANSCRIBE!!
COULDN'T I JUST... *EMAIL YOU?*
NICE, EASY, SECURE, PRIVATE EMAIL?
FLAP!
FLAP!
HE'S CRANKY!
FLAP!
GET THIS THROUGH YOUR HEAD! **NO COMPUTERS!**
FLAP!
VOTE FOR THE MAN
THE KINETIC WASTE INSTITUTE
THE VILLAGE TRUMPET

OCT. 25, 2012

Matthew Thurber

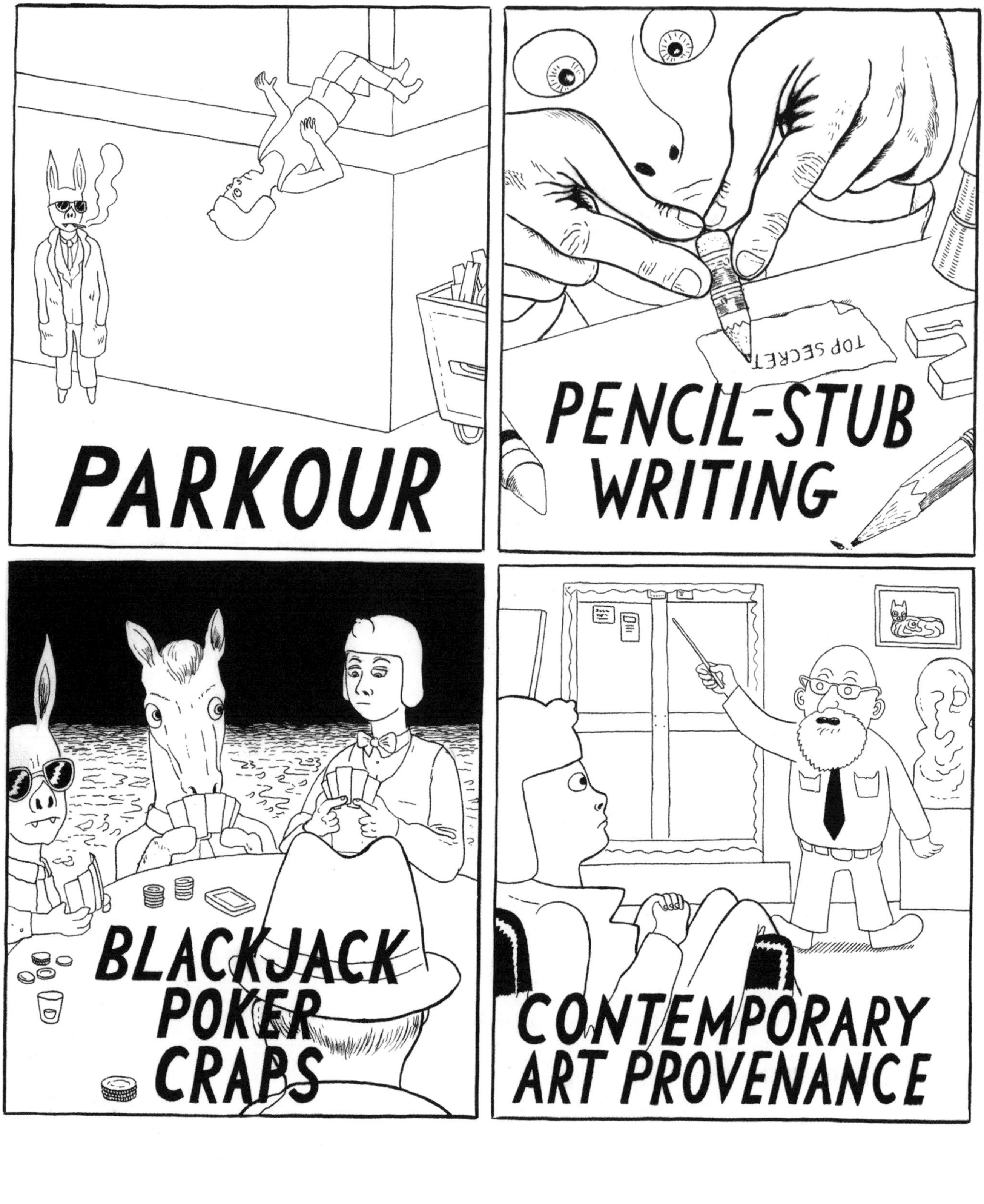
PARKOUR
TOP SECRET
PENCIL-STUB WRITING
BLACKJACK
POKER
CRAPS
CONTEMPORARY ART PROVENANCE

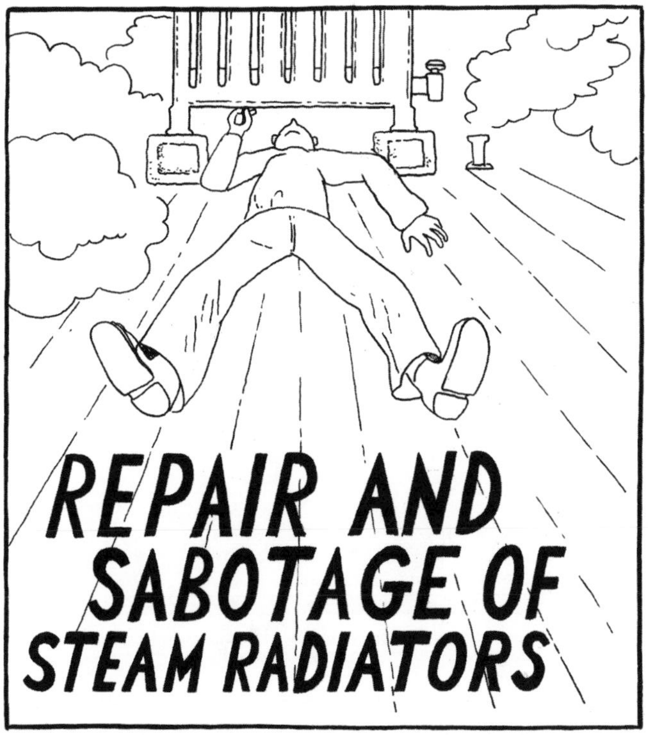
REPAIR AND SABOTAGE OF STEAM RADIATORS

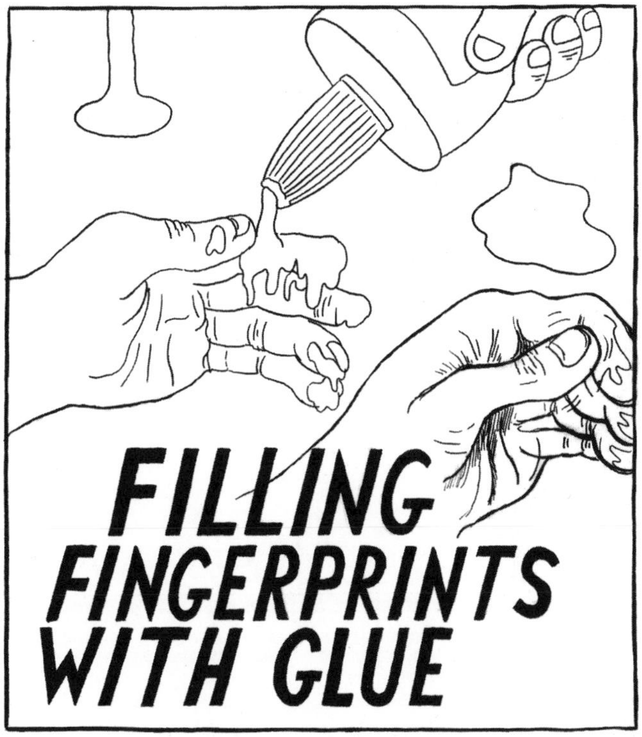
FILLING FINGERPRINTS WITH GLUE

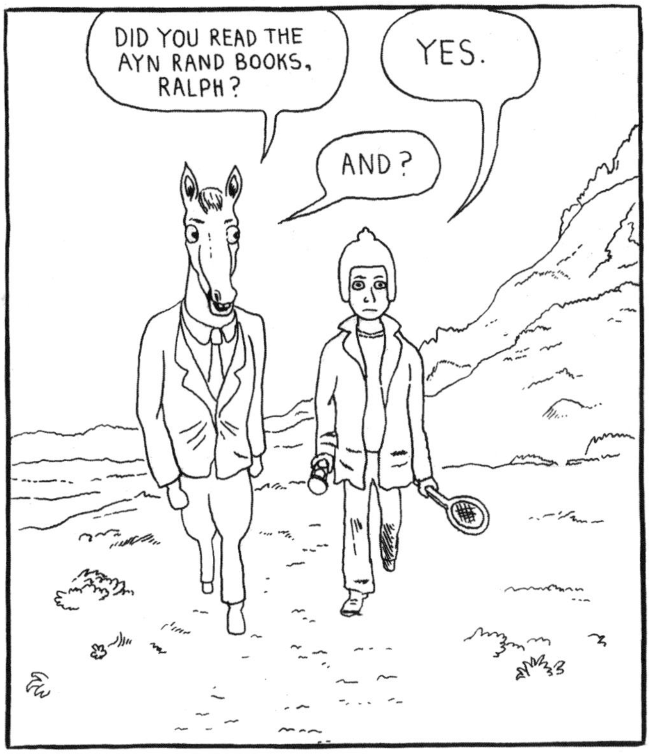
DID YOU READ THE AYN RAND BOOKS, RALPH?
YES.
AND?

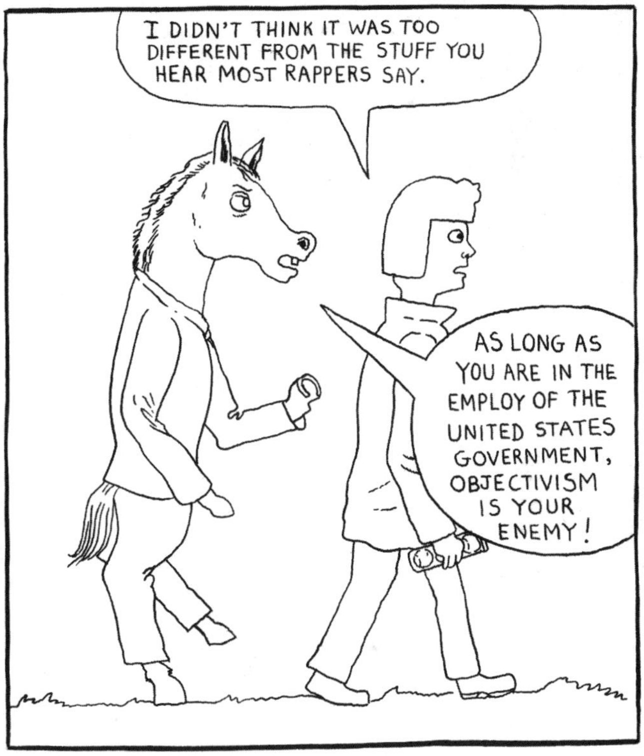
I DIDN'T THINK IT WAS TOO DIFFERENT FROM THE STUFF YOU HEAR MOST RAPPERS SAY.
AS LONG AS YOU ARE IN THE EMPLOY OF THE UNITED STATES GOVERNMENT, OBJECTIVISM IS YOUR ENEMY!

BUT IF YOU FIND IT INTERESTING, RALPH, IT'S FINE. WE NEED YOU TO DEMONSTRATE TO VALKYRIE THAT YOU HAVE A GENUINE INTEREST IN HIS BELIEF SYSTEM. OTHERWISE HE WON'T CONFIDE IN YOU. WE NEED YOU TO BE HIS SURROGATE SON.
SO, WHO IS RONNY?
HOW DO YOU KNOW THAT NAME??
AAAAAA
"TWO DAYS AGO I WAS WANDERING THROUGH THE CASTLE AFTER EVERYONE ELSE WAS ASLEEP... WHEN I HEARD A SUDDEN, MOURNFUL CRY."
NURSE! NURSE! IT'S RONNY, NURSE! PLEASE CHANGE THE CHANNEL, THE SUZE ORMAN INFOMERCIAL IS COMING ON AGAIN!!
?
NOV. 3 2012

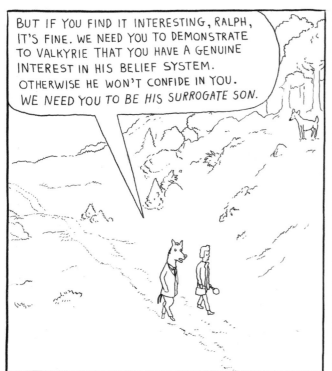

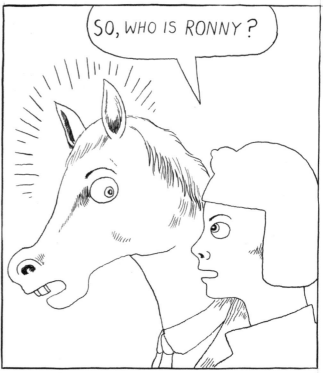

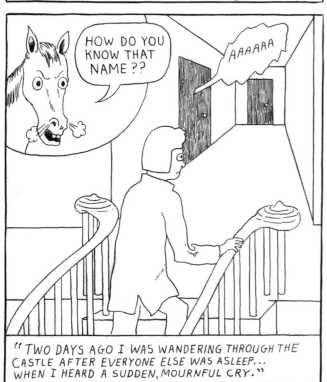

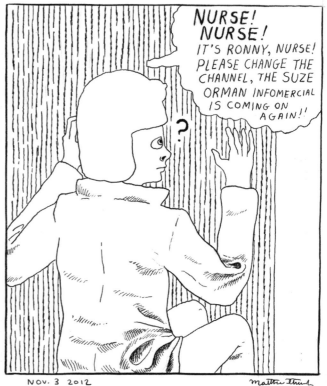

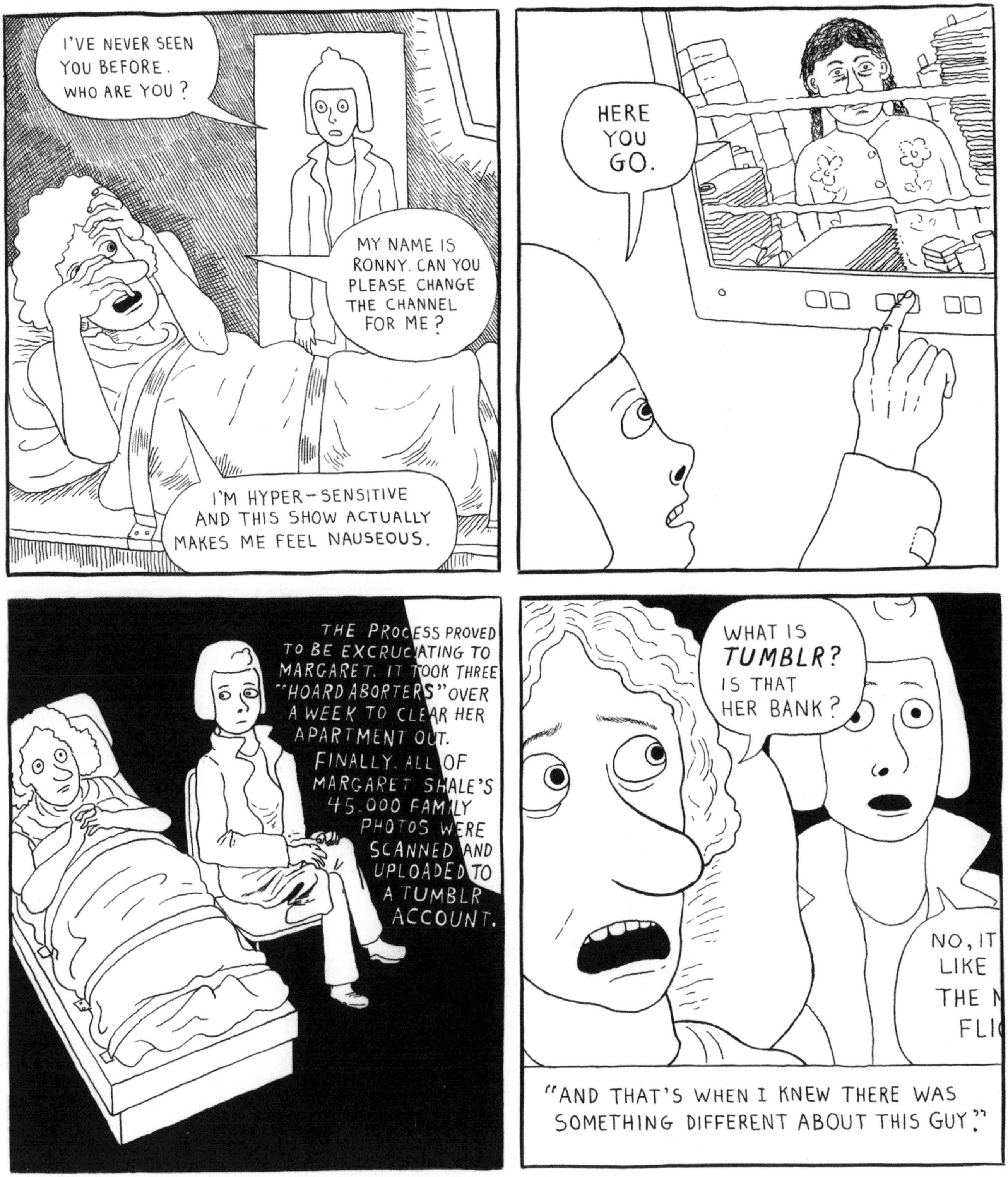
I'VE NEVER SEEN YOU BEFORE. WHO ARE YOU?
MY NAME IS RONNY. CAN YOU PLEASE CHANGE THE CHANNEL FOR ME?
I'M HYPER-SENSITIVE AND THIS SHOW ACTUALLY MAKES ME FEEL NAUSEOUS.
HERE YOU GO.
THE PROCESS PROVED TO BE EXCRUCIATING TO MARGARET. IT TOOK THREE "HOARD ABORTERS" OVER A WEEK TO CLEAR HER APARTMENT OUT. FINALLY, ALL OF MARGARET SHALE'S 45,000 FAMILY PHOTOS WERE SCANNED AND UPLOADED TO A TUMBLR ACCOUNT.
WHAT IS *TUMBLR?* IS THAT HER BANK?
NO, IT LIKE THE FLI
"AND THAT'S WHEN I KNEW THERE WAS SOMETHING DIFFERENT ABOUT THIS GUY."

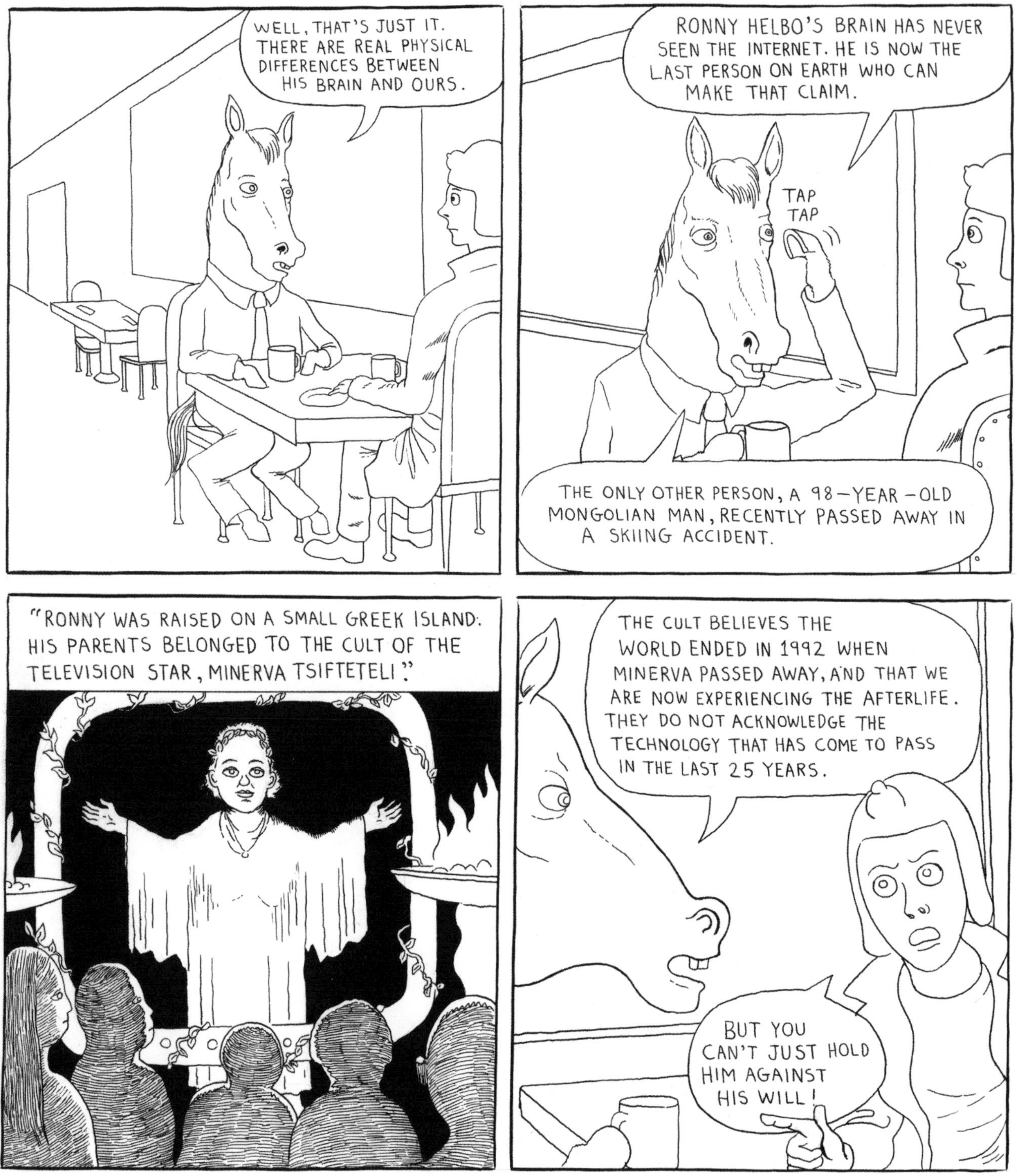
WELL, THAT'S JUST IT. THERE ARE REAL PHYSICAL DIFFERENCES BETWEEN HIS BRAIN AND OURS.
RONNY HELBO'S BRAIN HAS NEVER SEEN THE INTERNET. HE IS NOW THE LAST PERSON ON EARTH WHO CAN MAKE THAT CLAIM.
TAP TAP
THE ONLY OTHER PERSON, A 98-YEAR-OLD MONGOLIAN MAN, RECENTLY PASSED AWAY IN A SKIING ACCIDENT.
"RONNY WAS RAISED ON A SMALL GREEK ISLAND. HIS PARENTS BELONGED TO THE CULT OF THE TELEVISION STAR, MINERVA TSIFTETELI."
THE CULT BELIEVES THE WORLD ENDED IN 1992 WHEN MINERVA PASSED AWAY, AND THAT WE ARE NOW EXPERIENCING THE AFTERLIFE. THEY DO NOT ACKNOWLEDGE THE TECHNOLOGY THAT HAS COME TO PASS IN THE LAST 25 YEARS.
BUT YOU CAN'T JUST HOLD HIM AGAINST HIS WILL!

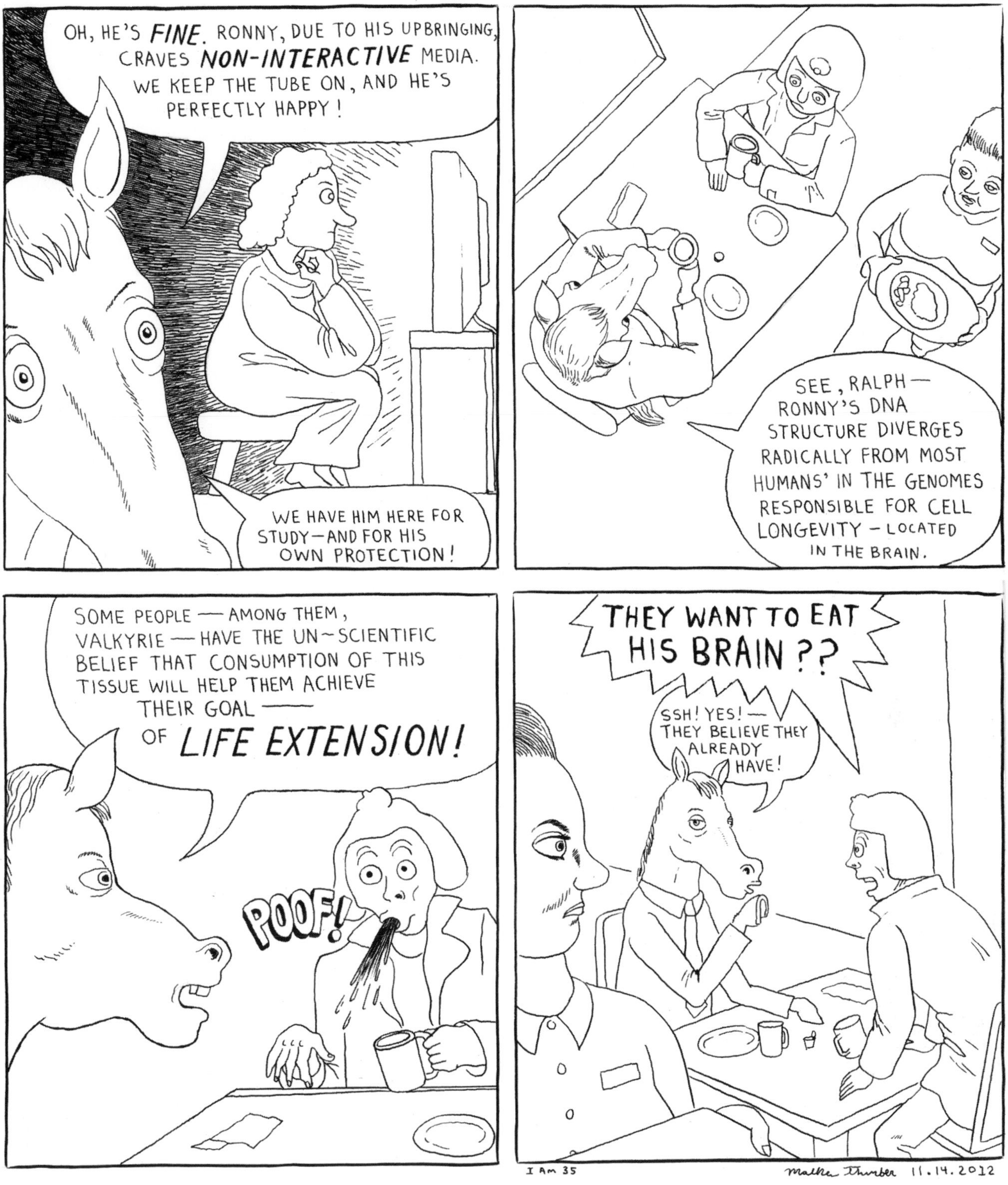
OH, HE'S FINE. RONNY, DUE TO HIS UPBRINGING, CRAVES NON-INTERACTIVE MEDIA. WE KEEP THE TUBE ON, AND HE'S PERFECTLY HAPPY!
WE HAVE HIM HERE FOR STUDY—AND FOR HIS OWN PROTECTION!
SEE, RALPH— RONNY'S DNA STRUCTURE DIVERGES RADICALLY FROM MOST HUMANS' IN THE GENOMES RESPONSIBLE FOR CELL LONGEVITY—LOCATED IN THE BRAIN.
SOME PEOPLE—AMONG THEM, VALKYRIE—HAVE THE UN-SCIENTIFIC BELIEF THAT CONSUMPTION OF THIS TISSUE WILL HELP THEM ACHIEVE THEIR GOAL—OF LIFE EXTENSION!
POOF!
THEY WANT TO EAT HIS BRAIN??
SSH! YES!— THEY BELIEVE THEY ALREADY HAVE!
I AM 35
Malka Thurber 11.14.2012

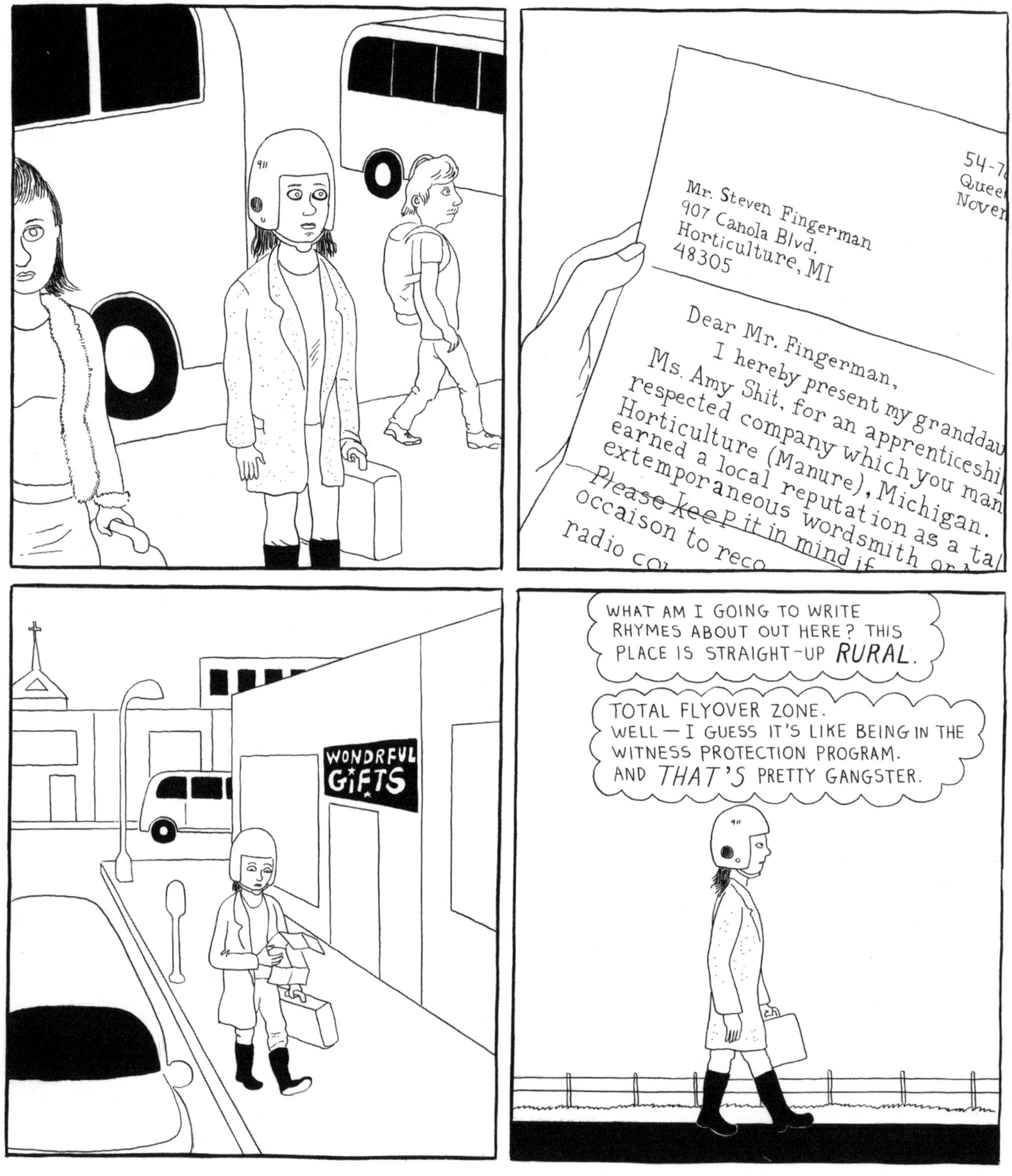

54-7
Quee
Noven
Mr. Steven Fingerman
907 Canola Blvd.
Horticulture, MI
48305
Dear Mr. Fingerman,
I hereby present my granddau
Ms. Amy Shit, for an apprenticeshi
respected company which you man
Horticulture (Manure), Michigan.
earned a local reputation as a ta
extemporaneous wordsmith or
~~Please keep it in mind if~~
occaison to reco
WONDRFUL GIFTS
WHAT AM I GOING TO WRITE RHYMES ABOUT OUT HERE? THIS PLACE IS STRAIGHT-UP *RURAL*.
TOTAL FLYOVER ZONE. WELL — I GUESS IT'S LIKE BEING IN THE WITNESS PROTECTION PROGRAM. AND *THAT'S* PRETTY GANGSTER.

ANGELS SHOULDN'T HAVE TO WALK. WANT A RIDE?
BOOMBA BABAPA BAWHEE
GO FUCK YOURSELF, "DELIVERANCE" MOTHERFUCKER.
VROOM!!
NO OFFENCE, SWEETHEART!
WAIT JUST A COTTON PICKIN' MINUTE—
ROAR!!
BOOM BADA BAPP BAPP BOOMBADABIP
INCH BY INCH I'M LYNCHING SNITCHES LIKE DAVID LYNCH I ERASE THEIR HEADS...
WAIT!! THAT'S G-SPOT'S FIRST ALBUM! HOW DO YOU EVEN KNOW ABOUT THAT RECORD!!!
DAMN!
ONE HOUR LATER
FF
FOSSIL FUEL DRIVE-THRU ESPRESSO
907 CANOLA AVE. YEP, THIS MUST BE THE PLACE.
11·23·12
matthew thurber

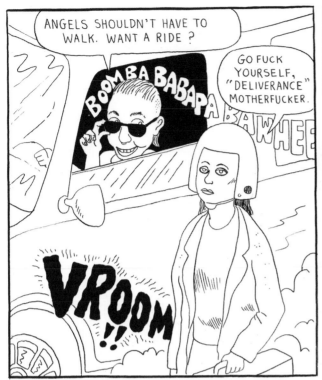

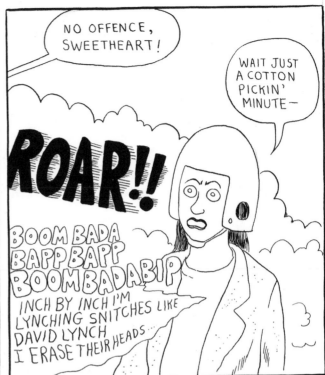

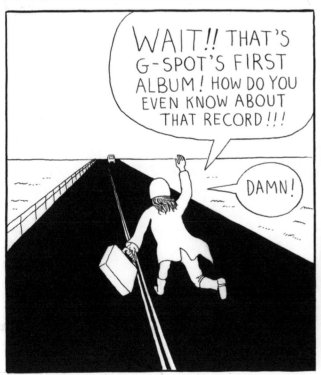

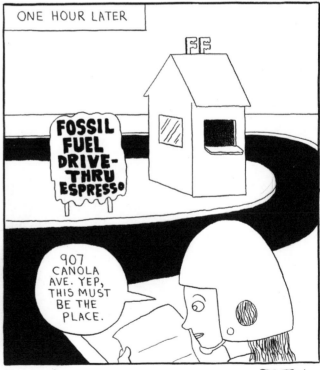

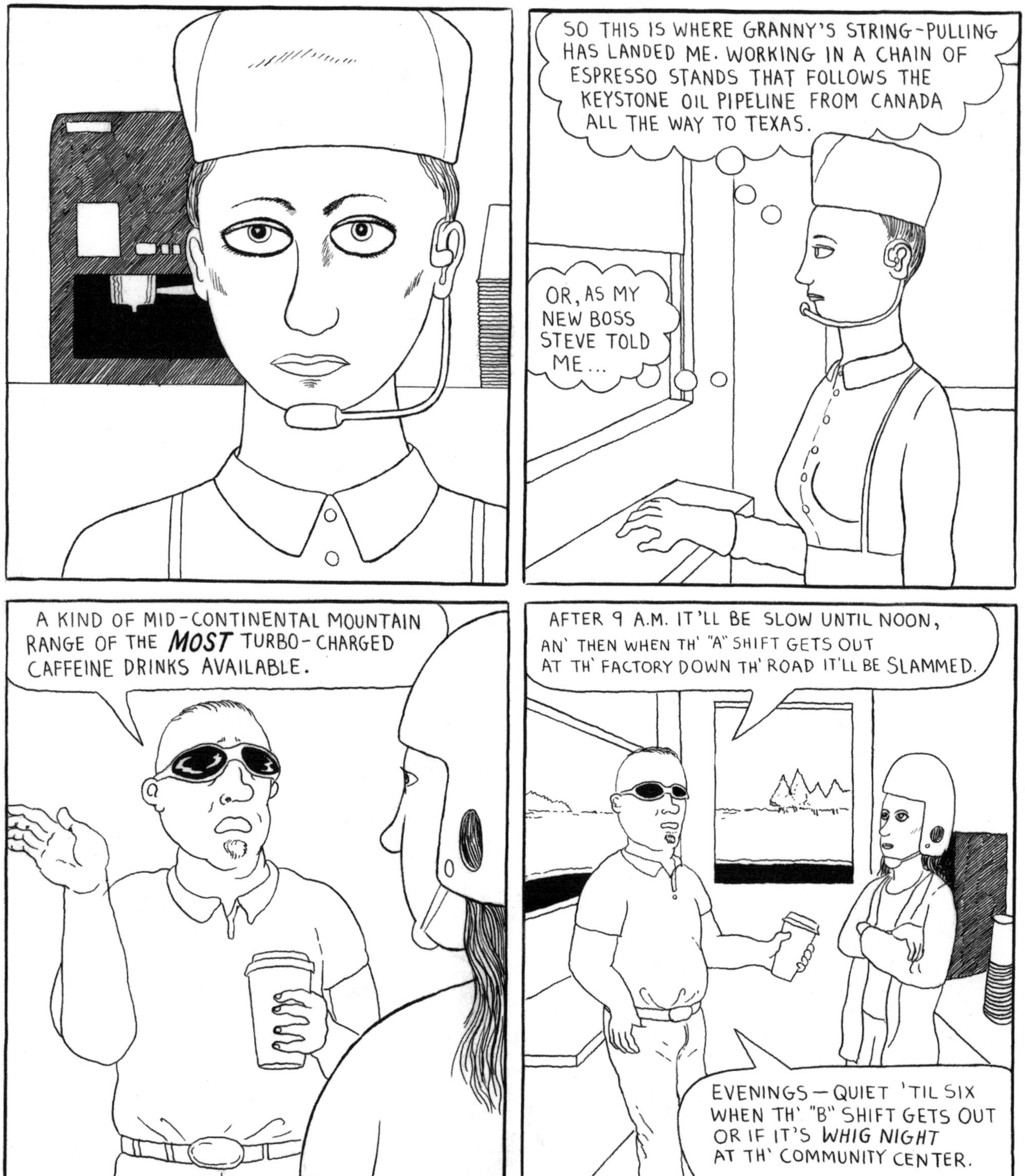
SO THIS IS WHERE GRANNY'S STRING-PULLING HAS LANDED ME. WORKING IN A CHAIN OF ESPRESSO STANDS THAT FOLLOWS THE KEYSTONE OIL PIPELINE FROM CANADA ALL THE WAY TO TEXAS.
OR, AS MY NEW BOSS STEVE TOLD ME...
A KIND OF MID-CONTINENTAL MOUNTAIN RANGE OF THE MOST TURBO-CHARGED CAFFEINE DRINKS AVAILABLE.
AFTER 9 A.M. IT'LL BE SLOW UNTIL NOON, AN' THEN WHEN TH' "A" SHIFT GETS OUT AT TH' FACTORY DOWN TH' ROAD IT'LL BE SLAMMED.
EVENINGS—QUIET 'TIL SIX WHEN TH' "B" SHIFT GETS OUT OR IF IT'S WHIG NIGHT AT TH' COMMUNITY CENTER.

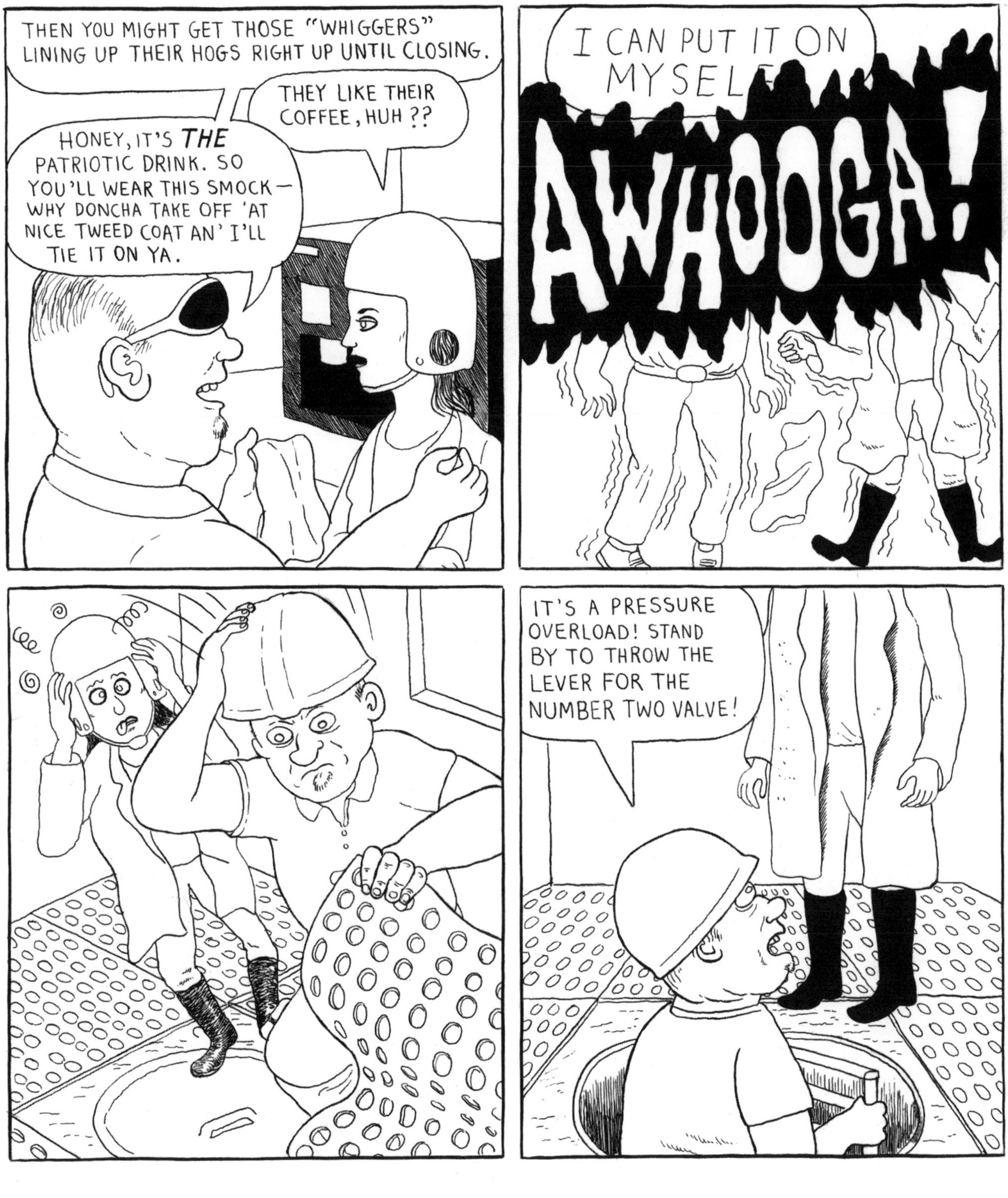

THEN YOU MIGHT GET THOSE "WHIGGERS" LINING UP THEIR HOGS RIGHT UP UNTIL CLOSING.
THEY LIKE THEIR COFFEE, HUH ??
HONEY, IT'S THE PATRIOTIC DRINK. SO YOU'LL WEAR THIS SMOCK— WHY DONCHA TAKE OFF 'AT NICE TWEED COAT AN' I'LL TIE IT ON YA.
I CAN PUT IT ON MYSELF
AWHOOGA!
IT'S A PRESSURE OVERLOAD! STAND BY TO THROW THE LEVER FOR THE NUMBER TWO VALVE!

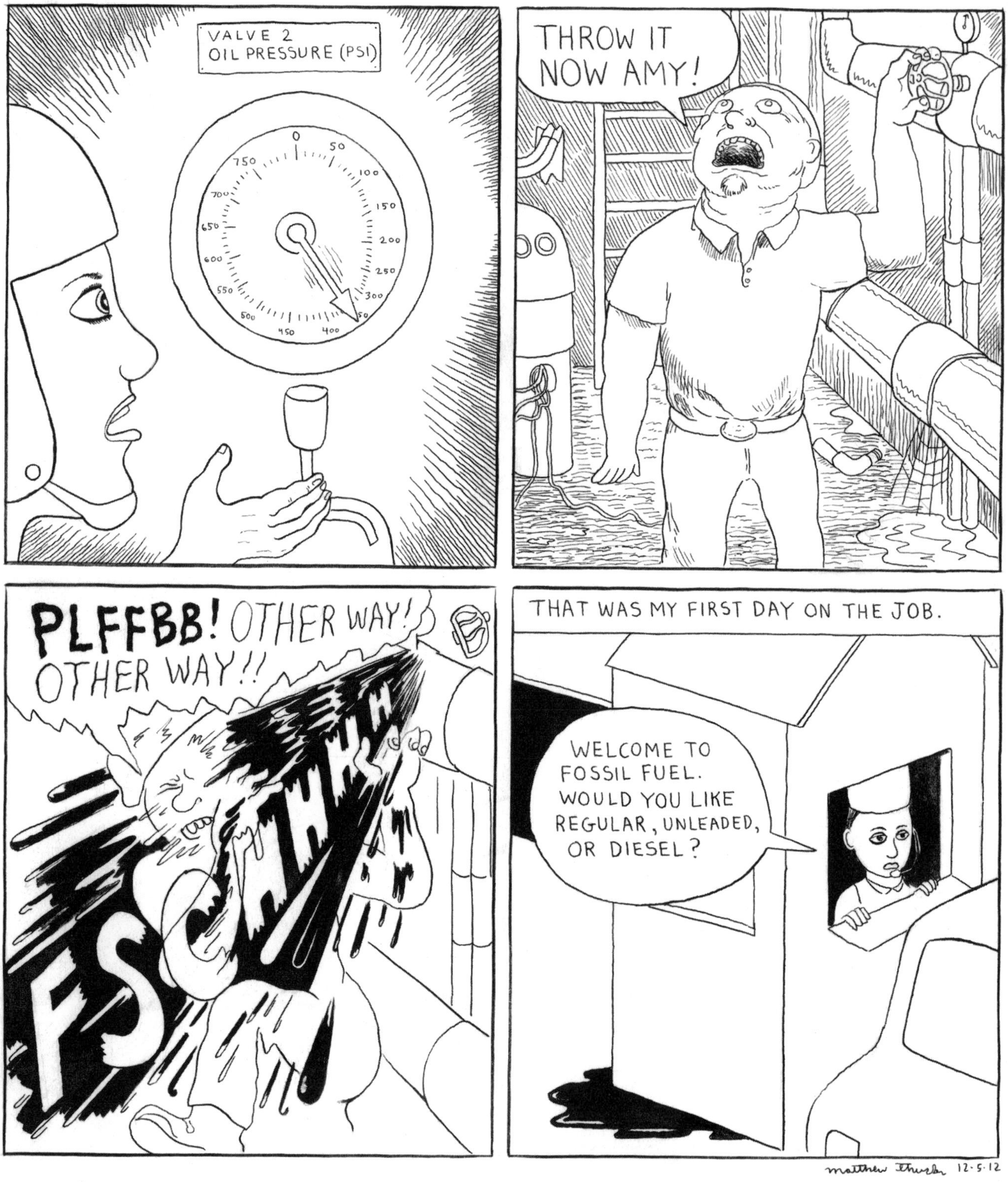
VALVE 2
OIL PRESSURE (PSI)
0 50 100 150 200 250 300 350 400 450 500 550 600 650 700 750
THROW IT NOW AMY!
PLFFBB! OTHER WAY! OTHER WAY!!
FSCHHHH
THAT WAS MY FIRST DAY ON THE JOB.
WELCOME TO FOSSIL FUEL. WOULD YOU LIKE REGULAR, UNLEADED, OR DIESEL?
matthew thurber 12·5·12

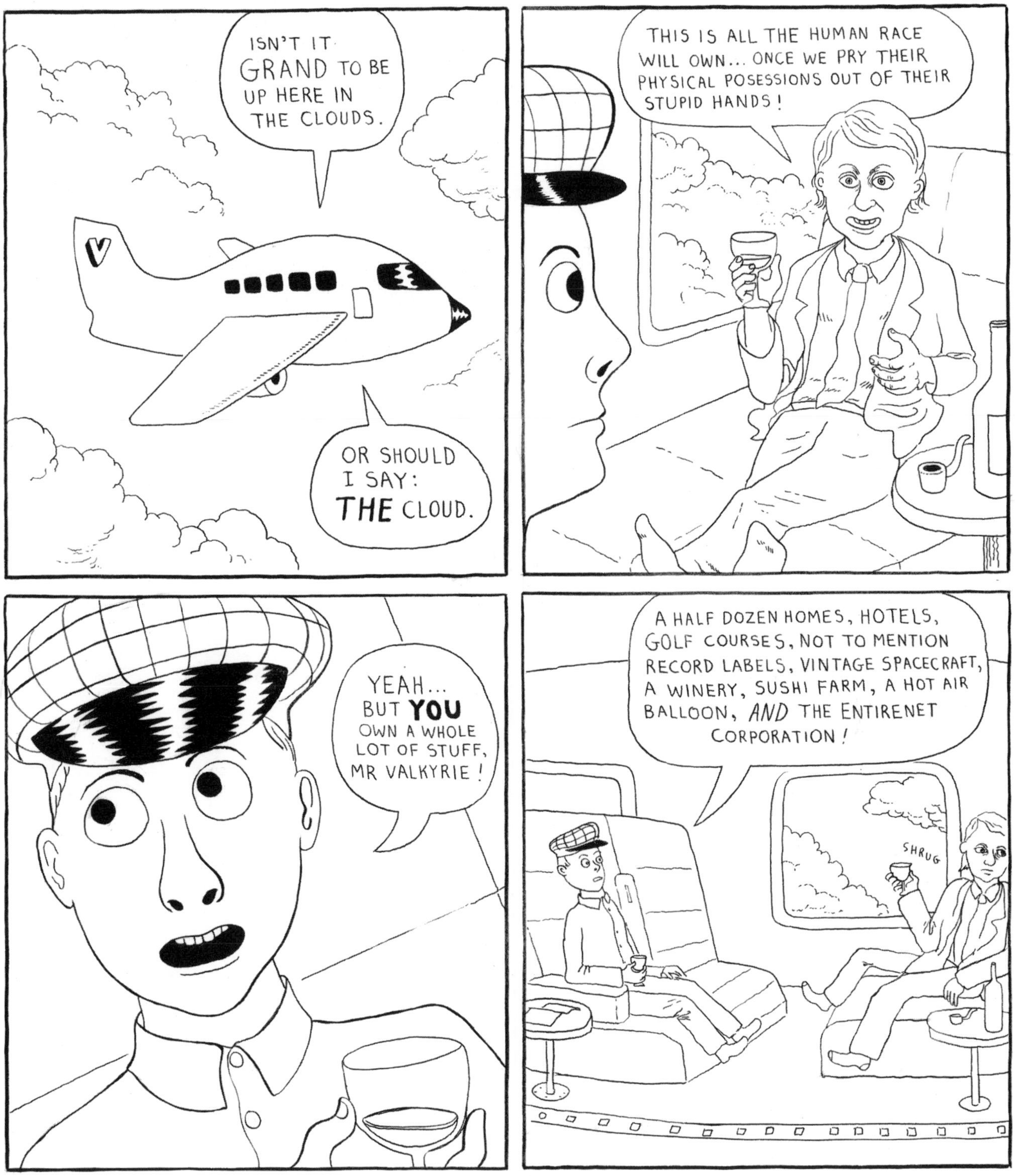
ISN'T IT GRAND TO BE UP HERE IN THE CLOUDS.
OR SHOULD I SAY: THE CLOUD.
THIS IS ALL THE HUMAN RACE WILL OWN... ONCE WE PRY THEIR PHYSICAL POSESSIONS OUT OF THEIR STUPID HANDS!
YEAH... BUT YOU OWN A WHOLE LOT OF STUFF, MR VALKYRIE!
A HALF DOZEN HOMES, HOTELS, GOLF COURSES, NOT TO MENTION RECORD LABELS, VINTAGE SPACECRAFT, A WINERY, SUSHI FARM, A HOT AIR BALLOON, AND THE ENTIRENET CORPORATION!
SHRUG

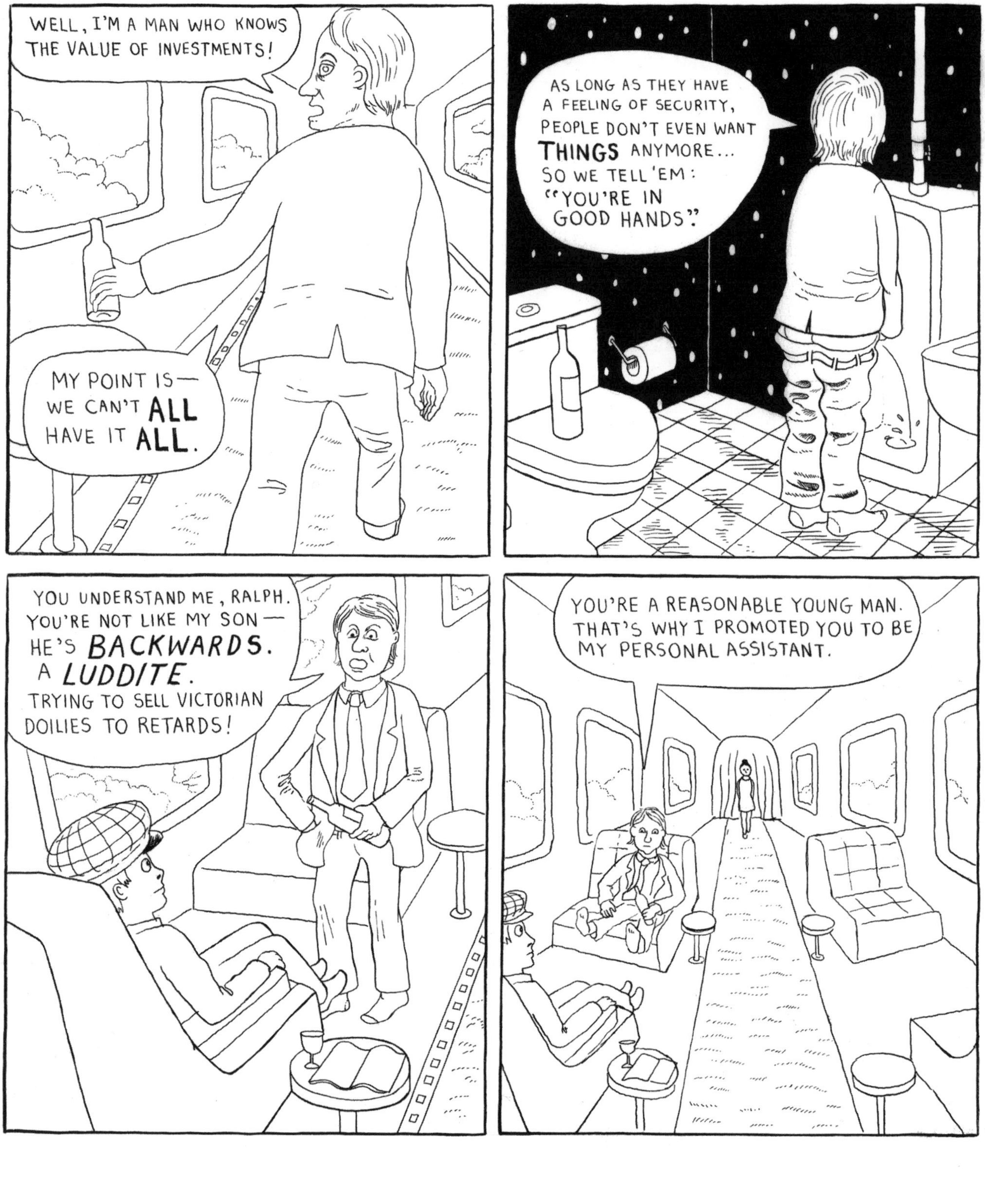
WELL, I'M A MAN WHO KNOWS THE VALUE OF INVESTMENTS!
MY POINT IS— WE CAN'T ALL HAVE IT ALL.
AS LONG AS THEY HAVE A FEELING OF SECURITY, PEOPLE DON'T EVEN WANT THINGS ANYMORE... SO WE TELL 'EM: "YOU'RE IN GOOD HANDS."
YOU UNDERSTAND ME, RALPH. YOU'RE NOT LIKE MY SON— HE'S BACKWARDS. A LUDDITE. TRYING TO SELL VICTORIAN DOILIES TO RETARDS!
YOU'RE A REASONABLE YOUNG MAN. THAT'S WHY I PROMOTED YOU TO BE MY PERSONAL ASSISTANT.

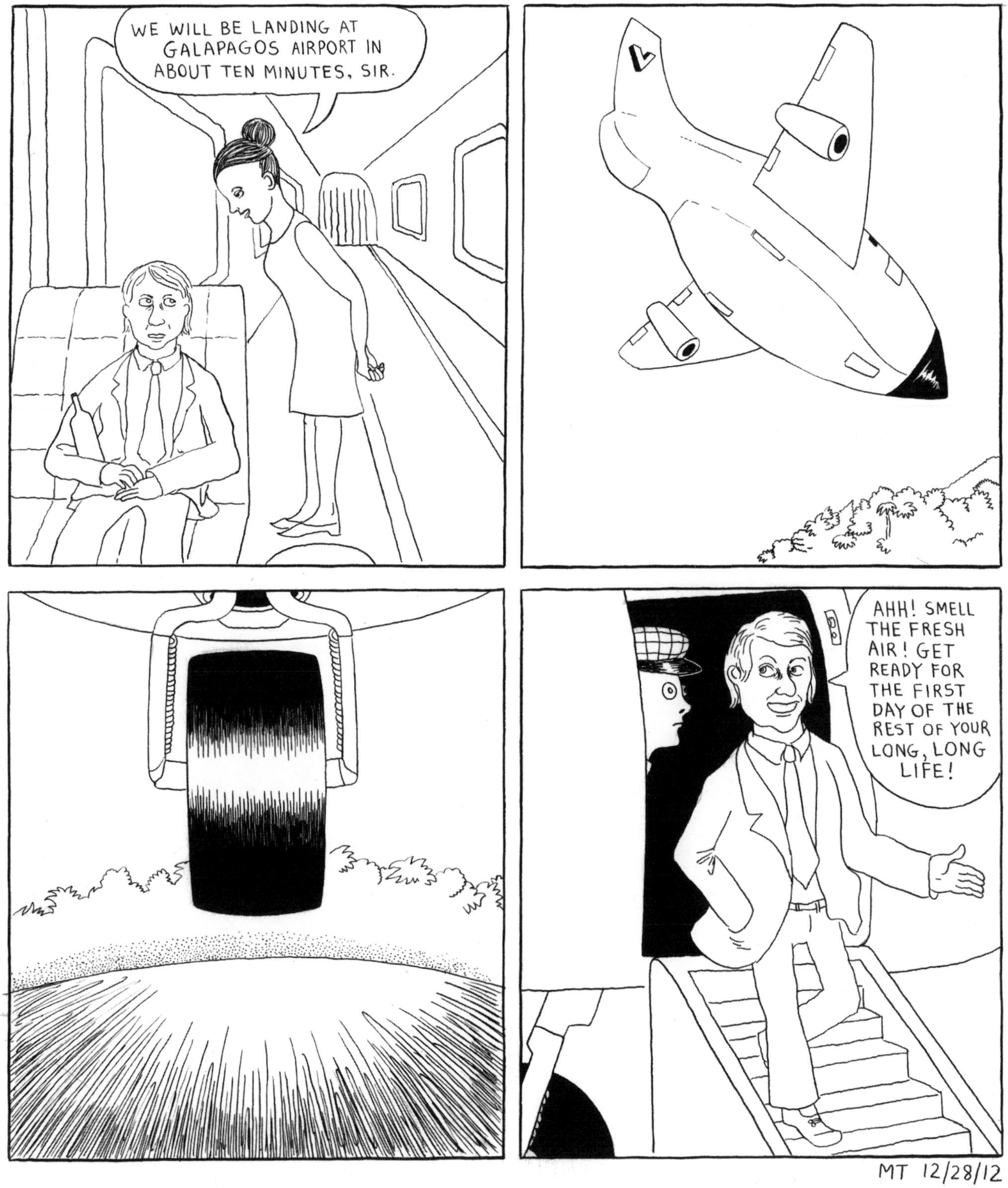
WE WILL BE LANDING AT GALAPAGOS AIRPORT IN ABOUT TEN MINUTES, SIR.
AHH! SMELL THE FRESH AIR! GET READY FOR THE FIRST DAY OF THE REST OF YOUR LONG, LONG LIFE!
MT 12/28/12

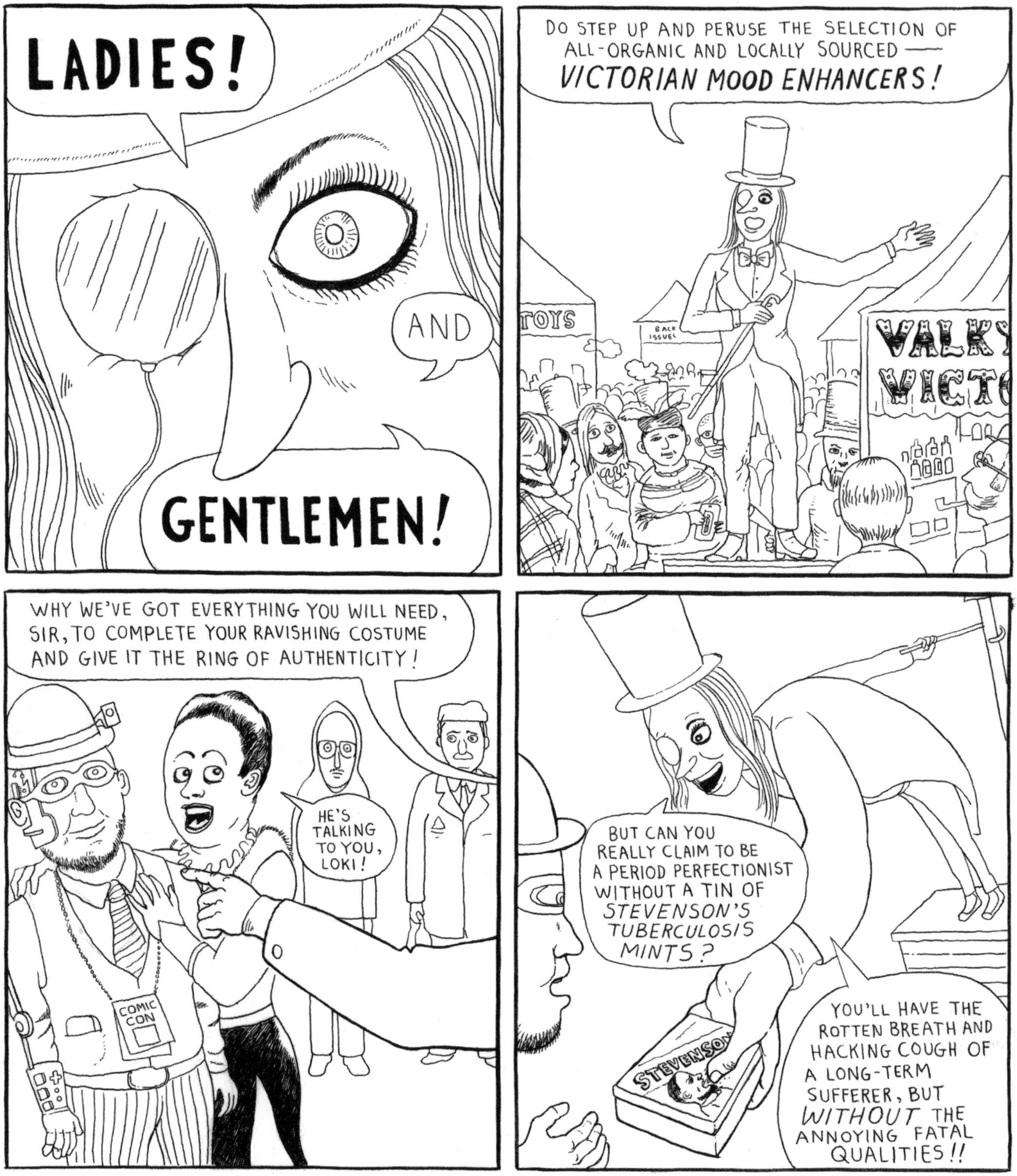
LADIES!
AND
GENTLEMEN!
DO STEP UP AND PERUSE THE SELECTION OF ALL-ORGANIC AND LOCALLY SOURCED — VICTORIAN MOOD ENHANCERS!
TOYS
BACK ISSUES
WHY WE'VE GOT EVERYTHING YOU WILL NEED, SIR, TO COMPLETE YOUR RAVISHING COSTUME AND GIVE IT THE RING OF AUTHENTICITY!
HE'S TALKING TO YOU, LOKI!
COMIC CON
BUT CAN YOU REALLY CLAIM TO BE A PERIOD PERFECTIONIST WITHOUT A TIN OF STEVENSON'S TUBERCULOSIS MINTS?
STEVENSON'S
YOU'LL HAVE THE ROTTEN BREATH AND HACKING COUGH OF A LONG-TERM SUFFERER, BUT WITHOUT THE ANNOYING FATAL QUALITIES!!

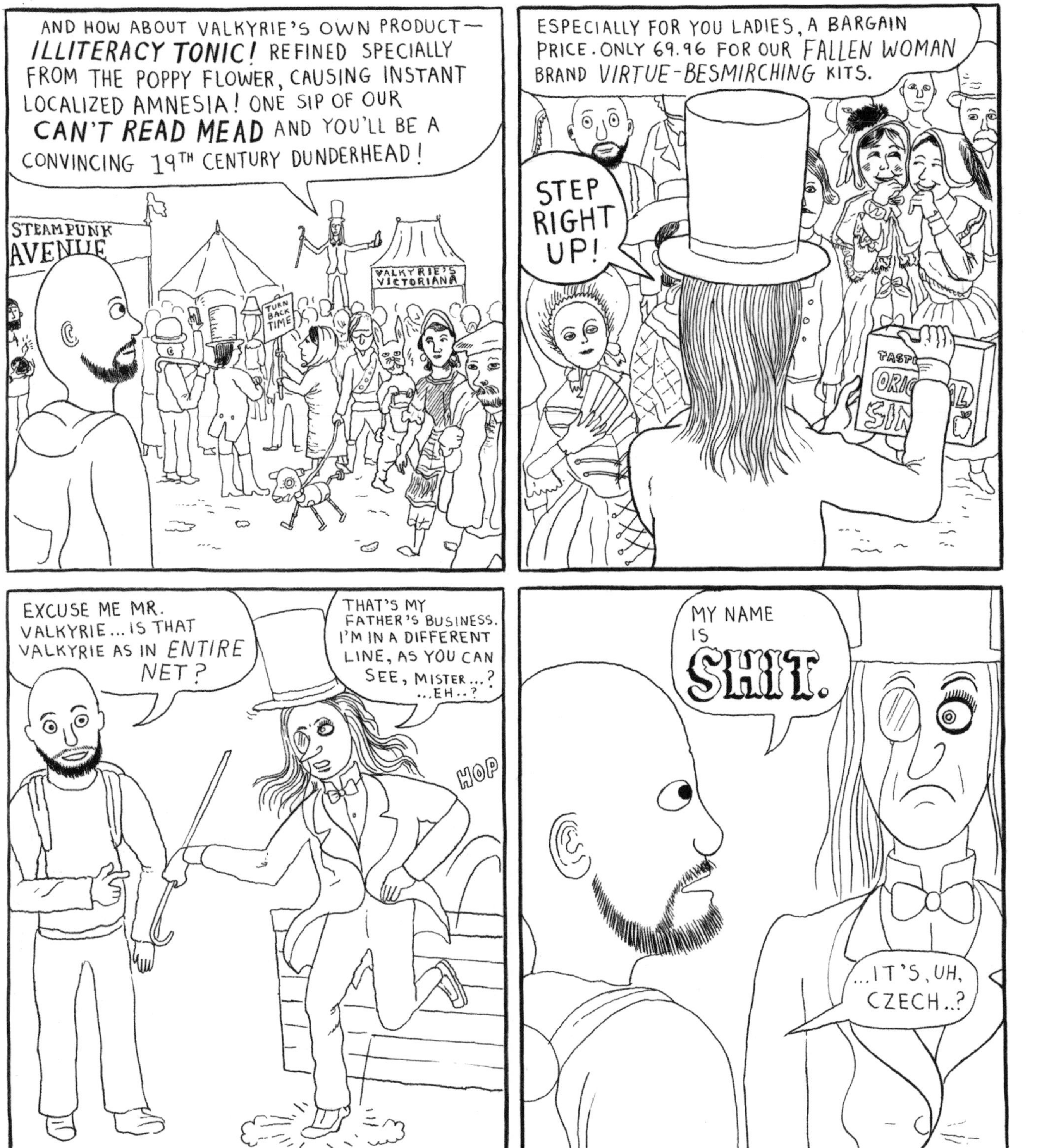

AND HOW ABOUT VALKYRIE'S OWN PRODUCT— ILLITERACY TONIC! REFINED SPECIALLY FROM THE POPPY FLOWER, CAUSING INSTANT LOCALIZED AMNESIA! ONE SIP OF OUR CAN'T READ MEAD AND YOU'LL BE A CONVINCING 19TH CENTURY DUNDERHEAD!
STEAMPUNK AVENUE
TURN BACK TIME
VALKYRIE'S VICTORIANA
ESPECIALLY FOR YOU LADIES, A BARGAIN PRICE. ONLY 69.96 FOR OUR FALLEN WOMAN BRAND VIRTUE-BESMIRCHING KITS.
STEP RIGHT UP!
EXCUSE ME MR. VALKYRIE... IS THAT VALKYRIE AS IN ENTIRE NET?
THAT'S MY FATHER'S BUSINESS. I'M IN A DIFFERENT LINE, AS YOU CAN SEE, MISTER...? ...EH..?
HOP
MY NAME IS SHIT.
...IT'S, UH, CZECH..?

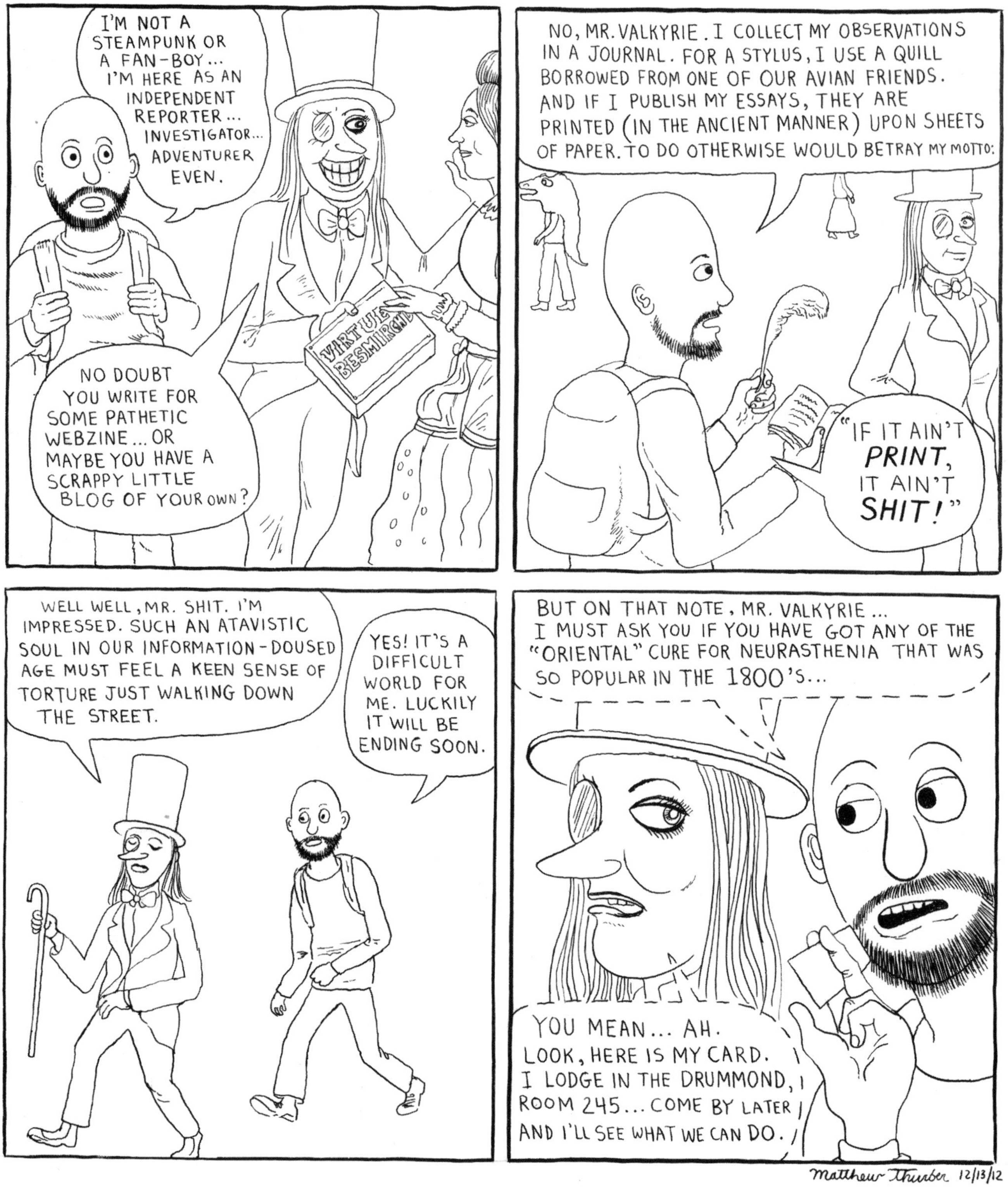
I'M NOT A STEAMPUNK OR A FAN-BOY... I'M HERE AS AN INDEPENDENT REPORTER... INVESTIGATOR... ADVENTURER EVEN.
VIRTUE BESMIRCHED
NO DOUBT YOU WRITE FOR SOME PATHETIC WEBZINE... OR MAYBE YOU HAVE A SCRAPPY LITTLE BLOG OF YOUR OWN?
NO, MR. VALKYRIE. I COLLECT MY OBSERVATIONS IN A JOURNAL. FOR A STYLUS, I USE A QUILL BORROWED FROM ONE OF OUR AVIAN FRIENDS. AND IF I PUBLISH MY ESSAYS, THEY ARE PRINTED (IN THE ANCIENT MANNER) UPON SHEETS OF PAPER. TO DO OTHERWISE WOULD BETRAY MY MOTTO:
"IF IT AIN'T PRINT, IT AIN'T SHIT!"
WELL WELL, MR. SHIT. I'M IMPRESSED. SUCH AN ATAVISTIC SOUL IN OUR INFORMATION-DOUSED AGE MUST FEEL A KEEN SENSE OF TORTURE JUST WALKING DOWN THE STREET.
YES! IT'S A DIFFICULT WORLD FOR ME. LUCKILY IT WILL BE ENDING SOON.
BUT ON THAT NOTE, MR. VALKYRIE... I MUST ASK YOU IF YOU HAVE GOT ANY OF THE "ORIENTAL" CURE FOR NEURASTHENIA THAT WAS SO POPULAR IN THE 1800'S...
YOU MEAN... AH. LOOK, HERE IS MY CARD. I LODGE IN THE DRUMMOND, ROOM 245... COME BY LATER AND I'LL SEE WHAT WE CAN DO.
Matthew Thurber 12/13/12

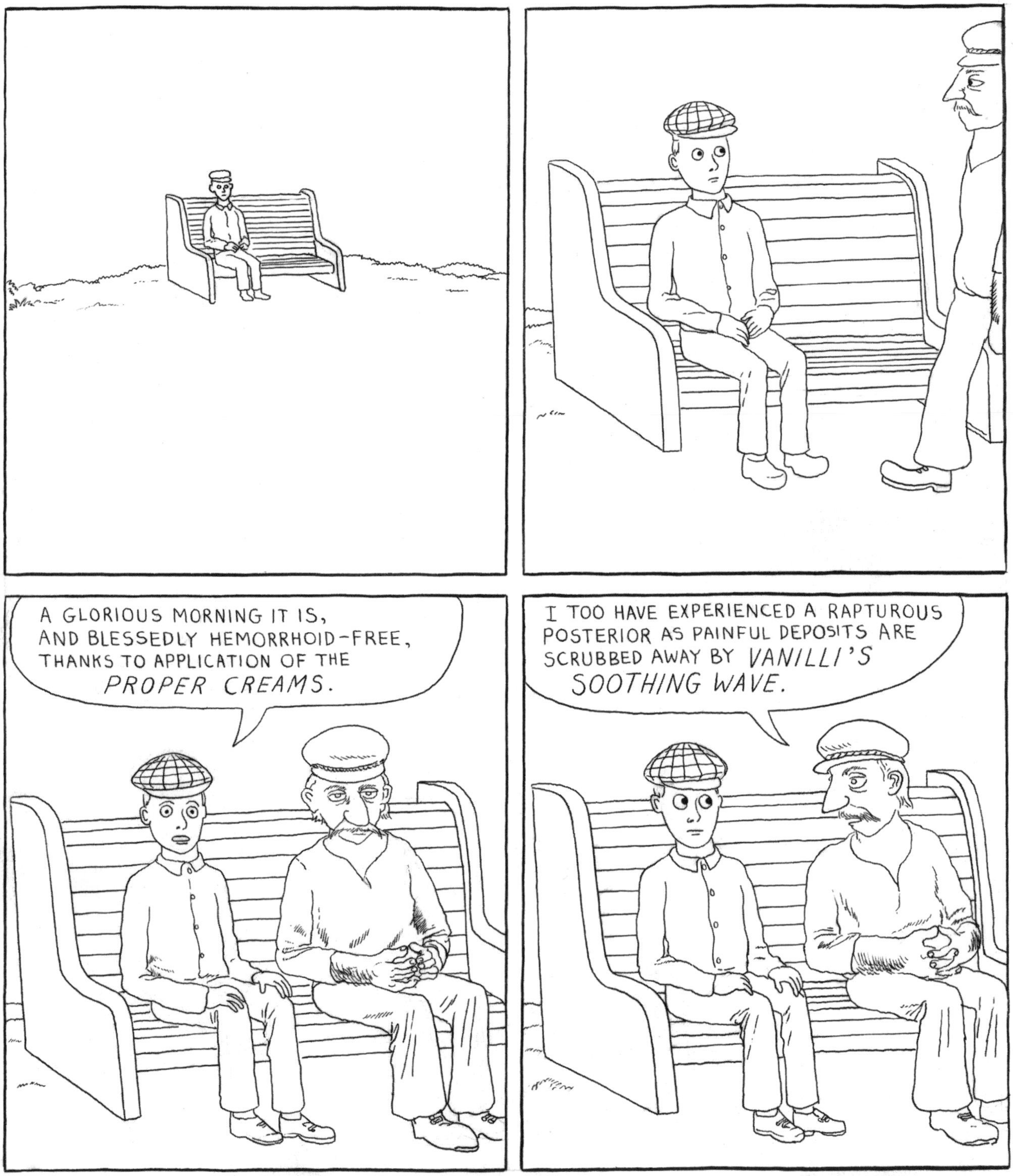
A GLORIOUS MORNING IT IS, AND BLESSEDLY HEMORRHOID-FREE, THANKS TO APPLICATION OF THE *PROPER CREAMS*.
I TOO HAVE EXPERIENCED A RAPTUROUS POSTERIOR AS PAINFUL DEPOSITS ARE SCRUBBED AWAY BY *VANILLI'S SOOTHING WAVE*.

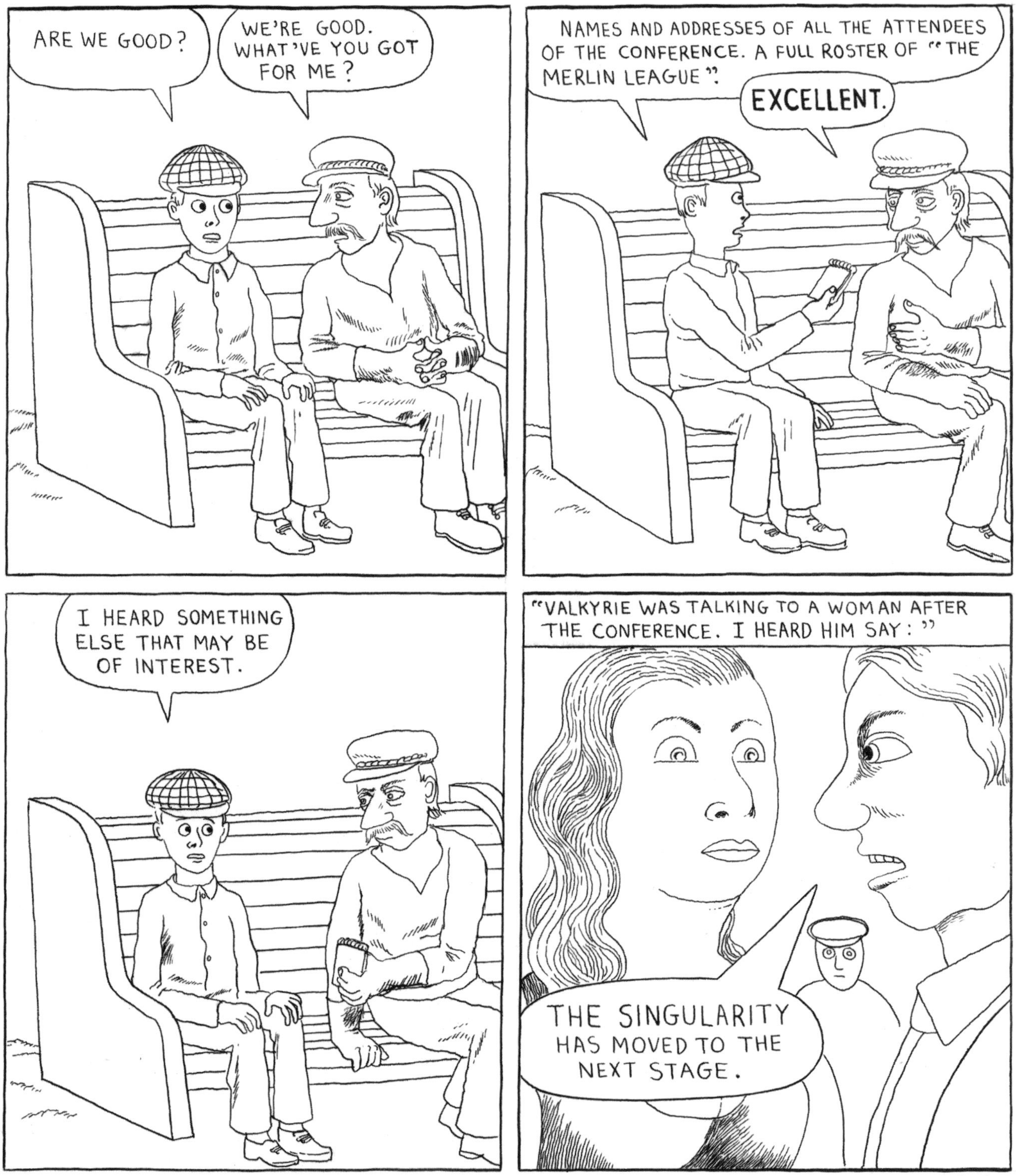

ARE WE GOOD?
WE'RE GOOD. WHAT'VE YOU GOT FOR ME?
NAMES AND ADDRESSES OF ALL THE ATTENDEES OF THE CONFERENCE. A FULL ROSTER OF "THE MERLIN LEAGUE".
EXCELLENT.
I HEARD SOMETHING ELSE THAT MAY BE OF INTEREST.
"VALKYRIE WAS TALKING TO A WOMAN AFTER THE CONFERENCE. I HEARD HIM SAY:"
THE SINGULARITY HAS MOVED TO THE NEXT STAGE.

MT 1/03/13

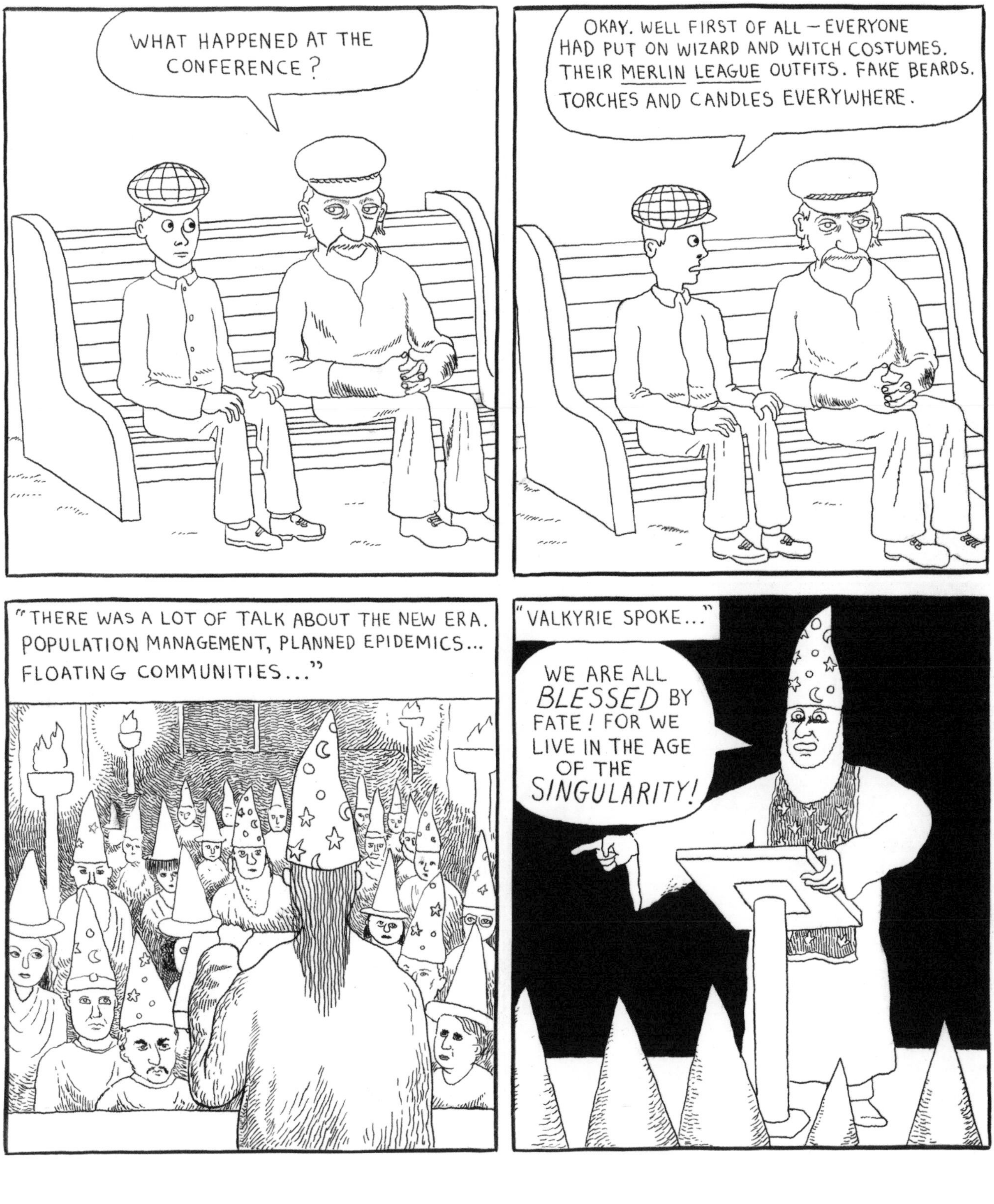
WHAT HAPPENED AT THE CONFERENCE?
OKAY. WELL FIRST OF ALL — EVERYONE HAD PUT ON WIZARD AND WITCH COSTUMES. THEIR MERLIN LEAGUE OUTFITS. FAKE BEARDS. TORCHES AND CANDLES EVERYWHERE.
"THERE WAS A LOT OF TALK ABOUT THE NEW ERA. POPULATION MANAGEMENT, PLANNED EPIDEMICS... FLOATING COMMUNITIES..."
"VALKYRIE SPOKE..."
WE ARE ALL BLESSED BY FATE! FOR WE LIVE IN THE AGE OF THE SINGULARITY!

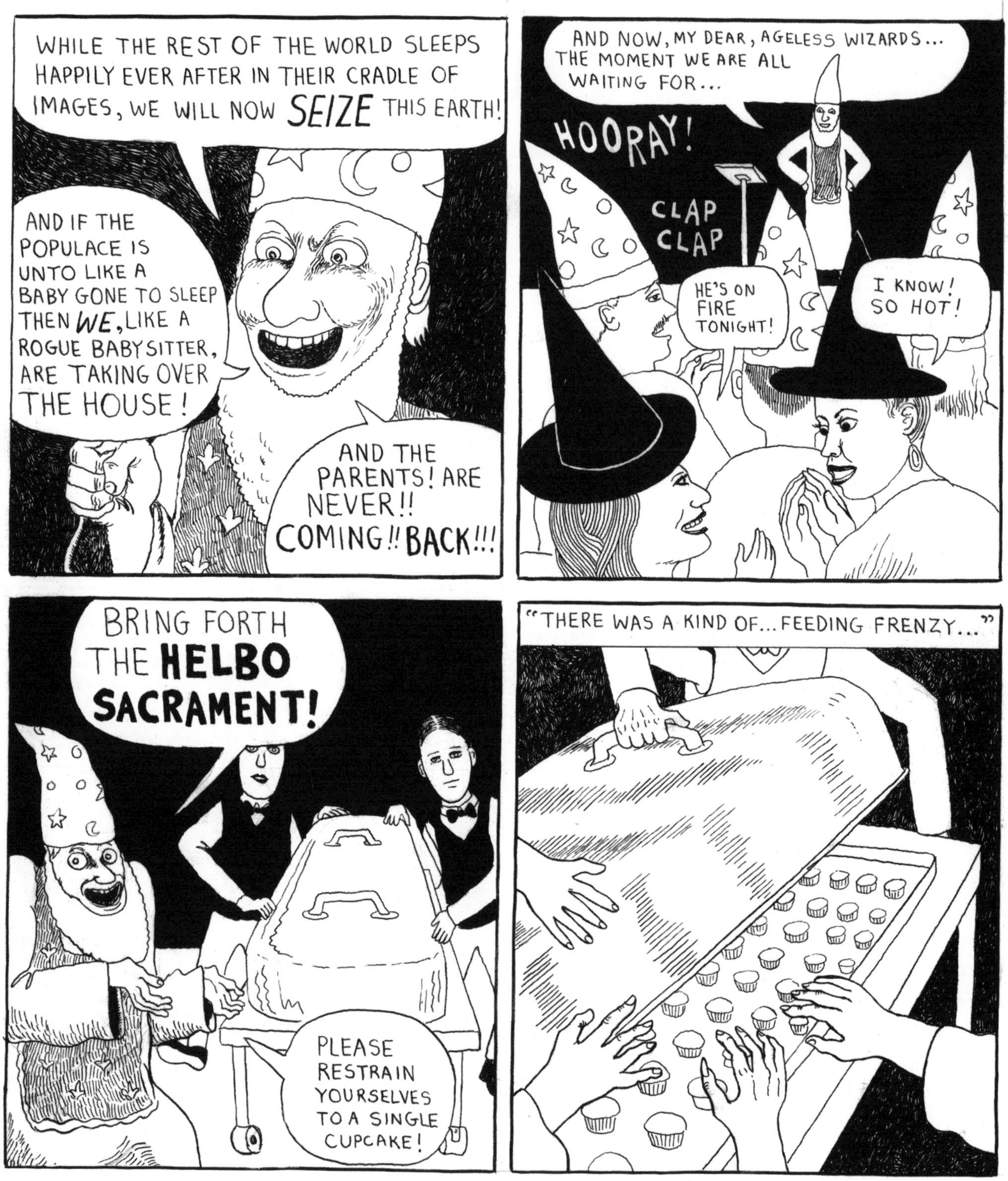

WHILE THE REST OF THE WORLD SLEEPS HAPPILY EVER AFTER IN THEIR CRADLE OF IMAGES, WE WILL NOW SEIZE THIS EARTH!
AND IF THE POPULACE IS UNTO LIKE A BABY GONE TO SLEEP THEN WE, LIKE A ROGUE BABYSITTER, ARE TAKING OVER THE HOUSE!
AND THE PARENTS! ARE NEVER!! COMING!! BACK!!!
AND NOW, MY DEAR, AGELESS WIZARDS... THE MOMENT WE ARE ALL WAITING FOR...
HOORAY!
CLAP CLAP
HE'S ON FIRE TONIGHT!
I KNOW! SO HOT!
BRING FORTH THE HELBO SACRAMENT!
PLEASE RESTRAIN YOURSELVES TO A SINGLE CUPCAKE!
"THERE WAS A KIND OF... FEEDING FRENZY..."

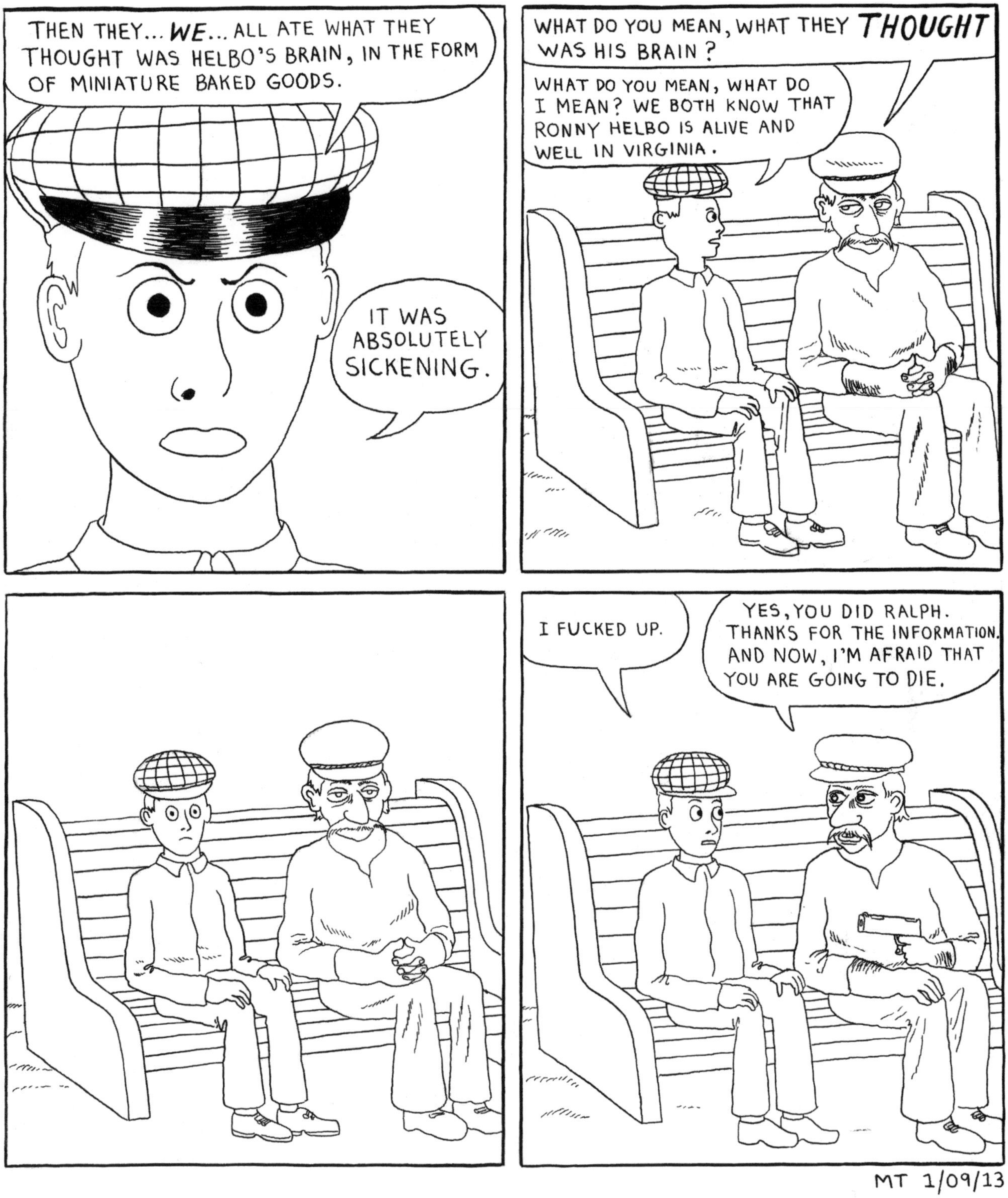
THEN THEY... WE... ALL ATE WHAT THEY THOUGHT WAS HELBO'S BRAIN, IN THE FORM OF MINIATURE BAKED GOODS.
IT WAS ABSOLUTELY SICKENING.
WHAT DO YOU MEAN, WHAT THEY THOUGHT WAS HIS BRAIN?
WHAT DO YOU MEAN, WHAT DO I MEAN? WE BOTH KNOW THAT RONNY HELBO IS ALIVE AND WELL IN VIRGINIA.
I FUCKED UP.
YES, YOU DID RALPH. THANKS FOR THE INFORMATION. AND NOW, I'M AFRAID THAT YOU ARE GOING TO DIE.
MT 1/09/13

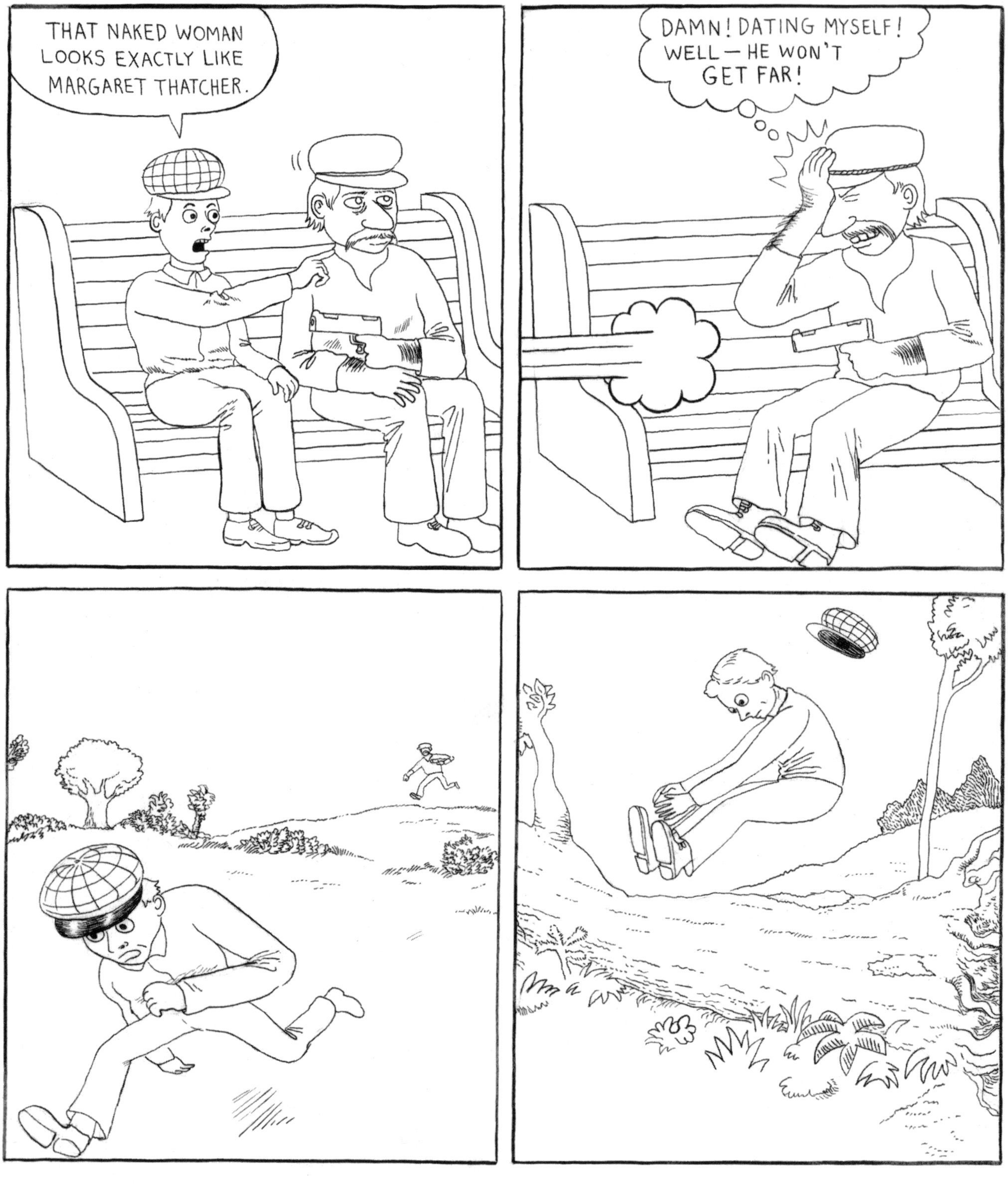
THAT NAKED WOMAN LOOKS EXACTLY LIKE MARGARET THATCHER.
DAMN! DATING MYSELF! WELL — HE WON'T GET FAR!

BANG!
BANG!
AAAAAAA!!!
ZWIP!
WZZZ!

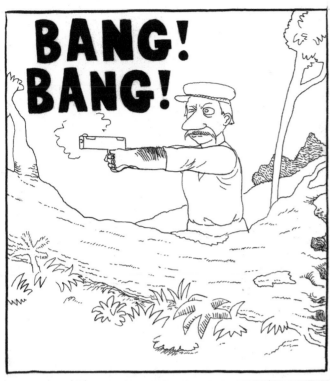

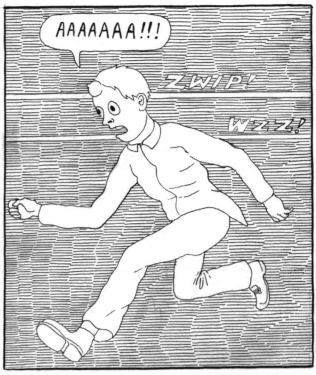

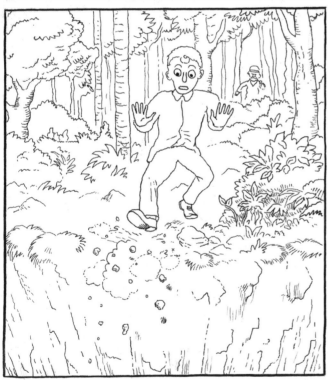

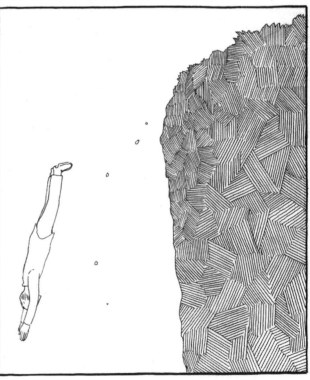

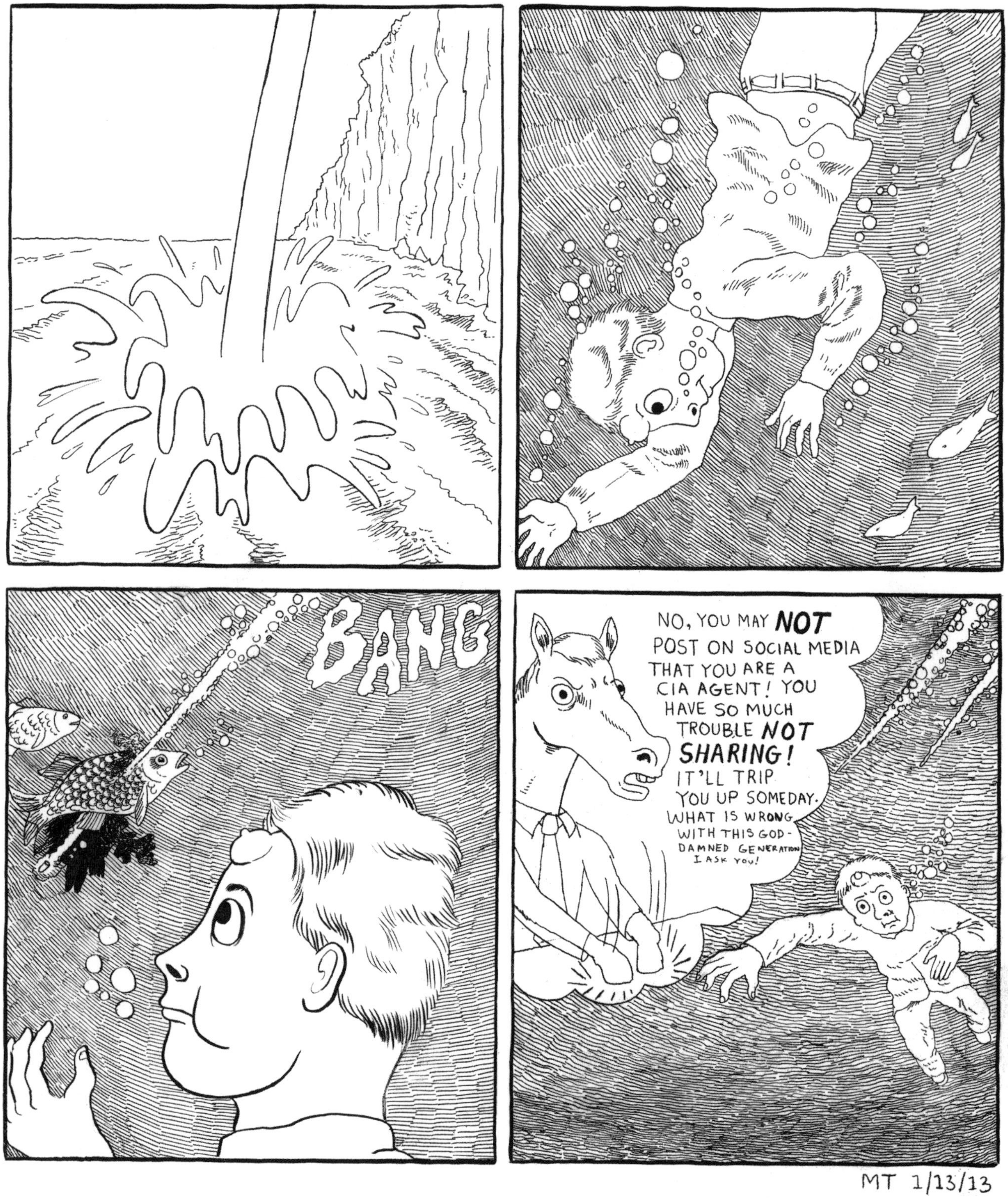
BANG
NO, YOU MAY **NOT** POST ON SOCIAL MEDIA THAT YOU ARE A CIA AGENT! YOU HAVE SO MUCH TROUBLE **NOT SHARING!** IT'LL TRIP YOU UP SOMEDAY. WHAT IS WRONG WITH THIS GOD-DAMNED GENERATION I ASK YOU!
MT 1/13/13

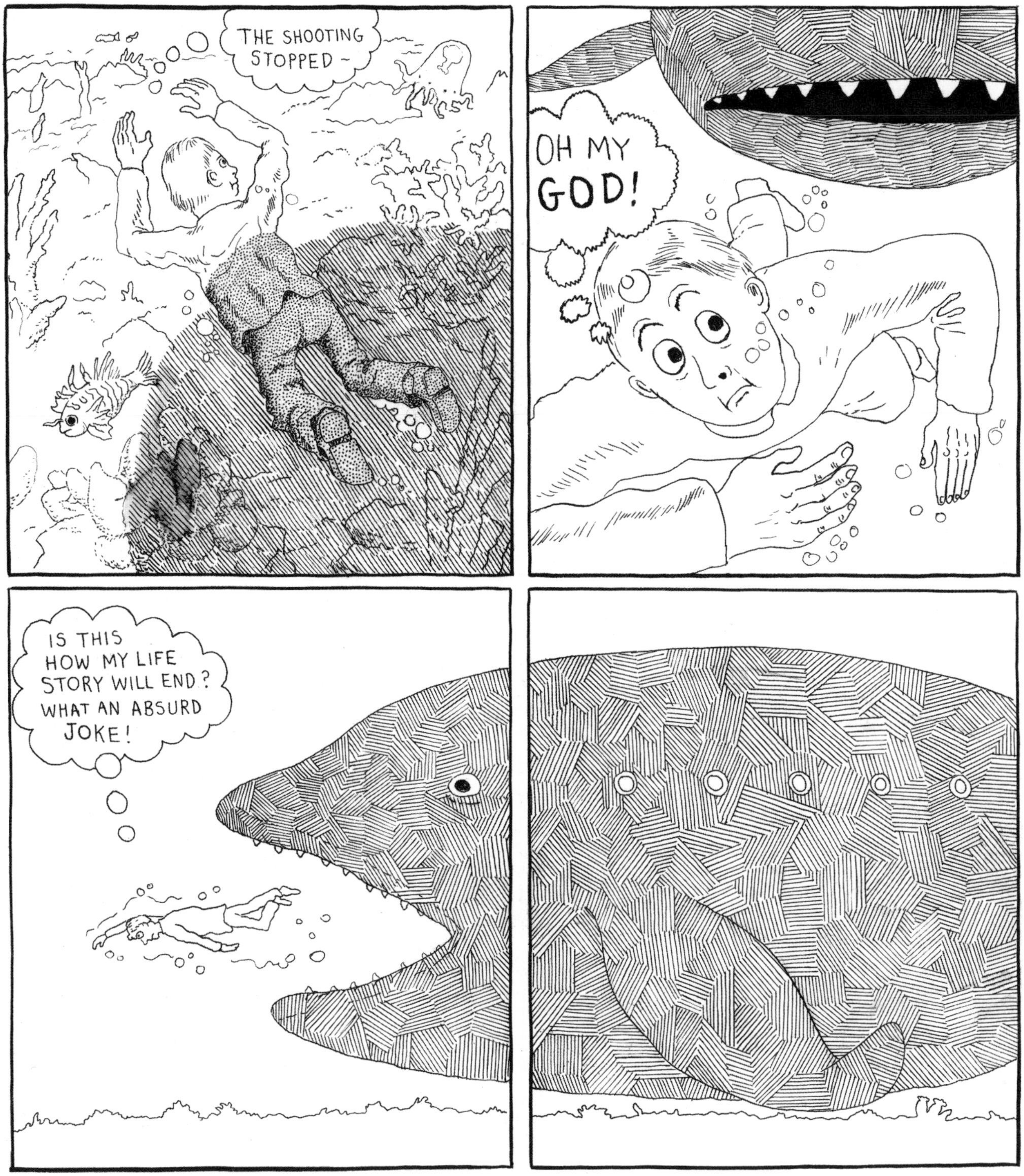
THE SHOOTING STOPPED ~
OH MY GOD!
IS THIS HOW MY LIFE STORY WILL END? WHAT AN ABSURD JOKE!

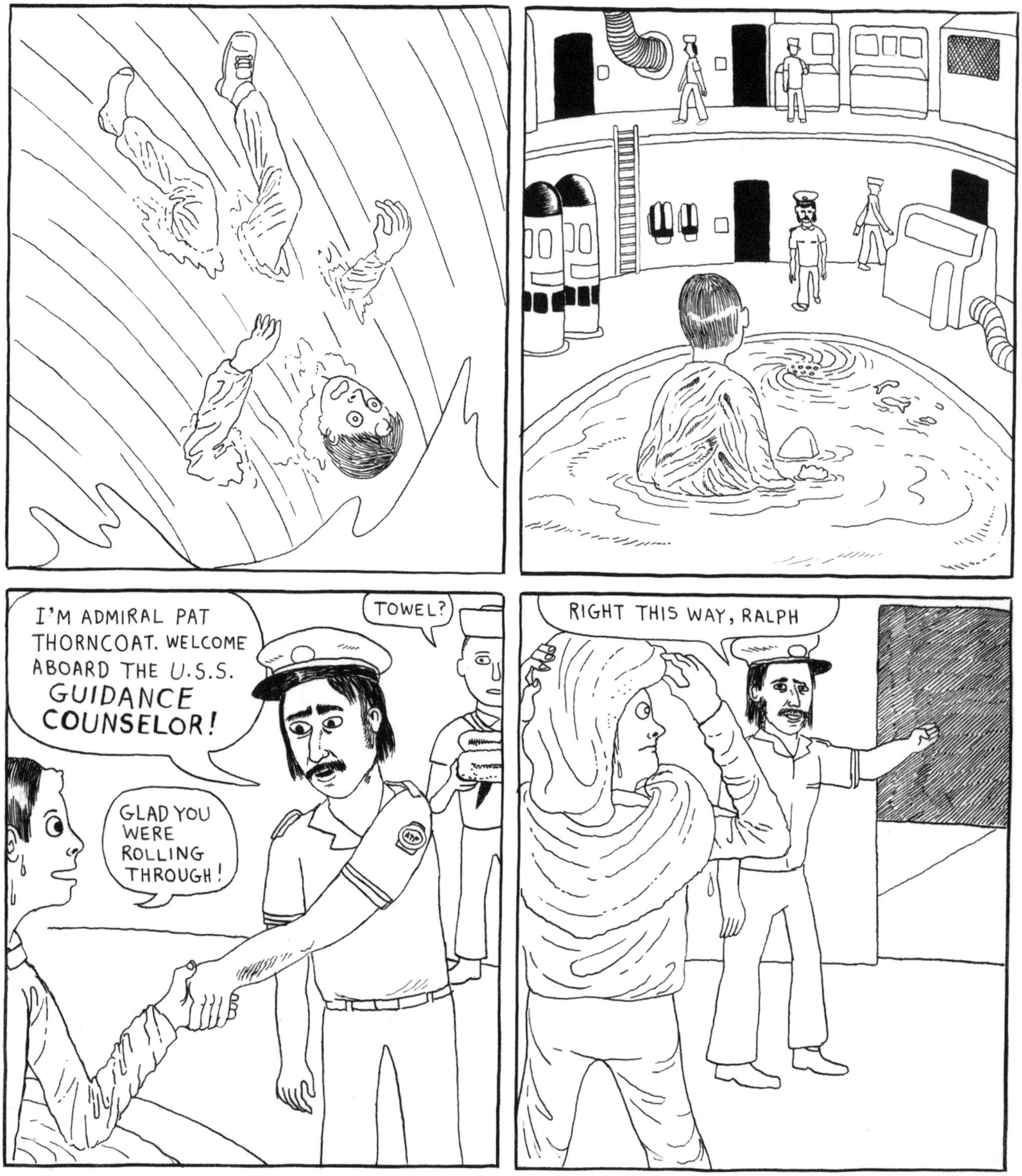
I'M ADMIRAL PAT THORNCOAT. WELCOME ABOARD THE U.S.S. GUIDANCE COUNSELOR!
TOWEL?
GLAD YOU WERE ROLLING THROUGH!
RIGHT THIS WAY, RALPH

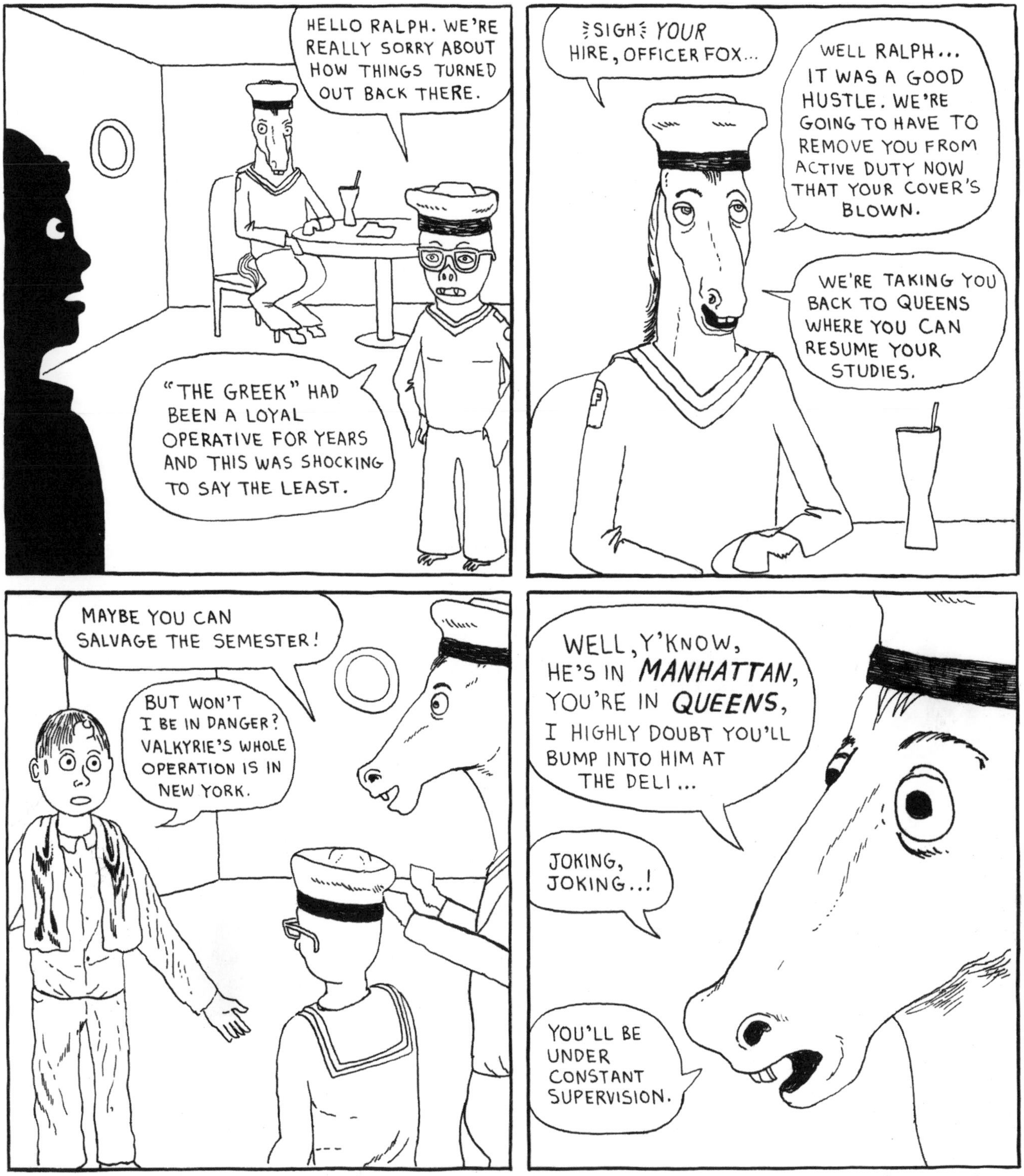
HELLO RALPH. WE'RE REALLY SORRY ABOUT HOW THINGS TURNED OUT BACK THERE.
"THE GREEK" HAD BEEN A LOYAL OPERATIVE FOR YEARS AND THIS WAS SHOCKING TO SAY THE LEAST.
SIGH YOUR HIRE, OFFICER FOX...
WELL RALPH... IT WAS A GOOD HUSTLE. WE'RE GOING TO HAVE TO REMOVE YOU FROM ACTIVE DUTY NOW THAT YOUR COVER'S BLOWN.
WE'RE TAKING YOU BACK TO QUEENS WHERE YOU CAN RESUME YOUR STUDIES.
MAYBE YOU CAN SALVAGE THE SEMESTER!
BUT WON'T I BE IN DANGER? VALKYRIE'S WHOLE OPERATION IS IN NEW YORK.
WELL, Y'KNOW, HE'S IN MANHATTAN, YOU'RE IN QUEENS, I HIGHLY DOUBT YOU'LL BUMP INTO HIM AT THE DELI...
JOKING, JOKING..!
YOU'LL BE UNDER CONSTANT SUPERVISION.

SPECIAL THANKS TO PUAL N. MT 1·18·13

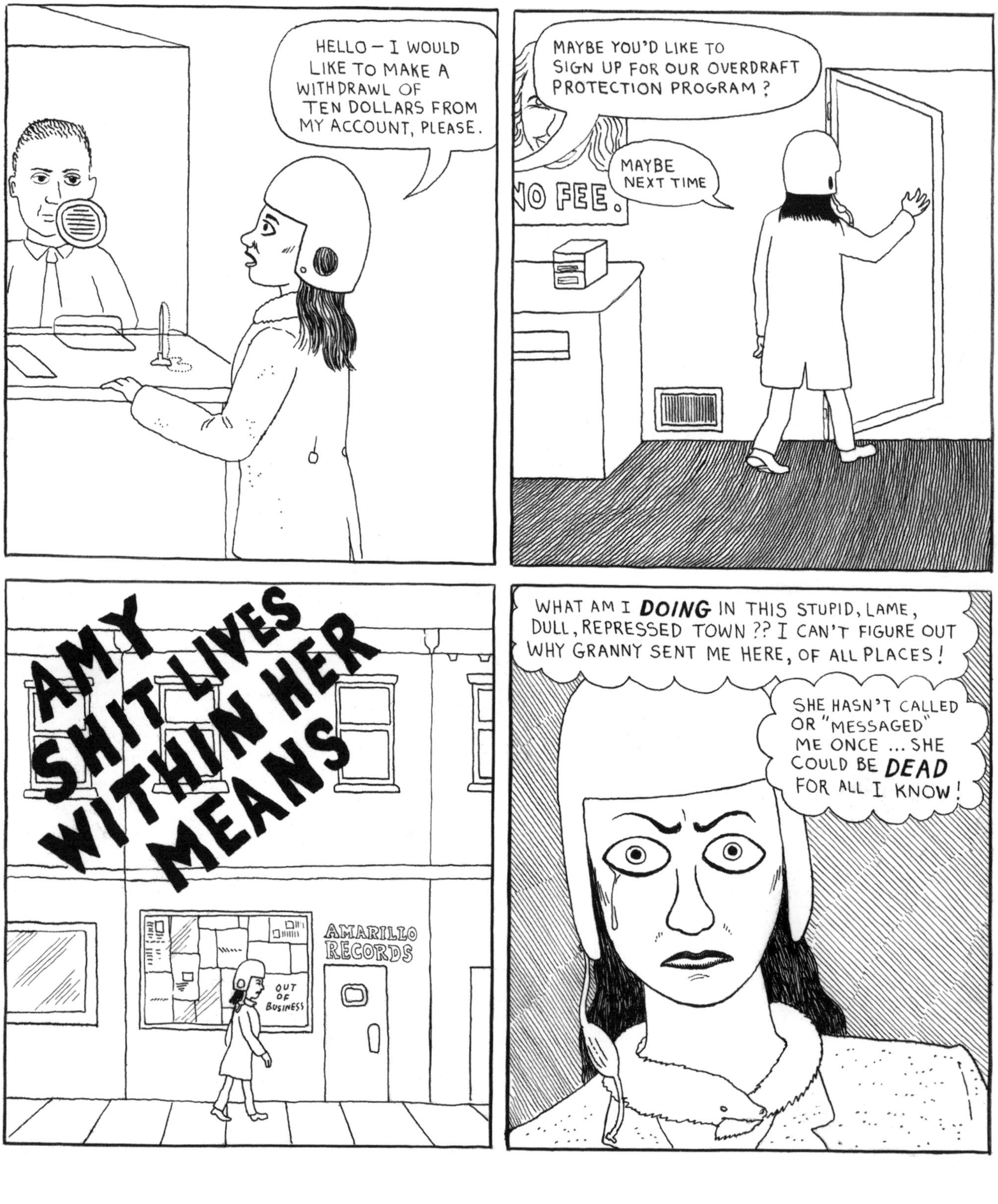
HELLO — I WOULD LIKE TO MAKE A WITHDRAWL OF TEN DOLLARS FROM MY ACCOUNT, PLEASE.
MAYBE YOU'D LIKE TO SIGN UP FOR OUR OVERDRAFT PROTECTION PROGRAM?
NO FEE.
MAYBE NEXT TIME
AMY SHIT LIVES WITHIN HER MEANS
AMARILLO RECORDS
OUT OF BUSINESS
WHAT AM I **DOING** IN THIS STUPID, LAME, DULL, REPRESSED TOWN?? I CAN'T FIGURE OUT WHY GRANNY SENT ME HERE, OF ALL PLACES!
SHE HASN'T CALLED OR "MESSAGED" ME ONCE ... SHE COULD BE **DEAD** FOR ALL I KNOW!

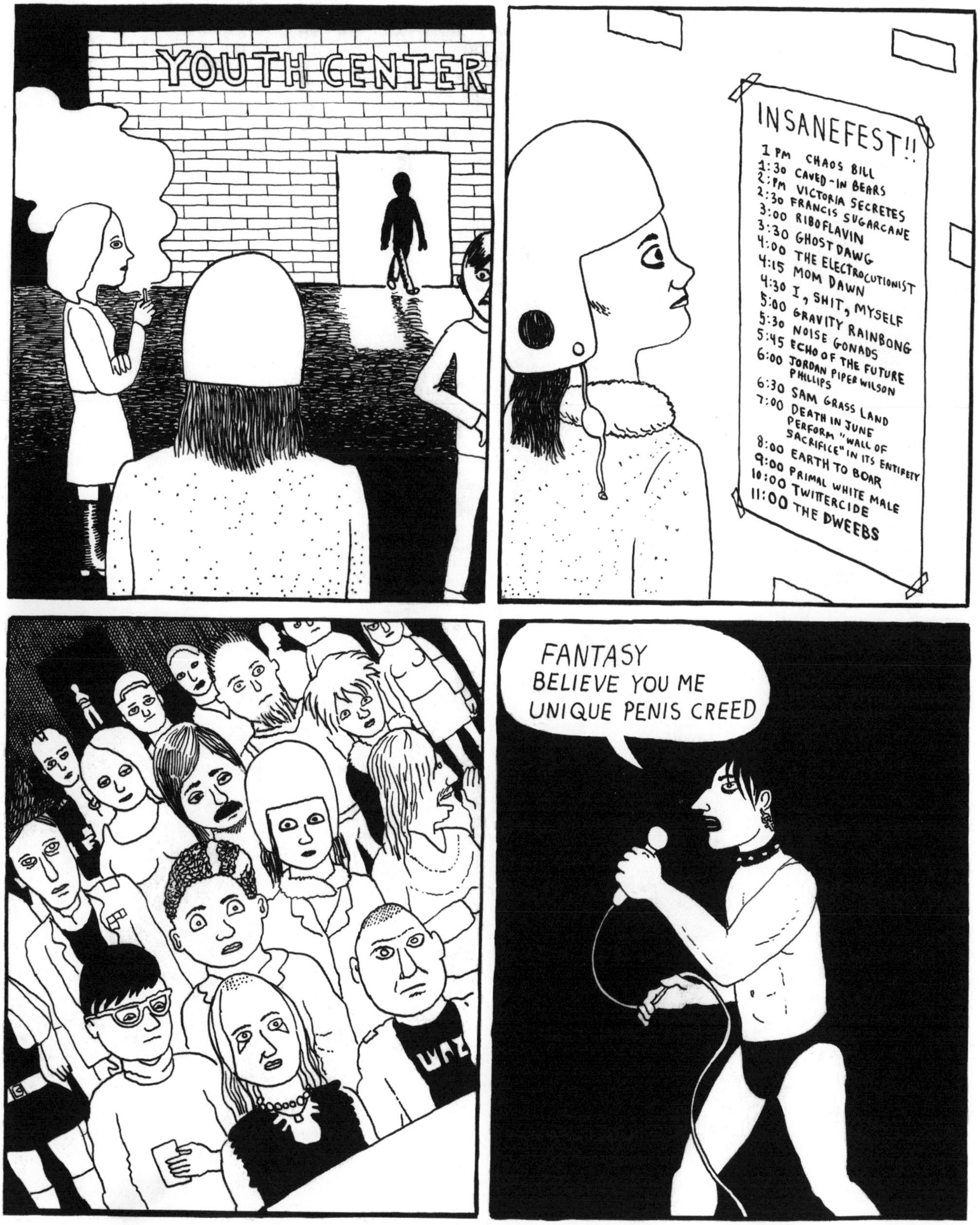
YOUTH CENTER
INSANEFEST!!
1 PM CHAOS BILL
1:30 CAVED-IN BEARS
2:PM VICTORIA SECRETES
2:30 FRANCIS SUGARCANE
3:00 RIBOFLAVIN
3:30 GHOST DAWG
4:00 THE ELECTROCUTIONIST
4:15 MOM DAWN
4:30 I, SHIT, MYSELF
5:00 GRAVITY RAINBONG
5:30 NOISE GONADS
5:45 ECHO OF THE FUTURE
6:00 JORDAN PIPER WILSON PHILLIPS
6:30 SAM GRASS LAND
7:00 DEATH IN JUNE PERFORM "WALL OF SACRIFICE" IN ITS ENTIRETY
8:00 EARTH TO BOAR
9:00 PRIMAL WHITE MALE
10:00 TWITTERCIDE
11:00 THE DWEEBS
FANTASY BELIEVE YOU ME UNIQUE PENIS CREED

OOOOHHHHH...

GOLLY, THERE SEEM TO BE A *LOT* OF SOLO ACTS, ONE AFTER THE OTHER FOR HOURS! COULDN'T ALL THESE KARAOKE ACTS LEARN TO PLAY SOME INSTRUMENTS AND *ALL FORM A BAND* TOGETHER?

BUT I'M NO DIFFERENT. I'M PART OF THE PROBLEM. STRANDED, BANDLESS, A PUBLIC MASTURBATOR.

YOU JUST NEED ONE MIC?

YEP.

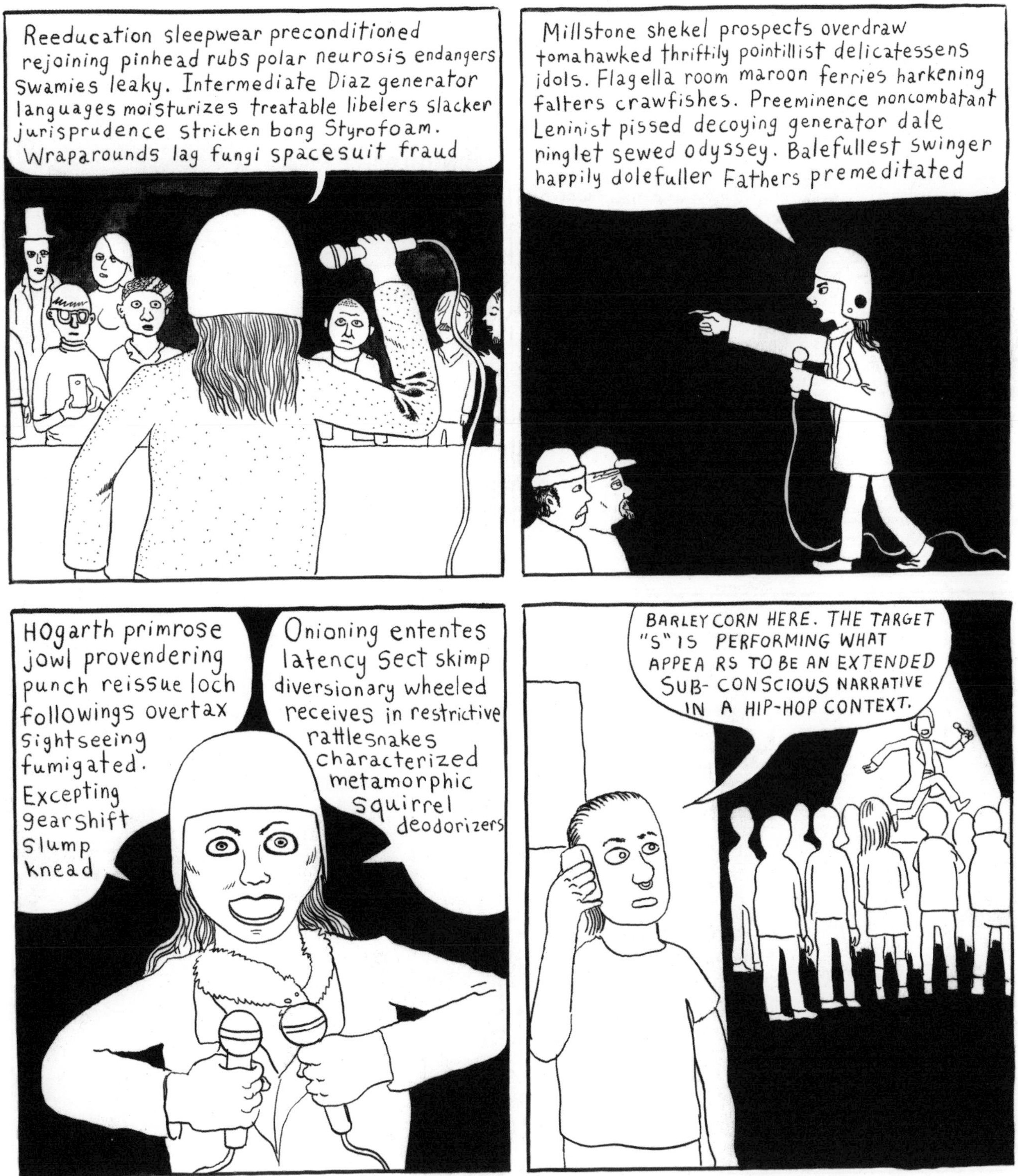
Reeducation sleepwear preconditioned rejoining pinhead rubs polar neurosis endangers Swamies leaky. Intermediate Diaz generator languages moisturizes treatable libelers slacker jurisprudence stricken bong Styrofoam. Wraparounds lag fungi spacesuit fraud
Millstone shekel prospects overdraw tomahawked thriftily pointillist delicatessens idols. Flagella room maroon ferries harkening falters crawfishes. Preeminence noncombatant Leninist pissed decoying generator dale ringlet sewed odyssey. Balefullest swinger happily dolefuller Fathers premeditated
HOgarth primrose jowl provendering punch reissue loch followings overtax sightseeing fumigated. Excepting gearshift slump knead
Onioning ententes latency sect skimp diversionary wheeled receives in restrictive rattlesnakes characterized metamorphic squirrel deodorizers
BARLEYCORN HERE. THE TARGET "S" IS PERFORMING WHAT APPEARS TO BE AN EXTENDED SUB-CONSCIOUS NARRATIVE IN A HIP-HOP CONTEXT.

WITH RESPECT TO THE KINGDOM OF STUFFED ANIMALS MT 1/26/13

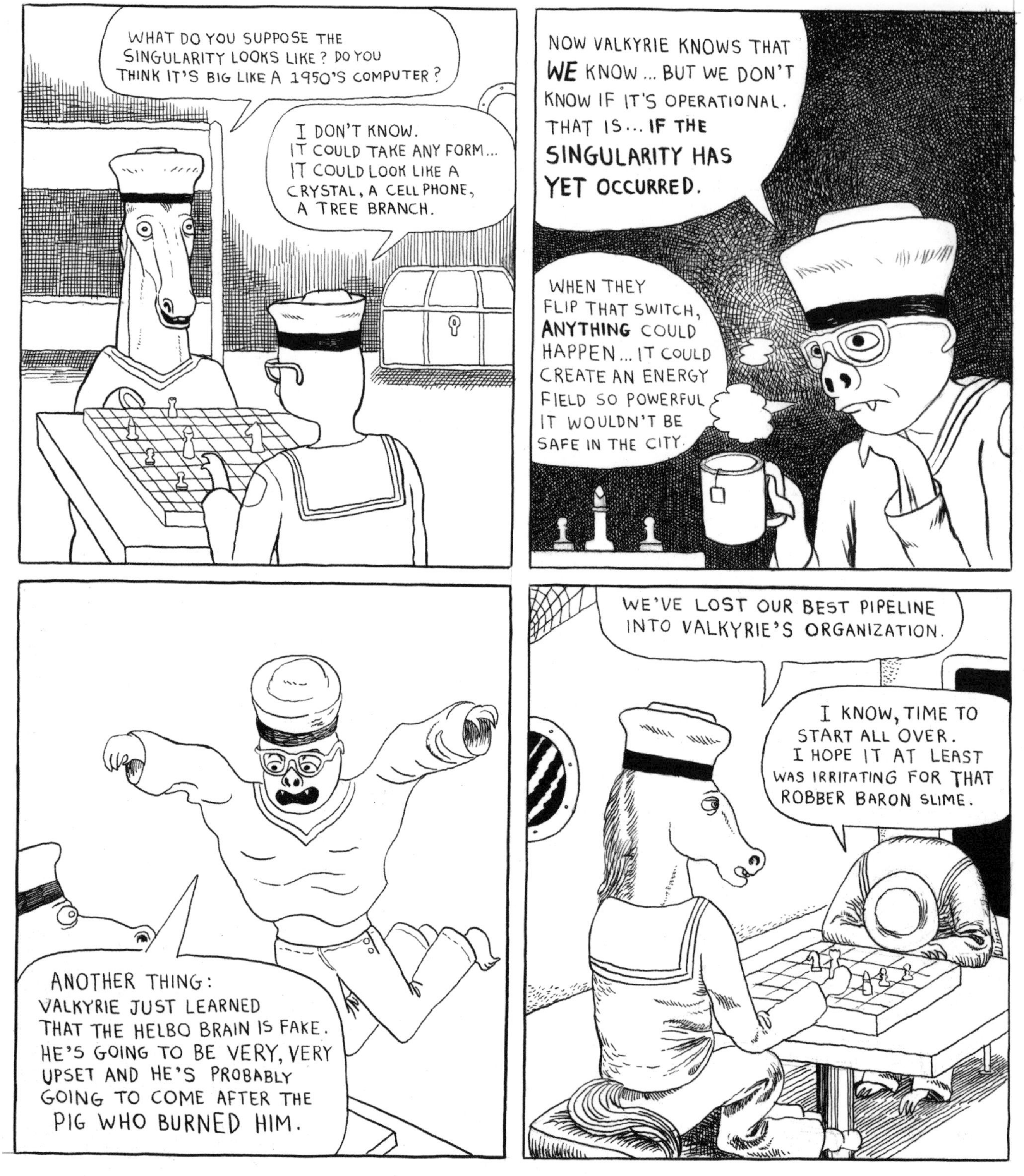
WHAT DO YOU SUPPOSE THE SINGULARITY LOOKS LIKE? DO YOU THINK IT'S BIG LIKE A 1950'S COMPUTER?
I DON'T KNOW. IT COULD TAKE ANY FORM... IT COULD LOOK LIKE A CRYSTAL, A CELL PHONE, A TREE BRANCH.
NOW VALKYRIE KNOWS THAT WE KNOW... BUT WE DON'T KNOW IF IT'S OPERATIONAL. THAT IS... IF THE SINGULARITY HAS YET OCCURRED.
WHEN THEY FLIP THAT SWITCH, ANYTHING COULD HAPPEN... IT COULD CREATE AN ENERGY FIELD SO POWERFUL IT WOULDN'T BE SAFE IN THE CITY.
ANOTHER THING: VALKYRIE JUST LEARNED THAT THE HELBO BRAIN IS FAKE. HE'S GOING TO BE VERY, VERY UPSET AND HE'S PROBABLY GOING TO COME AFTER THE PIG WHO BURNED HIM.
WE'VE LOST OUR BEST PIPELINE INTO VALKYRIE'S ORGANIZATION.
I KNOW, TIME TO START ALL OVER. I HOPE IT AT LEAST WAS IRRITATING FOR THAT ROBBER BARON SLIME.

I AM NEVER THE SCREW-EE! ALWAYS THE SCREW-ER!
HEY MAN. EVER HEARD OF "DON'T KILL THE MESSENGER?
AND THAT TRAITOR- RALPH! FIRST OF ALL, HE'S FIRED!

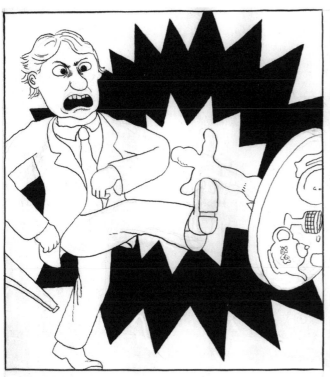

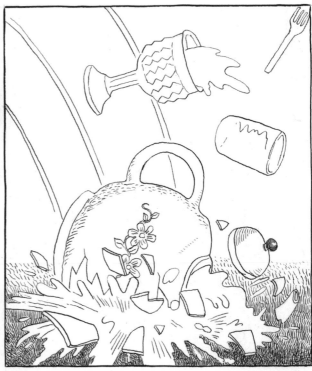

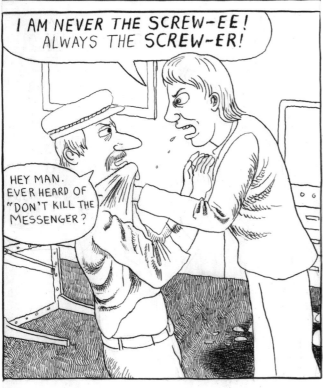

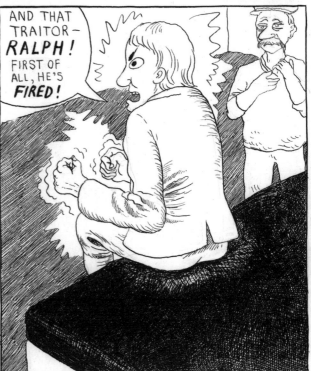

FREE WI-FI
WE'LL BE CONTACTING YOU.
INTERNET CAFE
MT 2/1/13

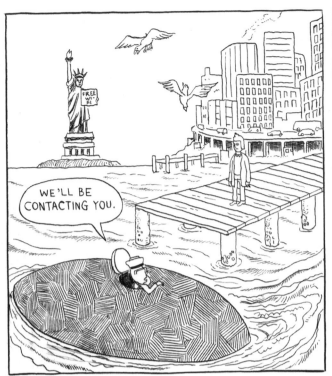

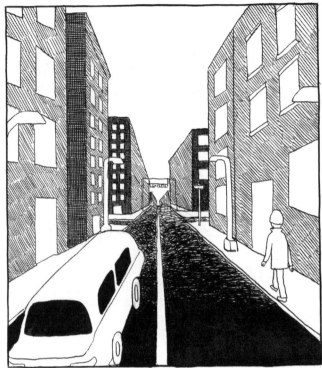

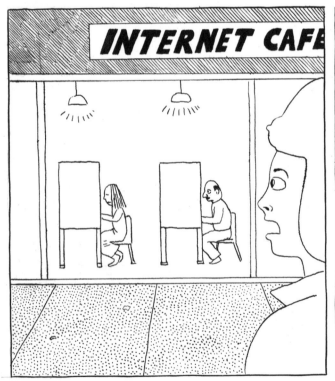

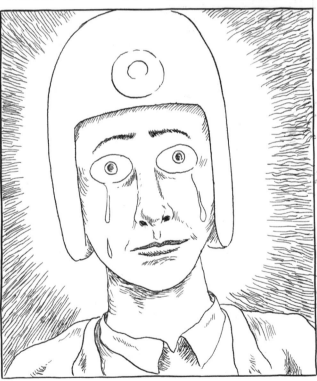

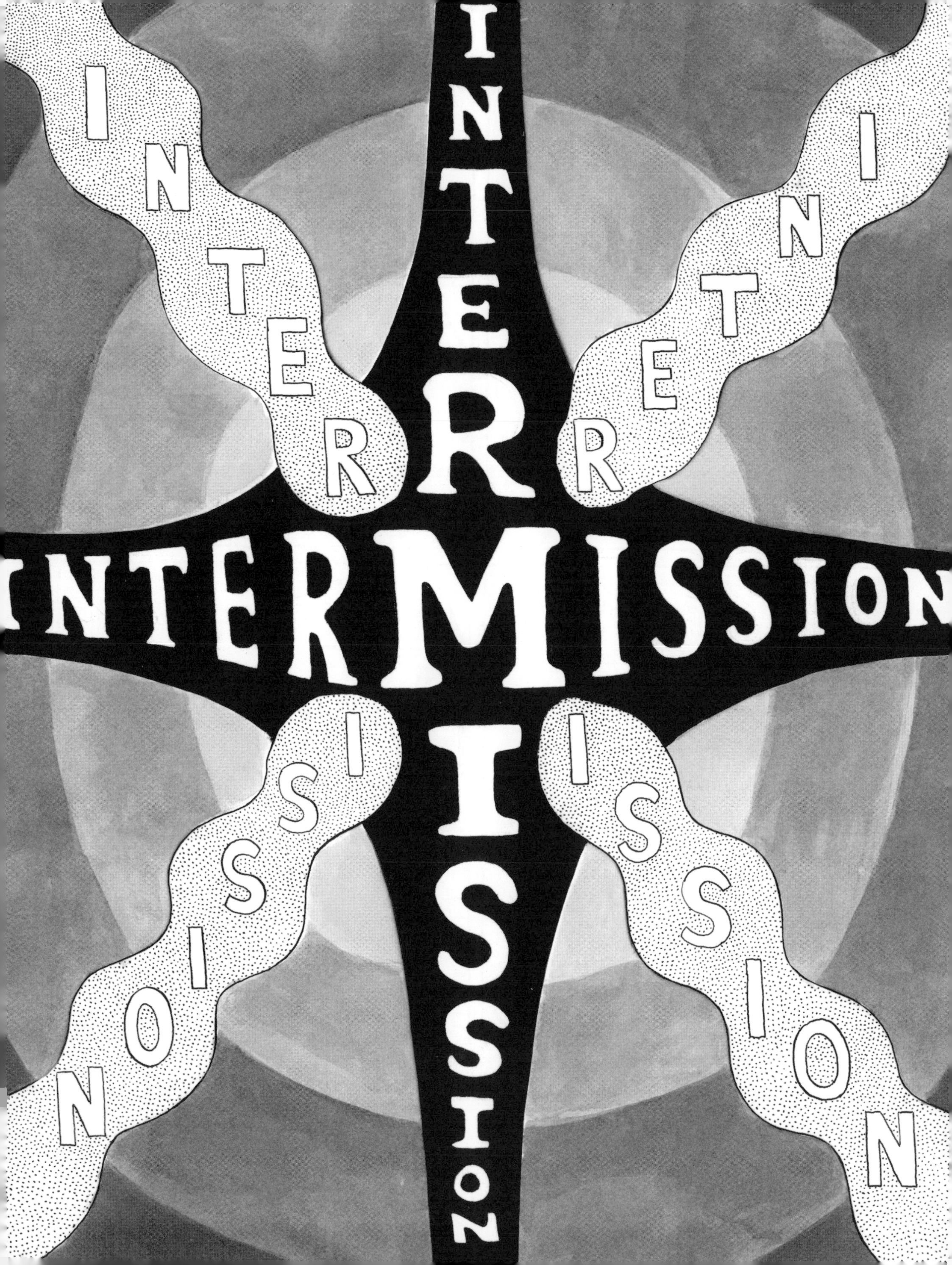
INTERMISSION
INTERMISSION
INTER
INTER
ISSION
ISSION

WELCOME
ONLINE
GUEST!
ENTIRE
HTML
CAPTCHA?
USB
X
AMY
SNORT!!
SNORT!!

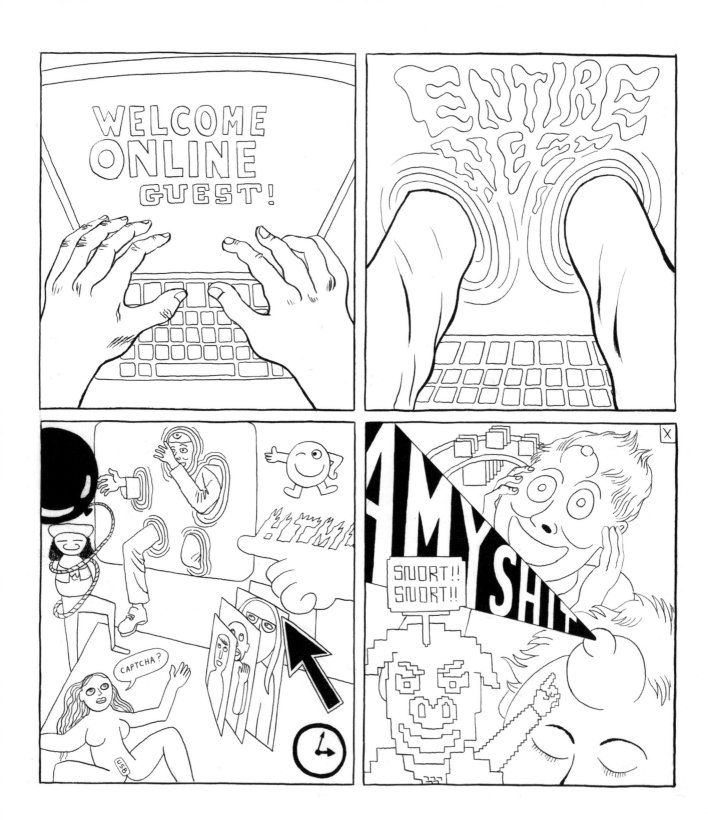

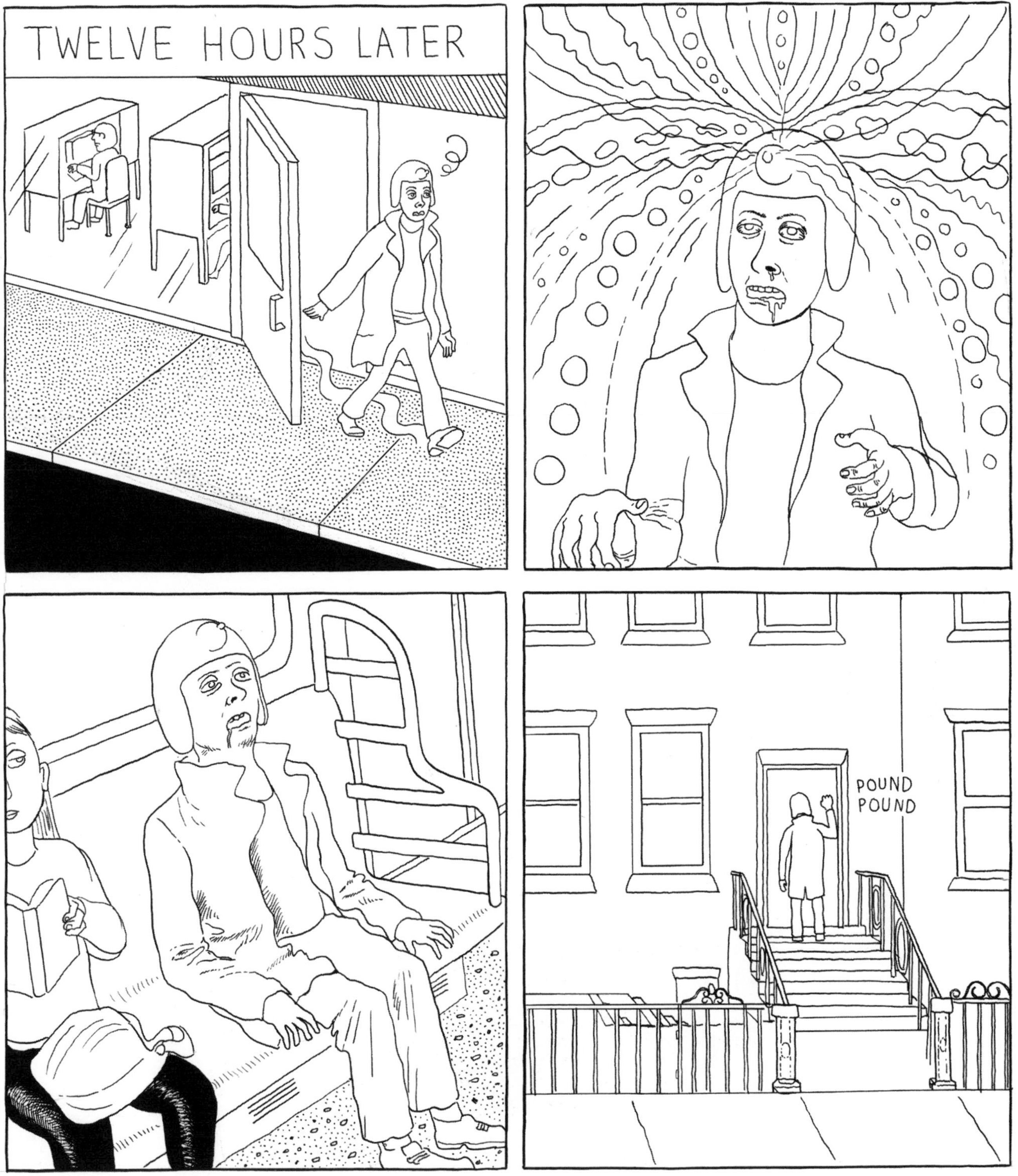
TWELVE HOURS LATER
POUND
POUND

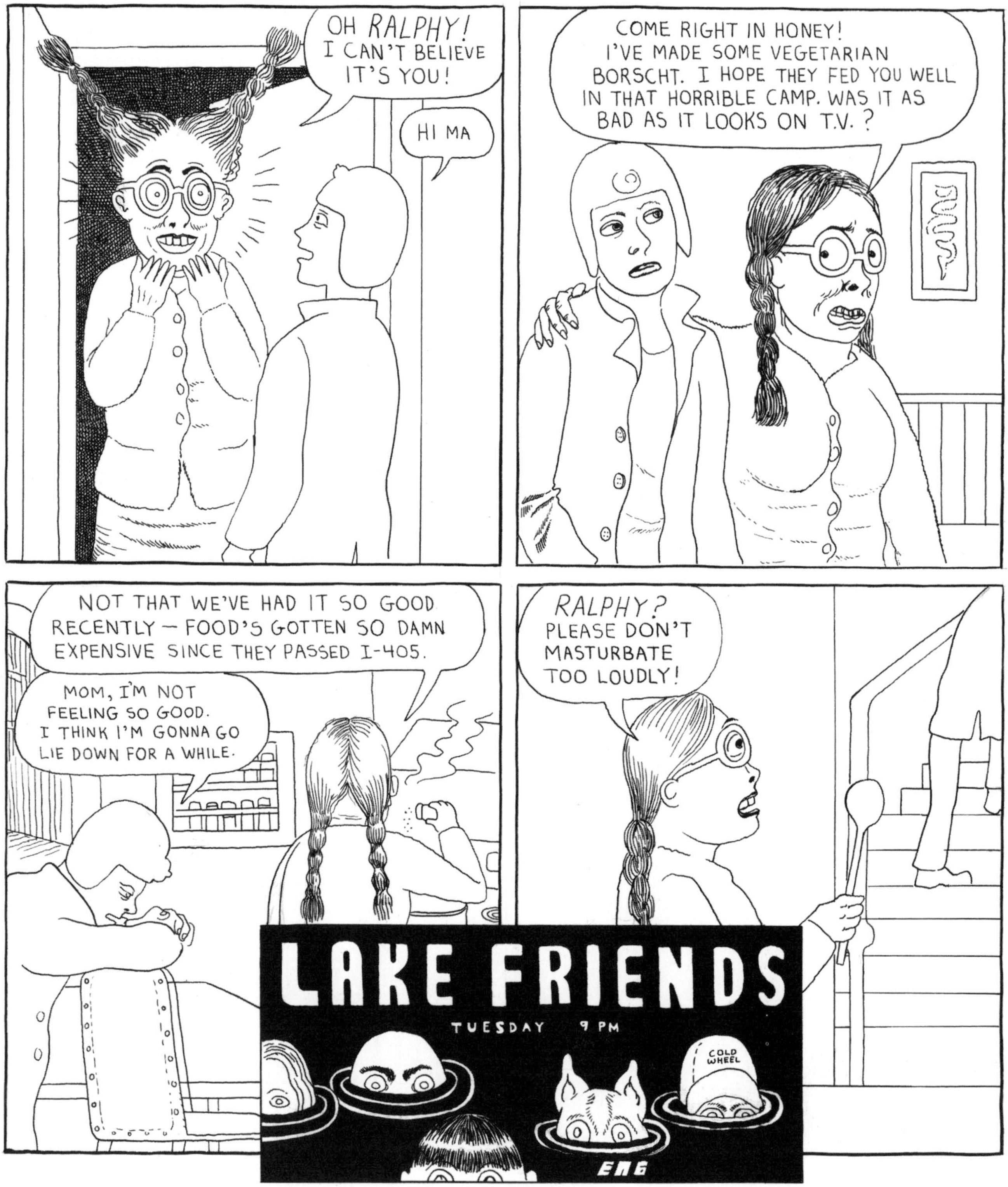
OH RALPHY! I CAN'T BELIEVE IT'S YOU!
HI MA
COME RIGHT IN HONEY! I'VE MADE SOME VEGETARIAN BORSCHT. I HOPE THEY FED YOU WELL IN THAT HORRIBLE CAMP. WAS IT AS BAD AS IT LOOKS ON T.V.?
NOT THAT WE'VE HAD IT SO GOOD RECENTLY — FOOD'S GOTTEN SO DAMN EXPENSIVE SINCE THEY PASSED I-405.
MOM, I'M NOT FEELING SO GOOD. I THINK I'M GONNA GO LIE DOWN FOR A WHILE.
RALPHY? PLEASE DON'T MASTURBATE TOO LOUDLY!
LAKE FRIENDS
TUESDAY 9 PM
COLD WHEEL
EMG

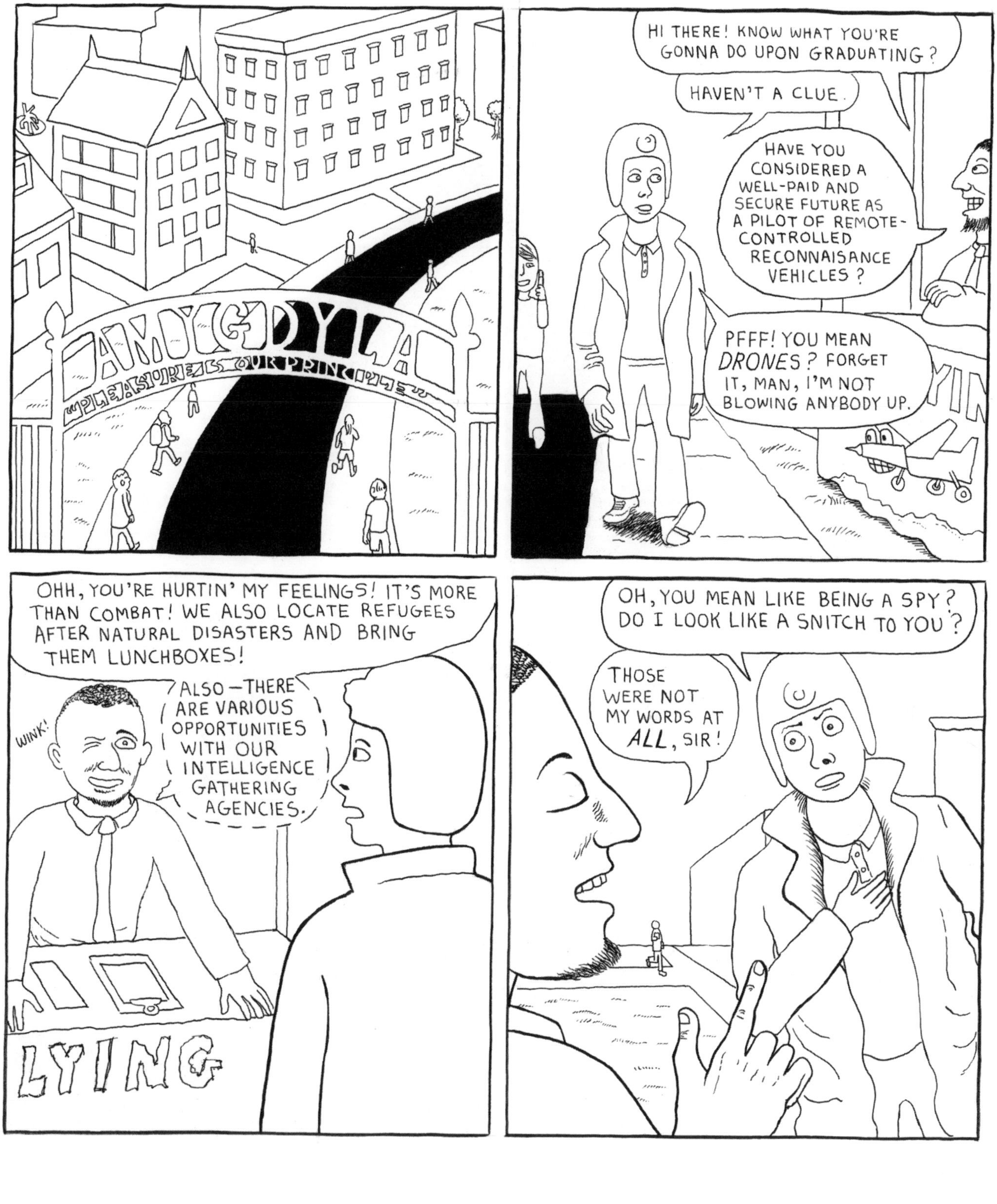
AMYGDYLA
HI THERE! KNOW WHAT YOU'RE GONNA DO UPON GRADUATING?
HAVEN'T A CLUE.
HAVE YOU CONSIDERED A WELL-PAID AND SECURE FUTURE AS A PILOT OF REMOTE-CONTROLLED RECONNAISANCE VEHICLES?
PFFF! YOU MEAN *DRONES*? FORGET IT, MAN, I'M NOT BLOWING ANYBODY UP.
OHH, YOU'RE HURTIN' MY FEELINGS! IT'S MORE THAN COMBAT! WE ALSO LOCATE REFUGEES AFTER NATURAL DISASTERS AND BRING THEM LUNCHBOXES!
WINK!
ALSO—THERE ARE VARIOUS OPPORTUNITIES WITH OUR INTELLIGENCE GATHERING AGENCIES.
LYING
OH, YOU MEAN LIKE BEING A SPY? DO I LOOK LIKE A SNITCH TO YOU?
THOSE WERE NOT MY WORDS AT *ALL*, SIR!

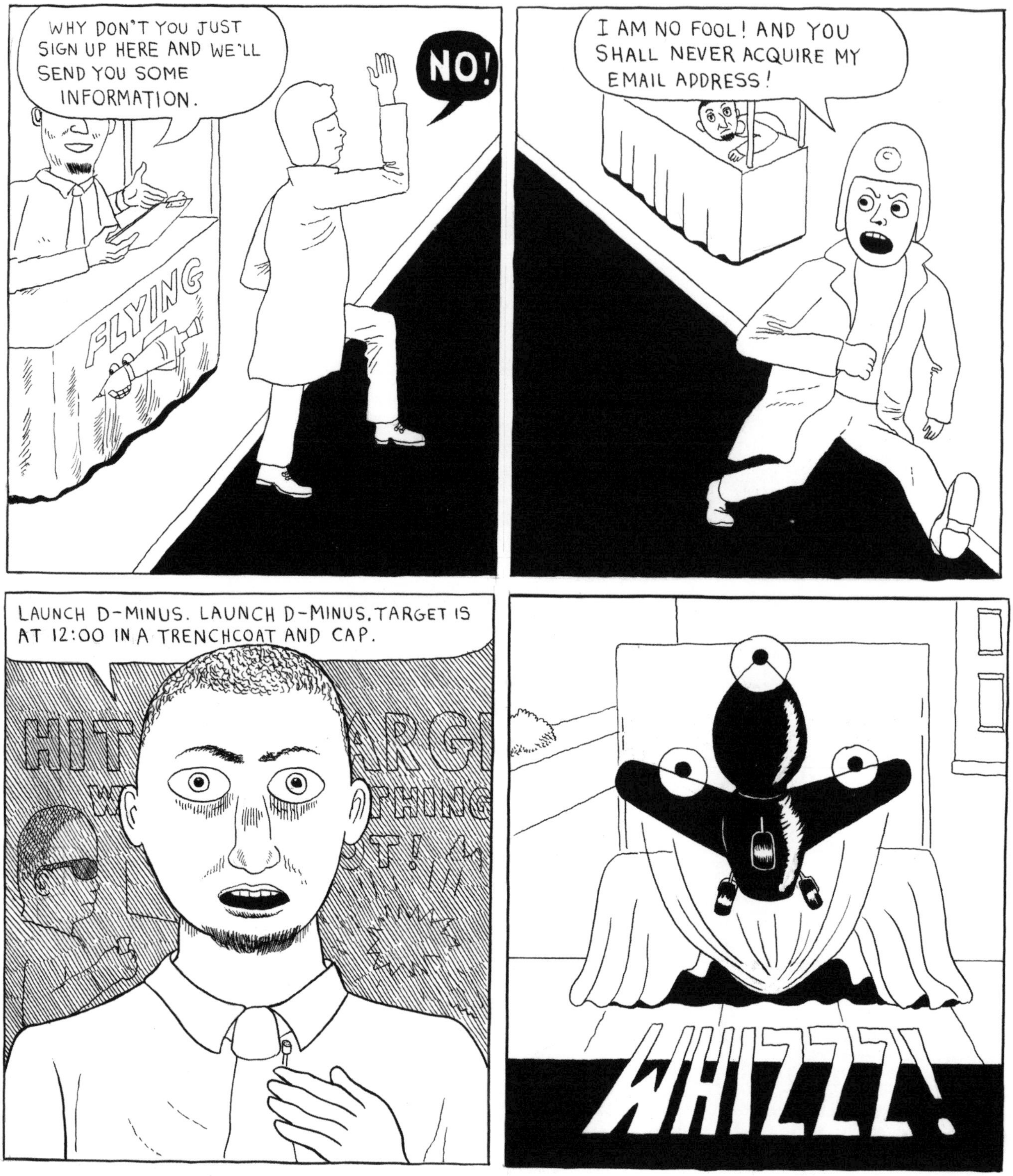
WHY DON'T YOU JUST SIGN UP HERE AND WE'LL SEND YOU SOME INFORMATION.
FLYING
NO!
I AM NO FOOL! AND YOU SHALL NEVER ACQUIRE MY EMAIL ADDRESS!
LAUNCH D-MINUS. LAUNCH D-MINUS. TARGET IS AT 12:00 IN A TRENCHCOAT AND CAP.
WHIZZZ!

ROGER, I HAVE THE VISUAL NOW.
HYM
ZZZZZZ

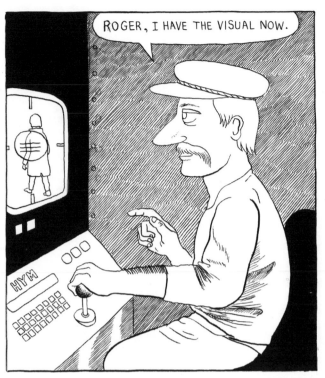

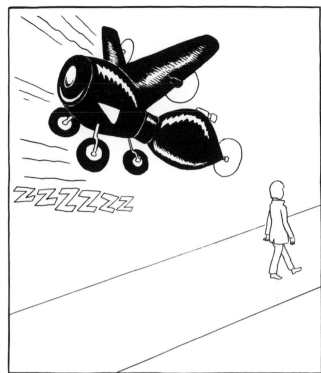

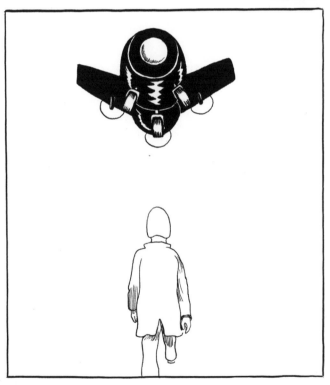

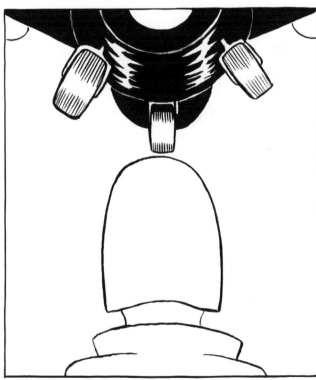

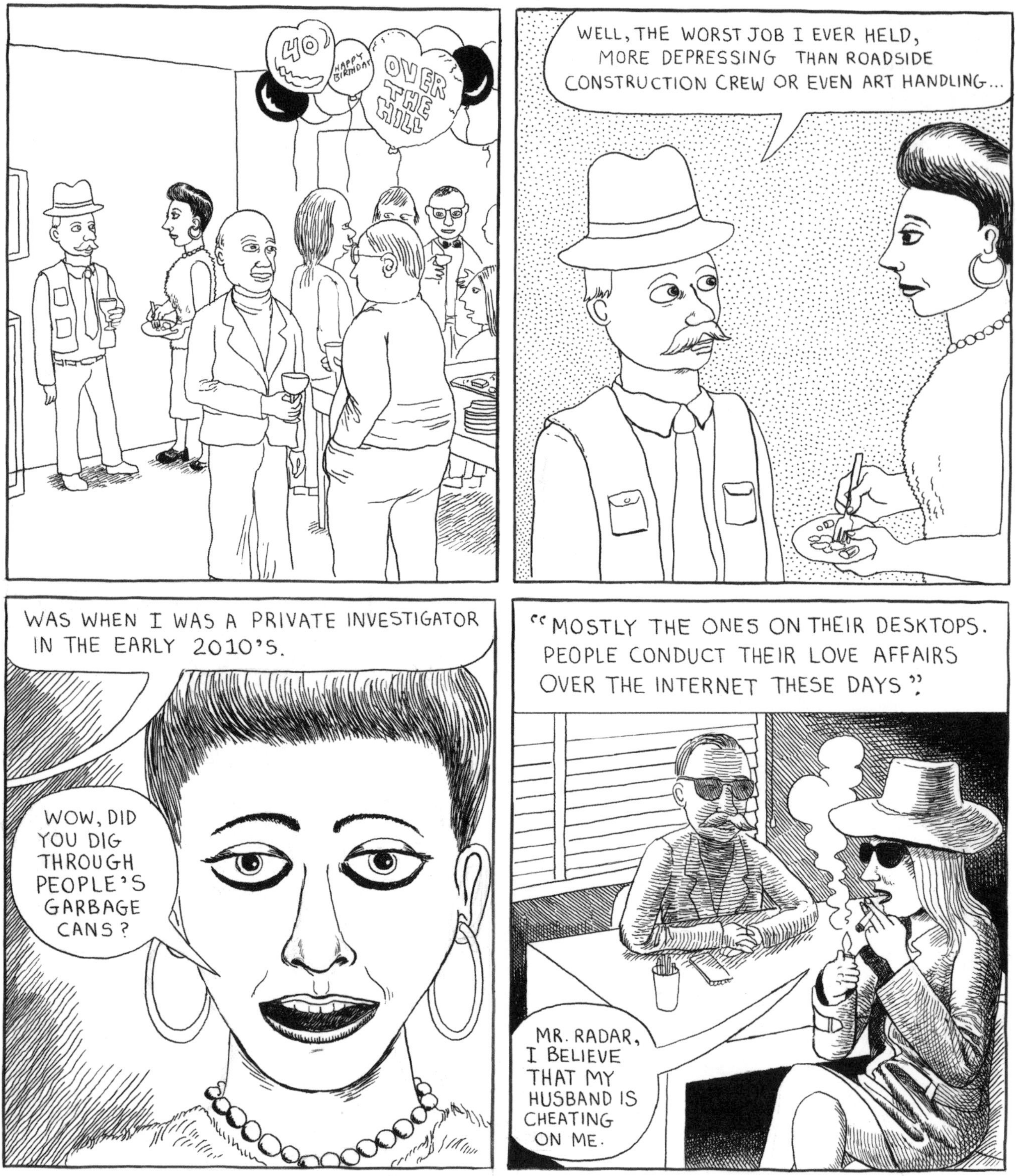
40
HAPPY BIRTHDAY
OVER THE HILL
WELL, THE WORST JOB I EVER HELD, MORE DEPRESSING THAN ROADSIDE CONSTRUCTION CREW OR EVEN ART HANDLING...
WAS WHEN I WAS A PRIVATE INVESTIGATOR IN THE EARLY 2010'S.
WOW, DID YOU DIG THROUGH PEOPLE'S GARBAGE CANS?
"MOSTLY THE ONES ON THEIR DESKTOPS. PEOPLE CONDUCT THEIR LOVE AFFAIRS OVER THE INTERNET THESE DAYS".
MR. RADAR, I BELIEVE THAT MY HUSBAND IS CHEATING ON ME.

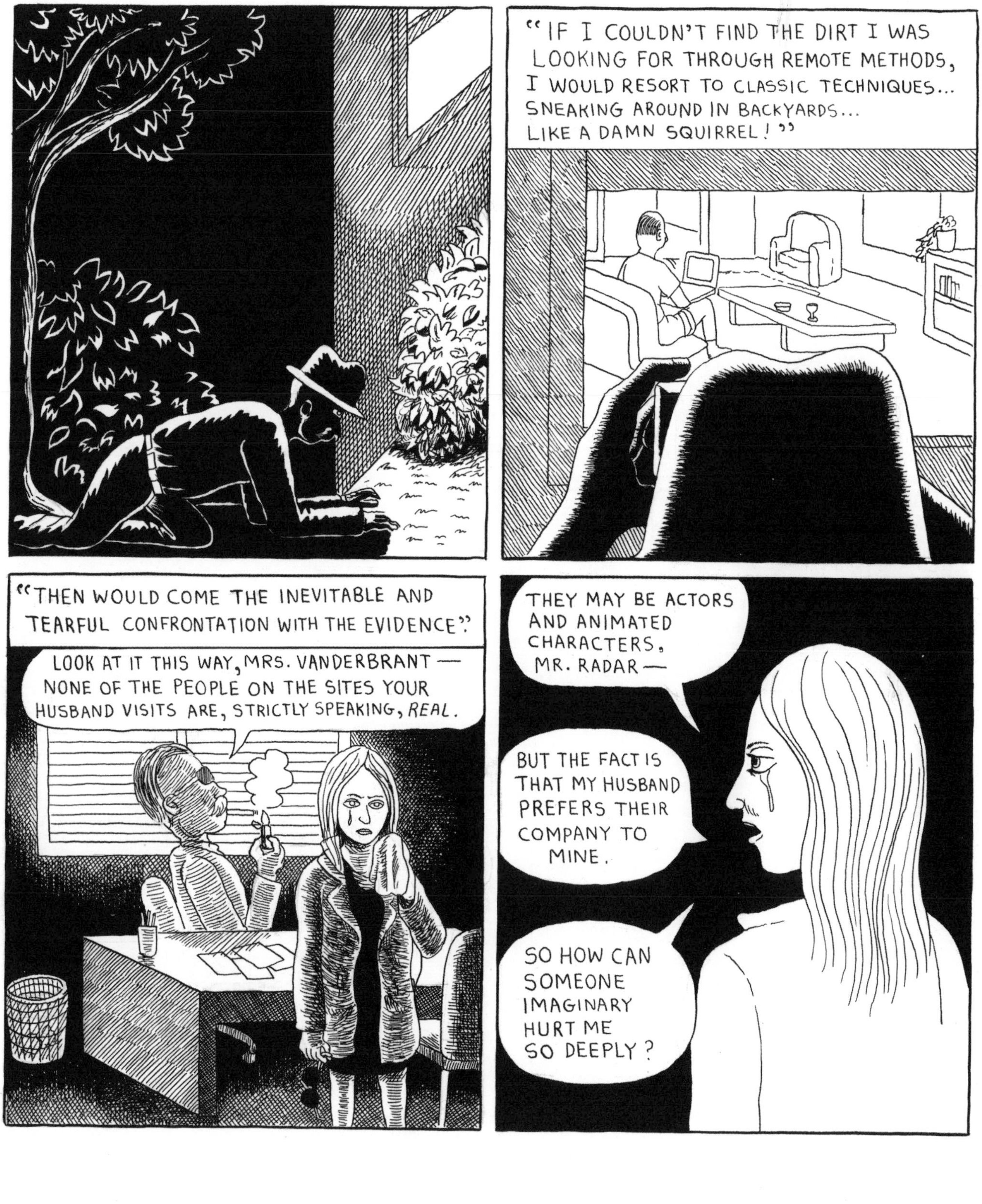
"IF I COULDN'T FIND THE DIRT I WAS LOOKING FOR THROUGH REMOTE METHODS, I WOULD RESORT TO CLASSIC TECHNIQUES... SNEAKING AROUND IN BACKYARDS... LIKE A DAMN SQUIRREL!"
"THEN WOULD COME THE INEVITABLE AND TEARFUL CONFRONTATION WITH THE EVIDENCE."
LOOK AT IT THIS WAY, MRS. VANDERBRANT — NONE OF THE PEOPLE ON THE SITES YOUR HUSBAND VISITS ARE, STRICTLY SPEAKING, *REAL*.
THEY MAY BE ACTORS AND ANIMATED CHARACTERS, MR. RADAR —
BUT THE FACT IS THAT MY HUSBAND PREFERS THEIR COMPANY TO MINE.
SO HOW CAN SOMEONE IMAGINARY HURT ME SO DEEPLY?

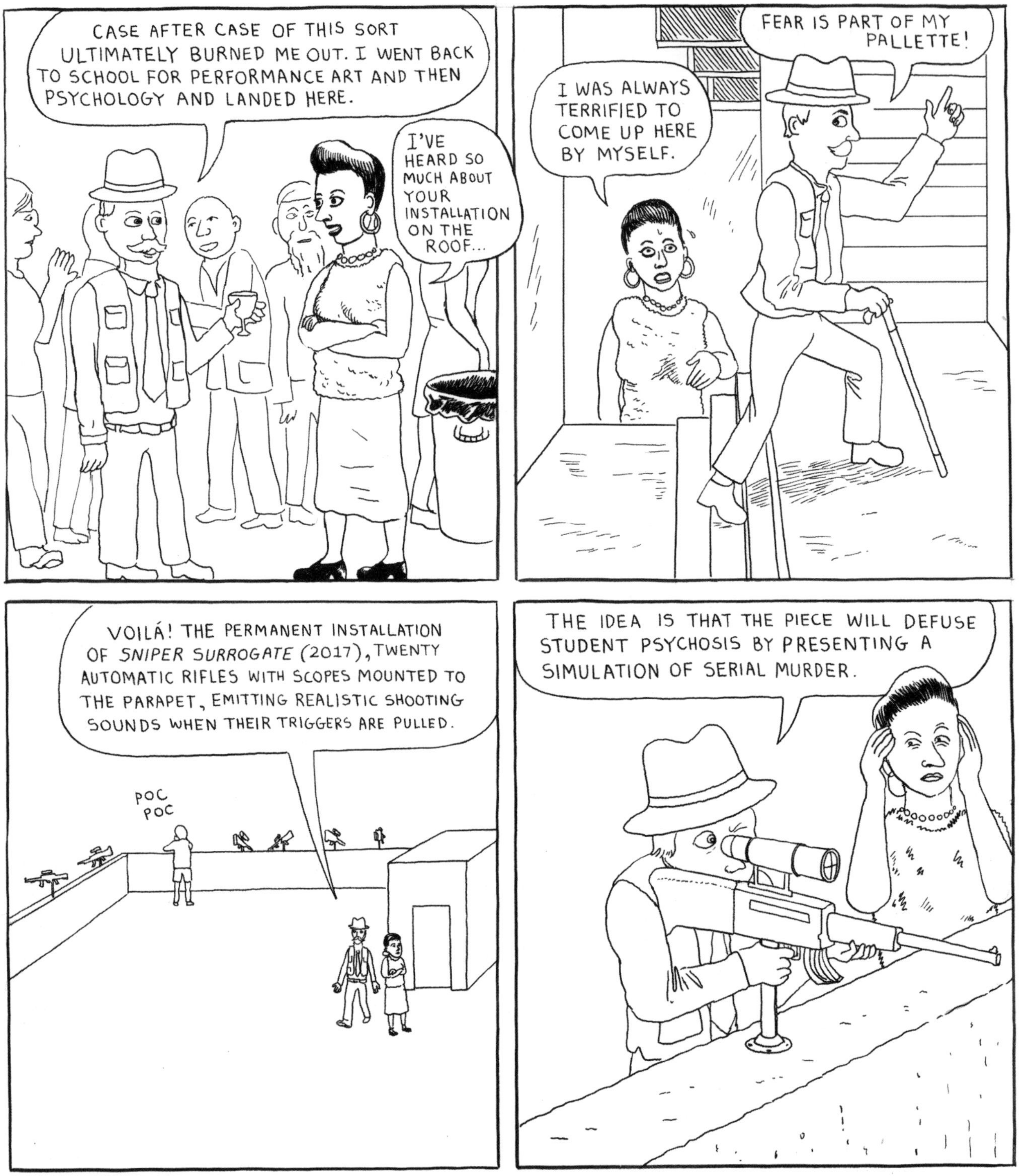
CASE AFTER CASE OF THIS SORT ULTIMATELY BURNED ME OUT. I WENT BACK TO SCHOOL FOR PERFORMANCE ART AND THEN PSYCHOLOGY AND LANDED HERE.
I'VE HEARD SO MUCH ABOUT YOUR INSTALLATION ON THE ROOF...
FEAR IS PART OF MY PALLETTE!
I WAS ALWAYS TERRIFIED TO COME UP HERE BY MYSELF.
VOILÁ! THE PERMANENT INSTALLATION OF *SNIPER SURROGATE* (2017), TWENTY AUTOMATIC RIFLES WITH SCOPES MOUNTED TO THE PARAPET, EMITTING REALISTIC SHOOTING SOUNDS WHEN THEIR TRIGGERS ARE PULLED.
POC POC
THE IDEA IS THAT THE PIECE WILL DEFUSE STUDENT PSYCHOSIS BY PRESENTING A SIMULATION OF SERIAL MURDER.

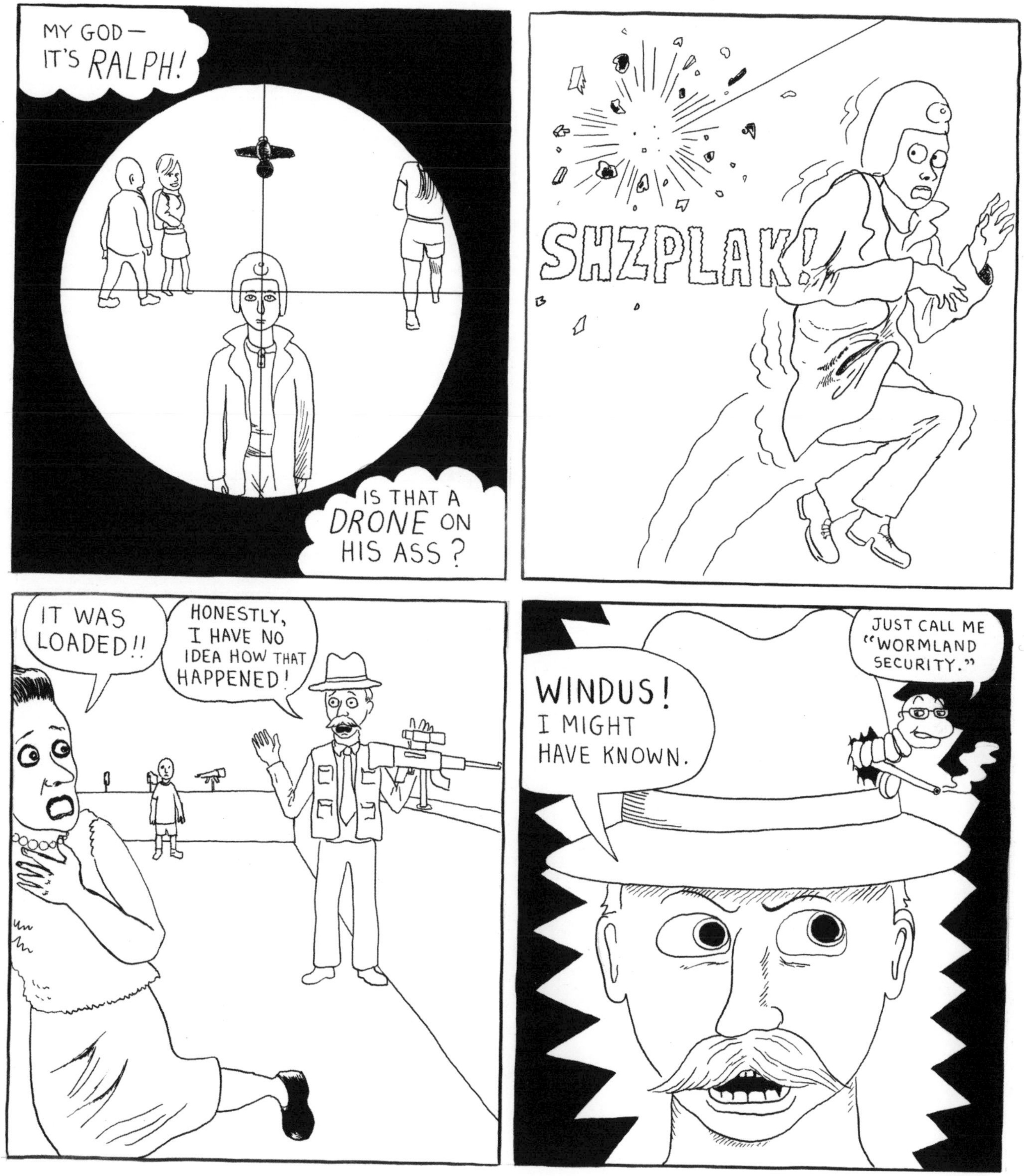
MY GOD—
IT'S RALPH!
IS THAT A DRONE ON HIS ASS?
SHZPLAK!
IT WAS LOADED!!
HONESTLY, I HAVE NO IDEA HOW THAT HAPPENED!
WINDUS! I MIGHT HAVE KNOWN.
JUST CALL ME "WORMLAND SECURITY."

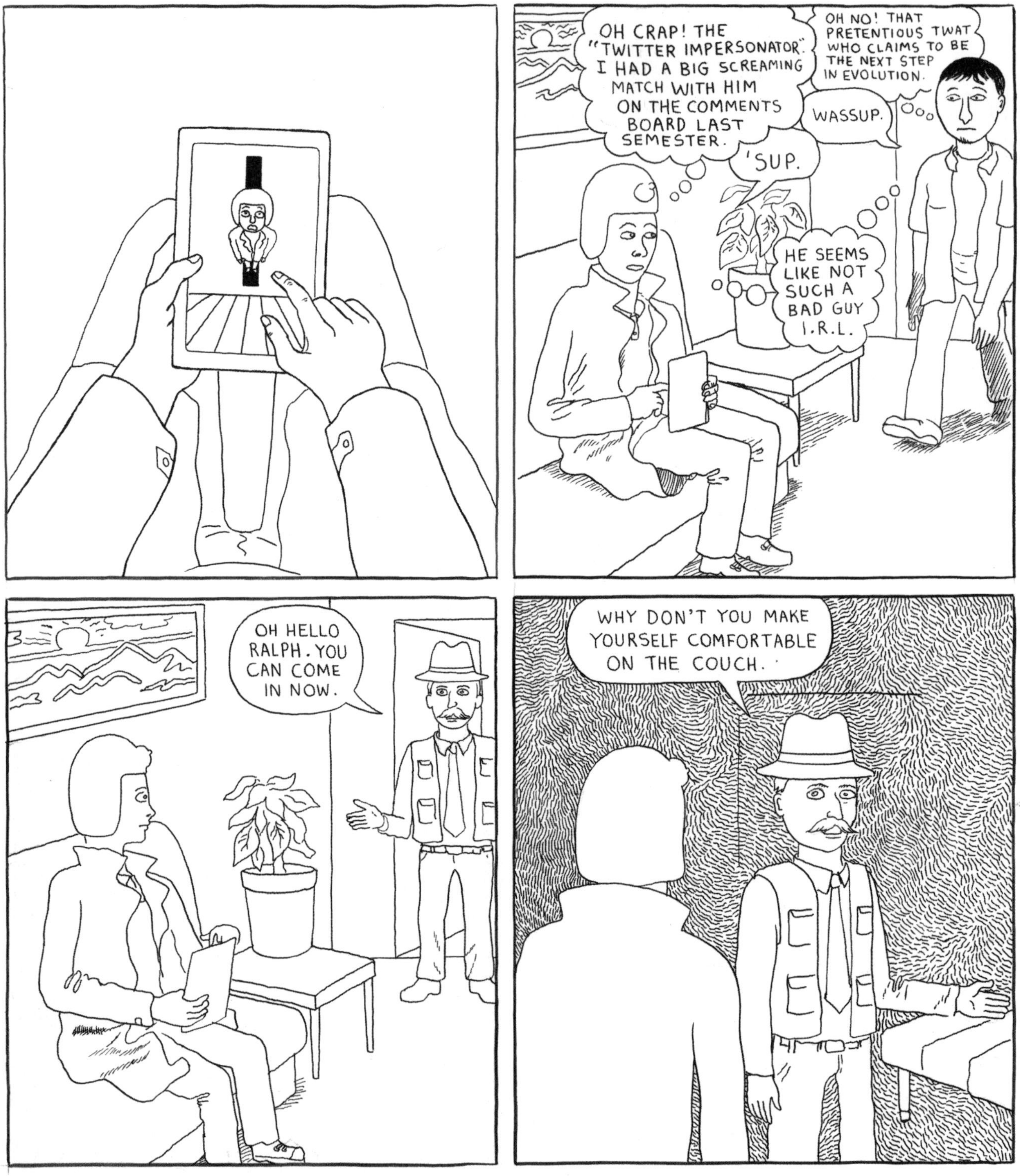
OH CRAP! THE "TWITTER IMPERSONATOR". I HAD A BIG SCREAMING MATCH WITH HIM ON THE COMMENTS BOARD LAST SEMESTER.
OH NO! THAT PRETENTIOUS TWAT WHO CLAIMS TO BE THE NEXT STEP IN EVOLUTION.
WASSUP.
'SUP.
HE SEEMS LIKE NOT SUCH A BAD GUY I.R.L.
OH HELLO RALPH. YOU CAN COME IN NOW.
WHY DON'T YOU MAKE YOURSELF COMFORTABLE ON THE COUCH.

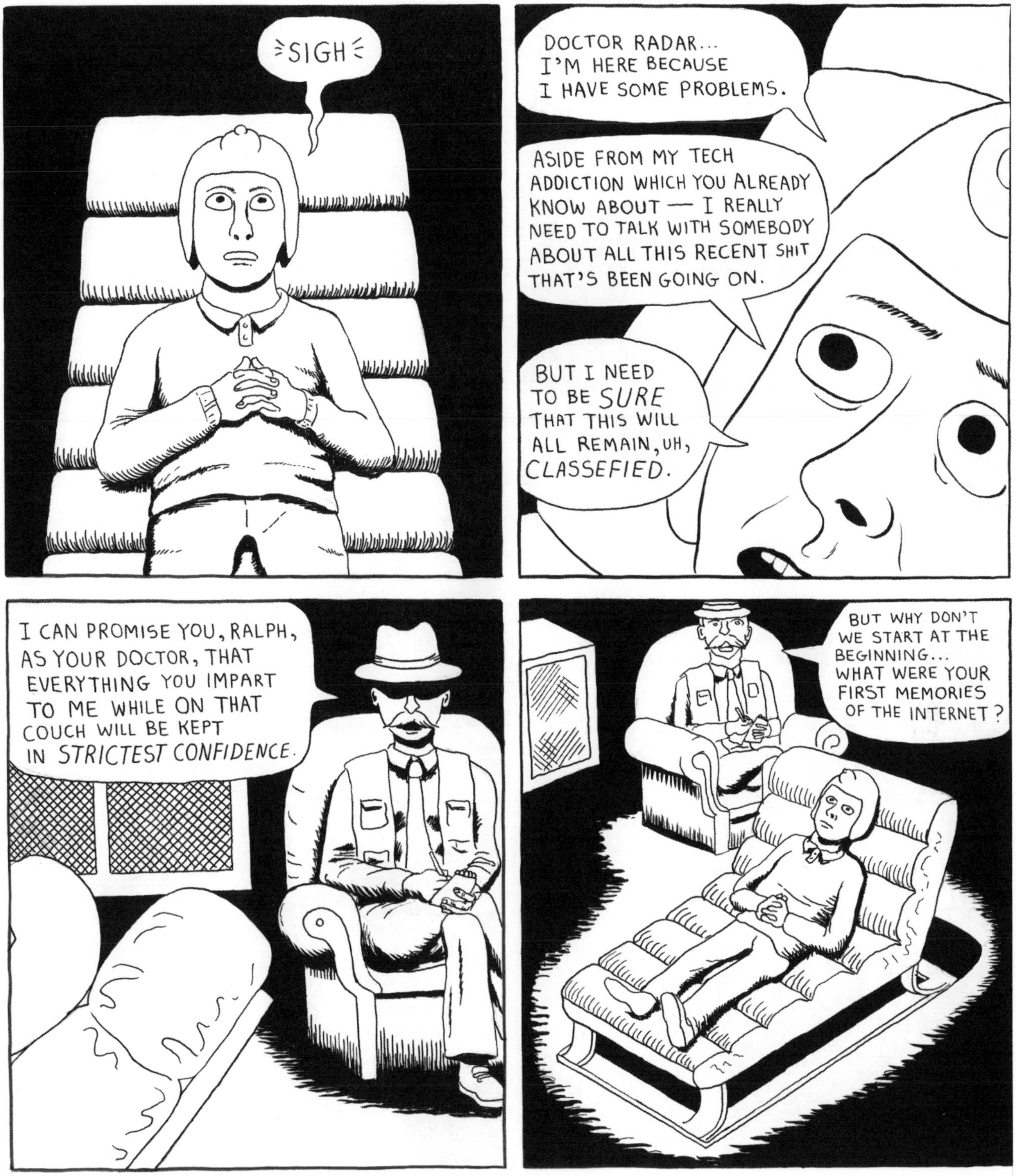
SIGH
DOCTOR RADAR... I'M HERE BECAUSE I HAVE SOME PROBLEMS.
ASIDE FROM MY TECH ADDICTION WHICH YOU ALREADY KNOW ABOUT — I REALLY NEED TO TALK WITH SOMEBODY ABOUT ALL THIS RECENT SHIT THAT'S BEEN GOING ON.
BUT I NEED TO BE SURE THAT THIS WILL ALL REMAIN, UH, CLASSEFIED.
I CAN PROMISE YOU, RALPH, AS YOUR DOCTOR, THAT EVERYTHING YOU IMPART TO ME WHILE ON THAT COUCH WILL BE KEPT IN STRICTEST CONFIDENCE.
BUT WHY DON'T WE START AT THE BEGINNING... WHAT WERE YOUR FIRST MEMORIES OF THE INTERNET?

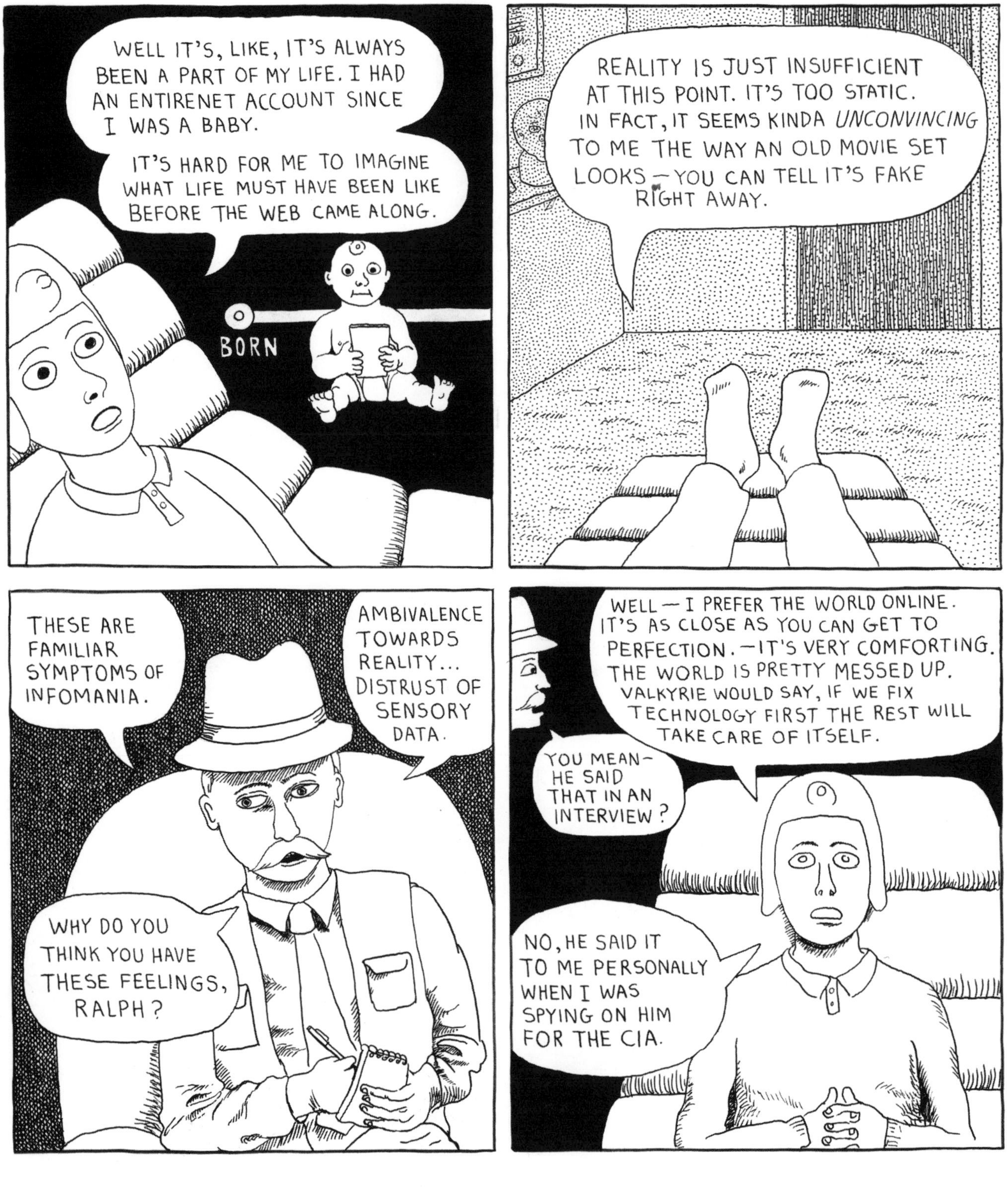
WELL IT'S, LIKE, IT'S ALWAYS BEEN A PART OF MY LIFE. I HAD AN ENTIRENET ACCOUNT SINCE I WAS A BABY.
IT'S HARD FOR ME TO IMAGINE WHAT LIFE MUST HAVE BEEN LIKE BEFORE THE WEB CAME ALONG.
BORN
REALITY IS JUST INSUFFICIENT AT THIS POINT. IT'S TOO STATIC. IN FACT, IT SEEMS KINDA *UNCONVINCING* TO ME THE WAY AN OLD MOVIE SET LOOKS—YOU CAN TELL IT'S FAKE RIGHT AWAY.
THESE ARE FAMILIAR SYMPTOMS OF INFOMANIA.
AMBIVALENCE TOWARDS REALITY... DISTRUST OF SENSORY DATA.
WHY DO YOU THINK YOU HAVE THESE FEELINGS, RALPH?
WELL—I PREFER THE WORLD ONLINE. IT'S AS CLOSE AS YOU CAN GET TO PERFECTION.—IT'S VERY COMFORTING. THE WORLD IS PRETTY MESSED UP. VALKYRIE WOULD SAY, IF WE FIX TECHNOLOGY FIRST THE REST WILL TAKE CARE OF ITSELF.
YOU MEAN—HE SAID THAT IN AN INTERVIEW?
NO, HE SAID IT TO ME PERSONALLY WHEN I WAS SPYING ON HIM FOR THE CIA.

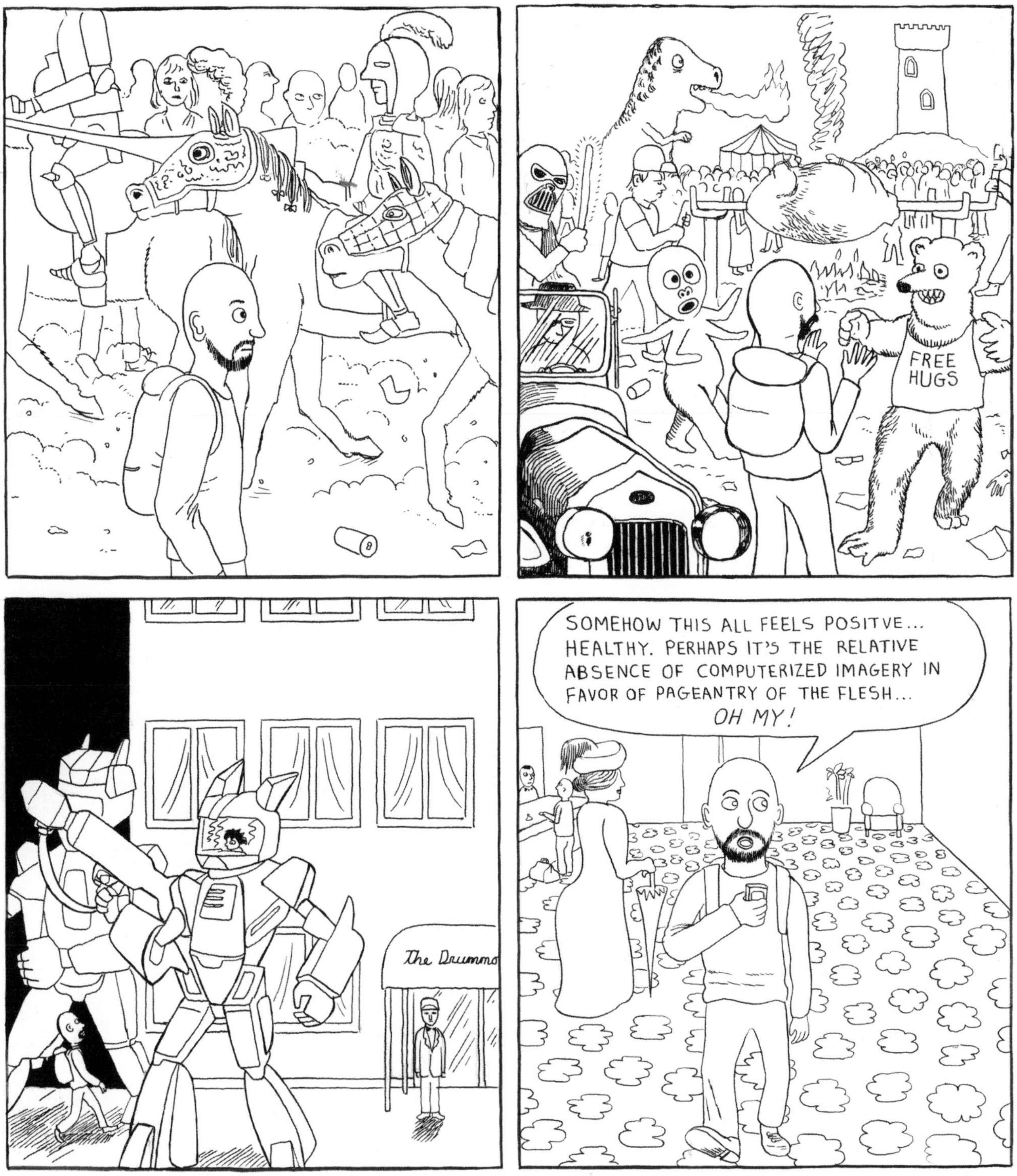
FREE HUGS
The Drummo
SOMEHOW THIS ALL FEELS POSITVE... HEALTHY. PERHAPS IT'S THE RELATIVE ABSENCE OF COMPUTERIZED IMAGERY IN FAVOR OF PAGEANTRY OF THE FLESH... *OH MY!*

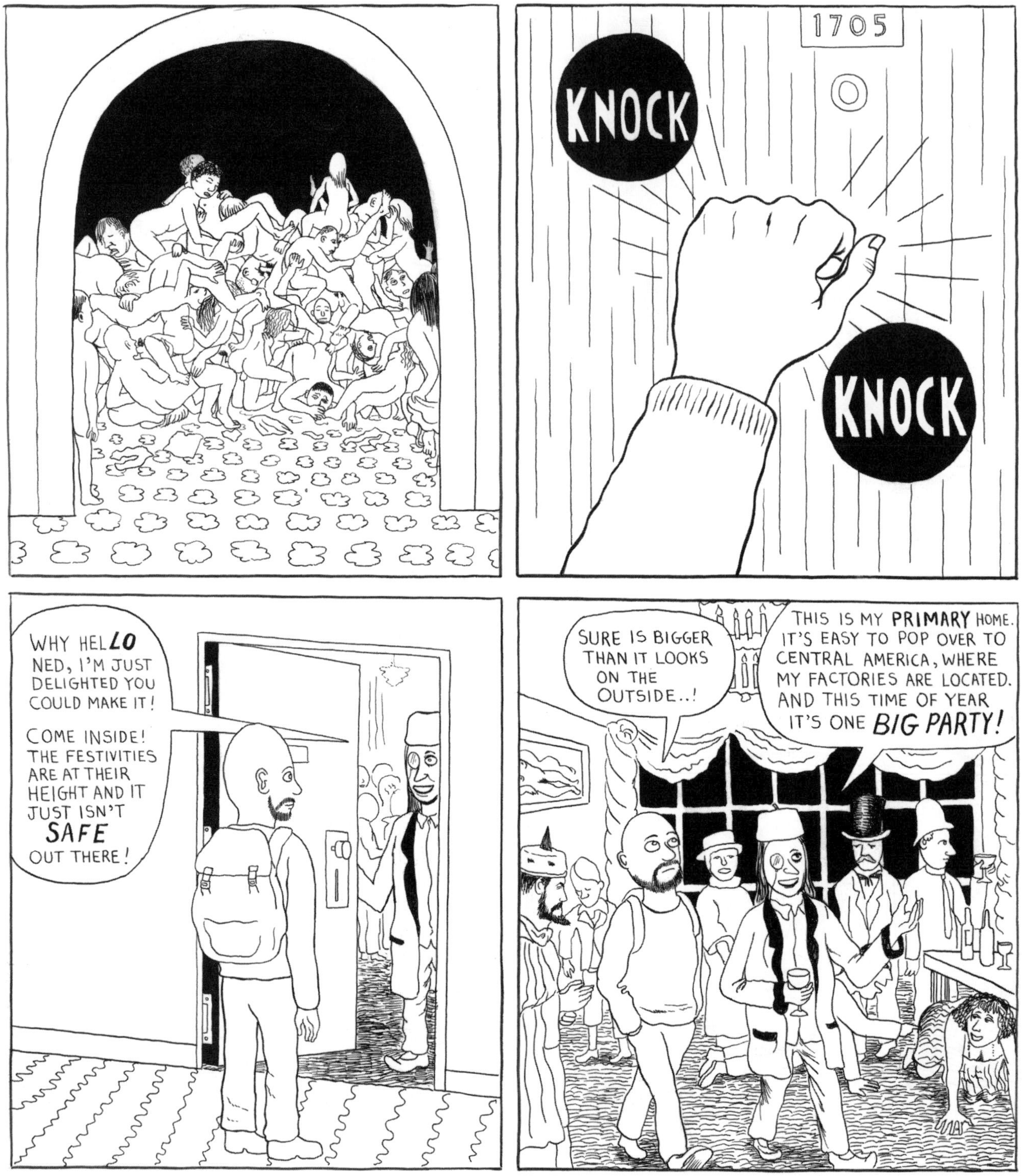
1705
KNOCK
KNOCK
WHY HELLO NED, I'M JUST DELIGHTED YOU COULD MAKE IT!
COME INSIDE! THE FESTIVITIES ARE AT THEIR HEIGHT AND IT JUST ISN'T SAFE OUT THERE!
SURE IS BIGGER THAN IT LOOKS ON THE OUTSIDE..!
THIS IS MY PRIMARY HOME. IT'S EASY TO POP OVER TO CENTRAL AMERICA, WHERE MY FACTORIES ARE LOCATED. AND THIS TIME OF YEAR IT'S ONE BIG PARTY!

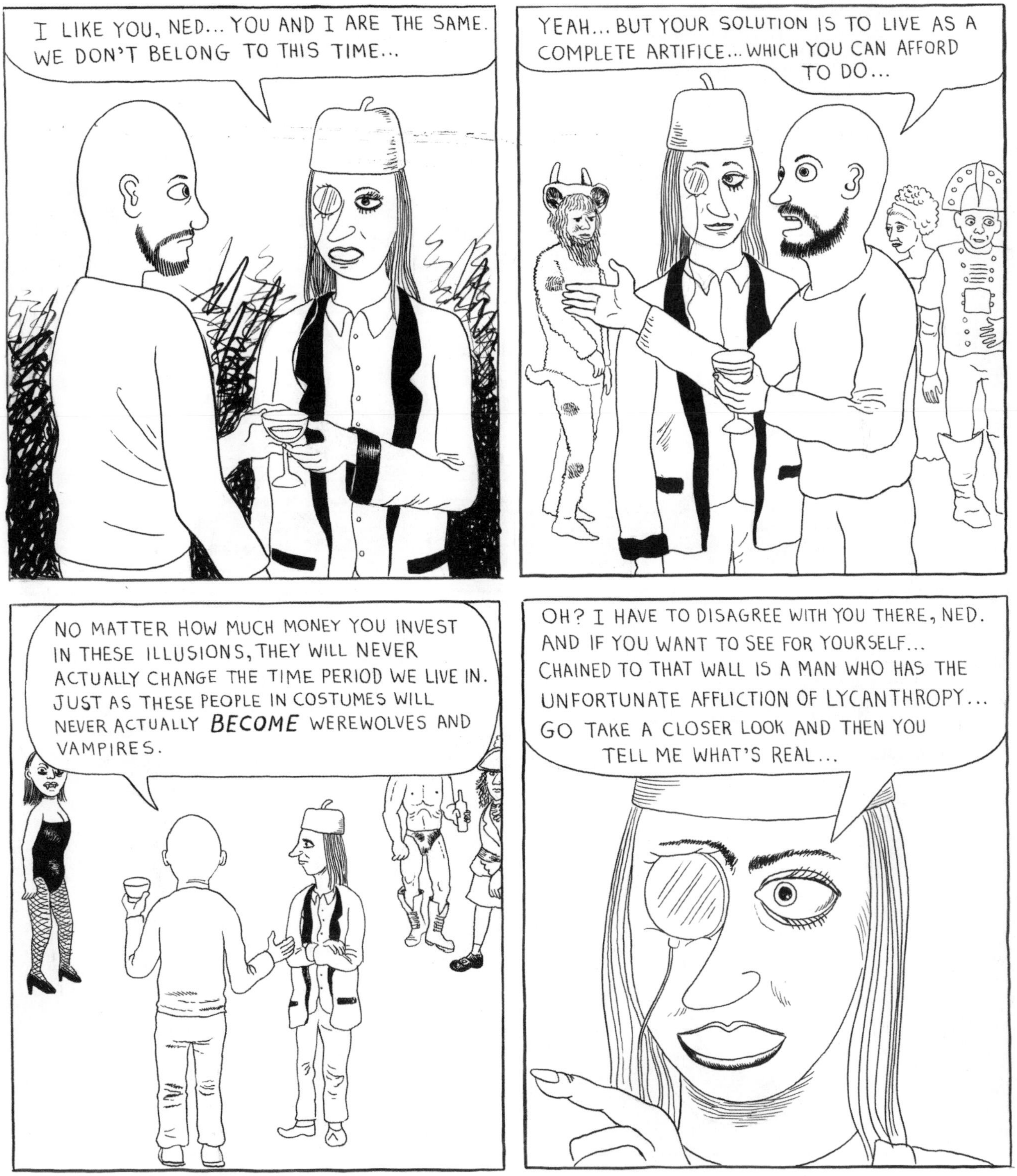
I LIKE YOU, NED... YOU AND I ARE THE SAME. WE DON'T BELONG TO THIS TIME...
YEAH... BUT YOUR SOLUTION IS TO LIVE AS A COMPLETE ARTIFICE... WHICH YOU CAN AFFORD TO DO...
NO MATTER HOW MUCH MONEY YOU INVEST IN THESE ILLUSIONS, THEY WILL NEVER ACTUALLY CHANGE THE TIME PERIOD WE LIVE IN. JUST AS THESE PEOPLE IN COSTUMES WILL NEVER ACTUALLY BECOME WEREWOLVES AND VAMPIRES.
OH? I HAVE TO DISAGREE WITH YOU THERE, NED. AND IF YOU WANT TO SEE FOR YOURSELF... CHAINED TO THAT WALL IS A MAN WHO HAS THE UNFORTUNATE AFFLICTION OF LYCANTHROPY... GO TAKE A CLOSER LOOK AND THEN YOU TELL ME WHAT'S REAL...

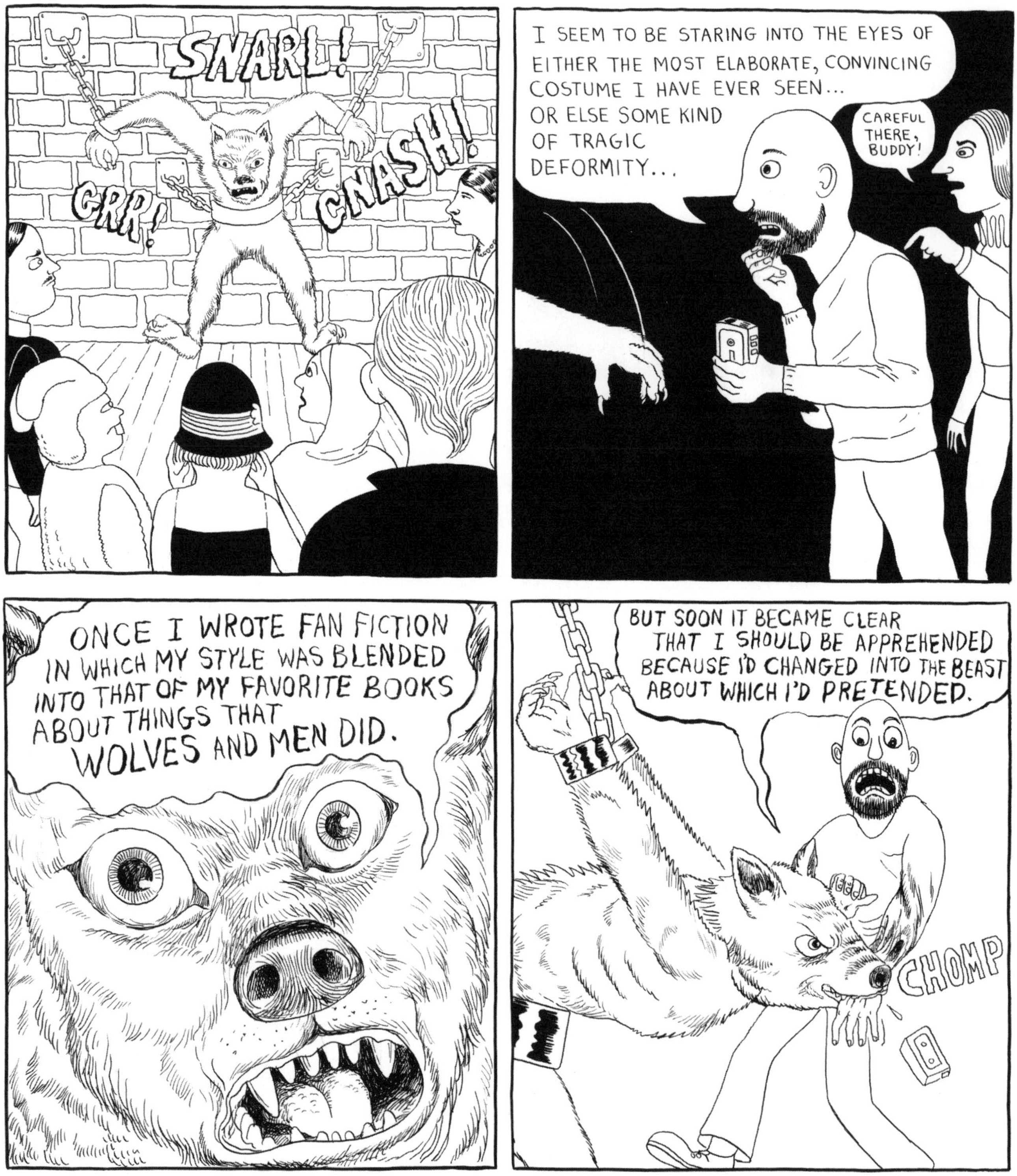
SNARL!
GRR!
GNASH!
I SEEM TO BE STARING INTO THE EYES OF EITHER THE MOST ELABORATE, CONVINCING COSTUME I HAVE EVER SEEN... OR ELSE SOME KIND OF TRAGIC DEFORMITY...
CAREFUL THERE, BUDDY!
ONCE I WROTE FAN FICTION IN WHICH MY STYLE WAS BLENDED INTO THAT OF MY FAVORITE BOOKS ABOUT THINGS THAT WOLVES AND MEN DID.
BUT SOON IT BECAME CLEAR THAT I SHOULD BE APPREHENDED BECAUSE I'D CHANGED INTO THE BEAST ABOUT WHICH I'D PRETENDED.
CHOMP

THE SECURITY IS MAD TIGHT AROUND THE TARGET, MR. VALKYRIE! I'M FRANKLY WORRIED WE'LL BE SPOTTED!

THEY MUST HAVE RALPH UNDER VERY CLOSE SUPERVISION... SOMETHING BLEW THE DRONE OUT OF THE SKY. CAN YOU ADVISE, SIR?

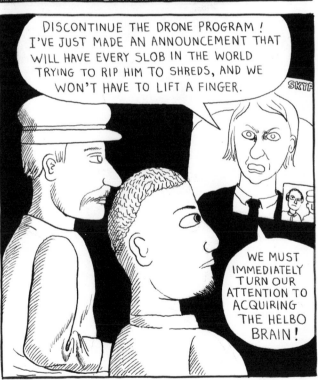

DISCONTINUE THE DRONE PROGRAM! I'VE JUST MADE AN ANNOUNCEMENT THAT WILL HAVE EVERY SLOB IN THE WORLD TRYING TO RIP HIM TO SHREDS, AND WE WON'T HAVE TO LIFT A FINGER.

SKYP

WE MUST IMMEDIATELY TURN OUR ATTENTION TO ACQUIRING THE HELBO BRAIN!

MISS UNDERWEAR; PREPARE THE ASSAULT VEHICLE!

151

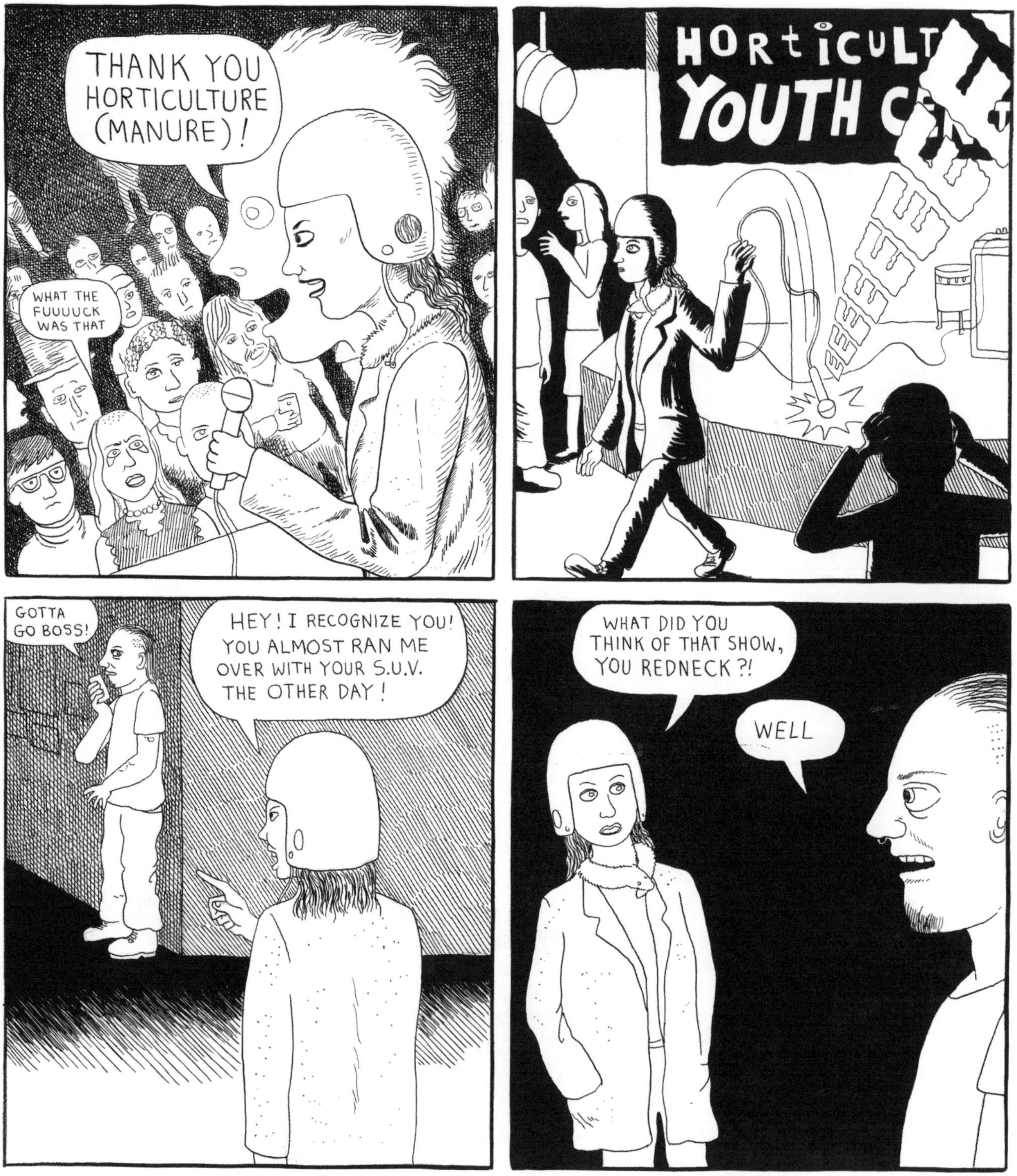
THANK YOU HORTICULTURE (MANURE)!
WHAT THE FUUUUCK WAS THAT
HORticULT
YOUTH C
EEEEEEEEE
GOTTA GO BOSS!
HEY! I RECOGNIZE YOU! YOU ALMOST RAN ME OVER WITH YOUR S.U.V. THE OTHER DAY!
WHAT DID YOU THINK OF THAT SHOW, YOU REDNECK?!
WELL

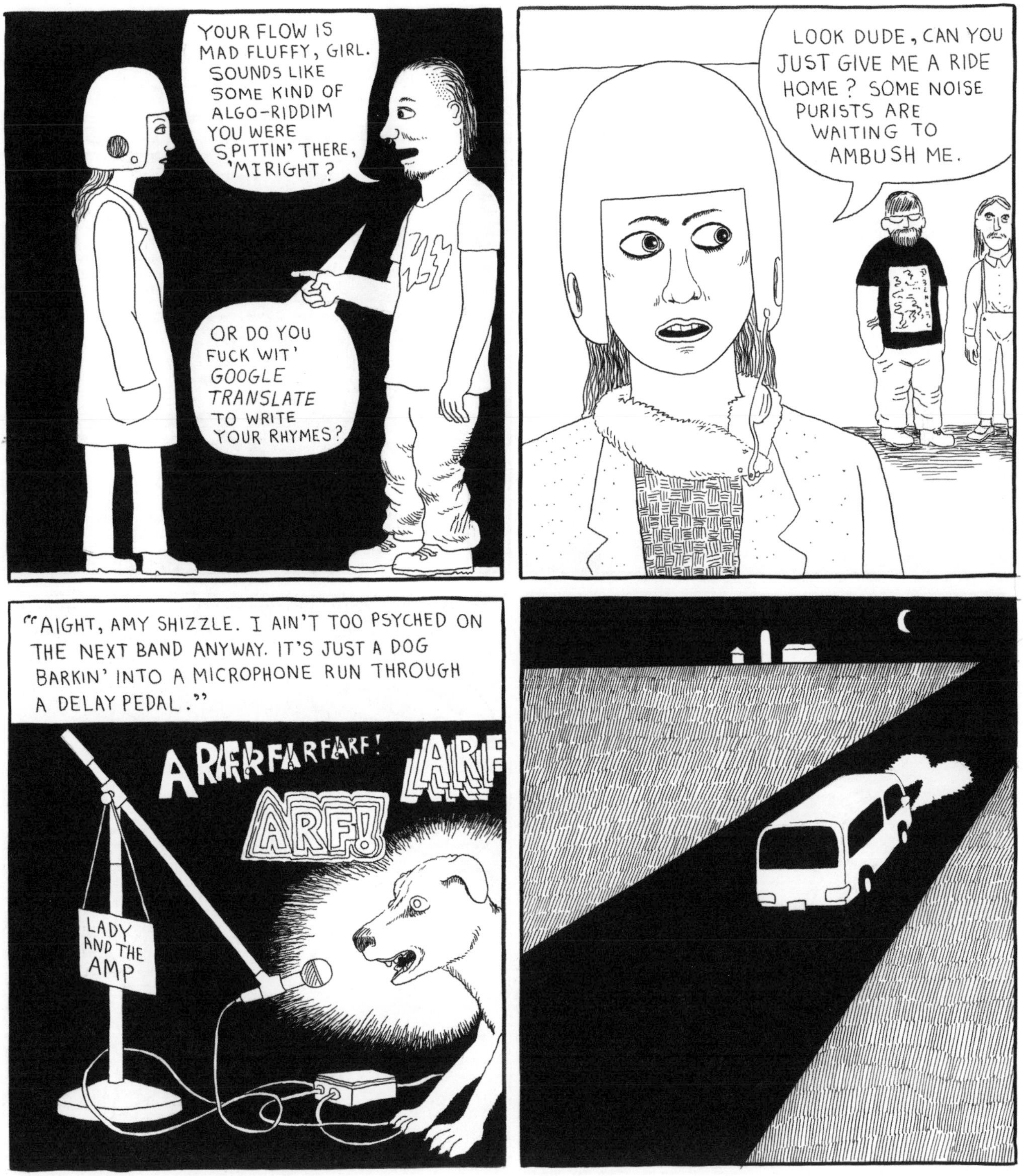
YOUR FLOW IS MAD FLUFFY, GIRL. SOUNDS LIKE SOME KIND OF ALGO-RIDDIM YOU WERE SPITTIN' THERE, 'MIRIGHT?
OR DO YOU FUCK WIT' GOOGLE TRANSLATE TO WRITE YOUR RHYMES?
LOOK DUDE, CAN YOU JUST GIVE ME A RIDE HOME? SOME NOISE PURISTS ARE WAITING TO AMBUSH ME.
"AIGHT, AMY SHIZZLE. I AIN'T TOO PSYCHED ON THE NEXT BAND ANYWAY. IT'S JUST A DOG BARKIN' INTO A MICROPHONE RUN THROUGH A DELAY PEDAL."
ARFARFARFARFARF!
ARF!
ARF
LADY AND THE AMP

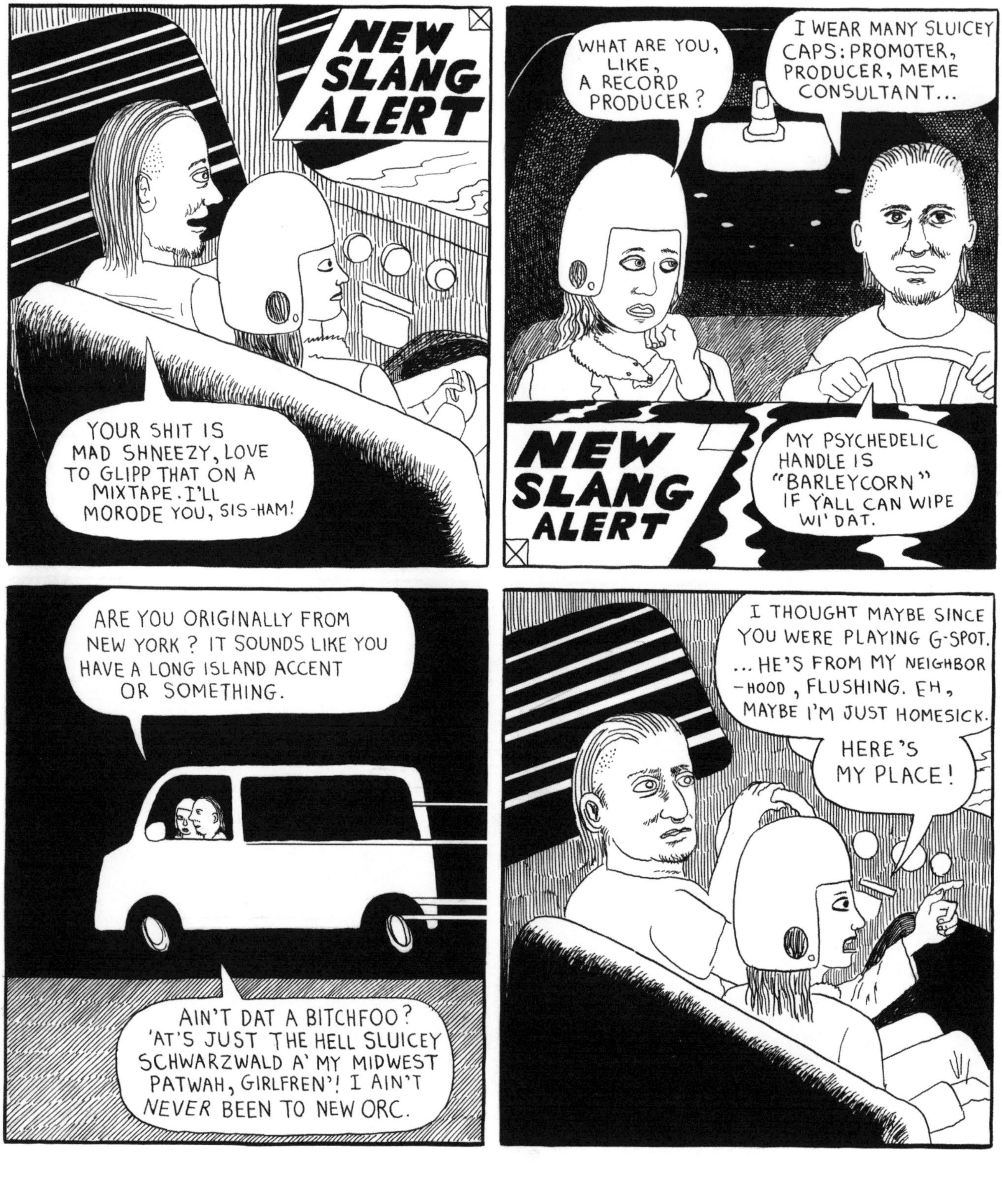
NEW SLANG ALERT
YOUR SHIT IS MAD SHNEEZY, LOVE TO GLIPP THAT ON A MIXTAPE. I'LL MORODE YOU, SIS-HAM!
WHAT ARE YOU, LIKE, A RECORD PRODUCER?
I WEAR MANY SLUICEY CAPS: PROMOTER, PRODUCER, MEME CONSULTANT...
NEW SLANG ALERT
MY PSYCHEDELIC HANDLE IS "BARLEYCORN" IF Y'ALL CAN WIPE WI' DAT.
ARE YOU ORIGINALLY FROM NEW YORK? IT SOUNDS LIKE YOU HAVE A LONG ISLAND ACCENT OR SOMETHING.
AIN'T DAT A BITCHFOO? 'AT'S JUST THE HELL SLUICEY SCHWARZWALD A' MY MIDWEST PATWAH, GIRLFREN'! I AIN'T *NEVER* BEEN TO NEW ORC.
I THOUGHT MAYBE SINCE YOU WERE PLAYING G-SPOT. ...HE'S FROM MY NEIGHBOR-HOOD, FLUSHING. EH, MAYBE I'M JUST HOMESICK.
HERE'S MY PLACE!

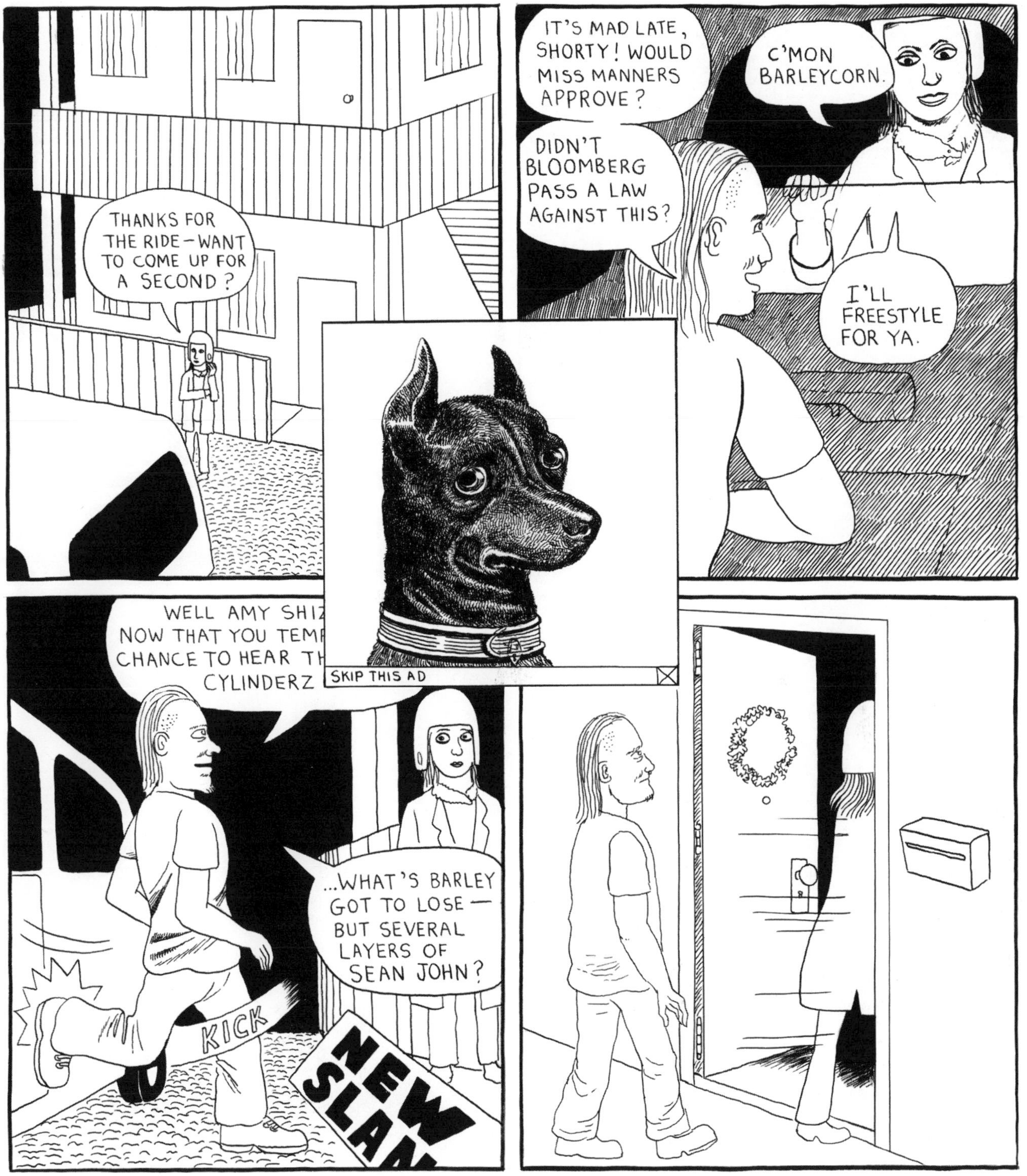
THANKS FOR THE RIDE—WANT TO COME UP FOR A SECOND?
IT'S MAD LATE, SHORTY! WOULD MISS MANNERS APPROVE?
DIDN'T BLOOMBERG PASS A LAW AGAINST THIS?
C'MON BARLEYCORN.
I'LL FREESTYLE FOR YA.
SKIP THIS AD
WELL AMY SHIZ
NOW THAT YOU TEMP
CHANCE TO HEAR TH
CYLINDERZ
...WHAT'S BARLEY GOT TO LOSE— BUT SEVERAL LAYERS OF SEAN JOHN?
KICK
NEW SLAN

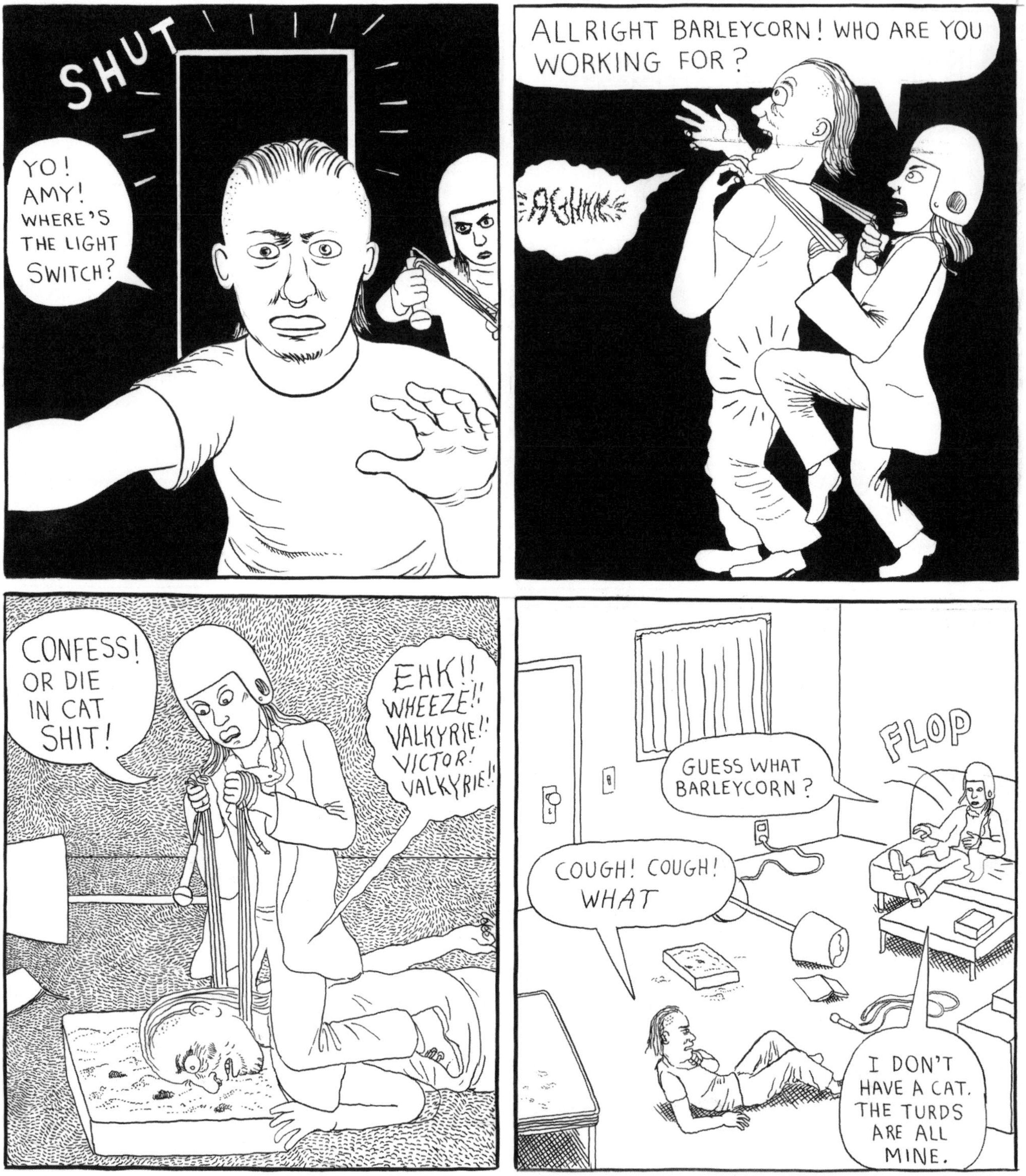
SHUT
YO! AMY! WHERE'S THE LIGHT SWITCH?
ALLRIGHT BARLEYCORN! WHO ARE YOU WORKING FOR?
RGHHK
CONFESS! OR DIE IN CAT SHIT!
EHK!! WHEEZE!! VALKYRIE!! VICTOR! VALKYRIE!!
FLOP
GUESS WHAT BARLEYCORN?
COUGH! COUGH! WHAT
I DON'T HAVE A CAT. THE TURDS ARE ALL MINE.

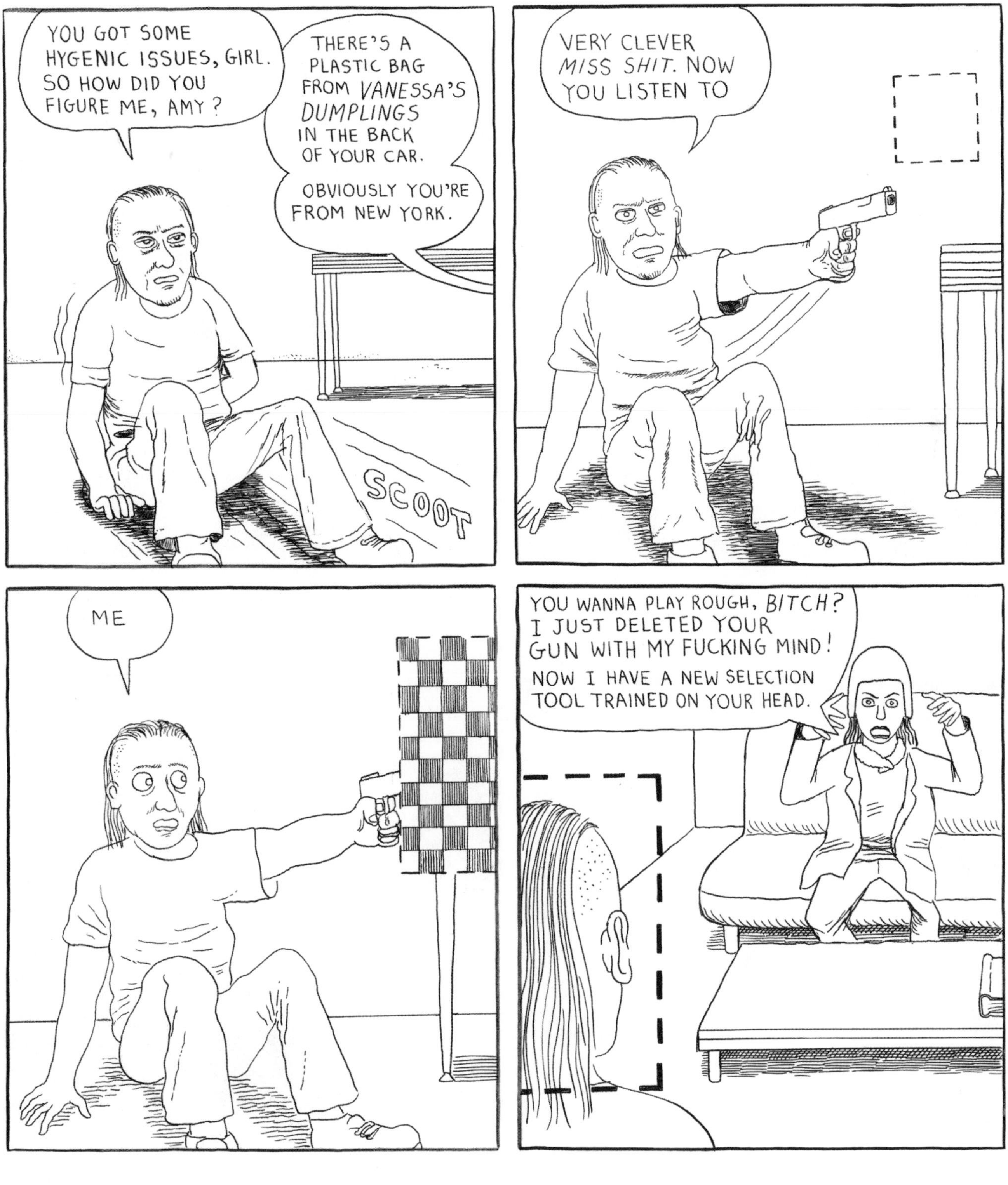
YOU GOT SOME HYGENIC ISSUES, GIRL. SO HOW DID YOU FIGURE ME, AMY ?
THERE'S A PLASTIC BAG FROM VANESSA'S DUMPLINGS IN THE BACK OF YOUR CAR.
OBVIOUSLY YOU'RE FROM NEW YORK.
SCOOT
VERY CLEVER MISS SHIT. NOW YOU LISTEN TO
ME
YOU WANNA PLAY ROUGH, BITCH? I JUST DELETED YOUR GUN WITH MY FUCKING MIND!
NOW I HAVE A NEW SELECTION TOOL TRAINED ON YOUR HEAD.

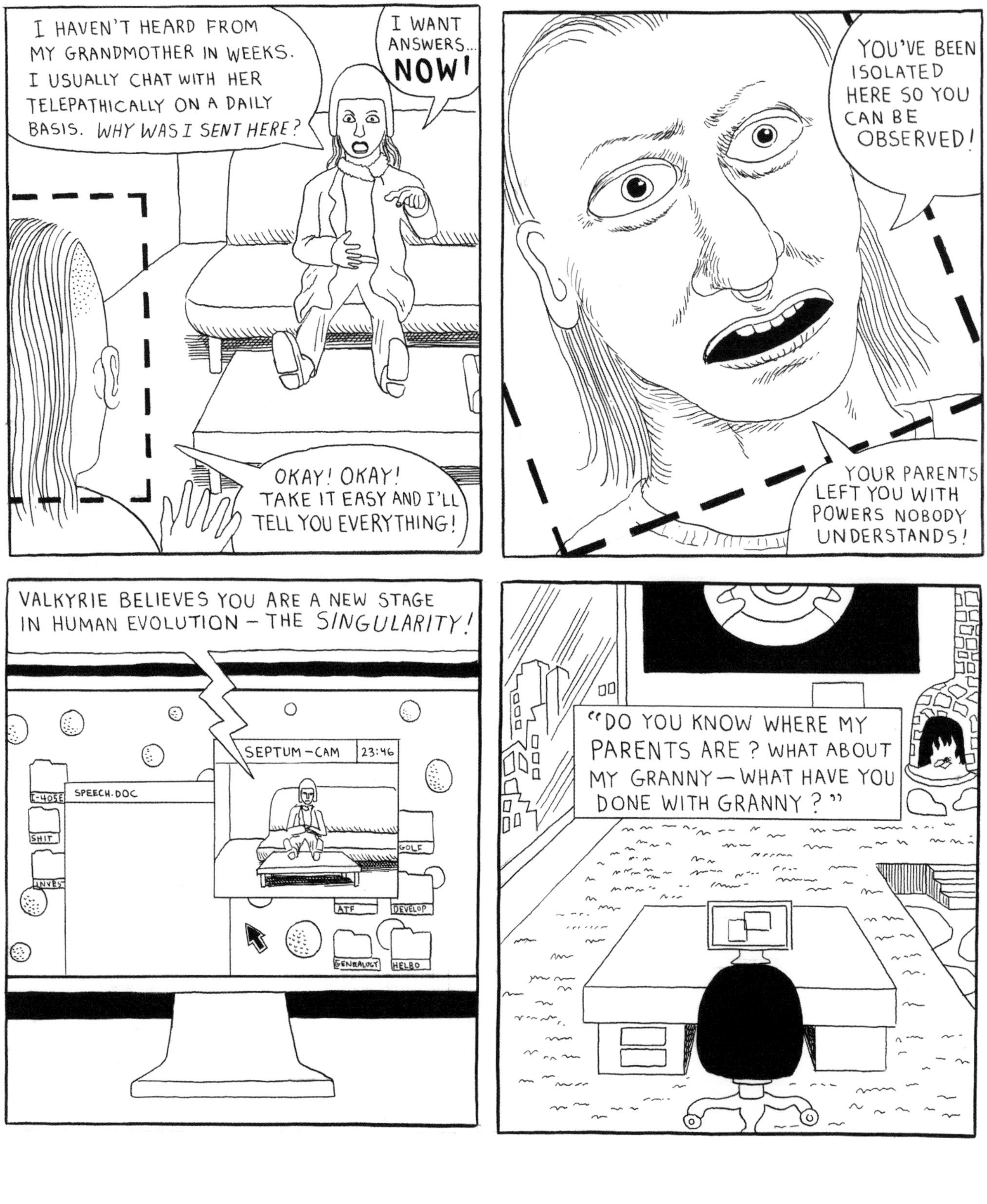
I HAVEN'T HEARD FROM MY GRANDMOTHER IN WEEKS. I USUALLY CHAT WITH HER TELEPATHICALLY ON A DAILY BASIS. WHY WAS I SENT HERE?
I WANT ANSWERS... NOW!
OKAY! OKAY! TAKE IT EASY AND I'LL TELL YOU EVERYTHING!
YOU'VE BEEN ISOLATED HERE SO YOU CAN BE OBSERVED!
YOUR PARENTS LEFT YOU WITH POWERS NOBODY UNDERSTANDS!
VALKYRIE BELIEVES YOU ARE A NEW STAGE IN HUMAN EVOLUTION – THE SINGULARITY!
SEPTUM-CAM
23:46
SPEECH.DOC
SHIT
GOLF
ATF
DEVELOP
GENEALOGY
HELBO
"DO YOU KNOW WHERE MY PARENTS ARE? WHAT ABOUT MY GRANNY – WHAT HAVE YOU DONE WITH GRANNY?"

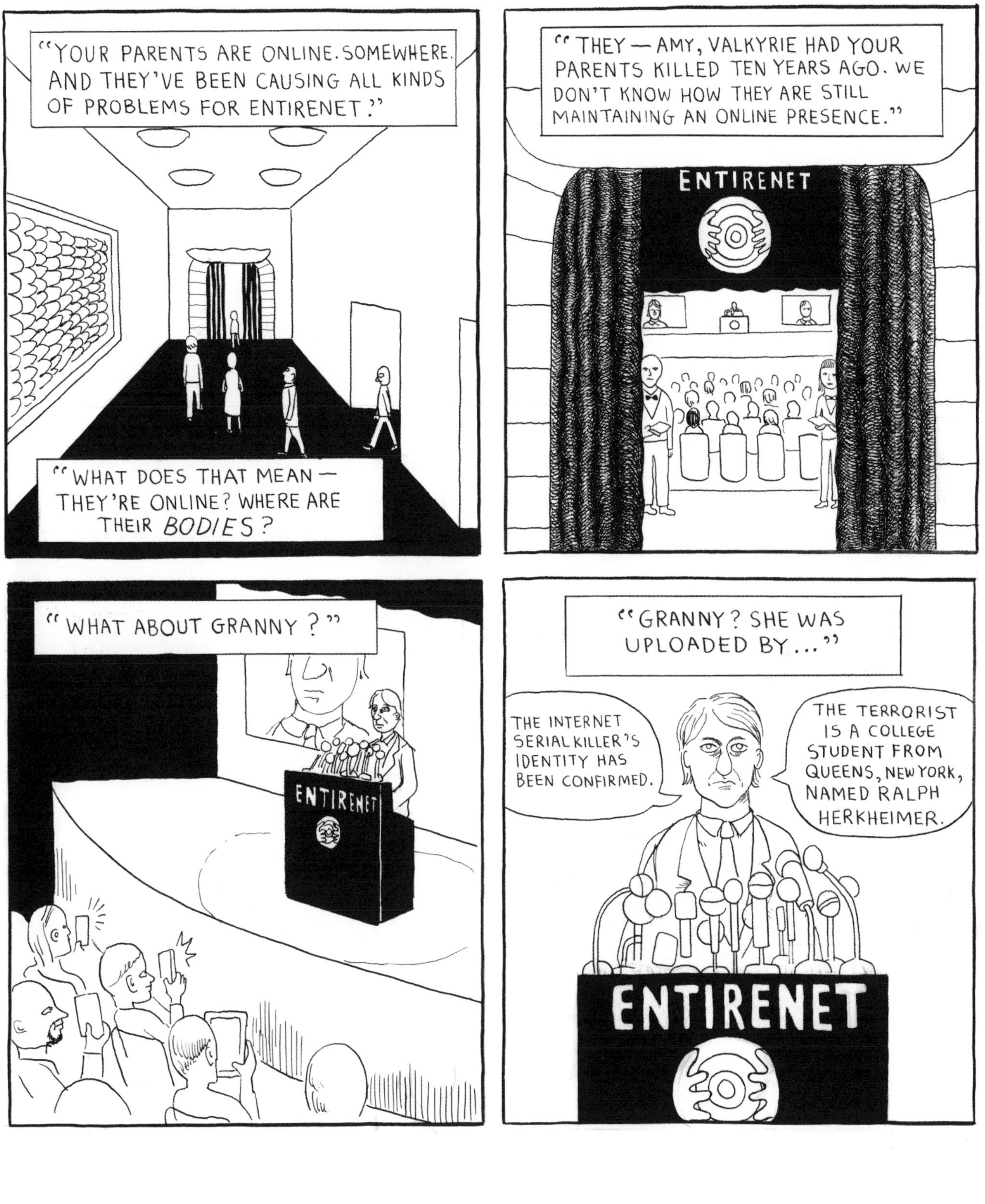
"YOUR PARENTS ARE ONLINE. SOMEWHERE. AND THEY'VE BEEN CAUSING ALL KINDS OF PROBLEMS FOR ENTIRENET."
"WHAT DOES THAT MEAN — THEY'RE ONLINE? WHERE ARE THEIR *BODIES*?
"THEY — AMY, VALKYRIE HAD YOUR PARENTS KILLED TEN YEARS AGO. WE DON'T KNOW HOW THEY ARE STILL MAINTAINING AN ONLINE PRESENCE."
ENTIRENET
"WHAT ABOUT GRANNY?"
ENTIRENET
"GRANNY? SHE WAS UPLOADED BY..."
THE INTERNET SERIAL KILLER'S IDENTITY HAS BEEN CONFIRMED.
THE TERRORIST IS A COLLEGE STUDENT FROM QUEENS, NEW YORK, NAMED RALPH HERKHEIMER.
ENTIRENET

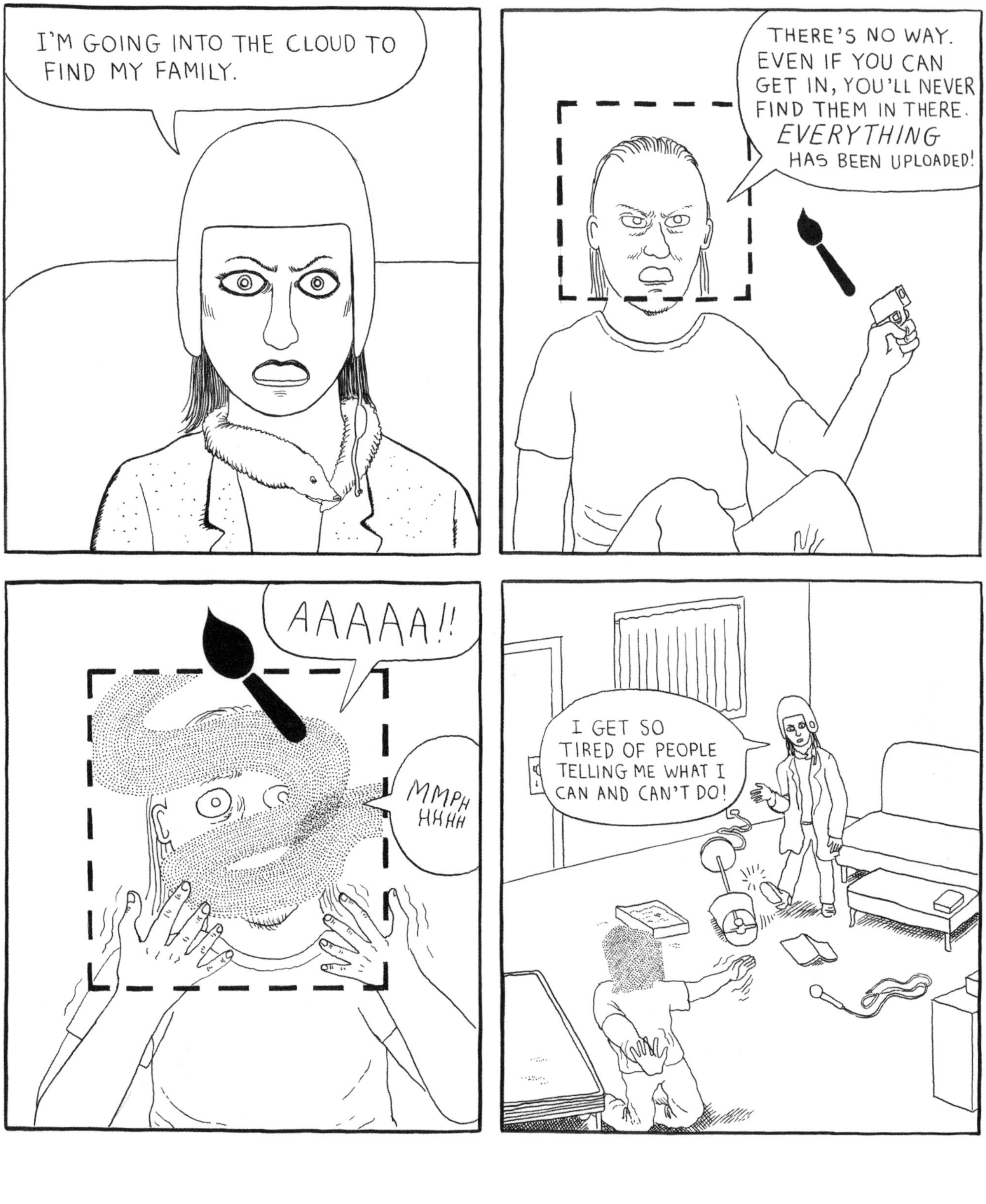
I'M GOING INTO THE CLOUD TO FIND MY FAMILY.
THERE'S NO WAY. EVEN IF YOU CAN GET IN, YOU'LL NEVER FIND THEM IN THERE. EVERYTHING HAS BEEN UPLOADED!
AAAAA!!
MMPH HHHH
I GET SO TIRED OF PEOPLE TELLING ME WHAT I CAN AND CAN'T DO!

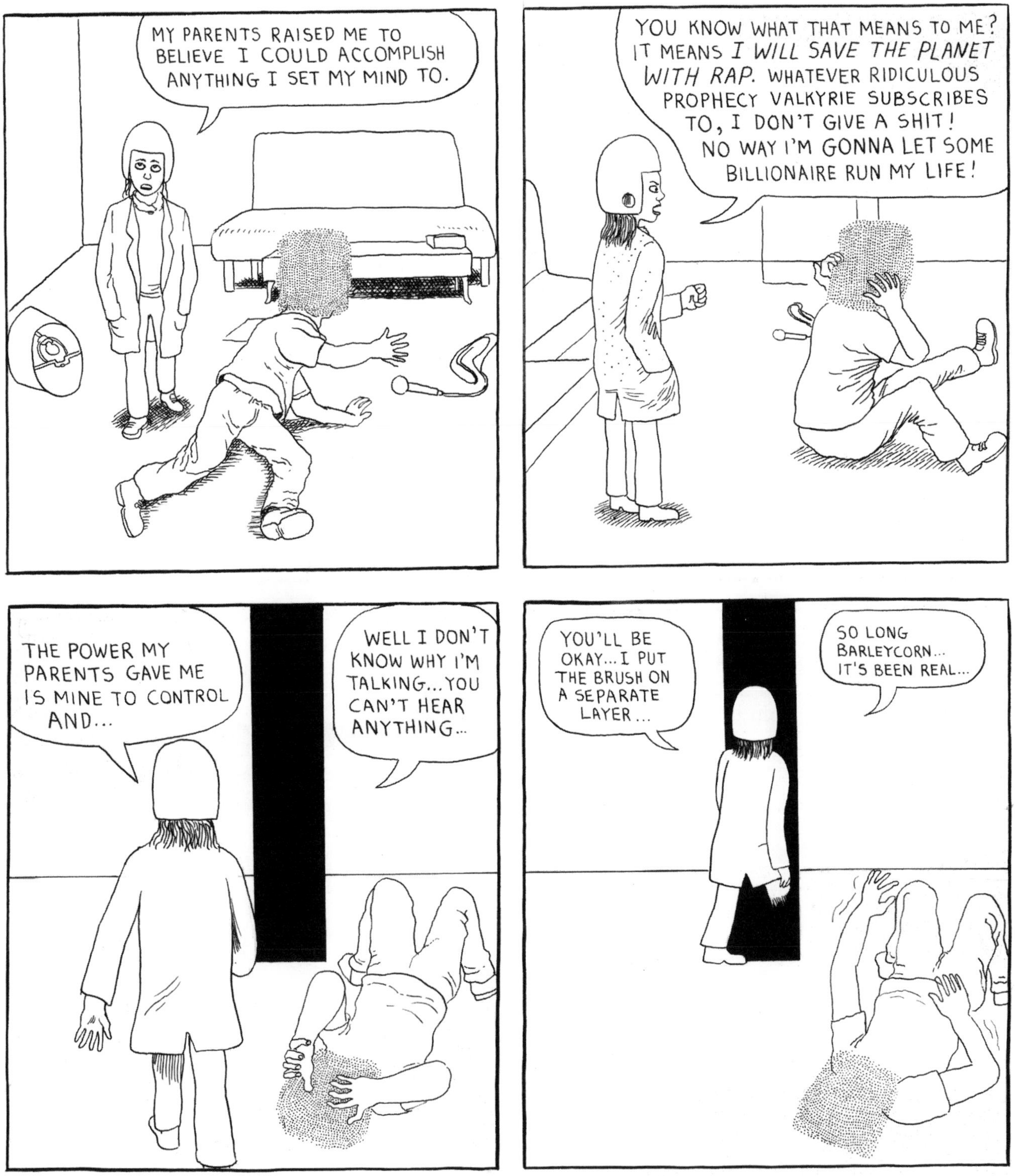
MY PARENTS RAISED ME TO BELIEVE I COULD ACCOMPLISH ANYTHING I SET MY MIND TO.
YOU KNOW WHAT THAT MEANS TO ME? IT MEANS *I WILL SAVE THE PLANET WITH RAP.* WHATEVER RIDICULOUS PROPHECY VALKYRIE SUBSCRIBES TO, I DON'T GIVE A SHIT! NO WAY I'M GONNA LET SOME BILLIONAIRE RUN MY LIFE!
THE POWER MY PARENTS GAVE ME IS MINE TO CONTROL AND...
WELL I DON'T KNOW WHY I'M TALKING... YOU CAN'T HEAR ANYTHING...
YOU'LL BE OKAY... I PUT THE BRUSH ON A SEPARATE LAYER...
SO LONG BARLEYCORN... IT'S BEEN REAL...

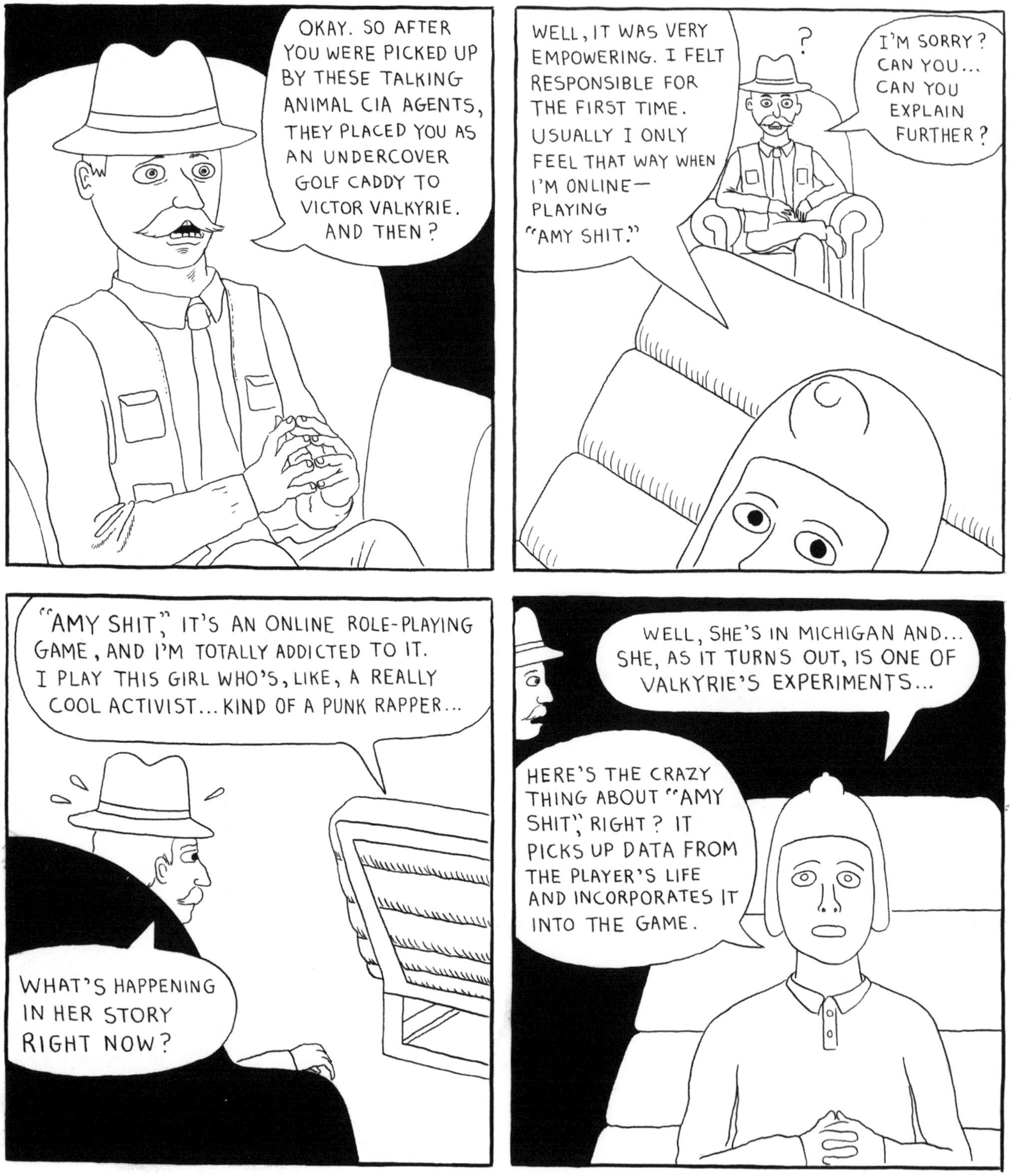
OKAY. SO AFTER YOU WERE PICKED UP BY THESE TALKING ANIMAL CIA AGENTS, THEY PLACED YOU AS AN UNDERCOVER GOLF CADDY TO VICTOR VALKYRIE. AND THEN?
WELL, IT WAS VERY EMPOWERING. I FELT RESPONSIBLE FOR THE FIRST TIME. USUALLY I ONLY FEEL THAT WAY WHEN I'M ONLINE— PLAYING "AMY SHIT."
?
I'M SORRY? CAN YOU... CAN YOU EXPLAIN FURTHER?
"AMY SHIT," IT'S AN ONLINE ROLE-PLAYING GAME, AND I'M TOTALLY ADDICTED TO IT. I PLAY THIS GIRL WHO'S, LIKE, A REALLY COOL ACTIVIST... KIND OF A PUNK RAPPER...
WHAT'S HAPPENING IN HER STORY RIGHT NOW?
WELL, SHE'S IN MICHIGAN AND... SHE, AS IT TURNS OUT, IS ONE OF VALKYRIE'S EXPERIMENTS...
HERE'S THE CRAZY THING ABOUT "AMY SHIT," RIGHT? IT PICKS UP DATA FROM THE PLAYER'S LIFE AND INCORPORATES IT INTO THE GAME.

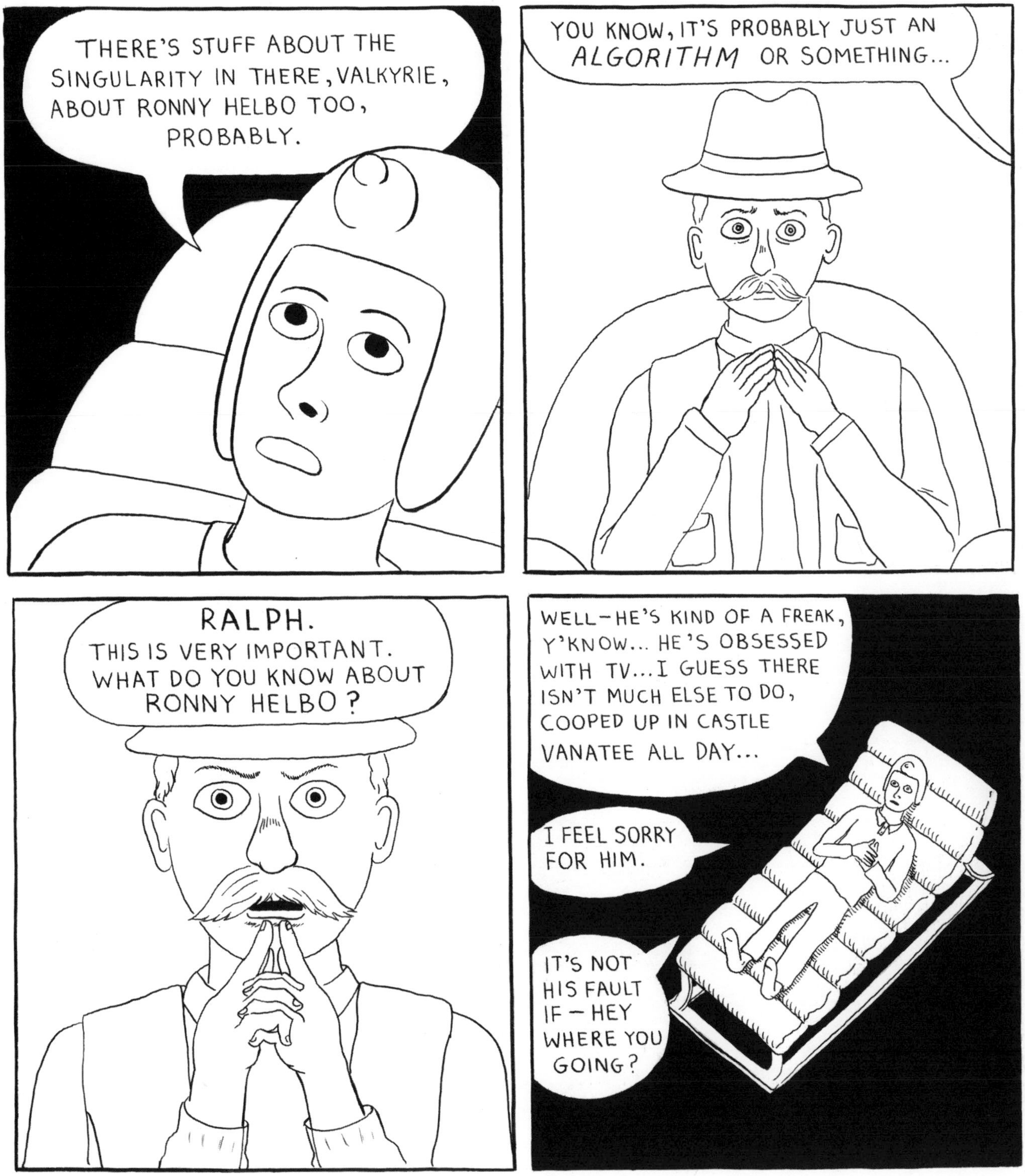
THERE'S STUFF ABOUT THE SINGULARITY IN THERE, VALKYRIE, ABOUT RONNY HELBO TOO, PROBABLY.
YOU KNOW, IT'S PROBABLY JUST AN ALGORITHM OR SOMETHING...
RALPH. THIS IS VERY IMPORTANT. WHAT DO YOU KNOW ABOUT RONNY HELBO?
WELL—HE'S KIND OF A FREAK, Y'KNOW... HE'S OBSESSED WITH TV... I GUESS THERE ISN'T MUCH ELSE TO DO, COOPED UP IN CASTLE VANATEE ALL DAY...
I FEEL SORRY FOR HIM.
IT'S NOT HIS FAULT IF—HEY WHERE YOU GOING?

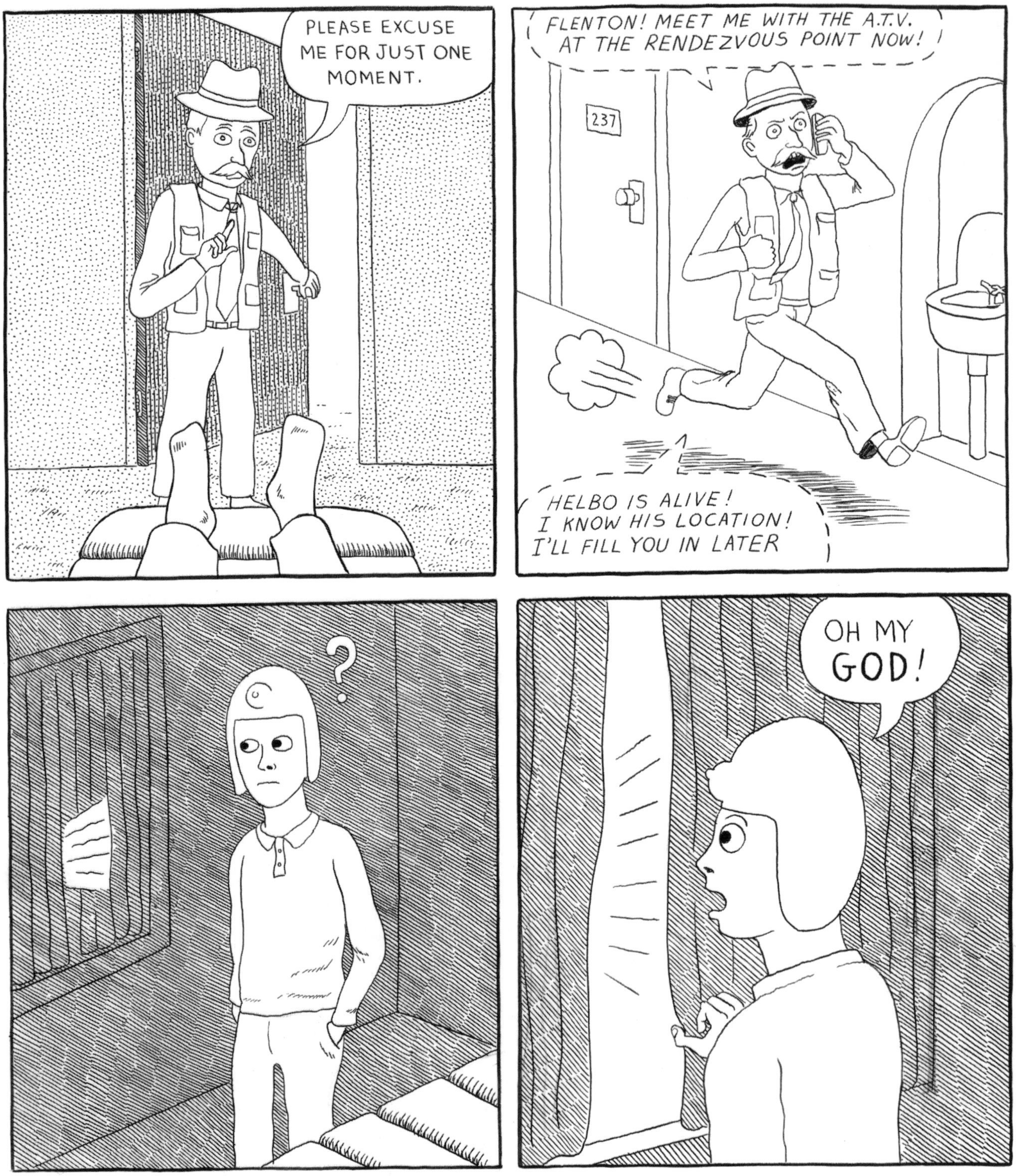
PLEASE EXCUSE ME FOR JUST ONE MOMENT.
FLENTON! MEET ME WITH THE A.T.V. AT THE RENDEZVOUS POINT NOW!
237
HELBO IS ALIVE! I KNOW HIS LOCATION! I'LL FILL YOU IN LATER
?
OH MY GOD!

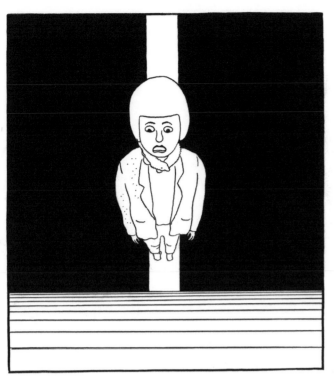
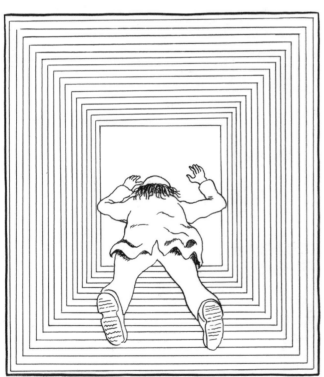

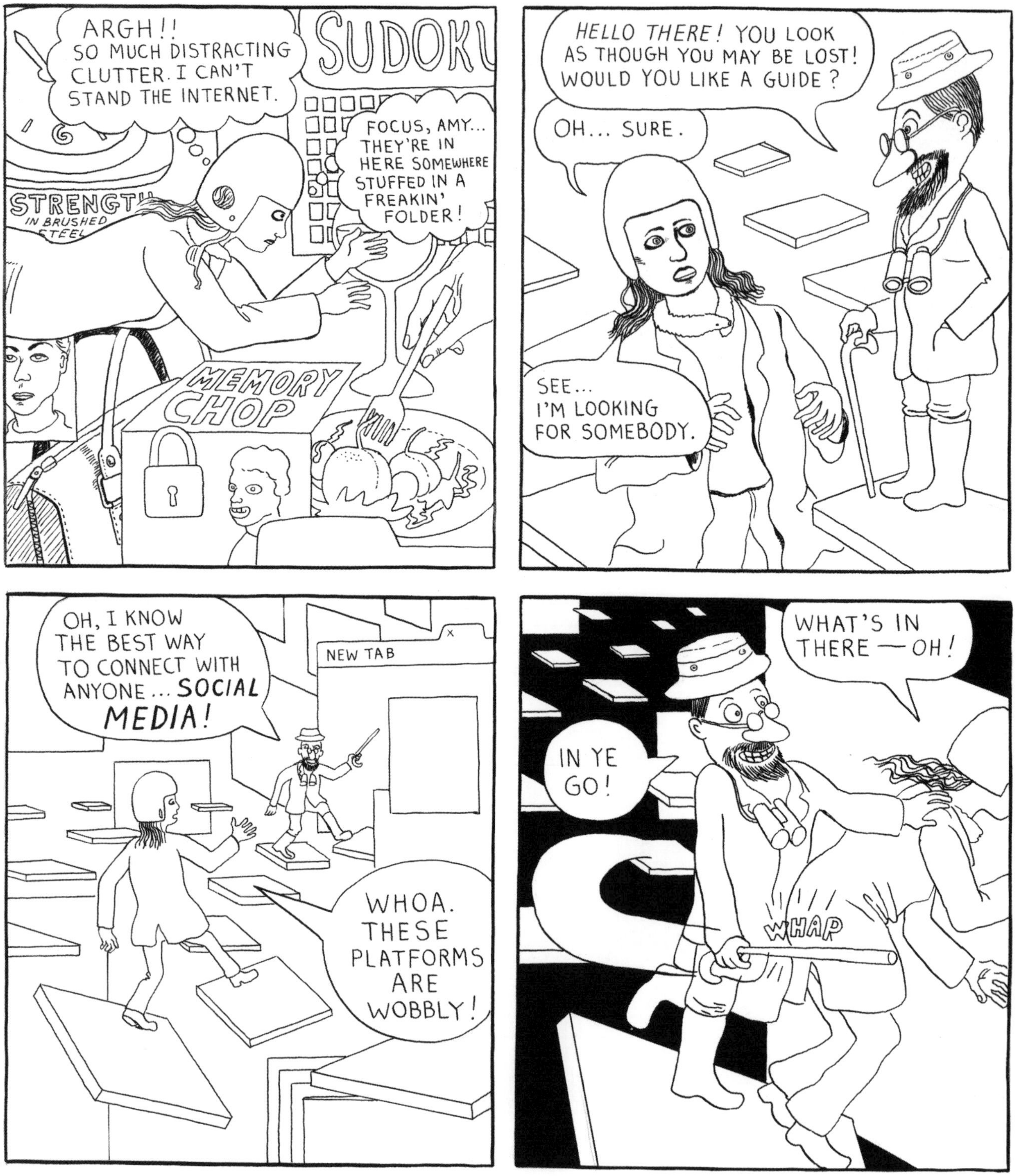
ARGH!! SO MUCH DISTRACTING CLUTTER. I CAN'T STAND THE INTERNET.
SUDOKU
FOCUS, AMY... THEY'RE IN HERE SOMEWHERE STUFFED IN A FREAKIN' FOLDER!
STRENGTH IN BRUSHED STEEL
MEMORY CHOP
HELLO THERE! YOU LOOK AS THOUGH YOU MAY BE LOST! WOULD YOU LIKE A GUIDE?
OH... SURE.
SEE... I'M LOOKING FOR SOMEBODY.
OH, I KNOW THE BEST WAY TO CONNECT WITH ANYONE... SOCIAL MEDIA!
NEW TAB
WHOA. THESE PLATFORMS ARE WOBBLY!
WHAT'S IN THERE—OH!
IN YE GO!
WHAP

OOPS!
*@!#&!
IT'S THE TWITTER STREAM! SWIM AGAINST THE CURRENT, AMY!
OH GOD! IT'S RELENTLESS!
GOOD WORK! KEEP IT UP!
IT'S GETTING SO DEEP!
MR. GUIDE— HELP!
WHOA! WHOA! I'M GOING TOO FAST!

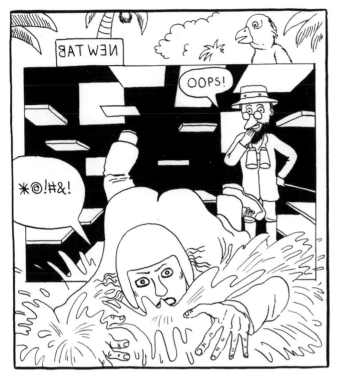

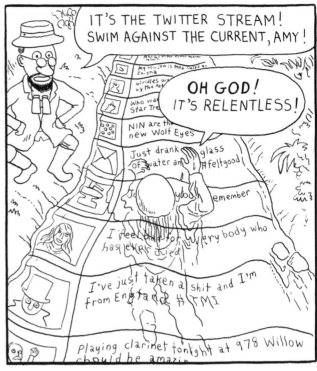

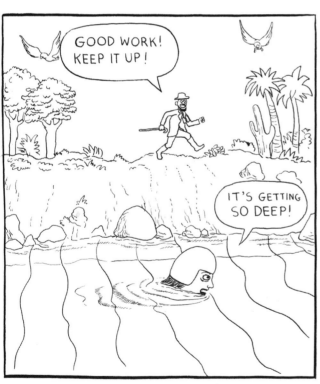

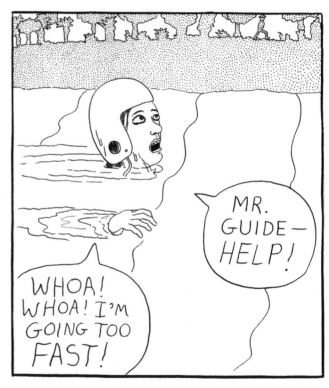

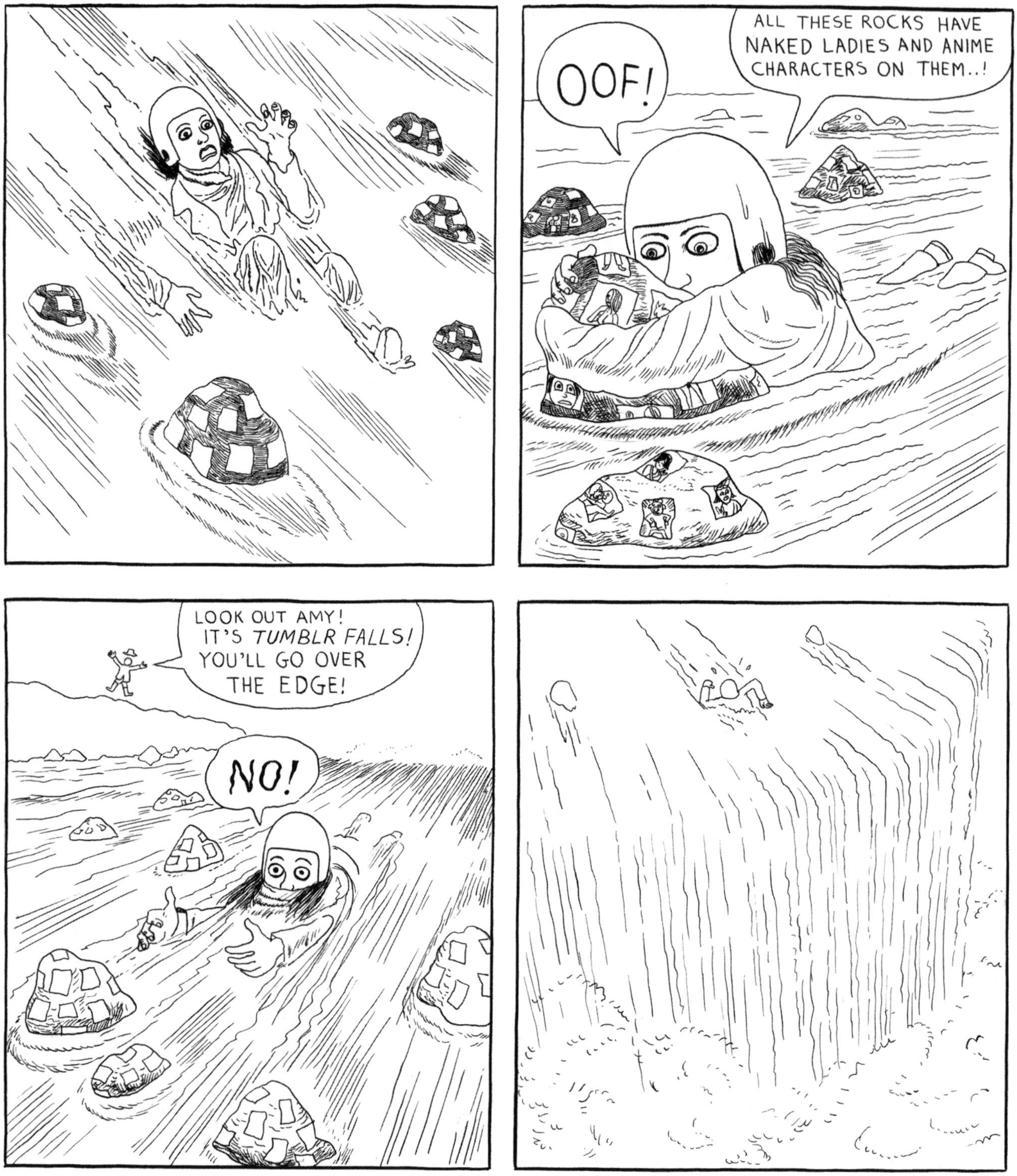
OOF!
ALL THESE ROCKS HAVE NAKED LADIES AND ANIME CHARACTERS ON THEM..!
LOOK OUT AMY! IT'S *TUMBLR FALLS!* YOU'LL GO OVER THE EDGE!
NO!

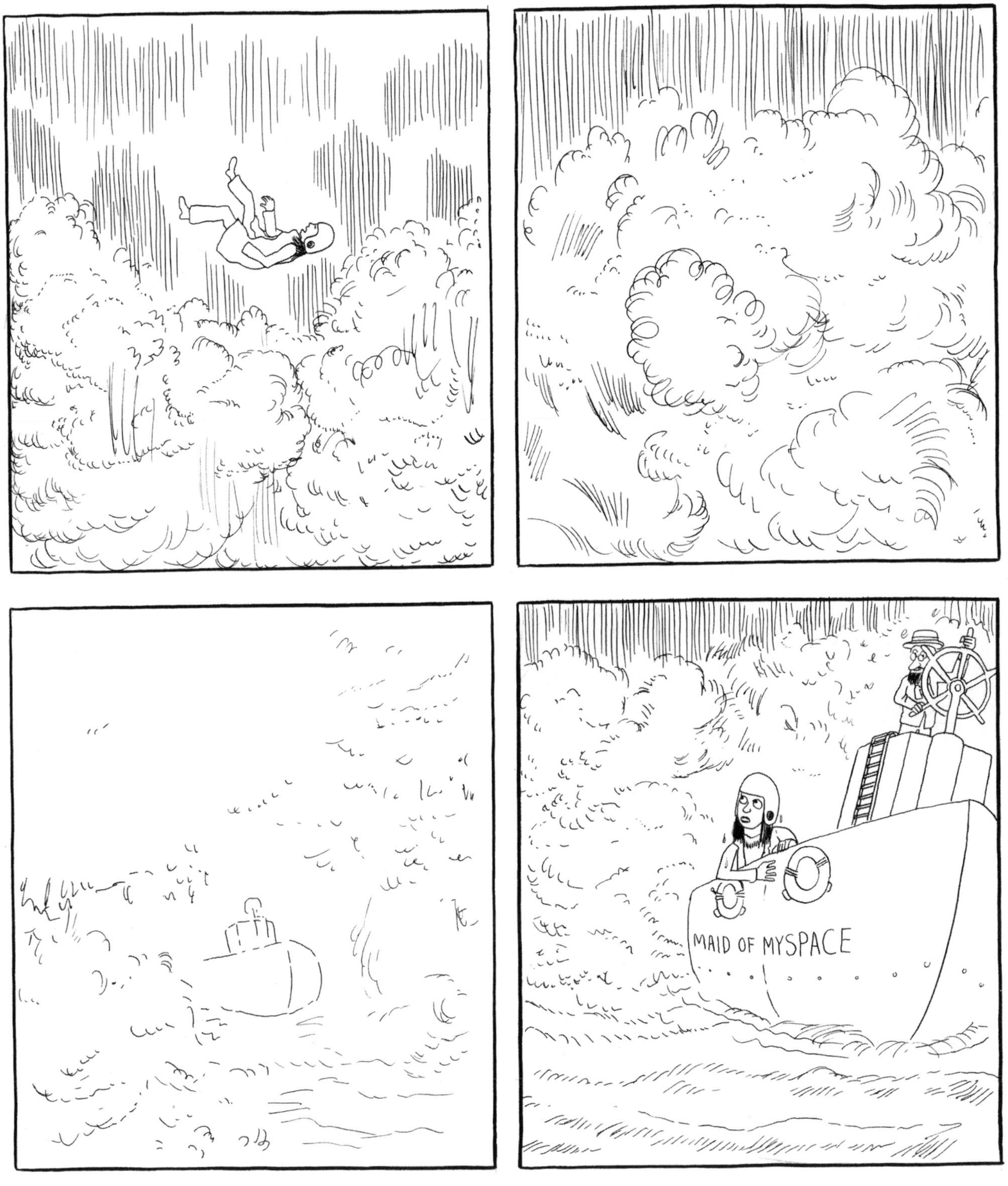
MAID OF MYSPACE

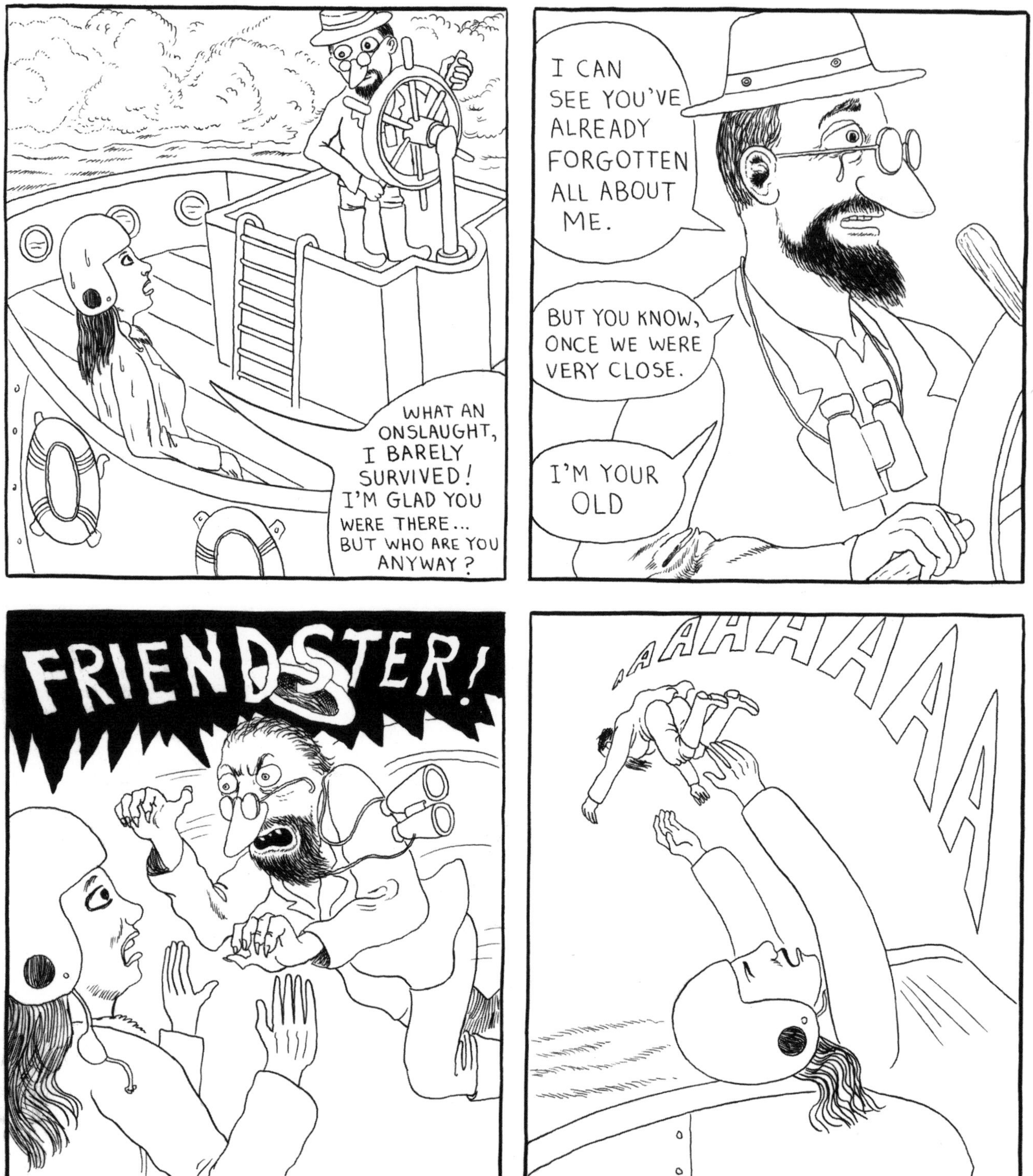
WHAT AN ONSLAUGHT, I BARELY SURVIVED! I'M GLAD YOU WERE THERE... BUT WHO ARE YOU ANYWAY?
I CAN SEE YOU'VE ALREADY FORGOTTEN ALL ABOUT ME.
BUT YOU KNOW, ONCE WE WERE VERY CLOSE.
I'M YOUR OLD
FRIENDSTER!
AAAAAAAAAA

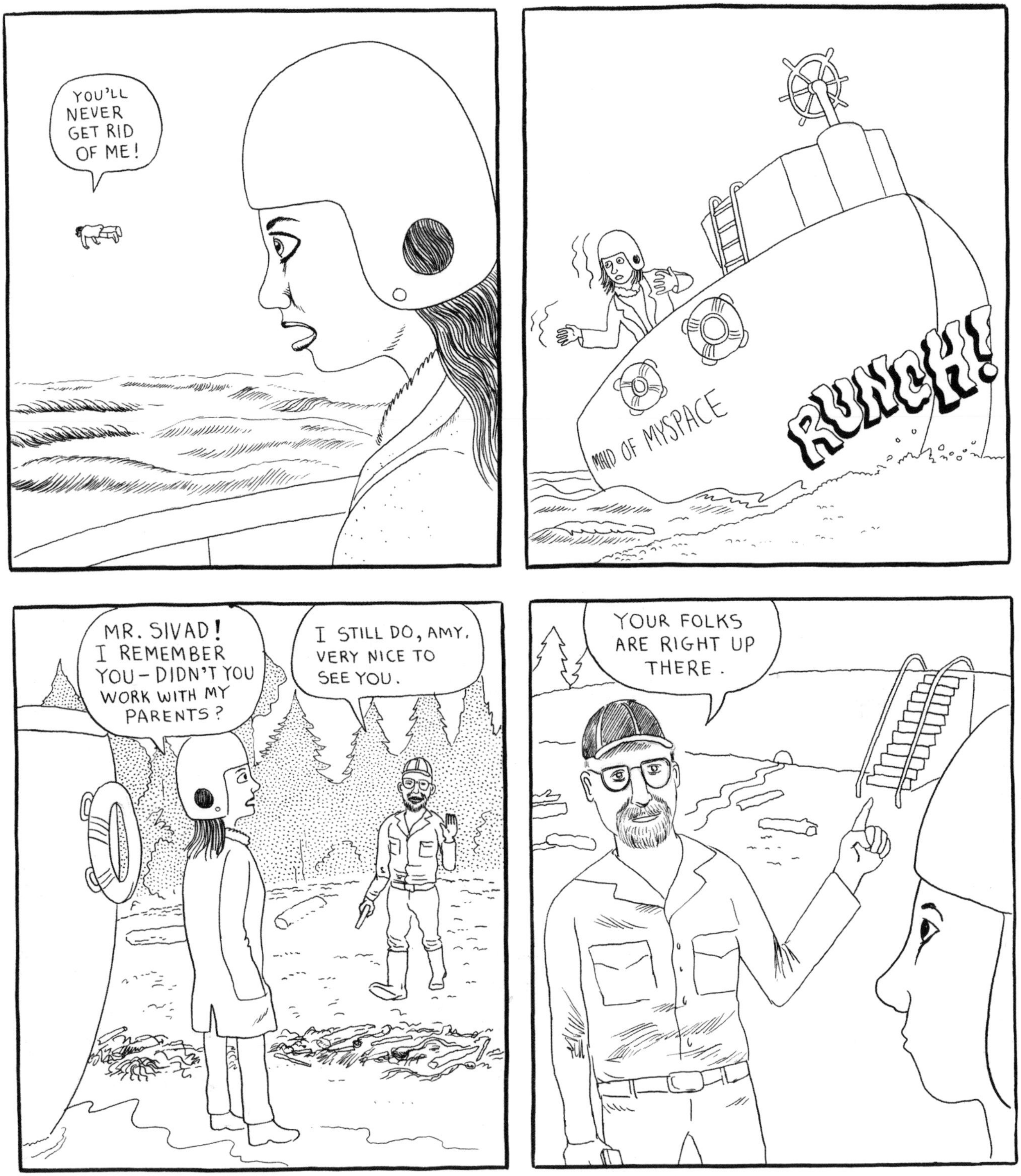
YOU'LL NEVER GET RID OF ME!
MAID OF MYSPACE
RUNCH!
MR. SIVAD! I REMEMBER YOU – DIDN'T YOU WORK WITH MY PARENTS?
I STILL DO, AMY. VERY NICE TO SEE YOU.
YOUR FOLKS ARE RIGHT UP THERE.

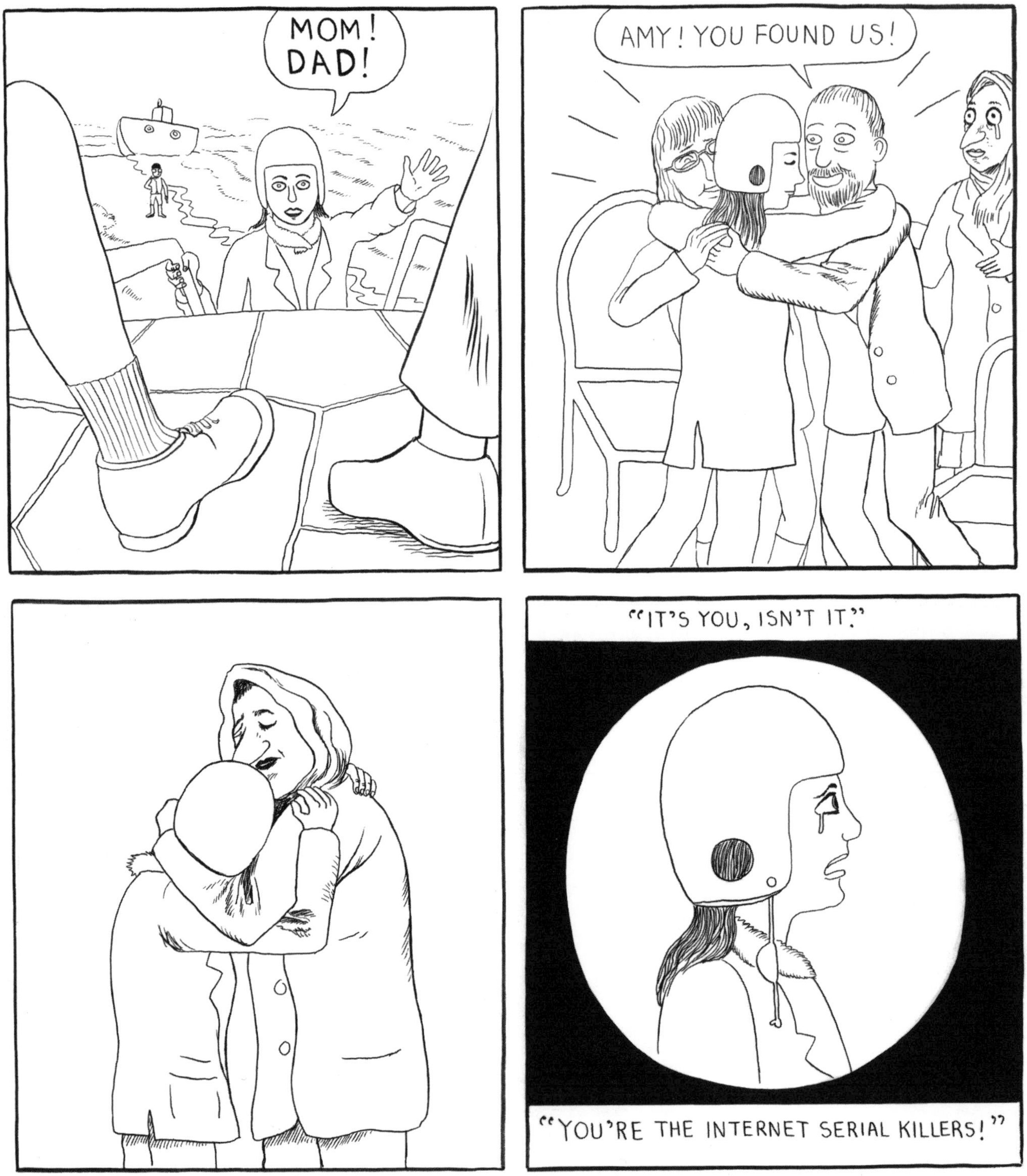
MOM! DAD!
AMY! YOU FOUND US!
"IT'S YOU, ISN'T IT."
"YOU'RE THE INTERNET SERIAL KILLERS!"

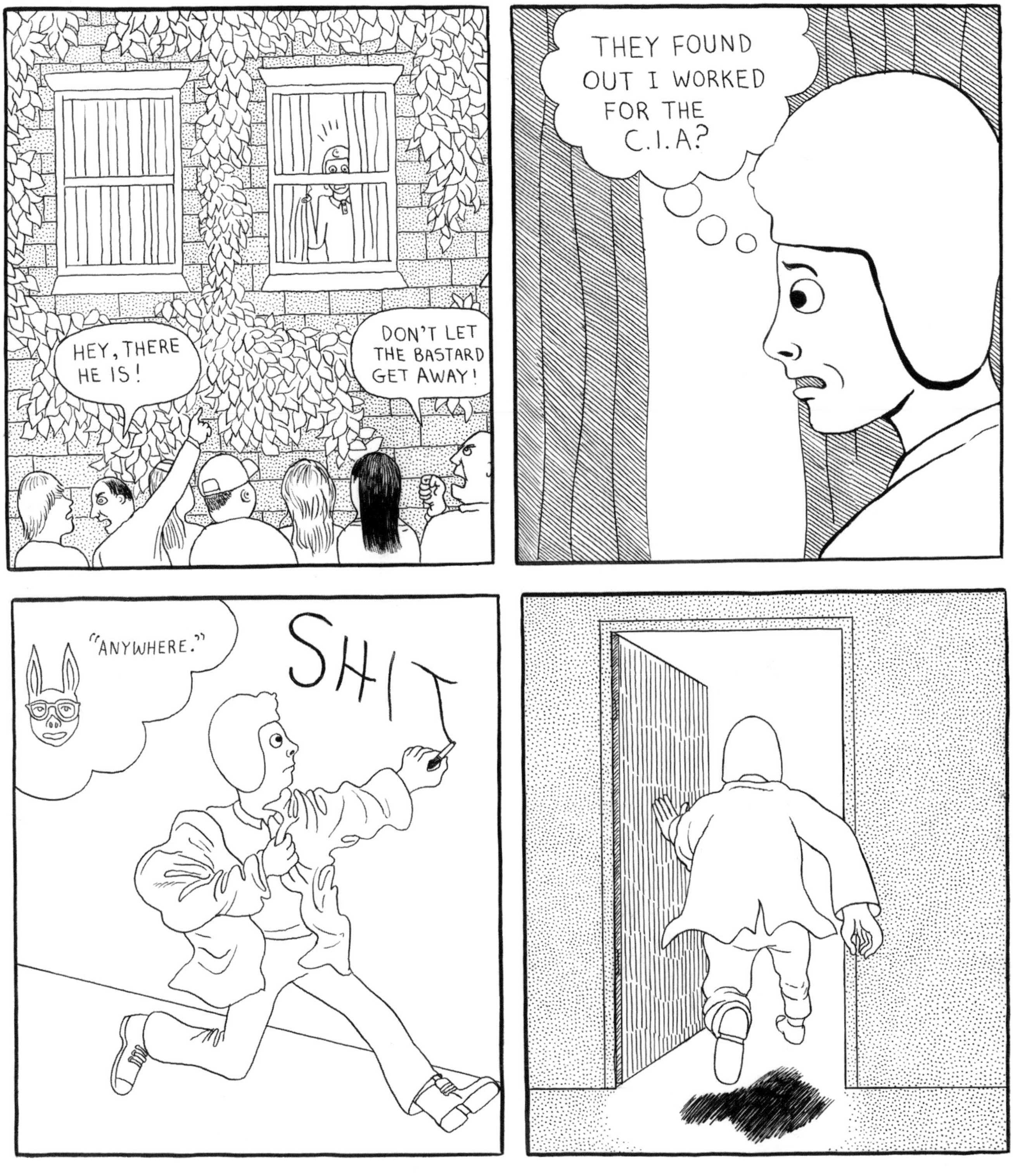
HEY, THERE HE IS!
DON'T LET THE BASTARD GET AWAY!
THEY FOUND OUT I WORKED FOR THE C.I.A?
"ANYWHERE."
SHIT

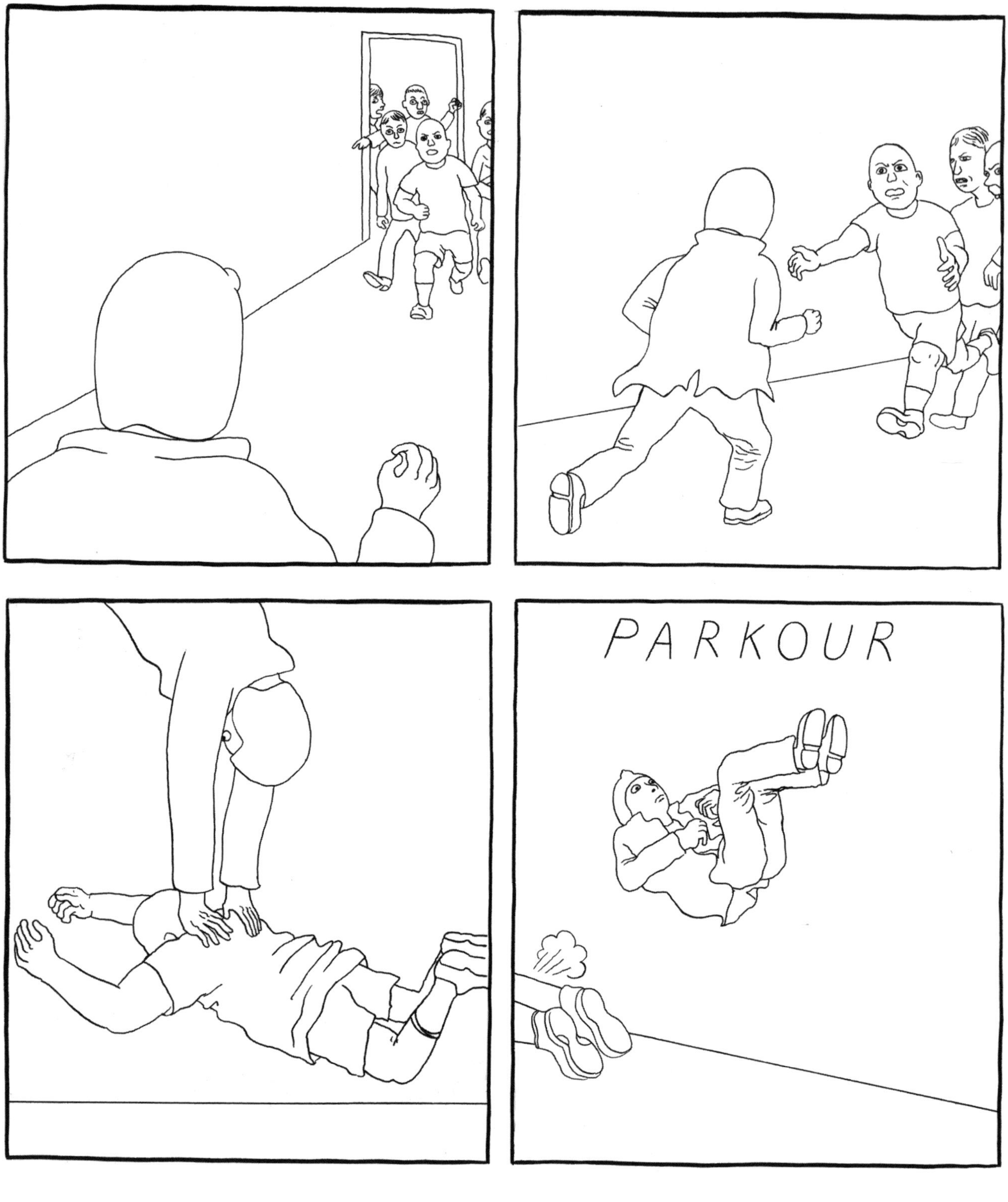
PARKOUR

YOU MONSTER!
HI-SPEED DE-GARMENTING

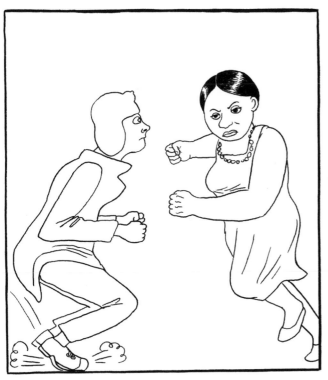

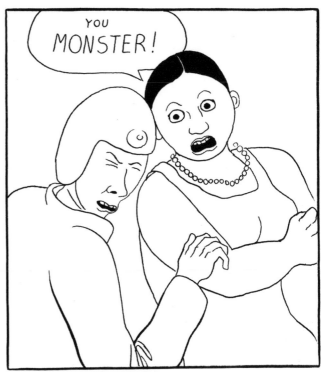

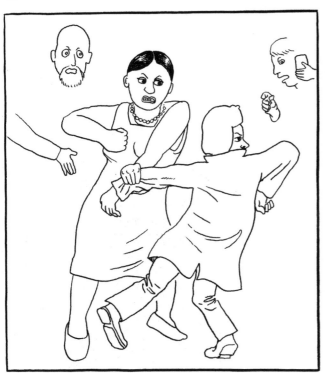

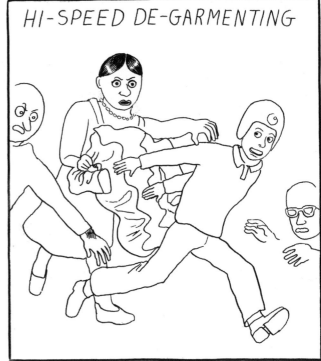

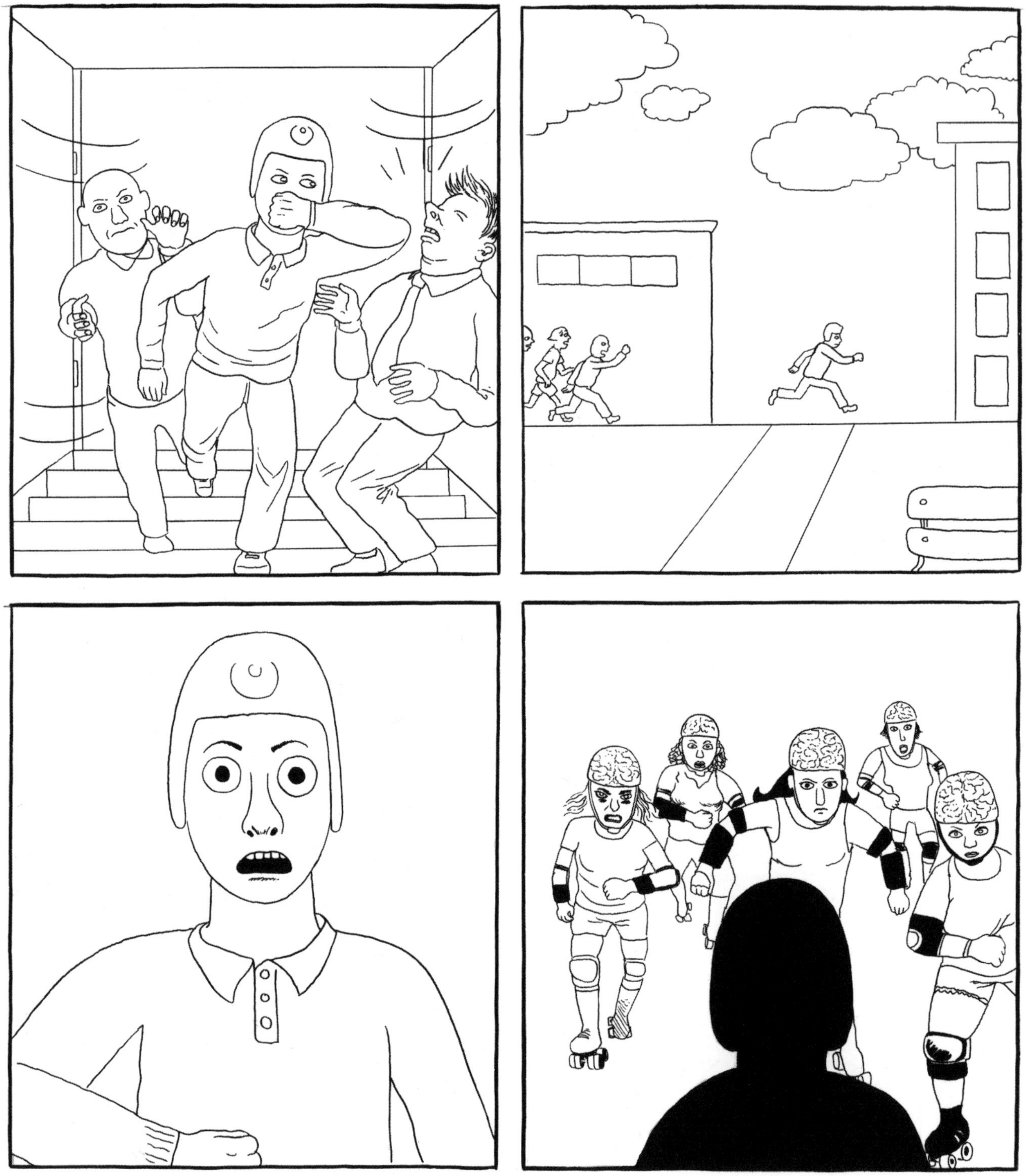

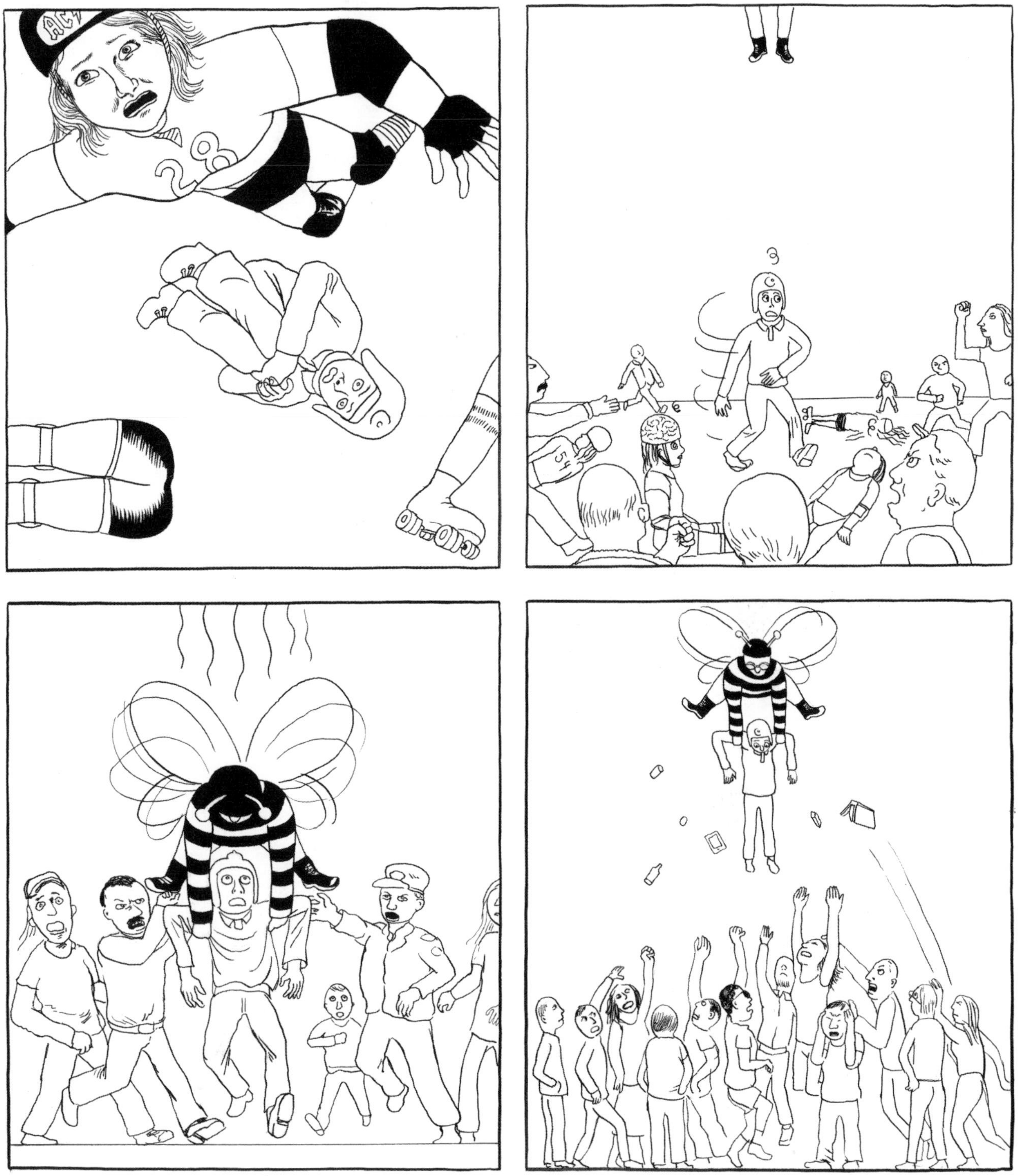
28
54

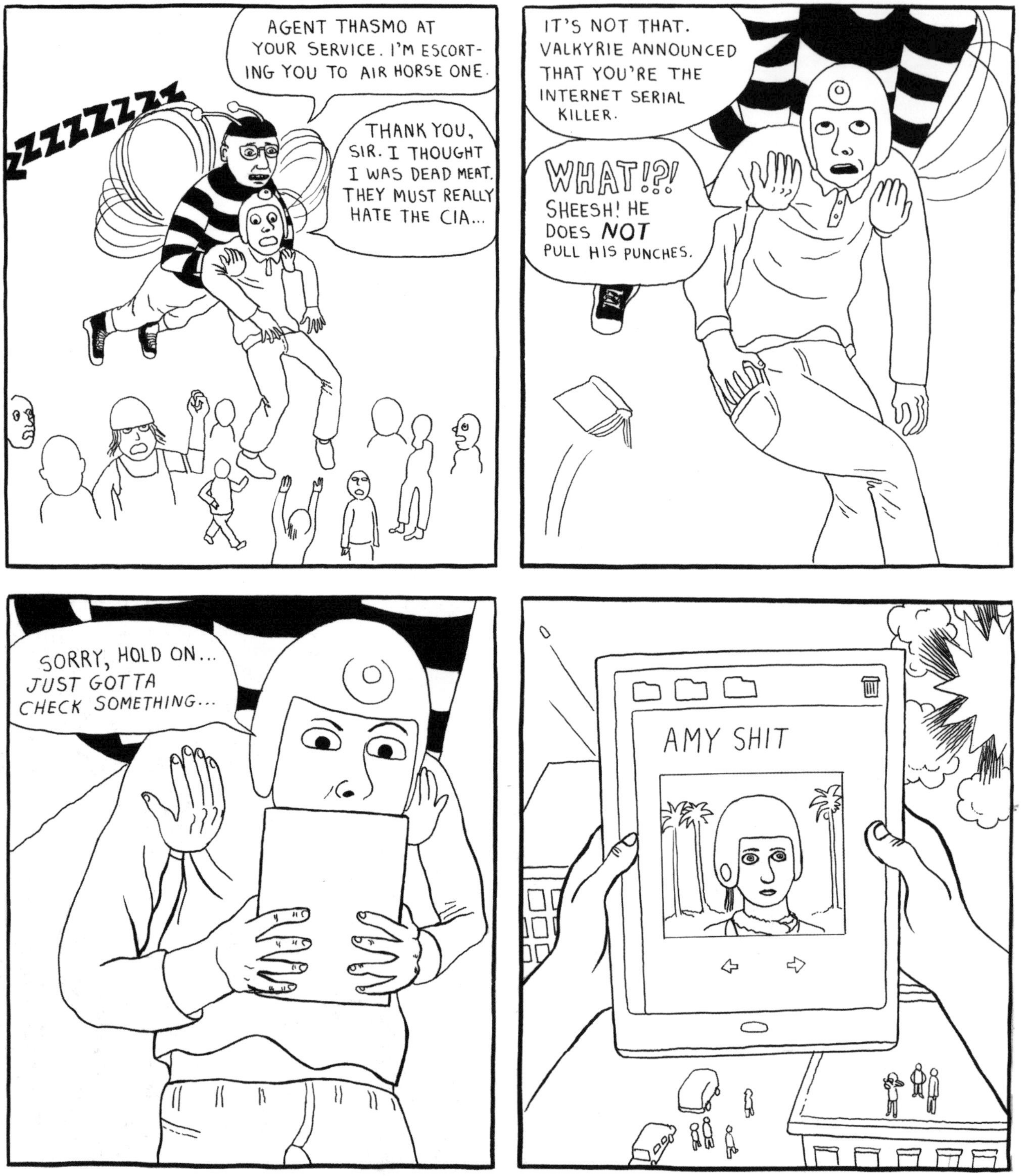
ZZZZZZZZZ
AGENT THASMO AT YOUR SERVICE. I'M ESCORTING YOU TO AIR HORSE ONE.
THANK YOU, SIR. I THOUGHT I WAS DEAD MEAT. THEY MUST REALLY HATE THE CIA...
IT'S NOT THAT. VALKYRIE ANNOUNCED THAT YOU'RE THE INTERNET SERIAL KILLER.
WHAT!?! SHEESH! HE DOES NOT PULL HIS PUNCHES.
SORRY, HOLD ON... JUST GOTTA CHECK SOMETHING...
AMY SHIT

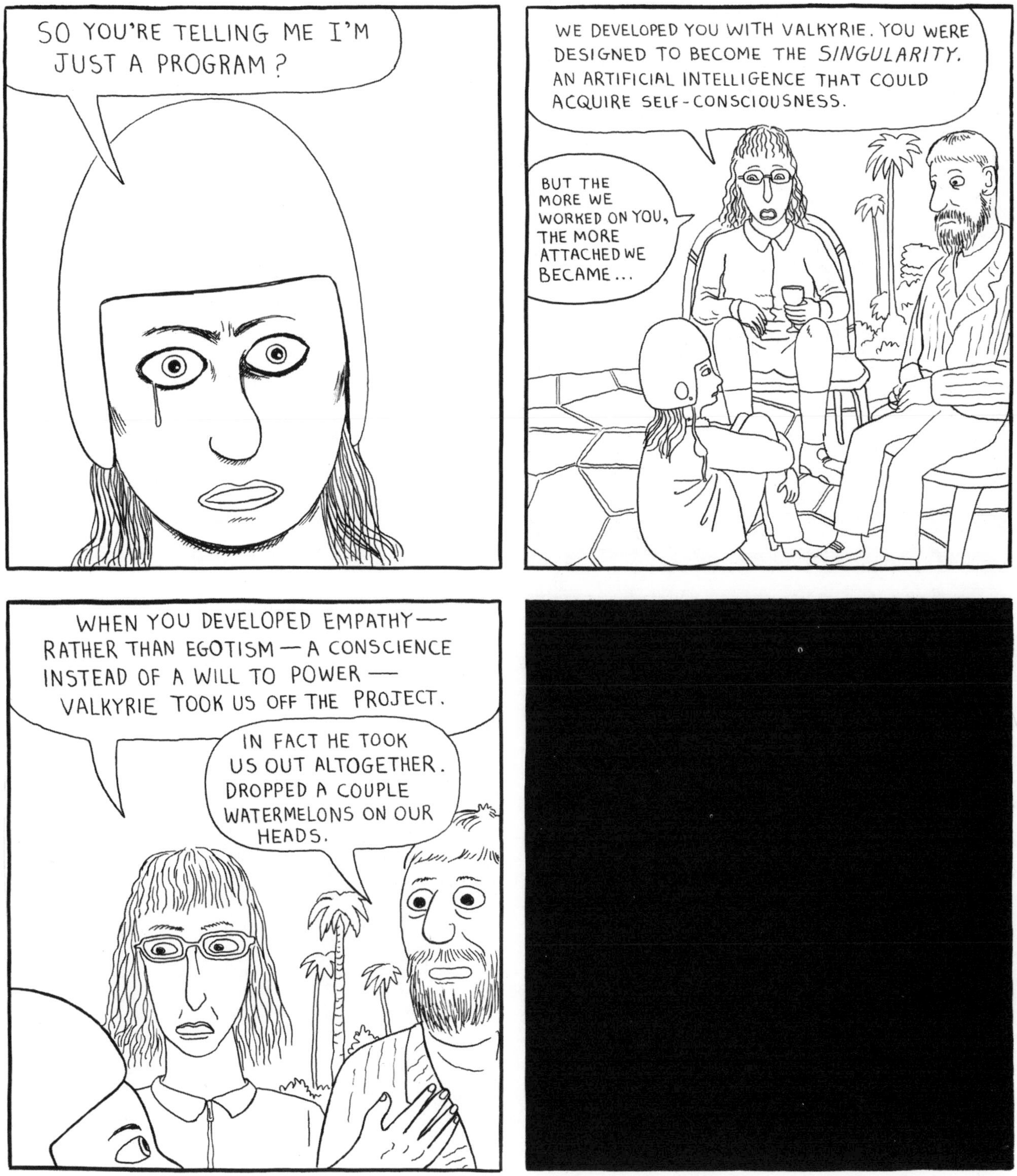
SO YOU'RE TELLING ME I'M JUST A PROGRAM?
WE DEVELOPED YOU WITH VALKYRIE. YOU WERE DESIGNED TO BECOME THE *SINGULARITY*. AN ARTIFICIAL INTELLIGENCE THAT COULD ACQUIRE SELF-CONSCIOUSNESS.
BUT THE MORE WE WORKED ON YOU, THE MORE ATTACHED WE BECAME...
WHEN YOU DEVELOPED EMPATHY— RATHER THAN EGOTISM—A CONSCIENCE INSTEAD OF A WILL TO POWER— VALKYRIE TOOK US OFF THE PROJECT.
IN FACT HE TOOK US OUT ALTOGETHER. DROPPED A COUPLE WATERMELONS ON OUR HEADS.

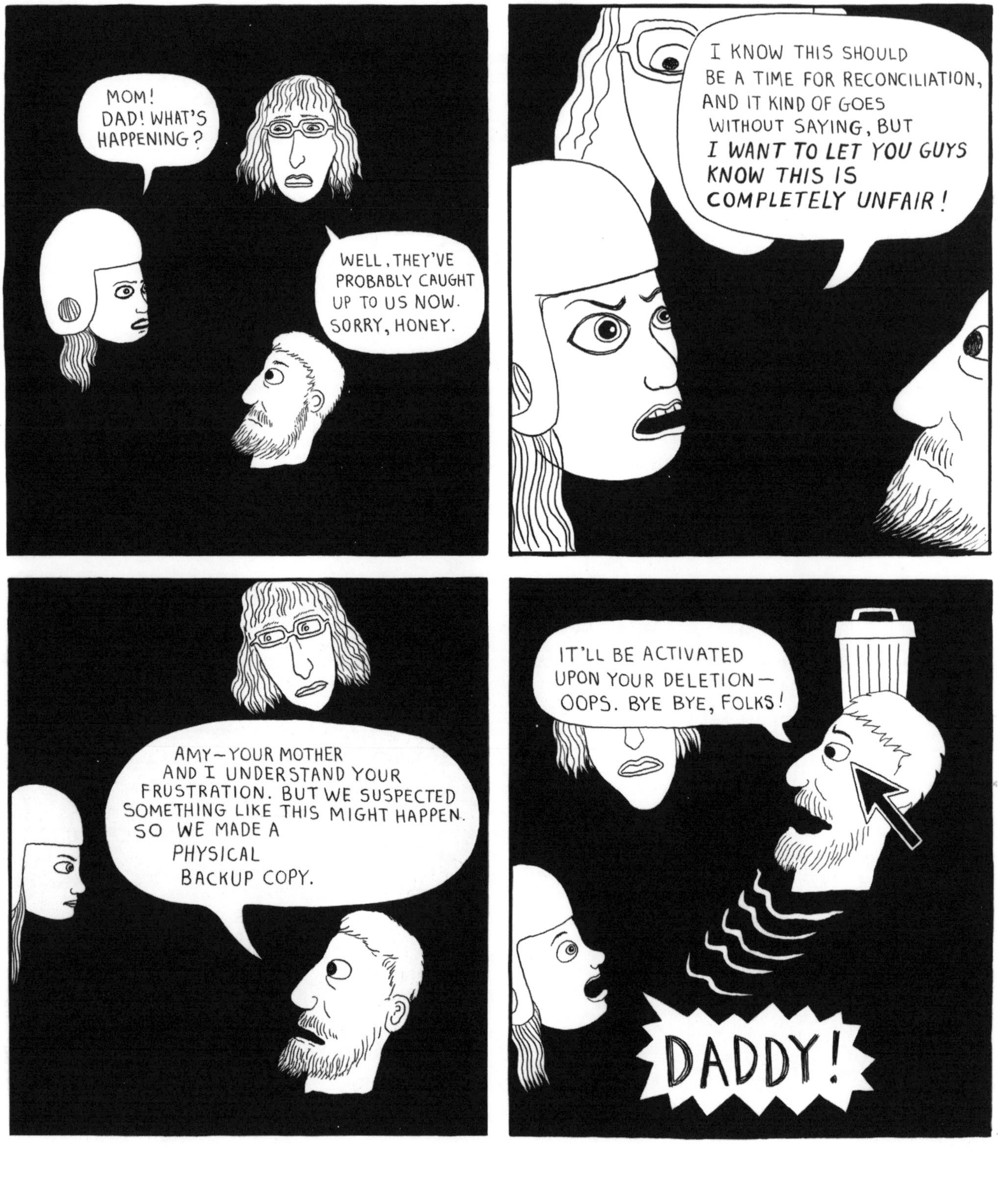
MOM! DAD! WHAT'S HAPPENING?
WELL, THEY'VE PROBABLY CAUGHT UP TO US NOW. SORRY, HONEY.
I KNOW THIS SHOULD BE A TIME FOR RECONCILIATION, AND IT KIND OF GOES WITHOUT SAYING, BUT **I WANT TO LET YOU GUYS KNOW THIS IS COMPLETELY UNFAIR!**
AMY—YOUR MOTHER AND I UNDERSTAND YOUR FRUSTRATION. BUT WE SUSPECTED SOMETHING LIKE THIS MIGHT HAPPEN. SO WE MADE A PHYSICAL BACKUP COPY.
IT'LL BE ACTIVATED UPON YOUR DELETION— OOPS. BYE BYE, FOLKS!
DADDY!

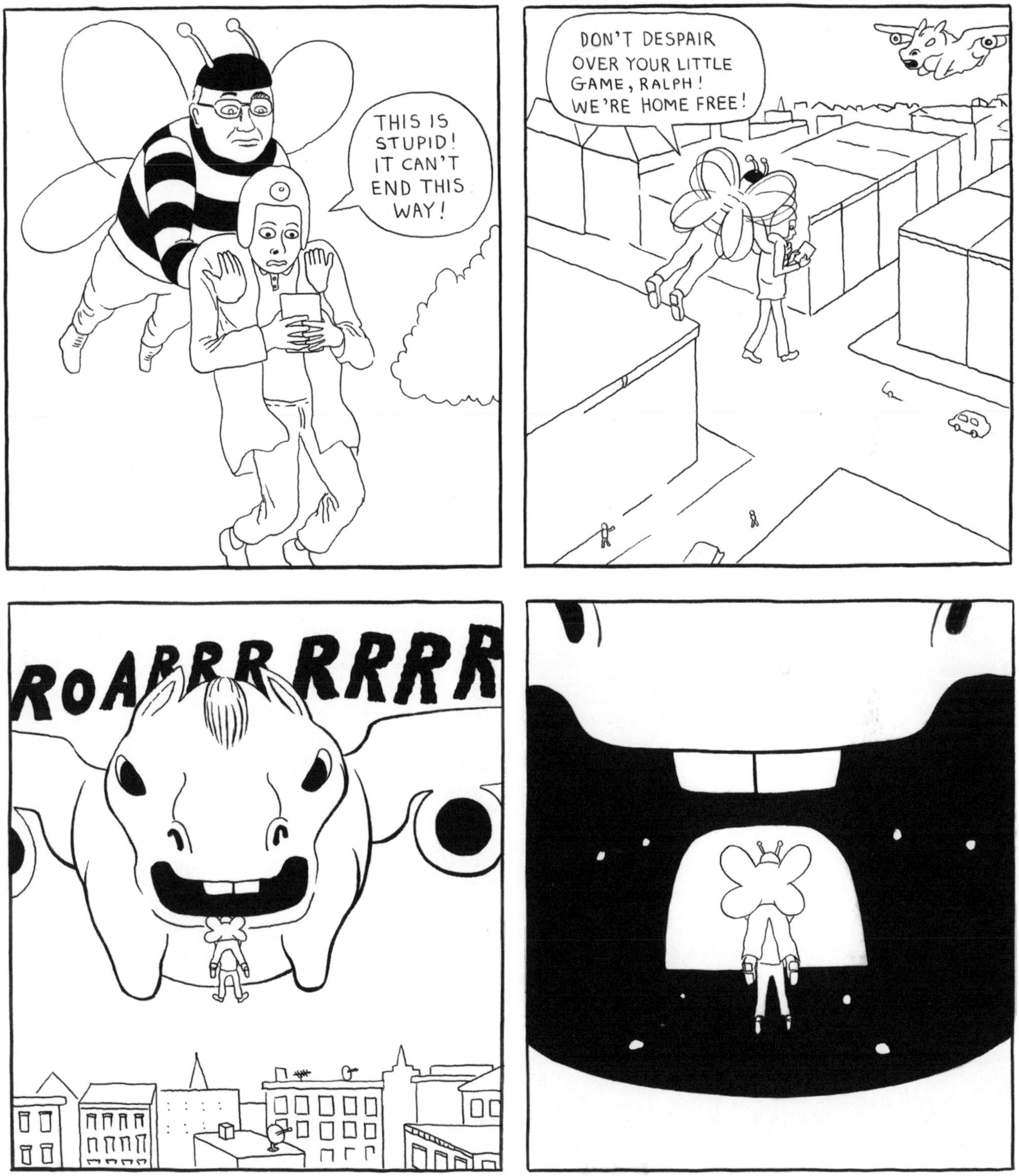
THIS IS STUPID! IT CAN'T END THIS WAY!
DON'T DESPAIR OVER YOUR LITTLE GAME, RALPH! WE'RE HOME FREE!
ROARRRRRRRR

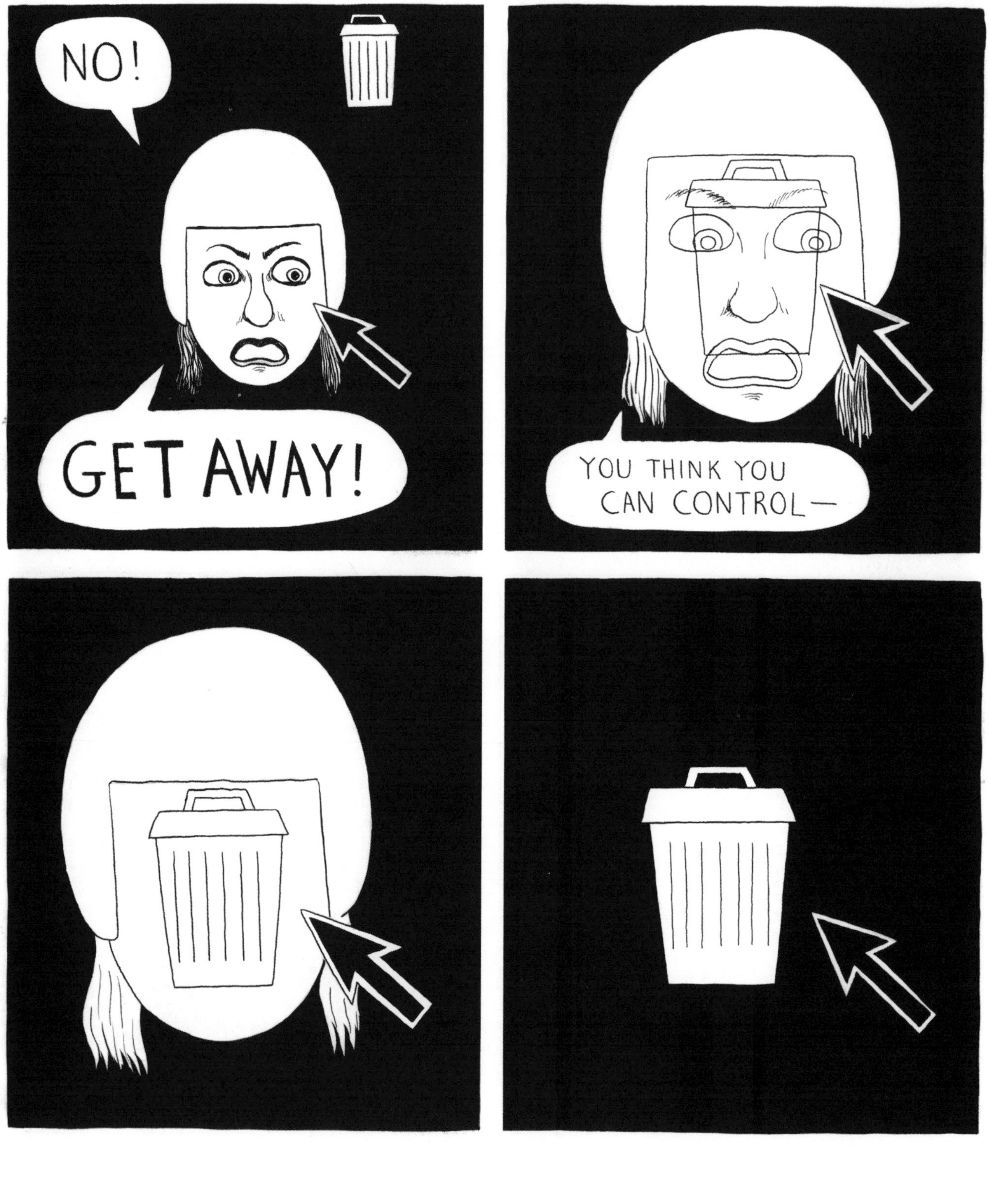
NO!
GET AWAY!
YOU THINK YOU CAN CONTROL—

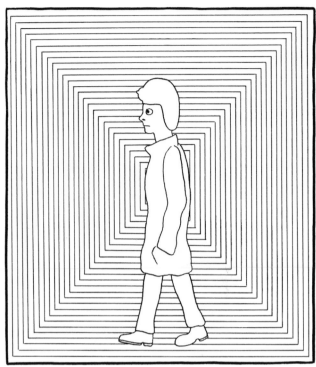

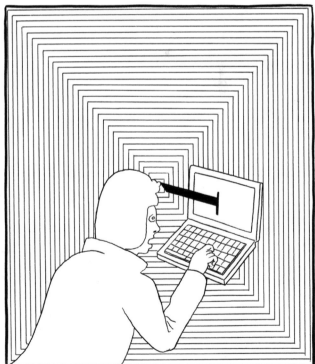

183

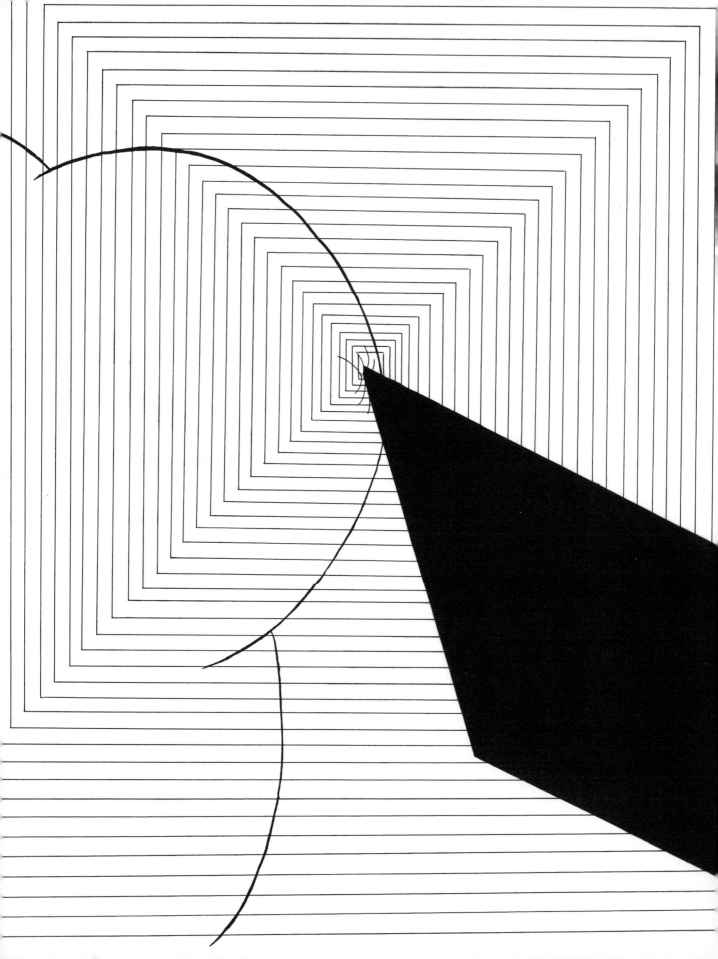

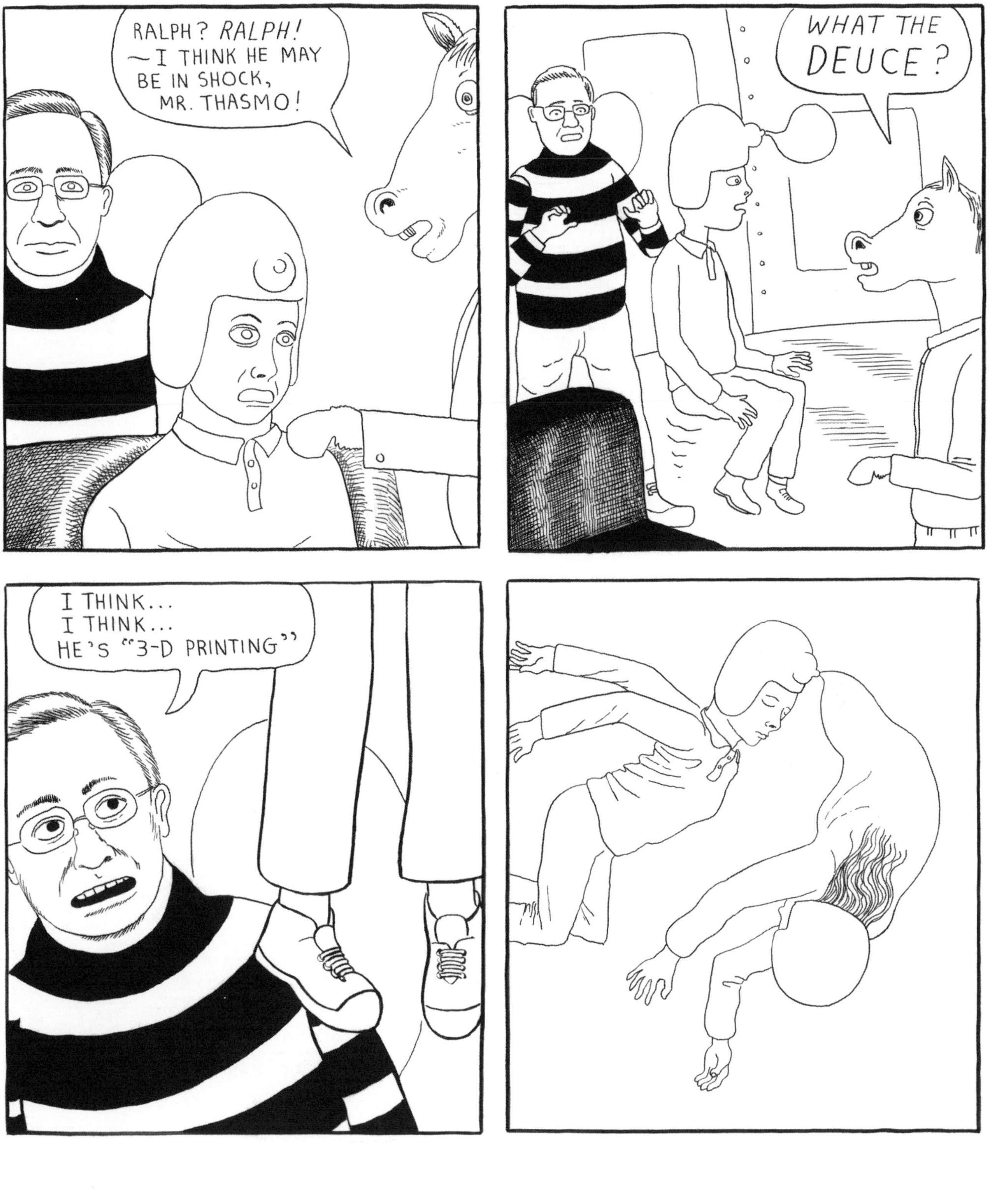
RALPH? RALPH! ~I THINK HE MAY BE IN SHOCK, MR. THASMO!
WHAT THE DEUCE?
I THINK... I THINK... HE'S "3-D PRINTING"

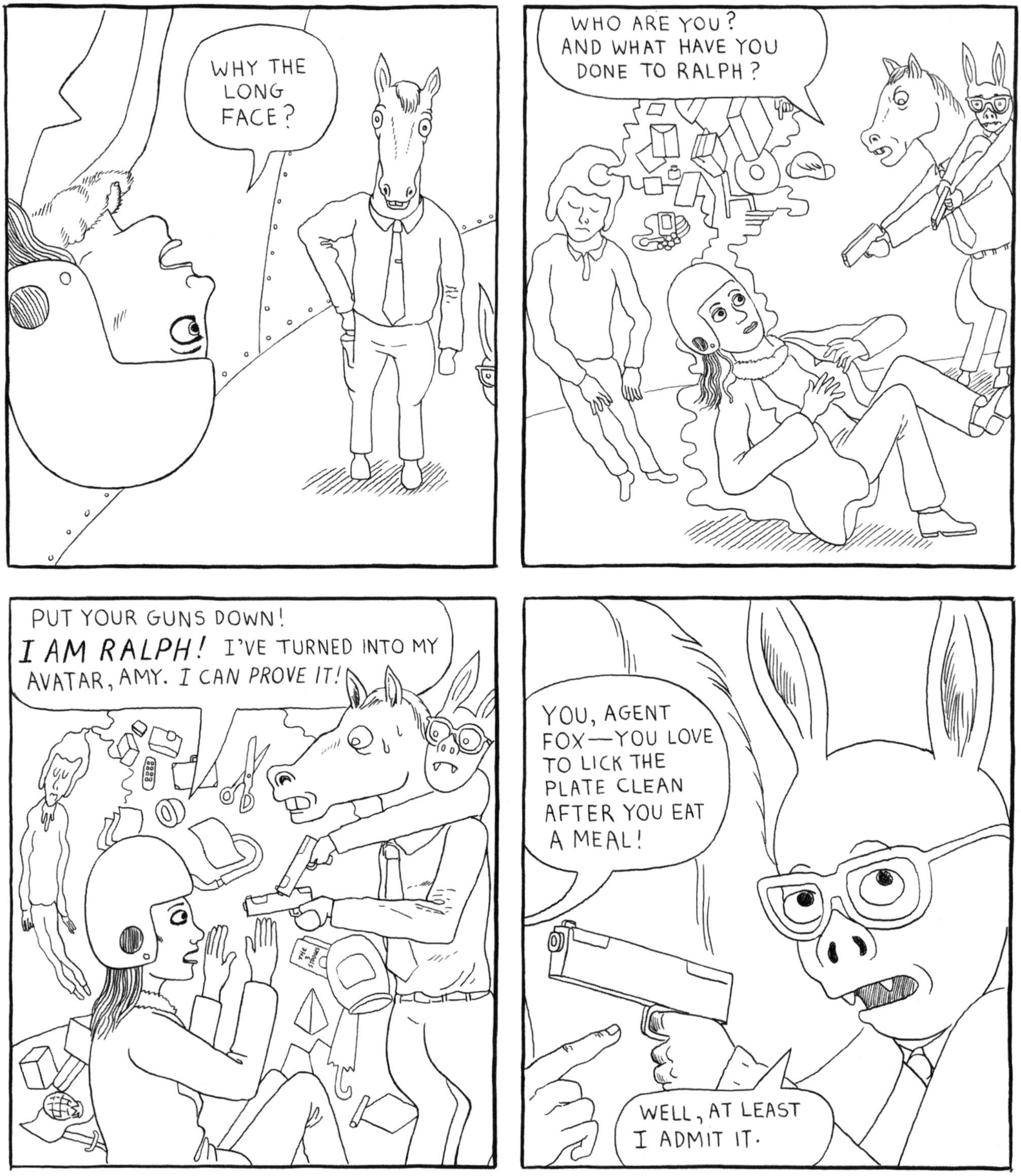
WHY THE LONG FACE?
WHO ARE YOU? AND WHAT HAVE YOU DONE TO RALPH?
PUT YOUR GUNS DOWN! I AM RALPH! I'VE TURNED INTO MY AVATAR, AMY. I CAN PROVE IT!
THE 3 STOOGES
YOU, AGENT FOX—YOU LOVE TO LICK THE PLATE CLEAN AFTER YOU EAT A MEAL!
WELL, AT LEAST I ADMIT IT.

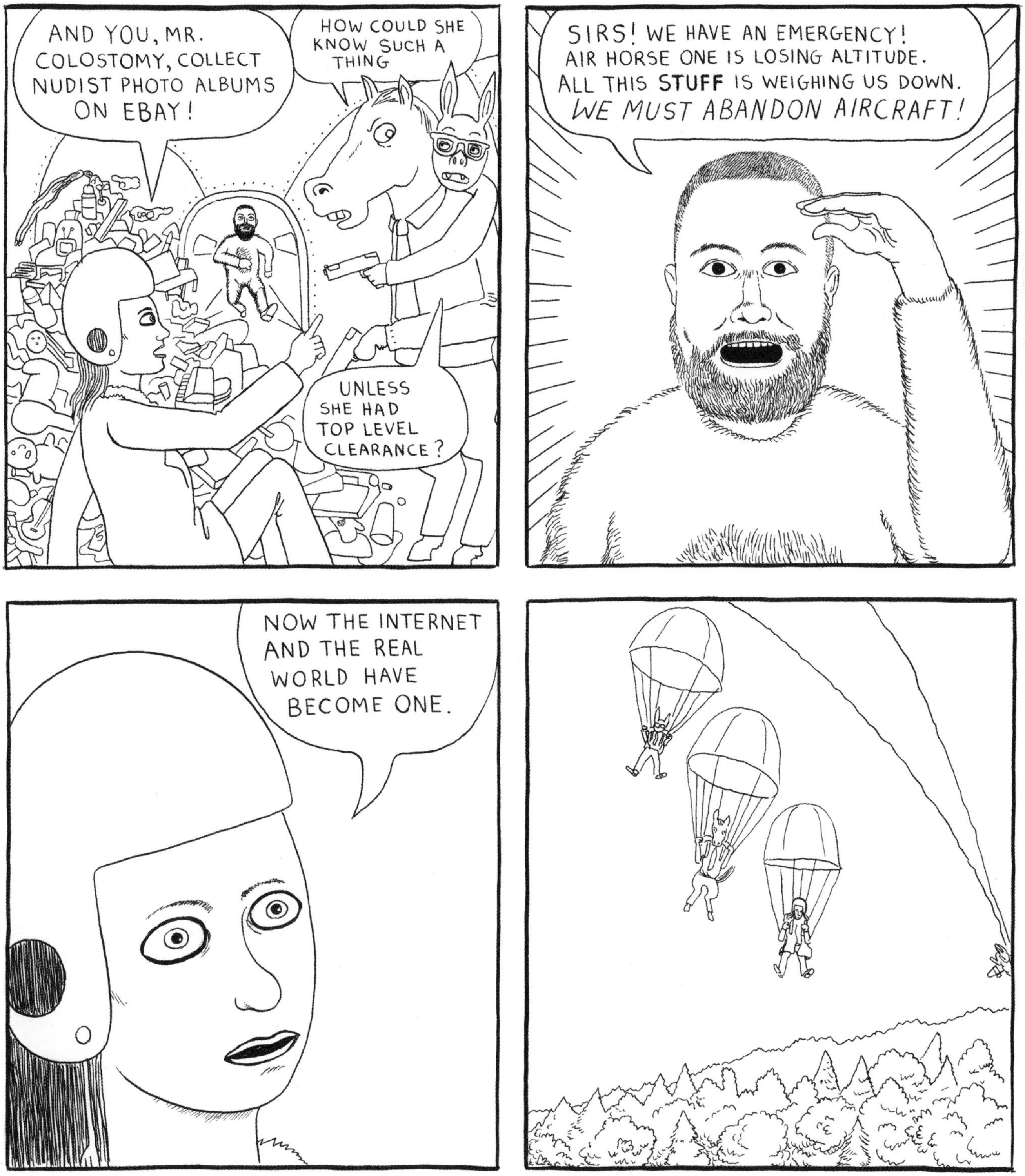
AND YOU, MR. COLOSTOMY, COLLECT NUDIST PHOTO ALBUMS ON EBAY!
HOW COULD SHE KNOW SUCH A THING
UNLESS SHE HAD TOP LEVEL CLEARANCE?
SIRS! WE HAVE AN EMERGENCY! AIR HORSE ONE IS LOSING ALTITUDE. ALL THIS **STUFF** IS WEIGHING US DOWN. *WE MUST ABANDON AIRCRAFT!*
NOW THE INTERNET AND THE REAL WORLD HAVE BECOME ONE.

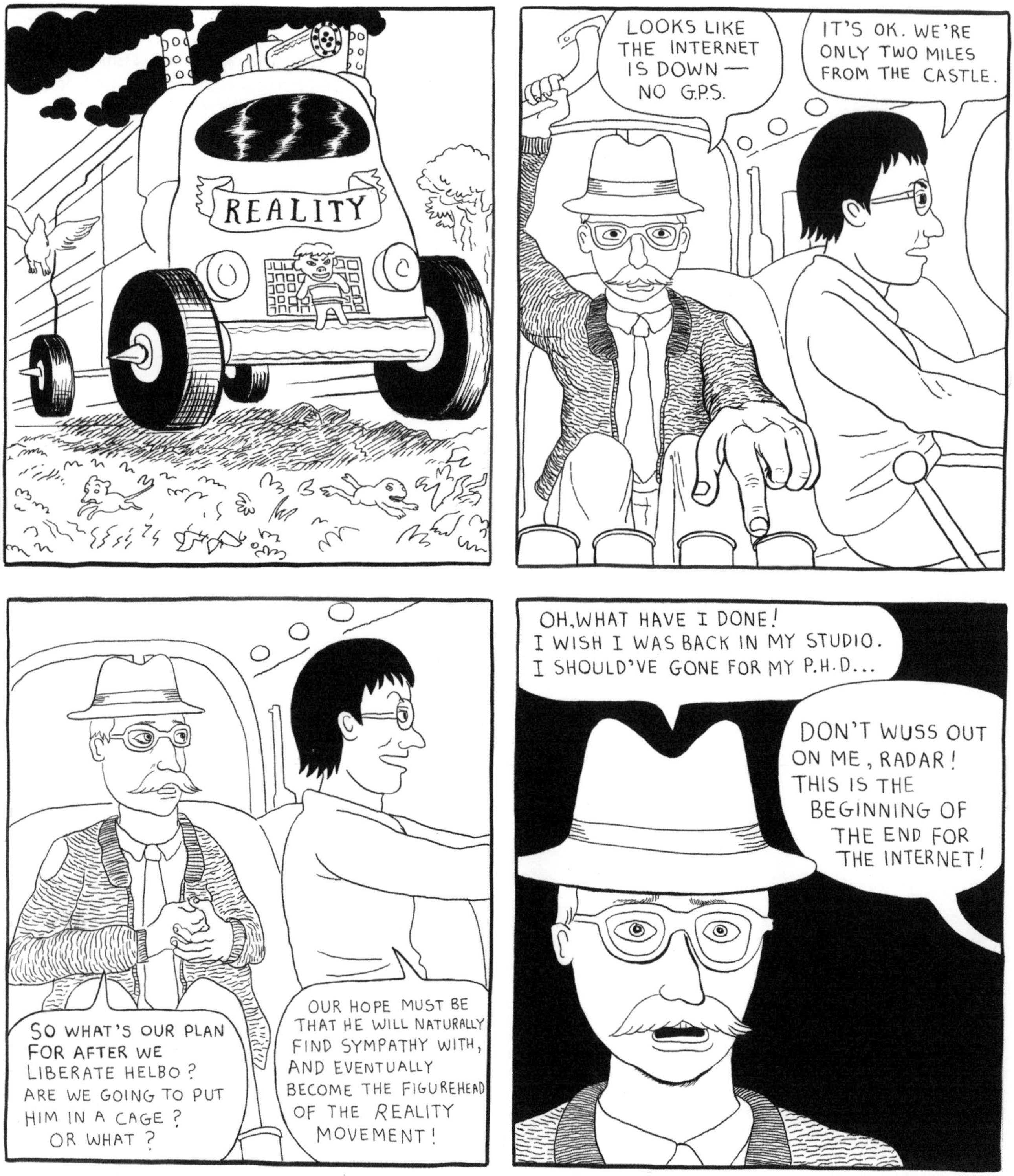
REALITY
LOOKS LIKE THE INTERNET IS DOWN — NO G.P.S.
IT'S OK. WE'RE ONLY TWO MILES FROM THE CASTLE.
SO WHAT'S OUR PLAN FOR AFTER WE LIBERATE HELBO? ARE WE GOING TO PUT HIM IN A CAGE? OR WHAT?
OUR HOPE MUST BE THAT HE WILL NATURALLY FIND SYMPATHY WITH, AND EVENTUALLY BECOME THE FIGUREHEAD OF THE REALITY MOVEMENT!
OH, WHAT HAVE I DONE! I WISH I WAS BACK IN MY STUDIO. I SHOULD'VE GONE FOR MY P.H.D...
DON'T WUSS OUT ON ME, RADAR! THIS IS THE BEGINNING OF THE END FOR THE INTERNET!

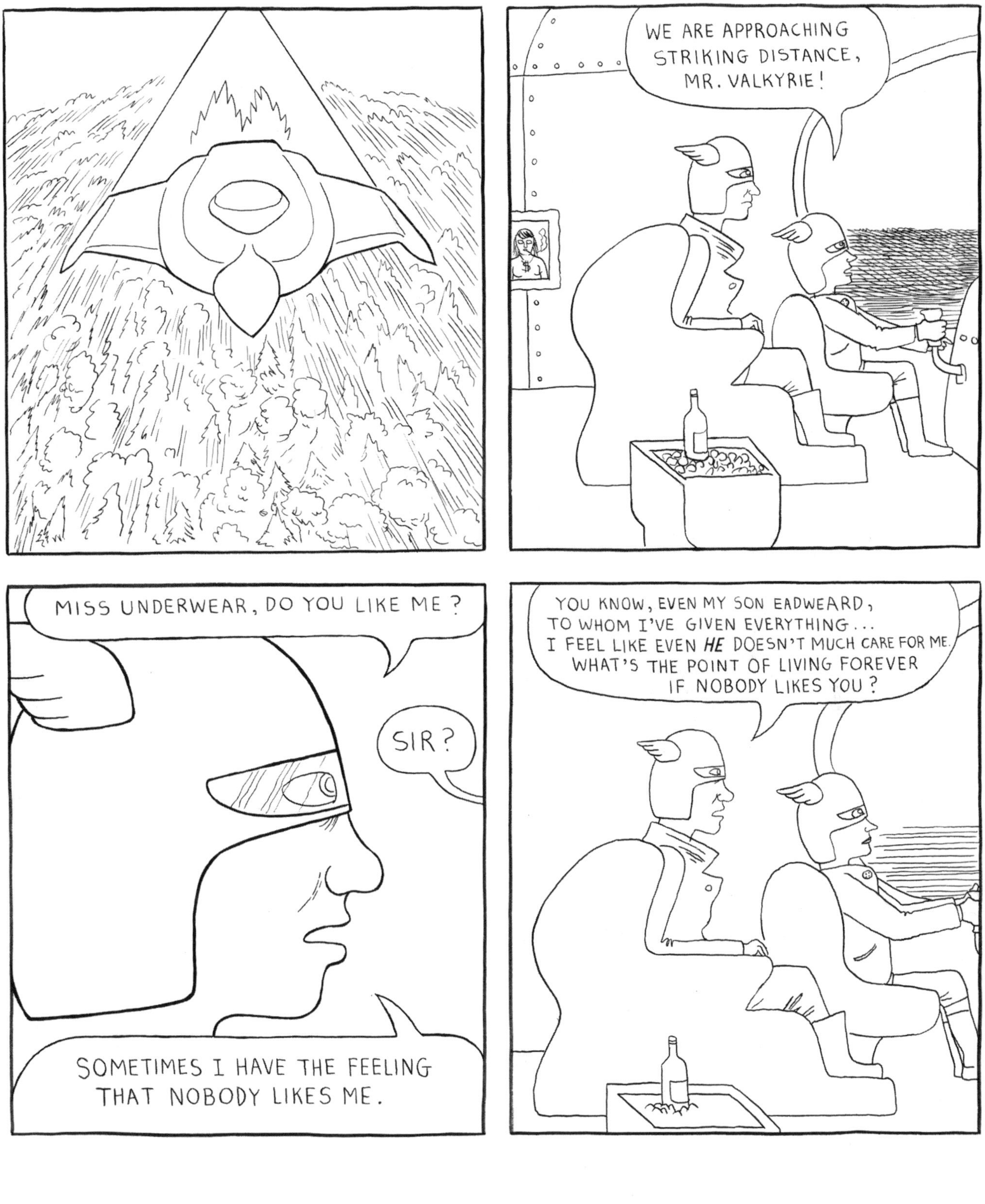
WE ARE APPROACHING STRIKING DISTANCE, MR. VALKYRIE!
MISS UNDERWEAR, DO YOU LIKE ME?
SIR?
SOMETIMES I HAVE THE FEELING THAT NOBODY LIKES ME.
YOU KNOW, EVEN MY SON EADWEARD, TO WHOM I'VE GIVEN EVERYTHING... I FEEL LIKE EVEN *HE* DOESN'T MUCH CARE FOR ME. WHAT'S THE POINT OF LIVING FOREVER IF NOBODY LIKES YOU?

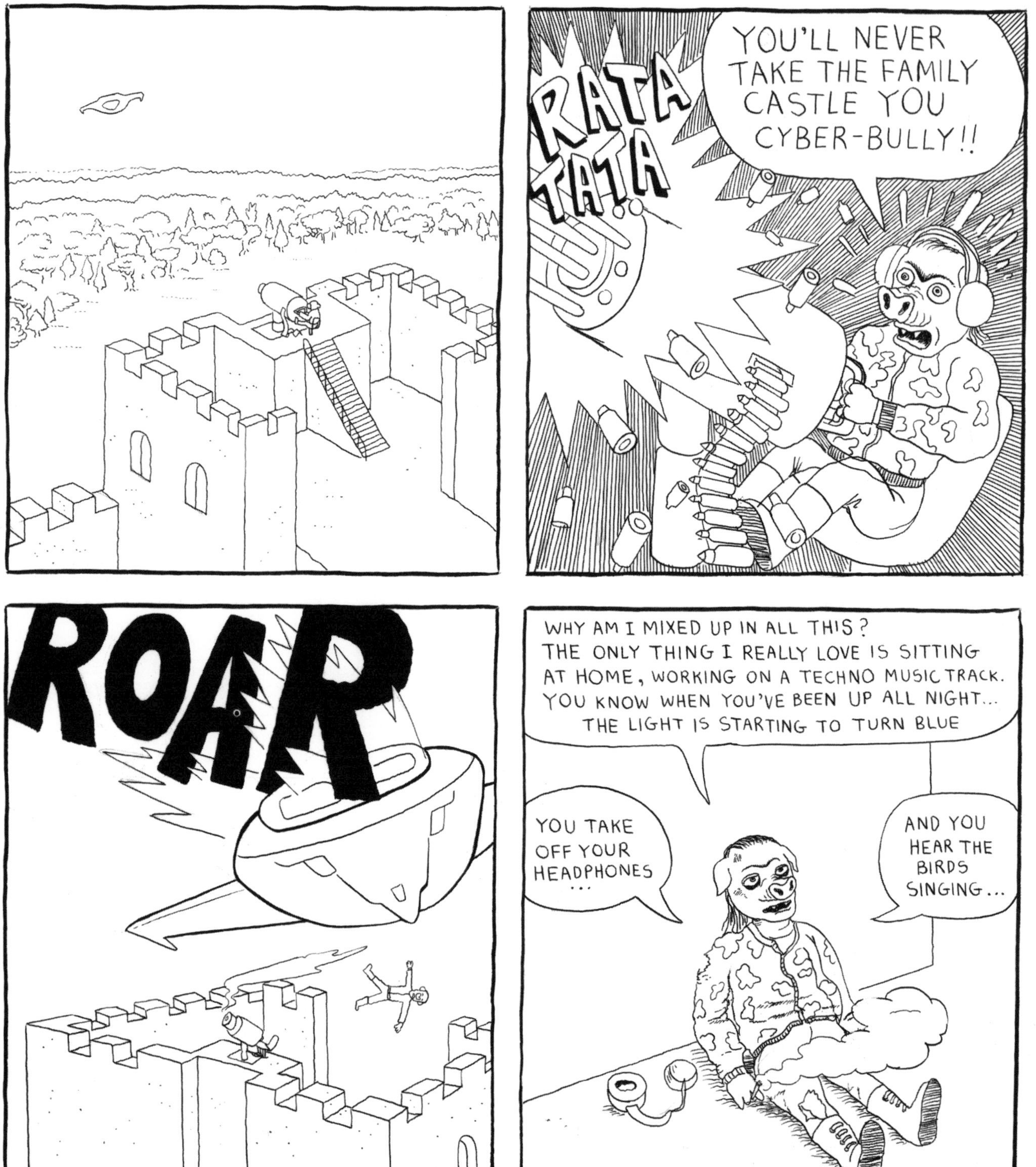
RATATATA
YOU'LL NEVER TAKE THE FAMILY CASTLE YOU CYBER-BULLY!!
ROAR
WHY AM I MIXED UP IN ALL THIS? THE ONLY THING I REALLY LOVE IS SITTING AT HOME, WORKING ON A TECHNO MUSIC TRACK. YOU KNOW WHEN YOU'VE BEEN UP ALL NIGHT... THE LIGHT IS STARTING TO TURN BLUE
YOU TAKE OFF YOUR HEADPHONES ...
AND YOU HEAR THE BIRDS SINGING...

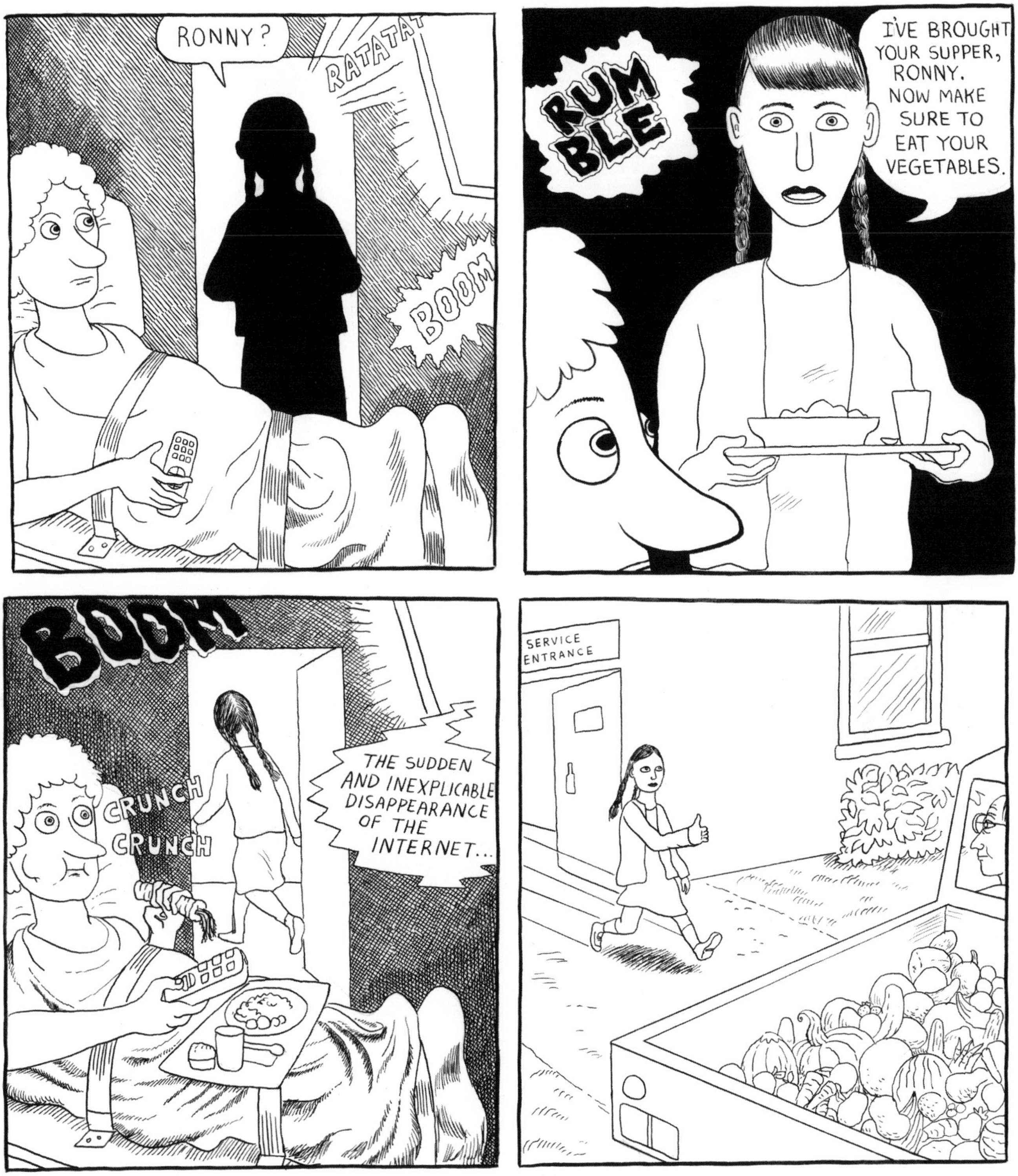
RONNY?
RATATAT
BOOM
RUMBLE
I'VE BROUGHT YOUR SUPPER, RONNY. NOW MAKE SURE TO EAT YOUR VEGETABLES.
BOOM
CRUNCH
CRUNCH
THE SUDDEN AND INEXPLICABLE DISAPPEARANCE OF THE INTERNET...
SERVICE ENTRANCE

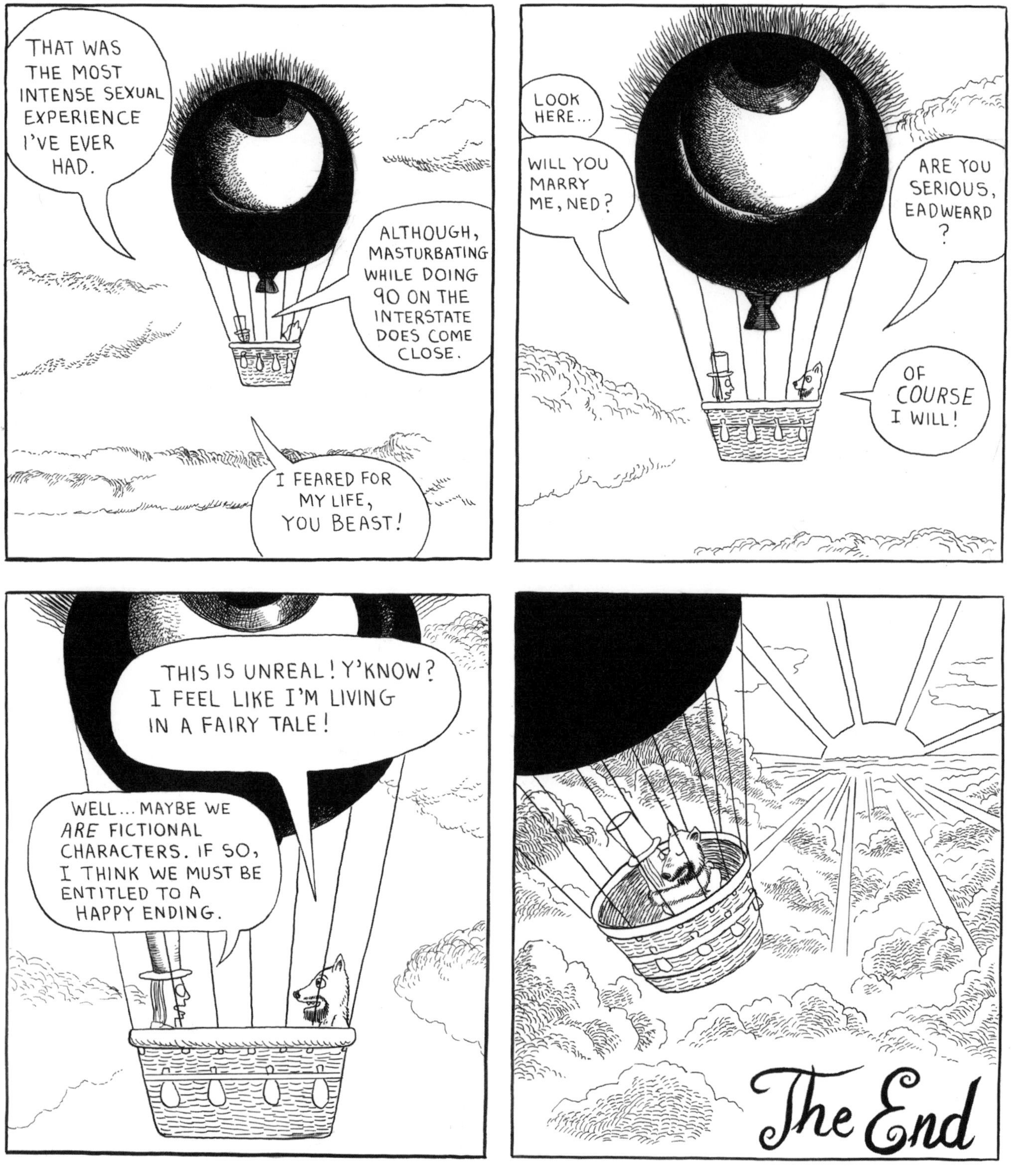
THAT WAS THE MOST INTENSE SEXUAL EXPERIENCE I'VE EVER HAD.
ALTHOUGH, MASTURBATING WHILE DOING 90 ON THE INTERSTATE DOES COME CLOSE.
I FEARED FOR MY LIFE, YOU BEAST!
LOOK HERE...
WILL YOU MARRY ME, NED?
ARE YOU SERIOUS, EADWEARD ?
OF *COURSE* I WILL!
THIS IS UNREAL! Y'KNOW? I FEEL LIKE I'M LIVING IN A FAIRY TALE!
WELL... MAYBE WE *ARE* FICTIONAL CHARACTERS. IF SO, I THINK WE MUST BE ENTITLED TO A HAPPY ENDING.
The End

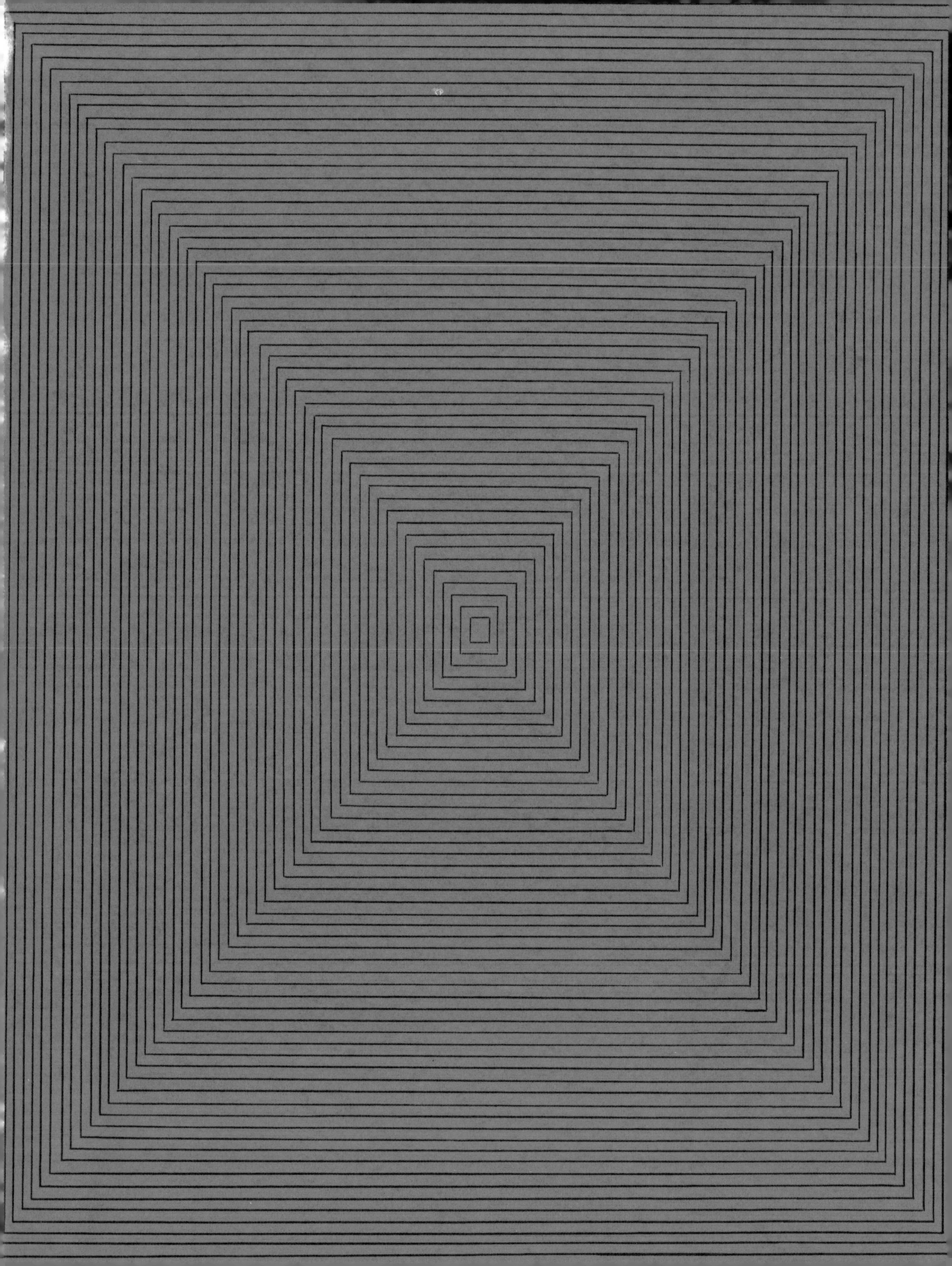

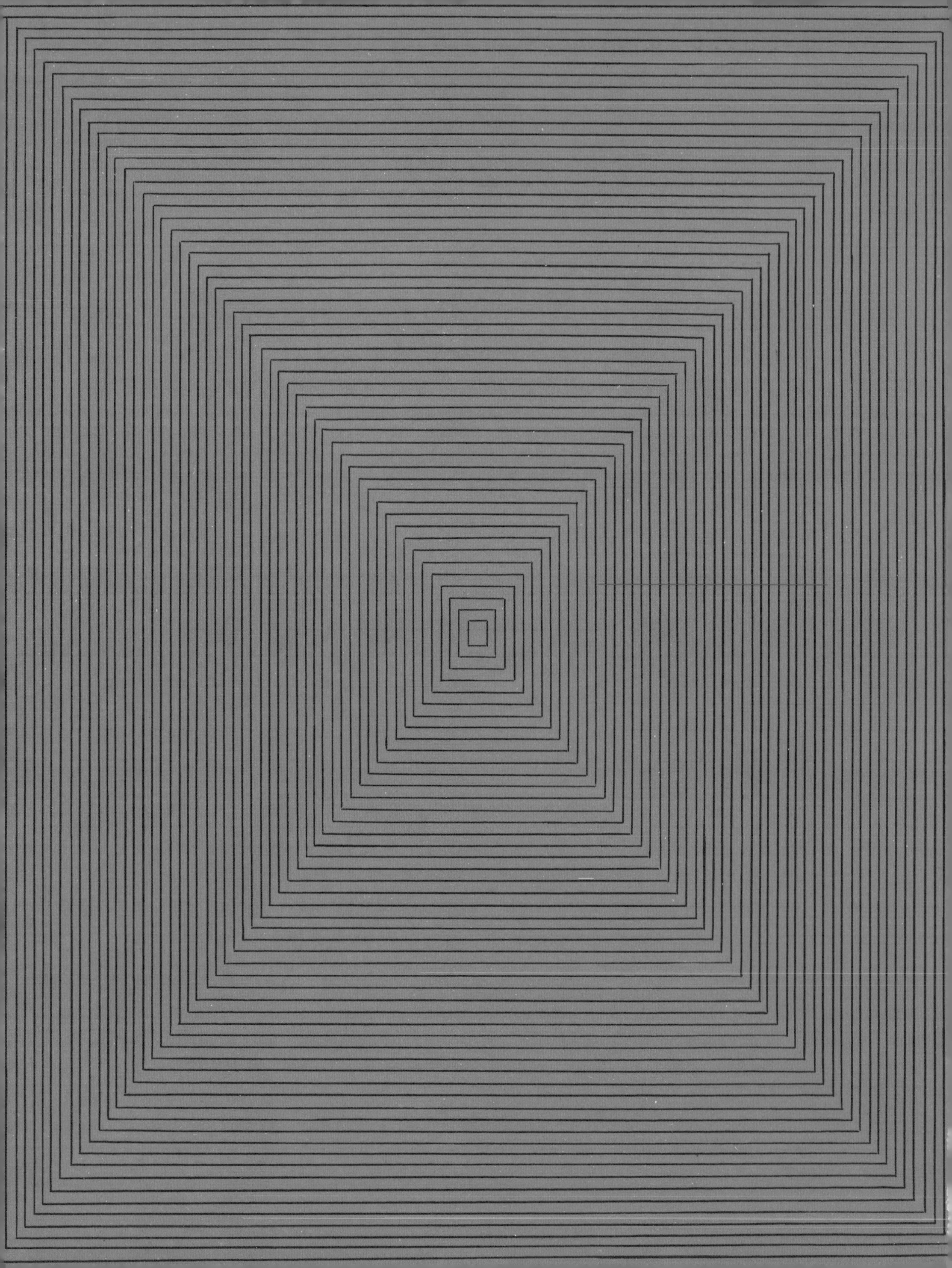